My life with the SA Defence Force

My life with the SA Defence Force

MAGNUS MALAN

PROTEA BOOK HOUSE
PRETORIA
2006

My life with the SA Defence Force

Magnus Malan

First edition, first impression 2006

Protea Book House

PO Box 35110, Menlo Park, 0102

1067 Burnett Street, Hatfield, 0083

protea@intekom.co.za

Typography and design by Chérie Collins

Cover photograph by Paul Alberts

Printed and bound by Paarl Print

Translation from the Afrikaans by Jan Schaafsma

ISBN 1-86919-114-5

© 2006 Magnus Malan

© All rights reserved. No part of this book may be reproduced without the permission of the publisher.

CONTENTS

Foreword		9
Abbreviations		16
Chapter 1	A life takes shape	19
Chapter 2	My military career begins in earnest (1953-1965)	33
Chapter 3	Appointment to command (1966-1972)	48
Chapter 4	Deputy Chief of the SA Army	63
Chapter 5	The National Service System	83
Chapter 6	Diverse challenges for the Chief of the SA Army	91
Chapter 7	An increase of terrorism across the border of South-West Africa	108
Chapter 8	Operation Savannah	117
Chapter 9	Basic requirements for a successful Defence Force	142
Chapter 10	Management and composition of the SA Defence Force	161
Chapter 11	Operational and related matters	185
Chapter 12	The National Security Management System	202
Chapter 13	Nuclear and related technological development	213
Chapter 14	Arsmcor, the other member of the Defence family	225
Chapter 15	Adapting to my new position as Minister of Defence	245
Chapter 16	The greatest battlefield victory of the SA Defence Force	261
Chapter 17	Desperate attempts to trump the SA Defence Force	287
Chapter 18	Two controversial matters: Dieter Gerhardt and the death of President Samora Machel	306
Chapter 19	The Eminent Person's Group and the Civil Co-operation Bureau	320

Chapter 20	The ANC: Origin, development and strategy	338
Chapter 21	Retirement from politics	364
Chapter 22	Operation Marion and the KwaMakutha court case	369
Chapter 23	Chemical and Biological warfare: Project Coast	391
Chapter 24	The SA Defence Force and the Truth and Reconciliation Commission	403
Chapter 25	Public reports of the TRC concerning the SA Defence Force	420
Chapter 26	Conclusion	432

End notes	436
Appendix A	457
Bibliography	468
Index	482

PHOTOGRAPHS

1	Magnus Malan meets Robert Kennedy, 1962.	44
2	Irrigation farm on the banks of the Okavango River.	103
3	A national serviceman in a classroom in the operational area of South-West Africa/Namibia.	104
4	A medical officer on duty in the operational area in South-West Africa/Namibia.	105
5	A pharmacy in the operational area.	106
6	*SAS President Steyn*.	127
7	The notorious Stalin Organ or 122 mm multiple rocket launcher.	139
8	Refuelling Cheetahs.	154
9	P.W. Botha, Punch Barlow and Wim de Villiers visiting a mortar section in the operational area.	162
10	The G6 gun.	165
11	The Mirage.	166
12	Strike craft on manoeuvres.	167
13	A church parade in the operational area.	178
14	SAMS practising the evacuation of casualties.	180
15	SADF officers, politicians and other civilians visit the operational area.	180-181

16	Captured armaments.	196
17	The RSA-3 missile.	220
18	Operation and control room, Overberg testing site.	221
19	Cmdt Piet Marais, Chairman of Armscor.	228
20	Cmdre Viljoen and the officers of *SAS Good Hope*.	229
21	The Bateleur rocket system.	232
22	The G5 cannon.	236
23	*SAS Drakensberg*.	237
24	The Seeker.	238
25	The Cheetah.	238
26	The Namacurra.	239
27	The Rooikat.	239
28	The Rooivalk.	242
29	Gen. Magnus and Mrs Margot Malan.	246
30	Captured BRDM-2 armoured vehicles.	254
31	Captured anti-aircraft guns.	254
32	Captured T-35 tanks.	255
33	Visitors to the operational area.	276-277
34	The G5 cannon deployed in the bush.	278
35	Battlefield after the SADF has dealt with enemy forces.	282
36	Mechanised infantry in Ratels near Techipa.	291
37	The South African negotiating team in Cairo.	293
38	Signing of the Trilateral Agreement on 22 December 1988 at UN Headquarters.	295
39	The communist spy Dieter Gerhardt and his Soviet handler, Grigori Shirobokov.	307
40	The accused in the KwaMakutha trial.	383
41	Defence Force members prepare for a chemical attack.	397
42	Gen. Magnus Malan testifying before the TRC.	407

MAPS

Map 1	Southern Africa.	Fly leaf
Map 2	South-West Africa/Namibia and its location in relation to the rest of Africa.	70
Map 3	Northern South-West Africa/Namibia and southern Angola.	111
Map 4	Northern South-West Africa/Namibia and Angola.	119

Map 5	The operational movements of Combat Group Orange to and from Bié during Operation Savannah.	129
Map 6	Subdivision of Southern Africa into operational areas.	153
Map 7	The enemy opened two fronts, one front from the north via Lucusse, and the other front from Cuito Cuanavale, both aimed at Mavinga and eventually Jamba.	265
Map 8	Operations Modular, Hooper and Packer: Deployment of enemy troops east of the Cuito River and the commencement of their march on Jamba through Mavinga.	268
Map 9	Cuban units in position in south-western Angola at Cahama, Xangongo, Techipa, Cuvelai and Cassinga.	288
Map 10	Northern South-West Africa/Namibia and Angola.	End paper

FOREWORD

There is an adage: "He who has no knowledge of the past, is like one without any memory." Every organisation, including the South African Defence Force, has its own history which should be preserved. I have written this book in answer to this call. For many years my life was so inextricably entwined with the Defence Force that the history of the Defence Force is almost my own history. My experiences in the Defence Force not only constitute my career history, but my personal history as well. This book is an attempt to talk about the Defence Force and its people, with whom I have worked and lived for a period of more than 40 years.

I still have a great need to thank all the men and women who served with me in various capacities. I wanted to record the facts about the role the Defence Force played in protecting our country, and in the successful transition to a new political dispensation, mainly because I have such a great appreciation for their input, and take such great pride in the achievements of the Defence Force.

This book focuses on the role played by the Defence Force in Southern Africa from about 1960 to 1994, but also includes accounts of many events of that time that in my opinion provide essential contextual information. I am referring mainly to people and events associated directly with the Defence Force. Interactions the Defence Force had with the Government of the time, with Parliament, Government departments, Armscor as well as the TRC, are explored. The battle wagged between the ANC Alliance, the PAC and SWAPO and the Defence Force are also investigated.

It would be impossible for me to capture all the important facts about the Defence Force in a single book. All that happened in Angola springs to mind. Many men and women could well say: "There are so many other military actions, adventures and events from the period between 1960 and 1994 that are not taken up in the book." Of course it is quite correct to say this, but in many cases there are good reasons why I could not include everything in the book.

The South African Defence Force (SADF) was replaced by the South African National Defence Force (SANDF) in 1994, and as a result there are very few informed bodies or persons able or willing to answer questions about, or allegations aimed at, the former organisation. Those who are able to talk with some authority about certain experiences in and exposure to the Defence Force are rapidly ageing, or are otherwise fading from the scene. If these events are not recorded now, it may soon be no longer possible to capture all the incidents and activities. Yet there is so much speculation and there are so many questions about events involving the Defence Force between 1960 and 1994 that still await answers. Unfortunately there has been little authoritative writing about Defence Force actions in this period to counter possible misperceptions, rumours and inaccuracies.

Some members of the SA Defence Force have been accused of capital offences, without any thorough investigation or proof. The KwaMakutha murders in KwaZulu-Natal and accusations arising from South Africa's biological and chemical capabilities are examples. In both these cases the accused were eventually tried and found not guilty. The experiences of these Defence Force members and their appearances before the Supreme Court and the TRC in the effort to prove their innocence, as well as the stigma that still clings to them, has compelled me to record certain facts in the interest of historical correctness.

I have personally experienced certain events, and this is why I felt the need not to silently accept the untruths about and contumely of an institution to which I, and thousands of others, have devoted a lifetime. A considerable part of South Africa's population was involved in the South African Defence Force in some capacity or another, and can claim a right to know what the Defence Force has to say with regard to, for example, the Samora Machel aircraft crash, the TRC's pronouncements and many other issues.

Most of the incidents recalled in the book occurred during the so-called struggle period. People often look back on that period without really taking into account the circumstances prevailing at the time. It is easy to judge events in retrospect, according to the norms of a world that had changed dramatically after the fall of the Berlin Wall in 1989, in other words, within the context of the disappearance of the Soviet Union's worldwide imperialistic-communist assault. Defence Force actions prior to 1990 are therefore often judged against the background of views and prejudices that exist today, consequently there are misconceptions that do not accord with the truths and realities of that time.

Hopefully the passage of time has quietened the intense feelings that were engendered by the struggle, so that the past can be judged more objectively. An account of that period, as seen from a military point of view, is therefore desirable and perhaps even essential. Furthermore I believe that the experiences I had during my youth and as a professional soldier have placed me in a better position to have an understanding of the thoughts and feelings of my fellow Defence Force members, even those at the most junior level.

When one's career takes one to a managerial level, one is kept busy with management matters that include planning, control and decision-making. This means that it is difficult to attend to the matters that one really cares about. I still reproach myself for not having adequately expressed my gratitude for the way in which loyal, disciplined Defence Force and Armscor members executed almost superhuman tasks in stressful conditions. They form part of a remarkable generation – the heroes of the recent past.

I have tried to maintain a style serving as tribute to the achievements of the Defence Force, while always keeping in mind the next-of-kin of those who paid the highest price. There are so many unsung heroes whose brave deeds will never be known, and others who carried out their daily tasks with dedication, making a quiet but essential contribution. I salute them: the men and women from all population groups who fought the battles both in and outside South Africa.

Many former Defence Force members, particularly those who were directly involved in operations, are often plagued by a nagging doubt: Were the proactive military actions worthwhile? My answer is an unequivocal YES! The policy of proactive military operations, and all that resulted from it, precluded the Defence Force from having to fight on its own soil, which explains why there is not a single ruin caused by war in South Africa. In this way, the Defence Force also ensured that the Marxist ideology espoused by the Soviet Union and its cohorts never took root in Southern Africa, and that they eventually had to beat a retreat. This, in itself, was a tremendous achievement. However, the most important achievement was that the Defence Force was able to create a climate in South Africa in which a new political dispensation could be peacefully negotiated.

We need to remember that the declared policy of the ANC Alliance, prior to 1990, was to use violence to make South Africa ungovernable, and in doing so to take over the reins. Blood had to flow. However, the Defence Force was too well trained, too well equipped and too well motivated to be swept aside. A security climate was created which promoted negotiations and created a situation in which the Defence Force was unbeatable. If this had not been the case, we would have been confronted with chaos, disruption and murder.

Few things in life give one greater inner satisfaction, mental pleasure and gratification, while simultaneously stimulating one's perseverance, self-sacrifice and enthusiastic willpower, than to be cemented together as a member of a team or highly motivated group while striving to achieve a common goal. This is even more so if one's country's future is at stake, and its survival depends on one's group achieving its goals. In such circumstances people are prepared to sacrifice themselves and to pay the highest price to save the country and its people. I find that this is when *esprit de corps* in all its glory triumphs. This is also how I experienced the SA Defence Force in all its diversity.

For this reason, I deem it a personal honour and privilege to dedicate this book to the national servicemen and members of the Citizen Force, Commando Force, the Permanent Force, the Auxiliary Services and the civilians of the Department of Defence. I do this regardless of whether they were members of the SA Army, SA Air Force, SA Navy, SA Medical Service or Armscor. These institutions deserve every honour, tribute and homage for their successes in the military field. They served the Defence Force and South Africa unselfishly, faithfully and loyally, which ensured that the South African constitution of the time was upheld. They also ensured that, from a military perspective, the revolutionary forces and their cohorts never gained the upper hand. From the onset of the struggle they delivered community service and developed good mutual human relations between all South Africans. Furthermore, they ensured the continued delivery of essential services in challenging times, thus creating the right climate for negotiations so that South Africa could decide its own future, by means of the ballot box – in an evolutionary way rather than a revolutionary one.

I thank and salute all members of the Defence Force who made considerable sacrifices and earned great honour and respect for their victories from their opponents, including the Soviet Union and the Cubans.

This was a Defence Force of which I, and the whole of South Africa, can still be justifiably proud.

In this book I have tried to briefly document some of the outstanding achievements of the Defence Force and the unique contributions made by Armscor. At the same time I have tried to correct certain misconceptions regarding the Defence Force, and to expose the myths created and allegations concerning the Defence Force in recent years.

Because the book is dedicated to those who participated in the battle, and because they deserve every compliment, it will be found that I often praise their efforts, but I will also record some disappointments.

The milieu in which the Defence Force was compelled to act at times, some of its actions as well as some misconceptions that have arisen and the accusations that have been levelled at it, are often too intricate to rebut with a simple explanation, particularly if the reader is not familiar with the Defence Force and the circumstances prevalent at the time. For the sake of clarity I will therefore repeatedly refer to the circumstances that dominated at a particular time, in the hope that these contexts will help to bring about greater understanding with regard to certain actions.

A few years ago, it was not advisable for me to react to certain allegations because of pending trials and TRC investigations and so on; therefore I remained silent. In the meantime the trials have been concluded, and the TRC's report has been made public, so I have fortunately been able to respond to many of these accusations and misperceptions.

These accusations were heart-rending to me, as I had tried out of inner conviction to devote almost my entire life to the security of our country. Many of the accusations were deliberately broadcast by persons with malicious intent in order to belittle the almost superhuman service rendered to our country and its people by the South African Defence Force.

I believe that it is now time to attempt countering the accusations. Therefore I am presenting facts that will hopefully allow readers to come to their own conclusion.

Because there is still a possibility of further judicial investigations against myself and certain members of the Defence Force, I cannot react to all accusations at this stage. I have to ward against prejudicing these members by any premature publication of facts at all cost.

At the peak of the physical military battle, I often instructed that journalists and writers should be invited to accompany the Defence Force on operations, or that they should be aided by means of briefings and question-and-answer sessions. F.J. du T. Spies's book *Operasie Savannah: Angola 1975-1976* (1989), for example, was a result of such invitations.

I tried, in this way, to ensure that what was happening on the battlefield should be recorded and thus be available for future historical purposes. Of course certain tactical actions and specifications regarding equipment had to be handled in accordance with the "need to know" principle.

The invitations ensured that the media was informed about what actually happened, and about the results of operations. For this reason, media reports and articles correspond, to a large extent, with the books published on important actions.

It was my goal to quash many of the untruths that have been told about the Defence Force in the past and to ensure that these untruths are not repeated in future. By carefully and responsibly recording the Defence Force's achievements, I wish to place it above any suspicion, and to ensure that the organisation receives all the acknowledgement and thanks that it deserves.

For the sake of convenience, I have used the following convention in this book: When a person is first mentioned in a particular chapter or section the full name is used, but thereafter only the surname is used. This should not be interpreted as suggesting any disrespect towards any person or organisation. The abbreviations of bodies and organisations appear in brackets after the first mention, and are then consistently used throughout. For the sake of convenience, a list of Defence Force abbreviations is provided. References to some sources are recorded by means of endnotes to each chapter, and a complete list of sources is provided at the end of the book.

ACKNOWLEDGEMENTS

During my period of service the SA Defence Force top management was always an outstanding team. Thank you for the support and wisdom that I could always rely on over the years, and again while writing this book. I particularly wish to thank Jan Schaafsma, the translator, Glenda le Cornu and Kathleen Peddle of Protea Book House, and Generals/Admirals Gert de Wachter, Jack Dutton, Raymond Holtzhausen, Dirk Marais, Hendrik Nel and André van Deventer for their help and advice.

Thanks to my family for their understanding, support and forbearance over all these years, but particularly while I was writing this book.

ABBREVIATIONS

ACVV	Afrikaanse Christelike Vrouevereniging (Afrikaans Christian Women's Association)	CSI	Chief of Staff Intelligence
		CVR	Cockpit Voice Recorder
Adv.	Advocate		
AEB	Atomic Energy Board	DF	Defence Force
AEC	Atomic Energy Corporation	DFDR	Digital Flight Data Recorder
ANC	African National Congress		
APLA	Military wing of the PAC		
Armscor	Armaments Corporation of South Africa	EPG	Eminent Person's Group
		ESCOM	Electricity Supply Commission
ATC	Air Traffic Control		
AG	Auditor-General		
AU	African Union	FAPLA	Forças Armadas Populares de Libertação de Angola
		FBI	Federal Bureau of Investigation (USA)
Bde	Brigade		
Bn	Battalion	FNLA	Frente Nacional de Libertação de Angola
Brig.	Brigadier		
		FRELIMO	Frente de Libertação de Moçambique
Capt.	Captain		
CBD	Central Business District		
CCB	Civil Co-operation Bureau	Gen.	General
Cmdre	Commodore	GOC	General Officer Commanding
CF	Citizen Force	GNU	Government of National Unity
CIA	Central Intelligence Agency	GRU	Glawnoye Razvedyvatelnoye Uprawleniye (Soviet Military Intelligence)
CODESA	The Convention for a Democratic South Africa		
Comdo	Commando		
Comdt/Cmdt	Commandant		
Col	Colonel	HQ	Headquarters
CSAAF	Chief of the SA Air Force		
CSADF	Chief of the South African Defence Force	IAEA	International Atomic Energy Agency

ABBREVIATIONS

ILS	nstrument Landing System	Poqo	PAC's military wing
ITB	Investigation Task Board	Pres.	President
ITU	Investigation Task Unit		
IFP	Inkatha Freedom Party	RENAMO	Resistência Nacional Moçambicana
JMC	Joint Management Centre; Joint Monitoring Commission (in SWA/Angola)	Recce(s)	Reconnaissance or Reconnaissance commandos
		RSA	Republic of South Africa
KGB	Komitet Gosudarstvennoy Bezopasnosti (Soviet Secret Police)	SA	South Africa
		SAAF	South Africa Air Force
KZN	KwaZulu-Natal	SABC	South African Broadcasting Corporation
		SACP	South African Communist Party
Maj.	Major	SADF	South African Defence Force
MDM	Mass Democratic Movement	SAMS	South African Medical Service
MI	Military Intelligence	SANDF	South African National Defence Force
MID	Military Intelligence Division		
Min.	Minister	SAVF	South African Women's Federation
MK	Umkhonto we Sizwe/Spear of the Nation	SAP	South African Police
MPLA	Movimento Popular de Libertação de Angola	SAS	South African Ship
		SF	Security Forces
MRL	Multiple Rocket Launcher	S Maj.	Sergeant-Major
		Spec. Forces	Special Forces
		SRC	Space Research Corporation
NCO	non-commissioned officer	SSC	State Security Council
NEC (ANC)	National Executive Committee	SW	South-West
		SWA	South-West Africa
NI	National Intelligence Service	SWA/N	South-West Africa/Namibia
NMS	National Management System	SWAPO	South-West African People's Organisation
NPMS	National Prosperity Management System	SWAWEK	SWA Electricity Corporation
NPT	Non-Proliferation Treaty		
NS	national service		
NSM	national servicemen	TRC	Truth and Reconciliation Committee
NSMS	National Security Management System		
		UDF	United Democratic Front
OAU	Organization of African Unity	UN	United Nations
Ops.	Operation	UNITA	União Nacional para a Independência Total de Angola
		UNO	United Nations Organization
PAC	Pan-African Congress	USA	United States of America
PF	Permanent Force	USSR	Union of Socialist Soviet Republics
PLAN	People's Liberation Army of Namibia (SWAPO's military wing)		

VHF	Very High Frequency	VLV	Woman's Agricultural Association
VIPs	Very Important Persons	VOR	Very high frequency omnidirectional radio range
VLU	Women's Agricultural Union		

Chapter 1

A LIFE TAKES SHAPE

EARLY CHILDHOOD (1930 – 1935)

One should always try to understand an entire life, and not only a part of it.

My earliest recollections are of Onderstepoort, where I was born on 30 January 1930. I was the eldest of four children; my sister was born eighteen months later, my brother seven years later and my youngest sister twelve years later.

I was named after my father's two brothers. Uncle Magnus, his eldest brother, was still a bachelor when he was killed in battle during World War I in what was then called South-West Africa. He was buried in Windhoek. Uncle André also died childless; there were rumours at a later stage that he had adopted children, but I have never been able to establish this beyond doubt. In order to perpetuate their memory, I was therefore given the names of these two childless uncles. My third name, which I acquired long after my birth, can be traced back to a time long before I was born.

The Malans originally came from the town of Mérindol near Avignon in south-east France. Jacques Malan, the first Malan to set foot on South African soil, was probably on board the *Berg China* which anchored in Table Bay on 4 August 1688. I say "probably" because an error in the *Berg China*'s passenger list has made is impossible to establish this beyond doubt. However, it *is* quite certain that he was one of 180 French refugees or Huguenots who arrived at the Cape between 1688 and 1694, as his name appears twice in Cape Archives documents concerning these French refugees. On 18 October 1694, he became owner of the farm La Motte in Franschhoek, and later also acquired the farm Morgenster, a portion of Willem Adriaan van der Stel's farm, Vergelegen.

When my eldest son was born, my father asked me to add a third name, "de Mérindol", to the names Magnus André that we had chosen for his grandson, maintaining that this would be "correct". Apparently it was an old French custom to add the name of the town where your ancestors came from, before your surname.

I agreed, on condition that my father should add this name to his own. He also agreed, on condition that I should add it to mine, which I did.

The newly born Magnus André was at that stage in no position to agree or disagree or to impose conditions, but he did exercise his rights as soon as he was able to. Without consulting anybody in the matter, Magnus André de Mérindol Malan used official channels to nullify the agreement between his father and grandfather, and emerged as simply André Malan. His brother, Charl Petrus Malan, then promptly added "de Mérindol" to *his* name, also without consulting anyone beforehand. It is good that the name given to someone should meet with that person's approval and perhaps it is not such a bad idea to have some control over one's own name; the Malans have been taking control of their own names for years. The Malans of Mérindol were Protestants, an apostasy for which the Roman Catholics punished them with the French word "malan" as a term of abuse. Instead of changing the name, however, the Malans retaliated by accepting it and using it with pride. (There is no way of knowing whether they consulted someone in the matter, or imposed any conditions.)

According to some authors (for example the noted South African genealogist Cor Pama), "malan" is the French word for "leper", but if so, it must be a very old word, because the modern French word for "leper" is "lépreux". It is possible that the old word refers to something or someone "unacceptable". In the early days the Malans often fled from France to Italy, and vice versa, to escape persecution. Eventually they were all but massacred in the town of Mérindol.

Talk to Italians today, and they will claim that Malan is an Italian family name. When I was a Cabinet Minister, the Italian community in South Africa made much of me, as if I were a lost son returned to the Italian bosom! They appointed Italian historians to research my personal history as well as that of the Malan clan, but I have no idea how reliable their version of this history is. The Malan society also did a great deal of research, even visiting France and Italy, and according to the 1988 edition of the Malan commemorative publication, the family name is associated with meanings such as "heretics" and "lepers", and, by extension, even with highwaymen! Despite this history, my father's pride in the old name meant a good deal to me, and I am happy to bear this name.

My father lectured in veterinary science at Onderstepoort, about 15 km north of Pretoria, and as a scientist he was also involved in agricultural research. The permanent inhabitants of Onderstepoort consisted mainly of scientists and their families who formed a small community on the banks of the Apies River. The only public transport was the passenger train from Pretoria which steamed northward past Onderstepoort. There were few motor cars, and the journey to Pretoria involved much more effort than it does nowadays.

There were no schools, shops or churches. The closest facilities of this nature – also rather limited – were in Pretoria North. The only local shop in Pretoria North despatched a truck to Onderstepoort once a week. The truck then went from house to house, with all the groceries displayed on the load bed, thus meeting the needs of the inhabitants.

The nearest church was the Dutch Reformed Church in Pretoria North, where I was baptised by the Rev. Loots.

The Onderstepoort community was dependent on each other for entertainment. My parents liked playing bridge and tennis, and my father also regularly competed in target-shooting competitions on the government rifle range. He was a good shot and won many prizes. I usually accompanied him to collect cartridge cases to play with. At that stage he was my only hero, and I idolised him.

I had many friends and we made maximum use of the community's swimming pool.

Perhaps the Onderstepoort children missed things that the city kids had, but there was a lot the city kids could envy us for. There were horses, cattle, donkeys and even one or two eland which were kept with the other animals in pens built from iron poles. There were also plenty of laboratory animals such as rabbits, guinea pigs, mice and rats.

When I was five years old, my parents decided that my father would continue with his duties at Onderstepoort, but that it was time we lived closer to schools. My father also needed more space to expand his well-organised backyard chicken-farming activities.

We left Onderstepoort, and this meant that we also had to leave behind the eland which had become so tame that it would eat grass from my hand and stand still so that I could scratch it.

SCHOOLDAYS (1936-1945)

Our new home was in the Moot, the region stretching along the southern reaches of the Magaliesberg. Many people are of the opinion that the northern side of the Magaliesberg marks the beginning of the Bushveld, and one does not argue with such people.

Our house in Mayville was built shortly after the Anglo-Boer War (1904) by one Fred Nicholson. This old house, called Mérindol from the moment we moved in, was surrounded by four morgen of land covered with trees, fields and gardens. The municipality classified it as an agricultural smallholding, but perhaps an estate would have been a better description.

Our turn for irrigation water from the communal furrow started at six o'clock on Sunday evenings, and lasted until six o'clock on Monday mornings. When I was a little older, I often irrigated the gardens and fields right through the night. All the fodder and irrigation water that was available made it possible for us to keep dairy cattle. I often helped my mother to make butter by turning the churn. This is why I still like buttermilk on my muesli for breakfast. And yes, cows mean that there were calves, and calves are there to be ridden, which resulted in many bad spills.

My father immediately started erecting permanent henhouses for a few thousand chickens. My mother was responsible for the four incubators, and for selling the chicks. There was always a shortage of hands when it came to running a farm of this nature and we kids had to help as soon as we were old enough to.

In spite of all the hard work we had enough time to play. The Magaliesberg was close and my friends and I, together with our dogs, clambered about in the mountains, pretending to be great explorers. We "discovered" caves, collected marula, wild plums and medlar to eat and to make jam and preserved fruit, dug up succulents and laid out rock gardens at home. We swam in the Apies River at the foot of the mountain, often after a hard day's climbing. And after good rains the Apies flowed so powerfully that it could easily drag you along for a few hundred metres.

At one stage I was an enthusiastic pigeon breeder with some pedigreed white fantails. When they sat preening, with their heads tucked back, and their breasts puffed up, I could easily catch them by hand. I also kept homing pigeons, and pitted them against my friends' pigeons in simple races. Our time-keeping was rather elementary, and it always felt as if my pigeons arrived home stone last. Not that it really mattered, because they were not purebred racing pigeons – my friends and I mostly swapped them amongst ourselves.

Bes was my horse at Mérindol, a Basotho mare with a very gentle disposition. I could ride her without saddle, bridle or rope. Admittedly, this was achieved only with a great deal of practice and patience and in the process I fell off many times.

My schooling started at Eloffsdal Primary. The principal, Mr Ebbie Swemmer, took an interest in the affairs of every child. His personality, and the way he handled his charges, made a life-long impression on me.

In December 1941 – my primary school days having just ended – I wanted to earn some money doing work during the holidays. My application to the A1 ice cream factory in Pretoria was successful. I was equipped with an ice cream cooler box mounted on a three-wheeled bicycle, and was off to Church Square. I was promoted within two weeks, which meant that my mode of transport was upgraded. I continued henceforth with a horse and cart, with the driver's seat mounted to the side. My new sales territory was the vicinity of the then Loftus Versfeld Rugby Stadium. My salary was calculated at four shillings and three pennies for every pound's worth (i.e. R2) of ice cream I sold. Thursdays after work was pay-day. There was only one hitch in this brief career: In the last week of that vacation I ate too much of the ice cream I was supposed to be selling, and had to pay in for missing merchandise.

Initially we attended the Sunday School at the Dutch Reformed congregation of Eloffsdal. When the new Eloffsdal West congregation was established, we went there because it was closer to home. My brother, my sisters and I were later confirmed in this congregation.

In 1942 I was sent to the hostel of Afrikaans Hoër Seunskool (Afrikaans Boys' High School) in Pretoria. At that time it was the only Afrikaans secondary school for boys in Pretoria. I would eventually have a great deal to do with two of the seven roommates I was assigned to. Alwyn Burger eventually became Chairman of the Prime Minister's Scientific Advisory Council, and Hendrik Schoeman and I would later become Cabinet colleagues.

Gerrit Viljoen, also to become a Cabinet colleague, was a senior pupil at the time.

Gerrit and Hendrik, in particular, had a great influence on me and my fellow-pupils in different ways. Gerrit was a formidable academic, and Hendrik was an entrepreneur who had no hesitation in proving his skills in practical ways.

From an early age, I wanted to be a soldier. In 1943 I read about the Union Defence Force, fighting in North Africa together with other Allied Forces. I so badly wanted to become a part of this winning team that I reported to the Physical Training Brigade at Roberts Heights (later Voortrekkerhoogte and even later Thaba Tshwane). A little later it dawned on me that this may have been a somewhat drastic and particularly untimely step. On my arrival the commanding officer – Col Danie Craven, a close friend of the family – smelt a rat. He pointed out to me that I did not have the required written permission from my parents, so I was forced to about turn and head straight home. I was 13, and had absconded from school. This hard truth was brought to my attention by my incensed father, who gave me a proper hiding to show me exactly what he thought of my initiative.

I was heart-broken. Wasn't the Physical Training Brigade established specifically to take in "difficult young men"...?

It was back to the old grind for me, but some things changed. My parents decided that for the time being the proper place for a difficult young man was his own home. Perhaps they also thought that the daily pedal of 10 km from our home to Afrikaans Hoër Seunskool compared favourably with exercising in the Physical Training Brigade, for which I had been prepared to sacrifice so much.

However, I also had some luck on my side. In those days there was little in the way of holiday work for schoolchildren, but during the December holidays of 1944 the General Post Office in Pretoria employed one of my friends and me. Using our own bikes, we had to deliver telegrams to the addressees as quickly as possible. The pay was good and there were many telegrams every day, most of them addressed to foreign embassies. The Russian embassy close to the Union Buildings was the most popular.

In the short school holiday of 1945 a few schoolmates and I helped to build a concrete dam for a primary farm school at Rooigrond near Lichtenburg as part of a Land Service camp. It was fun working in this rural atmosphere, and I was grateful for the manual skills I acquired in this way.

Ruiter in die Nag was one of the titles of the books on my bookcase and it stood among other books on the Anglo-Boer War, which had ended less than half a century before. Karl Kielblock, Mikro, Sangiro, and Johan van der Post were some of the authors that appealed to me. The profound longing for adventure in a military environment did not simply disappear overnight.

AT LAST: A MILITARY ENVIRONMENT (1946-1947)

In 1945 the Smuts Government decided that civil servants who were also members of the Afrikaner Broederbond had to resign from this secret organisation or from the civil service. In order to prove that it had nothing to hide, the Broederbond's executive council submitted a membership list to the Government. The council also gave the Government the assurance that it was not involved in, and was not planning, any activities directed against the State and had no wish to do so. Furthermore they requested the Government to confront members of organisations such as the Sons of England and the Freemasons with the same ultimatum that members of the Broederbond were facing. The Government ignored these pleas and stuck to its original standpoint.

My father was not prepared to give up his position at Onderstepoort, a government institution, or his membership of the Broederbond and consequently his services at Onderstepoort were summarily terminated, without a pension.

I was fifteen years old at the time, and would only understand the full implications of what had happened much later. My parents had suddenly lost their primary source of income, the security of my father's permanent appointment and any provision for their old age. They were now dependent on their chicken farming, which produced only a small income. Their two eldest children were in secondary school, their third child was in primary school, and their youngest was due to go to school soon.

I had never known my parents to be people who would sit back and wait for others to take care of their problems. This was probably instrumental in their giving me permission to leave Afrikaans Hoër Seunskool and join the Physical Training Brigade, where I would be able to complete my schooling free of charge. I would also be given a uniform and pay of one shilling (about 10c) per day – which at that time could buy a great deal more than today.

And so I reported to the Physical Training Brigade – again – in 1946. The unit had in the meantime moved to Kimberley, and had been transferred from the Department of Defence to the Union Department of Education, but Dr Danie Craven was still the principal.

The military environment that I had longed for, and eventually ended up in, provided me with a great deal more than I had anticipated. For the first time in my life I was confronted with boys who had known little or nothing of the security of a stable home environment. Not everyone arrived undamaged from the outside world at the Brigade. There were boys of good breeding, and there were those who already bore the scars of a hard life. Many Brigade members later committed offences and were transferred to reformatories. Others broke the law and were taken away by the police. The usual system of seniority that prevailed at other secondary schools was completely absent here, as seniority was determined by age and military rank. The matriculants were not necessarily the oldest group, and it was not unusual to find young men between the ages of 17 and 21 in the junior classes.

The Physical Training Brigade was, in size and organisation, a battalion which initially consisted of four companies, later of five. It was housed in a military camp dating back to World War II. This camp met all the Brigade's needs, as among other things it provided school facilities and staff housing. The camp's layout, buildings, playing fields, and facilities were ideal for the Brigade's purposes.

Platoon leaders (of which I became one in 1947) and section leaders reported to the company commander, who was a member of staff. Outside the school context we were responsible for the organisation and its members. We were also responsible for tidiness and cleanliness in the various company areas, mess halls and dormitories, for the movements of groups from one place to the next, and for conducting drill parades.

Military appointments were made with little or no reference to academic performance. Most staff members were appointed from the Union Defence Force. The organisation's spirit, culture and management were purely military-based.

The school buildings were situated west of the national road, which physically split the Physical Training Brigade in two. The school was subdivided into academic, commercial and technical sections, each with its own principal and teachers. Five hours per day, five days a week, were devoted to school, and the rest to physical training and sport.

Permission to leave the camp grounds, which were situated next to the airport about ten km from Kimberley, was granted only in exceptional cases, and we were allowed to go home only during the two long vacations of the year. The only way of making contact with people outside the camp was if you were selected as a member of a representative sports team that competed outside the camp's boundaries. With Danie Craven as principal it was quite natural that many excellent sportsmen worked at the Physical Training Brigade. Many of them excelled at provincial level, and some were even Springboks.

Thanks to teachers of this calibre I found myself in a favourable position to realise my sporting ambitions. I won the three major swimming items at the inter-company gala in 1947 and represented the Griqualand West under-17 athletics team in four items at the national championships. I broke the South African under-17 shot-putting record at an athletics meeting and also played baseball for the open club's first team.

Furthermore I played rugby in the school's first team and in the open club's second team, alongside Jack van der Schyff, who later became a Springbok. Amongst others, the first team also boasted players such as Floors Duvenage, Billy Anderson, St Elmo Wilken and Ronnie Ackerman. Danie Craven was writing his first book on rugby at the time, whilst coaching the club's first and second teams, and was thus able to put into practice many of his ideas and theories about rugby. It was an extremely instructive and interesting experience for us.

I did not perform very well academically. For various reasons I had to struggle with matric mathematics on my own, and I failed. In the context of the Physical Training Brigade, however, my academic achievements were actually not all that bad. It was the first time that matric exams were written at the institution. Only 5 of the 73 matrics in the class of 1947 passed, and I was grateful to be one of them.

In general there was little need for news in the Physical Training Brigade, so newspapers were not readily available. Very few of us could afford a radio and as theft was always a factor to keep in mind in camp, it would simply be foolish to have any expensive items. Nevertheless, my father gave me a small radio that I could lock away in my trunk to keep abreast of what was happening "outside" the Brigade. He also paid for a subscription to *Sondagnuus*, a new Sunday newspaper, which was posted to me.

Later on in my career I often came across former members of the Physical Training Brigade, and most of them were well-settled. On the other hand, a few ex-members of the Physical Training Brigade later paid the highest price for capital crimes.

In my two years in the Physical Training Brigade I had to learn to handle situations I had previously never been exposed to. This involved the most basic things, namely clothing and food.

Established guys from other companies quite often burst into the bungalows housing the Reception Company and offered newcomers an absurd price for any civilian clothes they may have brought with them. Should the newcomers refuse the offer, the amount – usually far less than a half-crown – was simply tossed on the bed to clinch the deal. If the newcomers offered any resistance, they were simply assaulted. If the unfortunate victim complained, the guilty parties received corporal punishment. The victim's reward was a repeat visit, but this time without the half-crown; furthermore the victim would not merely be assaulted, but would be beaten up thoroughly. As a result, complaints became few and far between. The situation did improve from about 1947 onwards, as the bullies were suspended for other offences, or left the Brigade of their own volition.

I really have no idea what I would have done had I been a victim of these men. Fortunately a friend had warned me, so when I got off the train and reported at arrival, I was dressed only in trousers and a shirt, without even a jacket.

I was less fortunate where food was concerned. The first time I walked into the mess hall, it was clear that the table manners that held sway, were not of any acceptable kind. As soon as the container of food was placed on the table, it was every man for himself. The strong guys therefore ate well, while the weaker ones had to make do with the crumbs. I may not have been one of the smaller fellows at the table, but I refused to grab for food, and began to lose weight rapidly.

With the money my parents later sent me, I started to buy dry bread and ginger beer from the local shop to satisfy my hunger in secret. The dry bread and ginger beer did not, however, still the frustration that was building up in me and of course the situation at table did not change.

Something needed to be done, and that something would clearly not come from my table companions. I asked myself why this was so, and reached the somewhat uncomfortable conclusion that it was because I had done nothing. By not intervening, and by secretly visiting the shop, I had withdrawn from the situation. It was high time I entered the arena. To ensure that we all survived, I had to do this in a way that tough men in tough circumstances would understand. This was my first and possibly my most important lesson on survival.

When next we met at table, I looked my table companions straight in the eye and made a suggestion, not a threat; the people I wanted to convince had grown up in a world where threats were the rule rather than the exception.

My suggestion had to be convincing not only to me, it had to convince the others at the table as well, so I proposed that at each meal a different person should get the chance to dish up for himself first, after which the dish of food would go down the line. It would then be someone else's turn to dish up first the next day. In practice this would mean that A, dishing up first today, will be last tomorrow and therefore will not take more than his share, because it will be B's turn tomorrow, and if A is too greedy, B will more than likely do the same.

This plan found favour with the guys.

Some time later a beehive crossed my path, or rather my path passed by a beehive that was situated alongside my jogging route, a few miles outside the camp in a eucalyptus plantation near Alexanderfontein. Somehow a fellow pupil had acquired this hive full of honey and working bees, and when he no longer wanted it, he sold it to me *voetstoots* (as is). I did not have the equipment to recover the honey, but he taught me how to do it at dusk, using an ordinary tobacco smoking pipe. Although I did sustain a few bee stings, I was fortunately not allergic. When I left Kimberley, I in turn sold the hive to one of the remaining pupils.

I sometimes wondered whether it was worthwhile staying at the Physical Training Brigade. However, had I left, I would never have learnt the lesson my table companions had unwittingly taught me. Because it involved far more than mere table manners, it was a lesson I would never have learned in an atmosphere of starched damask and silver cutlery.

Of course life at the Brigade showed little respect for human dignity. At that time, however, parlour conversations did not revolve around military institutions; the talk of the time involved domestic politics, whether one was a Smuts man or a Malan man. Perceived threats to the state still made reference to the Anglo-Boer War, at that time more than 40 years gone. Only much later would I understand what I was then too young to grasp: A military community is a concentrated version of a wider society, and it contains all kinds of people. The difference is that in a military community you do not get to choose your companions.

POST-SCHOOL YEARS: 1948-1953

Once back in Pretoria, my first priority was to pass Mathematics with matric exemption, and my second was to find permanent employment. Thanks to private tuition I passed Mathematics in 1948, and the Transvaal Provincial Department of Education employed me as a clerk, paying me a monthly salary of about £20. I also had to help with the chicken farming, but I did have some leisure time, which enabled me to play rugby for the Innesdal under-19 team in the Moot.

The Transvaal leader of the National Party, J.G. Strijdom, asked my father to make himself available for the Gezina constituency in the general elections due to take place on 26 May 1948. My father initially hesitated, mainly because responsibility for the chicken farm would rest fully on my mother's shoulders should he become involved in politics. Yet, after due deliberation, he did make himself available and was elected to the House of Assembly. The Mérindol farm operations continued, and with the help of a relative, my mother continued to manage all facets of the chicken farm. Father went to Cape Town early every year and stayed in lodgings. Apart from one or two long weekends, he was absent for six months, and the only communication was by telephone. A few years later my parents appointed managers to run the chicken farm so that Mother could accompany him to Cape Town to support him. By this time the public transport system had developed to such an extent that flights between Johannesburg and Cape Town had become commonplace.

I stayed on at Mérindol in 1948, and went to Stellenbosch in 1949. From 1950 onwards I was enlisted in the Union Defence Force and lived at Voortrekkerhoogte. My siblings remained at Mérindol until they, too, went to Stellenbosch for further studies.

I went to the University of Stellenbosch in 1949, staying in Marais House and completing the first year of my B.Com. degree. It was a good year, and I had many friends, amongst them Org Marais, who would later serve in the Cabinet with me. I enjoyed a busy student life, and played rugby and baseball for the Matie under-19 teams. A pleasant memory from those days (of which visible proof still exists today) was the holiday during which I helped to build an earth dam near Durbanville in the Cape as part of the University's Land Service Club. This dam was always full, and to this day wild ducks, red-knobbed coots and other waterbirds breed there.

Towards the end of that year the Union Defence Force advertised vacancies for candidate officers. One of the conditions was that if you were selected, you would have to obtain a university degree with military subjects. I had all the matric subjects needed to enrol for the degree, apart from Science (now known as Natural Science and Chemistry), but I passed this subject three months later and was selected as a candidate officer.

My official military career started in April 1950 when I commenced studies for a B.Mil. degree in the field of Natural Science at the University of Pretoria, while at the same time receiving military training at the South African Military College at Voortrekkerhoogte.

We received a salary from the Union Defence Force, as well as accommodation in the officers' mess, uniforms, transport to and from the university, books and more. The only limitation was that we were not allowed to represent the university at sport; we had to remain members of the Defence Force sports club.

All these perks were accompanied by another unexpected advantage, which probably had something to do with the fact that we attended class in uniform: The women students quite readily accepted our invitations. This did not improve our relations with the male students, but despite a few differences of opinion with the residents of Kollege House, which were settled with fire hoses, we enjoyed our campus life. During Rag we actually won first prize for our military float.

Johann Kriegler was one of my roommates during my studies. After his first year he decided to switch to studying Law. Much later he was one of the first judges to be appointed to the Constitutional Court, and he remained there until his retirement.

I was one of the first students to enrol for the B.Mil. degree. The course is still offered to this day, the only difference being that the Military Science faculty was transferred from the University of Pretoria to the University of Stellenbosch, and has since then functioned as the Military Academy at Saldanha. At the time the system was very successful. The subject choice has expanded since then, but the Military Academy still exists as a faculty of the University of Stellenbosch, which awards its degrees.

I obtained a B.Sc.Mil. degree in 1953, and was commissioned as a lieutenant in the South African Marine Corps of the Defence Force.

Chapter 2

MY MILITARY CAREER BEGINS IN EARNEST (1953-1965)

THE SA MARINES - ROBBEN ISLAND

As an officer, I was immediately transferred to Youngsfield in Cape Town. The Marines constituted a subdivision of the South African Navy and had a twofold task: to deploy anti-aircraft guns to defend key points or vulnerable areas against enemy air attacks, and to defend our harbours against attacks from enemy ships using coastal artillery.

Youngsfield housed the training school for the anti-aircraft section, and Robben Island, which fell under the authority of the Defence Force, accommodated the school for coastal defence training. On arrival at Youngsfield I heard that they were looking for an officer to help with training citizen force infantry recruits on Robben Island, and I immediately volunteered to be transferred there. It was rumoured that only a married officer stood a chance of being appointed, on the grounds that a bachelor would never be able to cope with the loneliness. I doubted that an instant marriage would offer any kind of solution, and in any case there was no suitable matrimonial candidate on the horizon, but nevertheless I went to see the Officer Commanding, Cmdt (later Gen.) Dunbar Moodie, and managed to persuade him to allow my transfer.

In the roughly two years I spent on Robben Island I forged friendships that would last me a lifetime. Capt. R.A. Edwards spent his free time imparting to me the basic knowledge required in practice of a young officer. His positive approach and the mutual respect that characterised his relationships made the greatest impression on me. He would rather respond to a request with a yes than a no. Such an approach does, of course, involve high risk, but at the same time responsibility is shared between the person making the request and the one acceding to it. In this way, more than mutual trust can be created, because the subordinate's self-confidence is also reinforced. Furthermore, opportunities for getting to know your fellow men more quickly are thus created. Capt. Ronnie Edwards retired years later as Adm. Edwards, Chief of the South African Navy. He is an outstanding gentleman and officer.

There was so much to do on Robben Island that this "lonely unmarried officer" seldom availed himself of the ferry to cover the ten kilometres across the sea to Cape Town. I fished, caught rock lobsters, went sailing and swam. I rebuilt and secured the island's rifle range to upgrade this training facility. Our Marine Bisley team was therefore able to thoroughly prepare for the annual Bisley in Bloemfontein. We also arranged local competitions. I improved my marksman talents to such an extent that I was selected for the Western Province shooting team.

The training was excellent. The course in repository and gun maintenance was one of the few opportunities to apply one's university education in practice. During this course a coastal gun had to be dismantled and serviced before being reassembled. There were no cranes or other hoists, only pulleys and wooden blocks. The gun barrel alone weighed 28 tons. My university Applied Maths stood me in good stead, and I was able to apply in practice what I had been taught.

The course stretched over several months, and covered the large-calibre 9,2-inch guns and their support systems in detail. On conclusion, I was placed in command of an operation to scuttle a ship about 10 000 yards off-shore, using these three guns. This was a rare opportunity.

The *Richard Bennet*, a veritable rust bucket of 227 tons, was donated by a private company for this purpose. The ship was no more than a hulk, as all useful accoutrements had been removed. One gun was manned by students from the course, and the other two by Marines from land bases in Cape Town and Simon's Town. A good deal of rivalry existed between the teams, as each crew wanted their gun to sink the ship.

These three-storey guns were highly sophisticated in terms of the technological standards of those days. The projectiles, which weighed 380 lbs (172 kg), were brought up from underground bunkers by hoists, and then slid along chutes. Everything worked automatically. Compressors rammed the projectile into the barrel. The only manual task was to place bags of propellants into the chamber. Factors such as the weather and distance, which could influence the accuracy of the projectile's flight, were calculated by means of radar and were automatically fed into the fire control system.

When the guns were ready, I gave the order to fire a shot. After the sighting shot I made some adjustments and ordered another shot. When this gun was on target, I ordered the crews of the other guns to join the action.

As the ship was empty, and most of the engine had been removed, the projectiles that hit the target smashed right through the hulk before exploding. As a result the ship floated for a long time, sinking very slowly, which meant that our target was visible for a much longer period.

After the 23rd shot the ship suddenly reared and disappeared beneath the green waves. I then decided that the student crew had won the competition, and that the other two teams had come second. The other gun crews just quietly smiled at this fabricated decision.

The development of rockets and missiles, and their more widespread use, have rendered obsolete the use of large-calibre guns for coastal defence. Even the biggest guns had a range of only about 18 miles (30 km). Rockets and missiles are far more flexible, and can be used over far greater distances.

When the government decided to disband the Marine Corps in 1955, I immediately applied to return to the South African Army as an infantryman, and I was transferred to the Army Gymnasium in Pretoria as a training officer. The gymnasium was organised into an artillery battery, an armoured squadron and an infantry company. The unit's trainees were all volunteers, most of them with matric, and they underwent a year's training in one of the three sub-units.

THE ARMY GYMNASIUM

I was appointed Officer Commanding the infantry company in 1956. Infantry training in platoon weapons meant that we camped out on the Elandsfontein training area west of Pretoria for long periods. Practical training and firing exercises kept us busy each day from dawn to dusk. We braaied in the evenings and slept under the stars in our sleeping bags. This time spent together cultivated a feeling of solidarity.

One morning a 2 inch mortar bomb exploded just above the barrel. As training officer I had been supervising the exercise, and I felt personally responsible for what had happened. Fortunately nobody was killed, but the mortar crew had been peppered with shrapnel, trainee Chris Wolmarans lost his kneecap, and I suffered a broken arm. Long after the event, a piece of shrapnel would fester anew, or someone would develop a pain, which meant that a piece of shrapnel had to be removed under anaesthetic. A weight lifted from my shoulders when the Board of Enquiry that the Department of Defence had appointed to investigate the incident found that that particular batch of imported mortar-bombs was defective. The rest of the mortar-bombs from this consignment were then destroyed by explosives.

ARMY HEADQUARTERS

Early in 1957 I was transferred to Army Headquarters in Pretoria as an intelligence officer. Among other things I had to help identify national key points, with the aim of convincing the owners or managers of such key points of the necessity for securing and protecting them. First, however, it was necessary to determine what a key point was, and which of its activities would constitute such a key point. Then it had to be decided where each key point fitted into the national priority list, and what the organisation had to provide to ensure safety and security.

Key points are of national importance, and identifying them proved to be an enormous and instructive task. It was a lengthy process, and it took a long time before we saw any light at the end of the tunnel. The priority list would also have to be updated continuously.

At that stage few organisations were concerned about security. The preparatory work done by the Army could only be of an advisory nature, and had to be done very discreetly in order to avoid panic. This is why it was advisable not to rely on correspondence, but to personally visit the organisations concerned and to explain the requirements. When I was transferred from this section in 1958, the process was still in its infancy.

AIDE-DE-CAMP

As only unmarried officers could be appointed as aides-de-camp (ADCs) to the Governer- General, I was instructed during the second half of 1958 to appear before the selection board for consideration. The two ADCs appointed to Dr E.G. Jansen were myself and Buks Crafford. Buks, who served with me, later became a general in the SA Airforce. He was a wonderful, cheerful man and an enthusiastic fighter pilot.

Our routine at the Governor's Residence was that one ADC was on call to Dr Jansen on a 24-hour basis, while the other served Mrs Jansen, but only during office hours. The two ADCs then swapped around. The one on call to Dr Jansen had to receive guests and accompany the Governor-General on all his public engagements, and the one serving Mrs Jansen accompanied her to her engagements. If Dr and Mrs Jansen left the house on an official engagement together, both ADCs accompanied them. The one on call to Dr Jansen had to scout ahead and make sure adequate arrangements had been made for the official function, and that protocol was adhered to.

Both ADCs lived in the Governor's Residence and partook of all meals with the Governor-General and his wife. At formal and informal functions we were usually seated at the main table in order to be immediately available. Customarily our presence was not required for official meetings, administrative matters and private events. These responsibilities, and regular formal and informal visits by the Prime Minister, Cabinet members, foreign visitors, local notables and politicians, gave one the opportunity to get to know the visitors and guests quite well.

It was customary for the Governor-General and his wife to pay an annual official visit to each of the country's provinces. On these occasions the couple and their staff travelled between Cape Town, Bloemfontein, Pretoria and Durban on the White Train. The Government kept up Governor's Residences in each of these cities to accommodate the Governor-General, his wife and their staff during these official visits. An annual state banquet was held at each of these residences for the diplomatic corps and local guests.

Mrs Jansen took the ADC appointed to her along on interesting private visits. She had a sound knowledge of Cape silver and furniture, other antiques and South African paintings. Accompanying her was invariably so informative that I always offered to go with her. One Saturday morning she bought a Cape silver salver at the flea market on the Parade as a gift to her son. She wanted to have the engraving on the salver removed and asked me to take it to a silver smith for this purpose. I thought this would be a good opportunity to test her expertise, and I asked her in what year the salver was made, and what she paid for it. A stamp on the bottom of a silver piece usually indicates the provenance and date, but sometimes even experts have difficulty pinpointing this information, even with the help of the stamp.

I asked the silver smith, who had no idea in which capacity I was there, to evaluate the item. His date corresponded with the one given by Mrs Jansen. However, his price was £2 higher than she had paid for it. I never again thought it necessary to test her knowledge.

MILITARY ACADEMY 1959

Before the end of my year in the Governor's Residence, I was transferred to the Military Academy in Saldanha on the insistence of the Defence Force, and was appointed second in command. Col (later Brig.) Piet de Vos was commander and Dean of the Faculty of Military Science. He was a capable academic and a very pleasant person, and we got on well together.

Towards the end of 1959 and early in 1960 there were clear signs of internal unrest and resistance organised by the ANC, with the potential to become violent. In March 1960, insurrection and demonstrations against particular laws occurred throughout the country. At this time the tragic incident at Sharpeville occurred, where 69 people lost their lives and many were wounded.

The Government declared a state of emergency and the Defence Force was put in a state of alert.

I was appointed as operations officer to Brig. Piet Jacobs, then Officer Commanding Western Province Command in the Castle in Cape Town. He was quick-tempered and straight-talking, but was a good commander who readily shared his knowledge and always knew what to do in particular circumstances.

During the early stages of these events, at a time when the Citizen Force and Commandos had not yet been fully deployed, there was a mass march to the Cape Town Central police station and Parliament. I was ordered to safeguard Parliament with the help of a group of storemen. The soldiers assigned to me had had years of experience of stock control, and they performed admirably at this task, but they knew next to nothing of weapons and riot control. I tried to quickly teach them the meaning of minimum force, and how to work together as a platoon. They showed great willingness when I deployed them at Parliament, but it is very fortunate that the march never spiralled out of control and was calmed before it posed any real threat to Parliament, with everybody dispersing peacefully.

Early in August 1960 I was nominated to attend an advanced military training course (known as the Army's Command and Staff Course) in Pretoria. This course was more or less one year in duration and required exceptionally hard work. The sections on the management and solution of military problems were very informative, and conventional and revolutionary warfare received special attention.

The decolonisation process, which was then playing itself out in Africa, was intensively analysed during the course, and the unrest in South Africa was discussed in this context. At the time, the South African government's apartheid policy was criticised both in Africa and internationally. The criticism, and incidents occurring in the country, made me realise that a more concentrated assault on South Africa would follow sooner or later. Consequently I had a growing interest in world affairs.

Many future top management figures in the Defence Force attended the Staff and Command Course, amongst them Capt. Constand Viljoen, who would later become a general and Chief of the South African Army, and later still Chief of the South African Defence Force; Maj. Bob Rodgers, later a general and Chief of the South African Air Force; Capt. André van Deventer, later general and Officer Commanding Operation Savannah (he was in command of the South African military forces in Angola in 1975-1976), and later still Chief of Finances of the South African Defence Force. When one works together for so long and under such pressure and tension, one gets to know everybody's strengths and weaknesses very well. With these officers, I felt, I could face any war and win.

South Africa became a Republic in 1961, an event which coincided with widespread unrest. The course was interrupted, and the students were despatched to the various areas of unrest. I was once again sent to the Castle in Cape Town to serve with Brig. Piet Jacobs.

For the duration of the unrest in the Western Province, which was limited to the Peninsula and surrounding Boland towns, I stayed at Brig. Jacobs' side. For the most part, we had Citizen Force and Commando units at our disposal. They were employed to quickly cordon off identified areas to prevent ringleaders from escaping and to give the police the opportunity to complete their task.

DEFENCE HEADQUARTERS

With the unrest quelled, I returned to the course with additional practical experience. On completion of the course in the spring of 1961, I was transferred to the office of the Director of Operations and Planning at the headquarters of the Chief of the Defence Force. Brig. Jacobs had been promoted to general, working with Brig. Jannie Burger at Defence Headquarters. (In my opinion Brig. Burger was one of the most hardworking and knowledgeable army officers we had at that time. His path to the top was assured. In 1966 he commanded the Defence Force's participation in the celebrations marking five years of the Republic at Monument Koppie. He died of a heart attack during the march-past: it was a blow to lose a good friend and valued colleague, especially during such celebrations.)

I worked in close collaboration with Brig. Jan Burger, and with his guidance we tried to determine the most extreme circumstances in which South Africa and South-West Africa could find themselves during a revolutionary onslaught. To do this we had to draw on the first local military appreciation that the Defence Force had compiled in 1960.

A military appreciation is a very important document drawn up to determine or indicate future security situations or actions. Various political, economic and security facts, factors, events and current trends, as well as situations at the national and international level, are considered to determine the expected future security situations and actions the country may face. It is an internationally acknowledged method which usually determines future military threats and actions quite accurately.[1]

We used the military appreciation in an attempt to determine whether there were enough Citizen Force and Commando units with suitable, properly trained manpower to meet such a future threat. Once the need had been determined, we had to attend to matters such as weapons and military equipment. Such an investigation is extremely time-consuming, but in view of the ever-escalating threat, the effort eventually paid off in that it assisted in the identification of a need for a more appropriate mindset within the Defence Force. It brought home the fact that certain preparations were necessary.

As for me, it was a time of war and love. I fell in love with a special girl from the Free State, Margot van der Walt, a public relations officer for the Rembrandt companies. After we learned to know each other thoroughly, we decided to get married on 2 February 1962.

At this stage I also farmed on the sideline. We had decided that the wedding reception should be held at the South African Military College, and agreed that I would take responsibility for arranging it, and would at the same time supply some of my own produce, for example mutton, in order to enjoy some of the fruits of my farming activities.

The college had excellent facilities for such occasions, such as tables that could be used for formal mess dinners. It was customary not to cover the whole table with white tablecloths, but to use long strips on which the cutlery was placed. On conclusion of the formal dinner, and before the toast was proposed, these narrow strips of tablecloth would also be removed, exposing a particularly beautiful tabletop. In my wisdom I decided not to use any tablecloths at all for our reception, so as not to hide the very attractive tabletops. However, after the reception one of the guests, a prominent and lovely elderly lady, pointed out to me that one does not place silver cutlery on bare wood. This left me with the same feeling of inadequacy concerning table manners that I had experienced years before at the Physical Training Brigade – I concluded that my knowledge of the finer details was lacking in some areas. I did find solace in the thought that my former comrades at the Brigade would probably not feel the slightest affront!

As for the rest, I thought everything was going well, until my bride asked me where the photographer was. Apparently I was supposed to have arranged for someone to take photographs of the ceremony. As a result we have no wedding pictures to speak of, and she still teases me about this (in good spirit, I hope).

THE AMERICAN EXPERIENCE

The South African Army regularly sent officers to foreign military institutions to ensure that South Africa kept up to date with the latest international military developments. As I was a major by then, I was sent to the USA in June 1962 to attend a command and staff course, and the South African Defence Force gave permission for my wife to accompany me.

The United States Army Command and General Staff College at Fort Leavenworth in Kansas is situated on the banks of the Missouri River, amid cornfields and cattle ranches. No US army officer can be promoted to the rank of general without having qualified at this college. Those who already have the relevant Bachelor's degree and then complete the command and staff course here, are entitled to a Master's degree. This was applicable to US citizens only, however.

About 900 senior US Army officers and about 100 officers representing the Air Force, Navy and Marine Corps attended the course. I represented South Africa, one of some 120 Allied officers from 55 countries.

The course was excellently planned, and the content was of the highest order. We attended classes or discussions for six hours per day, which required three or fours hours' preparation the previous night. Individual progress was regularly monitored by means of examinations.

A great deal of attention was paid to the analysis and management of conventional and revolutionary warfare. The use of nuclear, chemical and biological weapons formed part of the teaching. Various countries of the world served as reference for the customary military map exercises. Sometimes the US ambassador in the particular country made a presentation and introduced the discussion, to give the students a first-hand account of that country's historical background and prevailing circumstances.

An information sheet on the particular country was always handed out prior to a military map exercise. The information on South Africa was neither complete nor correct. For example, a photograph of Cape Town harbour dated from before the reclamation of the Foreshore and construction of the new harbour. Furthermore, according to the map, the Du Toitskloof Pass had not yet been completed. I was then asked to rewrite the information sheet, a challenge I did not shirk; I also led the discussion in this regard.

My wife and I rented a house about ten kilometres from "The Post", as the military institution was known. In the USA, when buying a car, ons can order a certain model a year before it is released. I decided to buy a 1963 model car, but it could only be delivered late in 1962, so we had to use public transport for a few months. This mode of transport was most inconvenient for someone attending classes, so I decided to buy a bicycle. In view of the high humidity in summer and the snow in winter nobody, but nobody, rides a bike in those parts of the USA. Motorists hooted at me and waved as they went past, and pedestrians cried out: "Look, a man on a bicycle!" This South African's biking exploits piqued my US colleagues' interest in South Africa, and resulted in friendships that have lasted until today.

At the time, South Africa's internal policy received rather sensational international news coverage and my wife and I were in strong demand to be present at local events, and even to appear on television. The appearances took a great deal of time and preparation, but were definitely worth it, as it forged sound relations.

The authorities created many opportunities for Allied students to meet politicians, high-ranking officials, business leaders and senior Defence Force officers. On one occasion the Allied officers were flown to Washington DC. Among other things, the ten-day period we spent there

My meeting with Robert Kennedy during my visit to Washington DC in 1962. He was the President's brother, and served as Attorney-General. As in South Africa, the USA's political system consists of three independent structures of authority, namely the executive, of which the President is the highest official, the judiciary and the legislature or Congress, consisting of the Senate and the House of Representatives.

was devoted to presentations, followed by internal discussions on the functioning of government, good governance, and the Democratic Party's political strategy for fostering better relations between the various population groups. There were also visits to the White House and government ministers (or secretaries, as they are known there).

During this visit I had a conversation with President J.F. Kennedy in the Rose Garden at the White House. The press often questioned me about this conversation, but I never responded – at the time a sense of discretion towards such a prominent figure precluded me from repeating any details of the discussion we had.

Pres. Kennedy enquired whether I was related to Sailor Malan – Adolf Gysbert Malan, who won renown for his exploits as fighter pilot and tactician in the British Royal Air Force during World War II. Kennedy knew Sailor Malan, which explained his interest. I answered that all Malans in South Africa were somehow related. (Sailor Malan, too, was a descendant of Jacques Malan, the patriarch referred to earlier.)

The conversation then shifted to South Africa, and I asked Kennedy whether he had read Clarence Randall's article "Give them time" in the new glossy edition of *Atlantic Monthly* – an unusually objective article on South Africa. Kennedy had not read it, but questioned me with obvious interest, and made some intelligent remarks. I later wrote him a letter and included the article. I worded my reference to our conversation in such a way that his secretarial staff would be compelled to consult him before deciding whether they would require his help in replying. Kennedy replied personally to my letter, however, thanking me for drawing his attention to the article, and wishing me every success.

Naturally I appreciated this gesture very much. It was consistent with the behaviour of the man at the White House that day: in contrast to some of his fellow party members, he did not turn his back on me when it became known that I was from South Africa, but was polite enough to have a chat with me. I do not want to express an opinion on everything that had been said and written about Kennedy in the years after his death, but I would like to add: He was truly well bred.

On the way back to Kansas we visited the Headquarters of the United Nations in New York for an information session, and also stopped at West Point, the US Army's foremost training facility for candidate officers, for a briefing. We ended the tour with a visit to the Pittsburgh industrial area.

On conclusion of the course in Kansas, I was transferred to the 35th Mechanized Division in Colorado Springs for valuable practical experience. There were manoeuvres during which the combat-ready division was airlifted to an area in the eastern United States and independently and immediately had to commence combat exsercises in the training area: about 10 000 men, with their tanks, armoured vehicles, artillery, helicopters and all other equipment had to be transported by air!

We returned to South Africa in the second half of 1963. As was usual after attending a military training course abroad, I was transferred to the South African Military College in Pretoria as a training instructor. I initially assisted with the training of officers for promotion, and then I became involved in the Command and Staff Course as a member of the directing staff. I was also asked to document what I learnt about the USA's military doctrine, organisation and development for the information of the staff and students.

BACK TO DEFENCE HEADQUARTERS

In 1964 my responsibilities increased at more than one level. Our first child, Madelein, was born at the end of that year, and I was transferred to the office of the Chief of the Defence Force as assistant military secretary. Among other things, my duties involved keeping minutes of the meetings of the General Staff Council (by way of explanation: The Chairman of the General Staff Council was the Chief of the South African Defence Force). I was also responsible for office administration and speech-writing for the Chief of the South African Defence Force. This meant that my family and I had to be in Cape Town during Parliamentary sessions.

In 1965 Gen. P.H. Grobbelaar, at that stage Chief of the South African Defence Force, was preparing for retirement. He wanted to make sure that units of the Defence Force to which sufficient time and funds had been allocated, were combat-ready. I had to accompany him during his personal tours of inspection to act as minuting secretary. This gave me a good grasp of the combat-readiness and morale of those units. Neither he nor I were impressed with the state of affairs, as many deficiencies were brought to light by the inspections.

In view of the spread of revolutionary warfare in Southern Africa, and in view of the complaints from South-West Africa about problems experienced in this regard, the Chief of the Army at the time, Gen. Pop Fraser, requested the new Chief of the South African Defence Force, Gen. R.C. Hiemstra, to release me from my secretarial duties and to despatch me to South-West Africa as Officer Commanding.

Before submitting this transfer request to the Chief of the Defence Force, Gen. Fraser asked my opinion about it. Because it would affect me personally, I found it difficult to judge the matter objectively. One of the reasons why I hesitated was that I had recently attended a very expensive course that lasted almost one year in the USA, dealing intensively with the command, management and deployment of large military capabilities. The financial outlay for the course was carried by the Army's budget, and therefore the Chief of the Army himself would have to decide whether the Army and Defence Force had enjoyed sufficient return on their investment.

Chapter 3

APPOINTMENT TO COMMAND (1966-1972)

SOUTH-WEST AFRICA

My name appeared on the annually circulated Army Transfer List at the end of 1965; I concluded that Gen. Fraser's request had been agreed to, and so I prepared to move my household to Windhoek. This was the first time I would have the privilege of commanding an independent unit or formation, the real desire or ambition of any military officer. Meanwhile, my wife and I were building our first house in Pretoria, but we looked forward to going to Windhoek, which we did after living in the house for only seven months.

My period of service ran from 1966 to early 1968. I was serving as the military officer commanding South-West Africa when the first shots were fired in that region. In my new capacity it was my responsibility to prepare all the region's inhabitants for the security threat, and to protect them against it.

Even at that early stage it was clear that the South-West African People's Organisation (SWAPO) wanted to conquer South-West Africa by revolutionary means, and that South-West Africa's Defence Force elements needed to be combat-ready. Because we were expecting SWAPO action, we were in a good position to prepare for a war that had not yet begun in earnest. We had time to prepare ourselves before matters got out of hand.

The vastness of the country and the population distribution had to be taken into account. By way of comparison, the country was about three quarters the size of South Africa, but it had a population equal to only about 4% of that of South Africa. The population was therefore far more sparsely distributed than was the case in South Africa.

I drew up an operational plan to counter the most severe possible onslaught, reorganised the existing Defence Force units, launched a recruitment drive and commenced local military training. The reaction was most encouraging. At the end of my period of service, there were more qualified counter-insurgency officers and non-commissioned officers in South-West Africa than in South Africa. The number of local commando units was increased from seven to fifteen during this reorganisation, and the complement of these voluntary elements more than doubled in size. The morale of the Defence Force members was excellent, and they all took part in the voluntary training exercises with great enthusiasm.

In 1966 the South African Police in South-West Africa received information that rebellious elements of the Herero tribe had decided, in conjunction with SWAPO leader Sam Nujoma, that he should pay a surprise visit to South-West Africa. The purpose of the visit was to embarrass the Administration of South-West Africa and at the same time, to encourage protest marches, unrest and violence aimed at the South-West African authorities in order to draw international attention to SWAPO as a liberation movement.

Sam Nujoma would arrive by plane from Lusaka on a specific afternoon, landing at the new Windhoek Airport about 50 km east of the city. A crowd of protestors would welcome Mr Nujoma and march to Windhoek with great fanfare to show the world that the South African authorities were no longer welcome in South-West Africa.

However, good footwork enabled the police to determine that the aircraft carrying the SWAPO leader would land at about eleven on the morning concerned. When the plane landed, none of his supporters had reached the airport yet, and his "welcoming committee" consisted of the Divisional Commissioner of Police, at that time Brig. Theo Crous, and I, as commander of the military forces in South-West Africa stationed in Windhoek. The pilot, named Nash, and Nujoma were the only people on the plane, and Nujoma was immediately arrested and taken away. His supporters arrived later that day, and were bitterly disappointed because they were under the impression that Nujoma had left them in the lurch. They returned to Windhoek without the slightest hint of protest or unrest.

What was to be done with the enemy's leader now? Apart from myself and the handful of policemen involved in this successful operation, nobody knew of his arrest. The next four or five days were spent deliberating and reflecting on the matter. After the Military Intelligence Division supplied an evaluation of enemy targets, which included Nujoma, we decided to send him back to Zambia on the same plane. One of the main reasons for this decision was that intelligence sources thought Nujoma would be of greater value to us amongst his own forces than in our hands.

One Friday afternoon, just before the office was about to close for the weekend, the signals officer rushed into my office: They were receiving a secret signal from the South African Army Headquarters in Pretoria marked "priority" and addressed to me. The signal was clearly urgent and contained very sensitive information that they the signallers busy decoding. The information in the signal indicated that there was a strong possibility that SWAPO was about to cross South-West Africa's border in one or more aircraft in order to demand the independence of South-West Africa from within its own borders.

For the purposes of the operation to neutralise this action, 2 Battalion Group in Walvis Bay was placed under my command, and three South African Air Force transport planes (C-130s) were made available. Keeping in mind the various airfields and pans where enemy planes could possibly land undetected and to save time, I ordered the Battalion Group to enter South-West-African territory as soon as possible by road and to proceed to the large airfield at Karibib, where they would receive further instructions. The aircraft would for the time being be stationed in Windhoek.

Although SWAPO never arrived, this pre-emptive exercise nevertheless had an interesting sequel. At that stage, Walvis Bay was still South African territory, and this substantial movement of South African armed troops into South-West Africa, involving a convoy of some 23 km in length, was probably the first large-scale South African Defence Force deployment in South-West Africa since World War I. Even though the International Court of Justice in The Hague was then deliberating the case involving South Africa's mandate over South-West Africa (which put great pressure on South Africa), there was, amazingly enough, very little reaction to this "invasion" of South-West Africa. This created a precedent, and probably helps to explain why the international community paid little attention to subsequent regular movements of armed South African troops in South-West Africa.

It took a great effort by all those involved to ensure that South-West Africa became combat-ready during my period of service. My family realised the gravity of the situation and willingly made sacrifices. There were four of us now, as our second child, André, was born in South-West Africa.

THE REVOLUTIONARY THREAT

A serious shortcoming at this stage was that the inhabitants of South-West Africa knew almost nothing of revolutionary warfare. They did not know what such a war was all about, or what challenges they were facing. In order to create public awareness of the dangers, and to explain the nature of the revolutionary threat, I travelled the length and breadth of South-West Africa, appeared at every possible public event and arranged information sessions.

At such public appearances and during military courses presented by the South-West Africa Command in Windhoek from 1967 onwards, the essence of revolutionary warfare had to be conveyed concisely but clearly. Without the proper background knowledge about the ways of the revolutionaries, it was almost impossible to understand the so-called struggle that would dominate events in Southern Africa for a long time to come. I therefore utilized the account given by Mao Zedong, the Chinese communist leader and founder of revolutionary warfare, as set out in his so-called Little Red Book.[1] To my mind, the following explanation serves as a good frame of reference:

A study of conflict in the 20th century shows that up until World War

II, countries entered into war with one another by issuing an official declaration of war. Conventional military forces then met one another on the field of battle to settle the dispute by force of arms.

Since then major doctrinal changes and new developments in the field of warfare had occurred. African countries such as Kenya, Algeria, Mozambique, Angola, Rhodesia (now Zimbabwe), South-West Africa (now Namibia) and South Africa already had first hand experience of some of these developments.

Mao Zedong explained revolutionary warfare in the following manner: "A revolution is not the same as a dinner, or writing an essay, or painting a picture, or stitching a piece of embroidery; it cannot be so refined, so peaceful and calm, so measured, good and well-mannered, controlled and benign. A revolution is the overthrowing, by violent means, of one group by another."

In a revolutionary war the ruling party or parties find themselves on one side. They wish to defend and maintain the constitution or a political system. On the other hand the opposing party or parties wish to overthrow and destroy the existing political system by violent means, in order to replace it with a new political dispensation. The opposing party uses the struggle to pursue its goal of a political victory by violently taking over the authority in the country.

Any country's population can be divided into three groups according to their view of or attitude towards the current political, ideological or constitutional system in that country:

(a) A small core group of ardent supporters of the current system, usually the government leaders and their immediate supporters.
(b) Another small core group with negative feelings towards the current political system, namely the opposition leaders and their immediate supporters.
(c) The third group, constituting the greatest mass of the population, which is not really emotionally attached to the political system. This group is neutral and does not necessarily take part in the political system, but may become involved if it is influenced, persuaded or intimidated.

According to Mao, the group opposing the current political system and wishing to replace it by revolutionary means, has to attempt overthrowing the small ruling group with violence in order to start a revolutionary war.

Both opposing groups will regard it as the highest priority to target the mass of unconcerned people (the so-called third group), to force them to leave their "neutral corner" and choose sides. The opposing parties will therefore try to shift the centre of gravity of political opinion over to their side by winning the support of the mass of the population and discrediting and defeating the ruling party.

To put it concisely: A revolutionary struggle mainly revolves around capturing the soul, heart, convictions and support of the population. Violence and intimidation characterises the climate in which such a revolutionary conflict occurs.

In the effort to retain the support of the population, the ruling party will accept certain restraints on its actions, while the revolutionary opposition accepts no restrictions.

Furthermore, the ruling party has to act within the laws of the country and certain acknowledged international conventions, such as the Geneva Protocol.

The ruling party cannot make promises and then not keep them. The party must properly fulfil its obligations and take note of the wishes of the population, taking into consideration factors such as law and order, security, job opportunities, the availability of housing, education, medical care, welfare, etcetera. In other words, the masses are constantly judging the ruling party on the way it is executing its responsibilities.

In contrast its opponents enjoy full freedom of movement and action. This group does not have to operate within the laws of the land. It may well threaten population groups or individuals with death, intimidate them, and even use the cruellest methods imaginable, such as necklacing, as long as these methods shock the population. Shock results in dismay, and dismay, in turn, is the forerunner of political capitulation.

The revolutionary opposition has no responsibilities. It can promise heaven and earth, because it cannot be held accountable while the conflict rages. When the opposition has achieved victory and has reached the struggle's objectives, what it promised is no longer of any importance. By then it has achieved its goals.

Such a revolutionary force has the further advantage that it can preach propaganda, spout negative criticism and spread lies during the struggle without being held accountable.

During the revolutionary period circumstances therefore favour the opposition party (or parties) rather than the ruling party. The results of revolutionary wars the world over support this statement.

That is why I maintained and propagated the view that in this type of conflict, in which attitudes are of prime importance, the attention of the state should be focused mainly on political and socio-economic matters (in the order of 80%), and to a lesser degree on security (in the order of 20%). Political and socio-economic matters are the areas of responsibility of the civil government departments. The Defence Force has always consistently propagated this view at its training facilities.[2]

Consequently, I repeatedly proclaimed in public that the conditions for stability in Southern Africa are to be found in law and order, proper political representation for all, job creation, educational opportunities, housing and social development. These priorities are equally important today, because human development and an improved standard of living hold the keys to success.[3]

This message, and a greater awareness of the nature of the onslaught, did help. Among other things it resulted in many citizens of South-West Africa voluntarily joining the Citizen Force and Commandos, undergoing training and actively participating in their activities. This contributed to an increase in the territory's preparedness.

THE MILITARY ACADEMY

The Minister of Defence, the Chief of the South African Defence Force and the Chief of the Army visited South-West Africa Command and the northern border with Angola in 1967. They were satisfied with the preparations and progress in South-West Africa – to such a degree that they decided to transfer me to the Military Academy in Saldanha, where I assumed command early in 1968.

My instructions were to ensure that officers of the proper calibre were trained to take on the challenges ahead.

Candidate officers of the Defence Force (i.e. Army, Air Force and Navy) were trained at the Military Academy. Those who successfully completed the three-year course were commissioned, and were awarded a B.Mil. degree by the University of Stellenbosch.

With the approval of the Defence Force and the University of Stellenbosch I adapted the training to make it more focused. I maintained that the first part of the course should determine whether a candidate shows the characteristics required of a Defence Force officer. At the same time there had to be development training and academic teaching which would be required later on in the candidate's career. This part of the course, under the competent leadership of Col (later Gen.) Raymond Holtzhausen, lasted six months. Those who passed could choose to be appointed as second lieutenant in the Defence Force, or to qualify for a B.Mil. degree after another two and a half years' training, and to serve in the Defence Force as full lieutenant.

The University of Stellenbosch approved the application for some of the subjects offered during the first six months of development training to be acknowledged as first-year university subjects. The Military Science Faculty undertook to adapt the subjects offered during the two and a half years' course in order to make them as practical as possible.

With regard to some of the challenges I encountered during the four years at this unit, I really found myself in deep water, but I received excellent professional advice, and was supported by a very capable staff. For example, I had to find a way of testing the potential of candidates' abilities as officers, over and above their academic results. There were no South African sources to advise me, as the Military Academy at Saldanha was the only one of its kind in South Africa. I therefore had to visit overseas academies and conduct intensive discussions. The conclusion was that one had to create circumstances in which one could observe the candidates' interpersonal reactions, and that additional facilities were essential.

A Letra course would help to foster the candidates' leadership abilities and assist in observing and testing their practical problem solving. The word "letra" is derived from "leadership training". Such a course usually consists of about twenty different practical problem situations that the participants as members of different teams need to solve. To illustrate with an oversimplified example: A man in a boat must ferry a goat, a cabbage and a lion across a river, but he can only transport two of them at a time. How do you get all of them to the other side unharmed? The solution to this type of problem, which usually carries a time restriction, can be explored in practice and observed on such a letra course. It is used to great effect at the military academies of some Western countries.

Furthermore I needed to find terrain where the candidates could be assessed in harsh conditions. After having studied the requirements for such terrain, I chose the Namib Desert, the oldest and driest desert in the world. The best know area in this desert contains red sand dunes, of which those at Sossusvlei are generally accepted as being the highest permanent dunes in the world – more than 300 m in height. Before the choice could be finalised, a team of observers needed to do a test run.

At that stage I had never attempted the Namib Desert on foot. Word had it that the last person to attempt an experimental crossing of the Namib Desert on foot – a South-West African German during World War II – did not survive. My conscience would never be clear if I were to send a team on such a mission without having experienced the desert myself.

Two officers at the Military Academy, Brig. J.D. Potgieter and the later Gen. Chris Thirion, together with the Academy S Maj. WO1 Erasmus, offered to accompany me. We started from Sossusvlei and headed southwest for Oyster Rocks. I had decided on this course because all the dunes on the route lay transversely across our route, which increased the difficulty, more so because the dunes followed one another without any hard sections to speak of in between. It was sand from start to finish, with no hard surfaces, so that one could not really hike, but rather stumble. An element of pressure was built in, as the exercise had to be completed within a specified time limit. It was certainly a stern test of one's physical and mental abilities!

Problem-solving, interpersonal relations, endurance and adaptation to a foreign environment formed part of the route. The terrain certainly rendered the desired results with regard to the training of the candidate officers that followed on our trial run.

As soon as the leadership corps of the South African Defence Force had approved the amended development and academic training, I organised a publicity weekend to present information about the Military Academy and the opportunities offered by the Defence Force to domestic and foreign journalists. The SABC was also invited; South Africa's television service was then in a preparatory phase, and was collecting material for broadcasting at a later stage. Its presence was therefore in the nature of an investment in future local TV broadcasts. Quite a few foreign television teams and journalists from local and foreign newspapers were present. It was a successful weekend of demonstrations, in-depth discussions and displays. The Military Academy's chaplain, Vic Borcherds, who was intimately involved in the arrangements and was knowledgeable about the media, calculated that about 20 to 30 million viewers world-wide tuned in to the programme. After this introduction we could pick and choose from amongst all the applicants.

At this stage I also instituted equitation as an additional challenge for candidate officers. Equitation makes great demands on the rider's ability to adapt to less sophisticated circumstances. Historically horses had proved to be of great operational value. An analysis of the looming threat in the South-West African operational area indicated that situations where a man on horseback would have an advantage, might soon occur.

Some time later, when I was Chief of the Army, it became clear that mounted troops were feared more than tanks or guns in South-West Africa. They proved to be a great psychological deterrent. Horses give the horsemen height, horsemen have the advantage of speed during follow-up or tracking operations, and the horses' heightened senses warn their riders if something is wrong.[4]

The success and experience gained from equitation at the Academy later supported my decision as Chief of the Army to establish a stud farm near De Aar. A few hundred mares and selected stallions did very well there. Horses for operational purposes were bought all over the country. A riding school (the South African Defence Force's Equestrian Centre) was established earlier on at Potchefstroom to train horsemen. Equestrian competitions provide popular television material worldwide, and consequently the Equestrian Centre at a later stage was able to project a positive image of the Defence Force to South African viewers.

Before my years at the Military Academy came to an end, our youngest child, Charl, was born at Saldanha, and the eldest started going to school there. I was transferred to Cape Town, but the children were not at all happy about the move. They had many friends in Saldanha, the beach was within walking distance, and life was carefree because their parents were readily accessible and, because it was safe, easily granted them permission to play with friends. It was paradise on earth for them.

WESTERN PROVINCE COMMAND

In 1972 I once again found myself in the Castle in Cape Town, this time as Officer Commanding Western Province Command. At that time the Command was responsible for a geographical area stretching from the Western Province to the Northern Cape up to the Orange River. A substantial number of Citizen Force and Commando units fell under my command. Given South Africa's vast rural areas, the Citizen Force and Commando units, with their knowledge of local circumstances, had a very important role to play. During inspections, meetings, order groups and personal and group discussions I tried to engender a greater awareness of the revolutionary onslaught, as I had done earlier in South-West Africa.

Many of the Citizen Force and Commando units could boast a glorious past, having fought in many battles. Units receive honours for participation in battles, and are judged, among other things, by lessons learnt in the use and application of tactics, personnel, time and place.

For example, Johannesburg's Light Horse Regiment received battle honours for its participation in the Battle of Elandslaagte and other battles during the Boer War. These honours are displayed on the unit's standard. During World War I the unit received honours for the Battle of Gibeon in South-West Africa, during World War II for its participation in the Battle of El Alamein, and once again for its more recent participation in the revolutionary war in South-West Africa, namely the "SWA 1975 to 1989" decoration. In the more than 100 years of its existence, this unit has garnered about 24 such battle honours.

Tradition was very important to some of these units and I was proud to be associated with them. Their leaders were very often volunteers, people who had already completed their statutory service of about twelve years, but chose to continue voluntary service in these forces. At a later stage I visited many of these units in the operational area, where they gave outstanding service.

At this stage nine months of national service was compulsory. I received criticism of the system, because national servicemen would physically work hard for the first three months, after which they would lounge about with very little physical exertion for the last six months.

As a substantial number of national servicemen received their training at the Youngsfield anti-aircraft base, I was in a good position to personally investigate this issue. It appeared that there were a number of causes for discontentment.

Fifty per cent of national servicemen had to be present in camp over weekends in order to maintain an adequate troop strength, should they be required for security purposes. Military camps therefore found themselves competing with commercial facilities in town in as far as weekend entertainment was concerned, and of course the Defence Force movies and swimming pool came a very poor second.

Another problem was that the first three months of national service involved far more physical training than the subsequent period. After the first three months the troops were fit and energetic, but the period that followed offered far less opportuity for physical activity. At the time sport was not regarded as time on duty, and there was very little encouragement for participation.

Moreover, most servicemen came from the Witwatersrand and were therefore far from home. It was quite understandable that they would have preferred to receive their training in a location more central than Youngsfield, which had served as the anti-aircraft training centre since World War II. Matters were complicated by the fact that anti-aircraft guns were far more likely to be deployed near cities and industrial complexes , and that most of these centres were situated in the north of the country. It would therefore have been more efficient to train servicemen from the northern provinces for such a purpose, because they would most probably be operationally deployed in their home area.

Unfortunately, it would have cost millions to move this training school. (Nevertheless such a move had to be included in future planning, and eventually did take place.)

I had a great deal of sympathy with the servicemen's frustration at having to spend weekends in camp. It reminded me of my days in the Physical Training Brigade – one was confined to camp without knowing why. It was only human that when servicemen looked back on their nine-month period of national service, they would judge the period as a whole, making no distinction between weekends and training during the week. Weekends in camp contributed greatly to expressions such as "we were busy for three months, and then we sat around doing nothing". Nobody could be blamed for questioning and disparaging the length and intensity of national service.

For various reasons, the intensity of the security threat in those years varied from one geographic area of South Africa and South-West Africa to the next. In my opinion, Army Headquarters needed to liaise more closely with the various Command Headquarters responsible for security in their areas, in order to paint a more accurate picture of the security threat and agree on the best counter-measures. This would result in a far more accurate assessment of the manpower and equipment, if any, required in the military camps over weekends. Closer liaison with the various Command Headquarters could even provide other solutions for problems encountered with the provision of manpower and equipment.

In order to solve the problem of servicemen in camps over weekends, I addressed submissions to the Chief of the Army, with the request that certain prescriptions should fall away in my command area, i.e. the geographical area that was my responsibility. I suggested that instead of warning the various commands of expected actions within their areas, a colour code system should be used, with green indicating that there was no restriction on national servicemen, yellow indicating certain restrictions on movement, and red indicating the most severe restrictions. It would then be the responsibility of Army Headquarters, in consultation with the area commander, to determine which restrictions should apply in a certain area. Adjustments could be made continually, thereby avoiding a system which was difficult to justify and sometimes even seemed unreasonable. The entire country need not always be in the same state of preparedness.

Another suggestion was that sport should be regarded as duty, so that participants could be credited for their participation. This would improve the Defence Force's performance in sport, and allow for excess energy to be dissipated. It would also contribute to the maintenance of fitness levels, and give servicemen more opportunities to meet the local people at sporting events. Once again, I recalled my days in the Physical Training Brigade and the solace I gained from sport. I tried to imagine myself in the position of the national servicemen – the same situation I had found myself in some 30 years before. I had no idea to what extent these suggestions would make their period of service more bearable; my recommendations was simply based on available options.

The Defence Force was probably one of the first sports clubs in the country where merit was the determining factor when selecting sports teams from amongst all population groups. As Officer Commanding in Cape Town I ordered the Western Province Defence Force Rugby Club to start selecting its teams on merit in 1972. In this regard I received very good advice and support from Cmdt (then Capt.) John Cupido. The Western Province Rugby Union's Jan Pickard gave these steps his active support, and as a result Western Province took the lead countrywide with regard to sport at provincial level. Other sporting codes and provincial teams later followed this lead.

In addition I suggested that the anti-aircraft school should be situated more centrally, for example in Kimberley or Bloemfontein, and that national servicemen should be permitted to work more hours during the week so as to earn longer weekends. This would make it possible for the servicemen to visit their homes more often and for longer periods of time.

Hitchhiking was against the policy of the Defence Force at the time. Many parents informed the Defence Force that their children were forbidden to hitchhike. If the Defence Force were to permit hitchhiking, and a serviceman were to be involved in an accident, the Defence Force would be held liable for vehicles and drivers over which it had absolutely no control. In practice, however, this policy offered neither the Defence Force nor the parents any peace of mind: Servicemen simply hitchhiked at will. In my opinion a fair division of responsibilities would be to everybody's advantage, and so I also requested that in certain circumstances official permission should be granted for national servicemen to hitchhike.

In order to lessen the homesickness, and to increase social interaction, I motivated women's organisations in and outside my geographical area of responsibility to invite servicemen to their homes or to community centres over weekends and to show greater appreciation for the sacrifices made by servicemen. Some of these women's organisations, amongst them the Defence Force's own Women's Organisation, various churches' women's organisations, the ACVV (Afrikaans Christian Women's Association), the SAVF (South African Women's Federation), the VLV (Women's Agricultural Association) and the VLU (Women's Agricultural Union) responded in a positive manner. Their contributions were highly appreciated.

I did not receive any reaction from Army Headquarters with regard to my submissions.

Chapter 4

DEPUTY CHIEF OF THE SA ARMY

At the end of 1972 I was transferred to Pretoria as Chief of Army Staff Operations, or Deputy Chief of the SA Army. Gen. Willem Louw, the Chief of the Army, telephoned me and informed me that he was transferring me to Pretoria with promotion to Chief of Army Operations. He was a man of few words, so the telephone conversation was over even before I could ask any questions.

On the one hand I was disappointed at the transfer. I have always had a soft spot for the Cape, even though I would probably always be a Blue Bull supporter. However, what weighed more heavily on my mind was that I would now find myself in a different work situation. I had been an officer commanding in various capacities for seven years, and was very grateful for the privilege, experience and exposure that this position afforded me. Unfortunately this transfer now meant the end of that privilege. I would no longer command and would simply become one more staff officer; one amongst many at headquarters in Pretoria. I would no longer be top dog, but would have to take on support responsibilities. In the Cape I was a big fish in a small pond, but in Pretoria I would simply be a small fish in a big pond. I had just begun to lay the foundation for my approach and inputs in this command, and now had to leave before my task was completed. I had just begun to get to know and appreciate the unit commanders, officers and senior non-commissioned officers, and suddenly, after a year, I had to take my leave of them. I had just arranged and conducted a successful informal interdepartmental get-together to develop better communication and sounder working arrangements with government departments in the Cape Town area.

The good news was that I would probably not be transferred from the Pretoria region any time soon. There were some matters I had referred to Army Headquarters for which I had not yet received replies, for example the matter concerning the national servicemen, and I would now be in a better position to achieve finality in this regard. Subconsciously the transfer also brought our children more peace and greater stability, because in the years ahead they would not have to change schools so often, and the family would have the opportunity to forge stronger ties. I therefore visited Pretoria at the first possible occasion to buy a house which was close to a primary school and a church, and from where I could commute to Army Headquarters fairly easily.

It had been fifteen years since I had last worked at Army Headquarters, and in the past eight years I had found myself in "outposts" such as South-West Africa, the Military Academy and the Castle in Cape Town. Each of these commands had been challenging in their own way. It took much more time and effort to adjust to the headquarters in Pretoria than I had expected. For example, Armscor had been established in the meantime, and I had to acquaint myself with new responsibilities, circumstances and personalities.

DEVELOPMENTS IN AFRICA

On my appointment to Army Headquarters, I gained easy access to sources of information that had previously been beyond my reach. I immediately regarded this as a good opportunity to update my rusty knowledge of Africa. At this stage is was becoming clear that danger zones were beginning to develop in countries to the north of South Africa, and that the security situation in South Africa would be influenced by political developments in neighbouring countries, Angola in particular. It was clear that the SA Army would sooner or later receive instructions to operate in areas where red lights were already flashing.

I began to immerse myself in the information available. At first I merely wanted to concentrate on recent events in Africa, particularly those with possible implications for future security operations. However, it soon became clear that if I wanted to have a proper perspective on and feeling for developments in Africa, I would have to study much more than the recent past. I therefore began compiling a schematic overview of historical events that had influenced Africa.

Africa was divided amongst seven great European powers at the Berlin West Africa Conference of 1885 under the chairmanship of German Chancellor Otto von Bismarck. The colonial powers never met again to discuss the decolonisation process, and apparently no informal attempts at co-operation took place either. It was as if they had lost the desire to rule.

The seeds of the decolonisation process can be found in the aftermath of World War II (1939-1945) and subsequent historical events. This war not only radically changed the histories of the Americas, Europe and the East, but also impacted on the history of Africa. In the wake of this devastating and exhausting war only two strong powers, or rather superpowers, remained, namely the United States of America (USA) and the Soviet Union (USSR). The pre-war European powers, namely Great Britain, France and Italy, regardless as to whether they were on the winning or losing side, could no longer hold their own as colonial masters in Africa and elsewhere in the world.

One of the most profound events of the post-war period was the struggle for independence in colonial empires, beginning with the Dutch East Indies Empire in Indonesia and ending with the Portuguese colonies in Africa and elsewhere. South Africa would not be spared these events. During World War II many men from the colonies served in the Allied Forces and in the process acquired military and leadership skills.

In the aftermath of the war, the cost of retaining their colonies became too great for most of the European mother countries. The citizens of colonial European powers had already experienced six years of hardship during World War II, followed by a decade of post-war depression. They were no longer prepared to bear great economic burdens and undergo compulsory military service in order to subjugate indigenous populations. The small interest groups that benefited from colonial empires could no longer rely on the support of their own citizens.

In the post-war years small groups of indigenes who enjoyed exposure to Europe came into contact with the Marxist argument that Europe's prosperity was based on the exploitation of colonial populations. On their return to their home countries these educated and energetic individuals often engendered political awareness amongst larger groups of people in the colonies, organising them and advocating racial equality and independence.

The pursuit of independence gained momentum in Africa only from 1956 onwards, but before the end of the 20th Century all former colonies on the continent were independent. African nationalism washed over the continent and influenced all of Africa from Cairo to the Cape from the 1960s onwards, and the movement lasted for the rest of the 20th Century. The decolonisation process received a boost when the Union of Independent African States, then known as the African Union, came into being in Accra under the leadership of Kwame Nkrumah of the Gold Coast (later Ghana). Eight independent African states joined the organisation and demanded the immediate independence of all African states. Three more meetings were held in 1959 and 1960, during which South Africa's apartheid system was also harshly criticised.

The development of the Soviet Bloc of states in Eastern Europe, and the outbreak of the Cold War, further tipped the scales in favour of the independence of African states. The Cold War engendered intense tension between the Soviet Union (USSR) and the United States of America (USA) as well as their satellites and supporters. There was never any military conflict between these great powers, but deadly rivalry existed in the fields of politics, economics and propaganda. The USSR, with its Marxist ideology, and the USA, with its capitalist democracy, competed fiercely for the support of Third World countries, resulting in the spread of the Cold War to Africa.

Joseph Stalin had stated Russia's desire for world domination as early as 1923, and subsequent Soviet leaders echoed the sentiment that there could be no world peace unless the Marxist ideology was firmly entrenched the world over. This constituted the biggest threat to the sovereignty of all states in the Free World, of which South Africa was one.[1]

Certain intermediate goals on the road to world domination were identified. Southern Africa was one of these intermediate goals, and this resulted in the communist onslaught on Southern Africa, with control over the area as the ultimate goal. On more than one occasion Leonid Brezhnev, later leader of the Soviet Union, declared: "Our goal is to control the two treasure chests on which the West depends – the energy treasure chest of the Persian Gulf, and the mineral treasure chest of Central and Southern Africa."[2] If one takes into account the variety and quantity of minerals over and above strategic minerals found in Southern Africa, it is easy to understand the importance of control over this mineral treasure chest.

At that stage Angola, Northern and Southern Rhodesia, Botswana and Mozambique could still be relied on as as buffer states between South Africa and the newly liberated and militant states to the north of these neighbours. As early as 1960, in his "Winds of Change" speech delivered during a visit to South Africa, Harold Macmillan, at that time Prime Minister of Britain, warned that the wind of national awareness was blowing through Africa, and that South Africa had to take note of it. South Africa soon began to feel the force of these winds – not only on its own soil, but also in its mandated territory, South-West Africa.

Soviet policy towards Africa was quite clear-cut. The USSR and its allies had to become the overwhelming influence in Africa, and do all in their power to contribute towards the fall of the "imperialist bastion" in the south of the continent and the establishment of Marxist governments throughout this area.

The Organisation of African Unity (OAU) was established in Adis Abeba in Ethiopia in 1963 as the successor to the African Union. From the start this organisation expressed itself forcefully against apartheid and racial discrimination in South Africa. Its members formed a powerful pressure group to isolate South Africa internationally, and have it expelled from the United Nations Organisation (UNO). Under the influence of the Soviet Bloc, the OAU and UNO, the states of Southern Africa increasingly campaigned in support of the revolutionary onslaught. Zambia, Botswana, Zimbabwe and Mozambique, in particular, eventually permitted the African National Congress (ANC) Alliance to operate clandestinely from their soil in order to commit acts of terrorism in South Africa.

The impressive amount of attention the Soviet Union gave to Africa, the amount of research it did, and the extent of its aid to movements involved in the "armed struggle" becomes clear from an imposing publication of 440 pages entitled *The armed struggle of the peoples of Africa for freedom and independence.* This detailed study was compiled by a team of writers of the Soviet Ministry of Defence's Institute for Military History, in co-operation with the Africa Institute and the Institute for Social Sciences in Moscow. The authors state the purpose of their work quite clearly: "The Soviet Union and associated Socialist countries are compelled to give continuous military and economic aid and political support to the peoples of Africa in their holy war against their oppressors ... and they regard it as their duty to support the holy war of the suppressed peoples and their legitimate wars of liberation against imperialism." Experts included the ANC in their highest category for freedom movements in this book. They believed that the combat-effectiveness of movements in this category was to a large extent determined by "the degree to which the views of the leadership correspond with Marxist-Leninist ideology, and the degree to which they co-operate with communist parties and Marxist-Leninist groups".[3]

The training of African leaders, including some from South Africa, commenced at the Africa Institute in Moscow as early as 1957 under a veteran expert on Africa, Prof. I.I. Potekhin. In addition, the Patrice Lumumba University in Moscow was established in 1960, where Third World students were indoctrinated and trained in the art of subversion and espionage.

SOUTH-WEST AFRICA

South Africa's mandate over South-West Africa (SWA) was the first issue (apart from its domestic policies) that placed the country in the international crossfire.

When World War I broke out in 1914, the British government requested South Africa to attack the German colony situated immediately north-west of it, which was then known as German South-West Africa. The objective was to occupy the harbours in that territory and to take over the powerful radio transmitter in Windhoek. The South African

Prime Minister, Gen. Louis Botha, acceded to the British request and quickly forced the German commander to surrender at Khorab.

World War I (1914-1918) officially ended after the Paris Peace Conference, that lasted for six months, and the signing of the Treaty of Versailles on 28 June 1919. Among other things, the terms of the Treaty included a Charter for the establishment of the League of Nations, and the re-allocation of former German territories. South-West Africa was ceded to South Africa, which was a member of the League of Nations by virtue of its status as a British dominion, as a so-called C Mandate territory. In terms of League of Nations stipulations such a C Mandate could not become an independent state, and the country to which a C Mandate was ceded could govern it as an integral part of its own territory.

South Africa's main function as holder of the mandate was to take responsibility for the welfare of the inhabitants of the territory. In my opinion South Africa faithfully implemented this mandate, as large amounts of taxpayers' money were spent in South-West Africa. South Africa was required to establish infrastructure such as railway lines, harbours, roads, bridges and airfields, and did so, footing most of the bill itself.

At the end of World War II Gen. Smuts wanted to incorporate the territory into South Africa, but encountered strong resistance from Third World leaders in the UNO, the new international organisation created as successor to the League of Nations. Mrs Vijayalakshmi Pandit, Indian ambassador to the UNO and sister of the Indian Prime Minister, Jawaharlal Nehru, was at the forefront of this resistance, which placed the South-West Africa question squarely in the international arena.

South Africa held the view that the UNO had not inherited the powers of the defunct League of Nations as far as stewardship of the mandate system was concerned, and that South Africa was under no obligation to transfer South-West Africa to UNO trusteeship. In years to come, the South-West Africa question would be referred to the International Court of Justice on various occasions. However, it was clear from the start that the UNO and the international community would only be satisfied once South Africa had surrendered control over South-West Africa.

MAP 2 SOUTH-WEST AFRICA/NAMIBIA AND ITS LOCATION IN RELATION TO THE REST OF AFRICA.

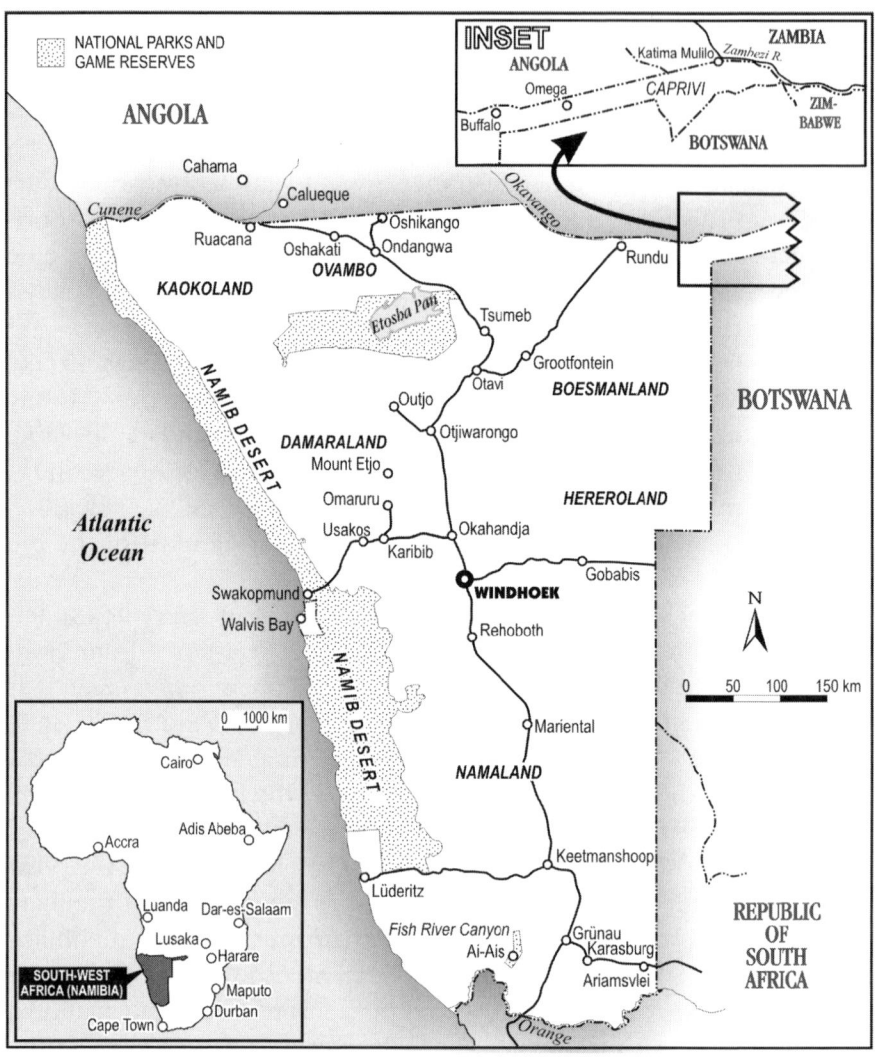

In a military sense South-West Africa south of Etosha, in other words south of the Red Line, was regarded as another South African province, and therefore the military organisation of the South African Defence Force in this area was similar to that in any other South African province. It consisted of a military headquarters, with Citizen Force and Commando units under its command; these Citizen Force and Commando members were inhabitants of South-West Africa. The South African Defence Act also applied to these members, and they were subject to the same national service as South Africans.

Over the decades the close relationship between South Africa and South-West Africa became even closer. The mandate entrusted to South Africa, the financial investments that South Africa made in South-West Africa, and that territory's economic dependence on South Africa, all contributed to the strong relationship of trust between the two countries. Furthermore South Africa was for seven decades directly involved in the administration of South-West Africa. No wonder that when the territory's security was threatened by terrorism from Angola, South Africa did not hesitate to come to South-West Africa's aid. Requests for aid from South-West Africa to combat terrorism came largely from leaders in the area north of the Red Line – Ovambos in particular.[4] In terms of the mandate South Africa was obliged to protect inhabitants in this area and to ensure that enemy elements, for example SWAPO, did not overthrow government authority by violent means.

The revolutionary struggle in South-West Africa had its origins in 1957 when Andimba or Herman Toivo ja Toivo – a World War II veteran – founded the Ovambo People's Organisation (OPO). It was a typical liberation movement of the time, with some members also supporting the South African Communist Party. Toivo was arrested for provocation in 1958, restricted to northern Ovamboland, and eventually jailed on Robben Island. Sam Nujoma assumed the presidency of OPO in 1959, and in 1960 changed its name to SWAPO.

The new name helped to consolidate support for the movement, and Ovambos, in particular, joined in large numbers; some 95% of SWAPO members who died or were taken prisoner during the South-West African border war were Ovambos.

In July 1961, an interim SWAPO headquarters was established in Dar es Salaam in Tanzania. Furthermore SWAPO created the People's Liberation Army of Namibia (PLAN) in 1962, and in so doing in effect ignited the border war. From the start South-West African/Namibian SWAPO leaders were committed to Marxism, and their weapons and training were supplied by communist countries.

At a SWAPO meeting in Dar es Salaam in 1963, Nujoma gave orders for strikes, sabotage and revolution in South Africa and South-West Africa. In their book about former South African Pres. P.W. Botha, *PW*, Dirk and Johanna de Villiers write:"This brought greater clarity to the communist plan to conquer Southern Africa. The southern pincer movement, which was already in operation in Angola and Mozambique with the help of Marxist terrorist movements, was to enclose South-West Africa and Rhodesia at a later stage."[5]

Ever more strident demands were made that South Africa should withdraw from South-West Africa. Liberia and Ethiopia, the only black members of the defunct League of Nations, brought a case against South Africa before the International Court of Justice, declaring that it was not fulfilling its obligations in terms of the mandate. However, the Court ruled that Ethiopia and Liberia had no real interest in the case, and had no right to become involved in it.

The nations of Africa would never accept such a ruling, and took the matter to the UNO's General Assembly. On 27 November 1966, the General Assembly unilaterally decided to end the mandate, and adopted Resolution 2145, which stated that South Africa had no right to administer the territory. South-West Africa would in future be the UNO's direct responsibility, and this body would administer it. South Africa rejected this resolution as illegal, and the General Assembly's reply to this reaction was a decision in 1968 that in future South-West Africa would,"in accordance with the wishes of the people", be known as Namibia. Furthermore a Committee and Commissioner for the territory were appointed.

Resolutions of the UNO's General Assembly cannot be enforced in any country. All member countries of the UNO are members of the General Assembly. On the other hand, the decisions of the UNO's Security Council, which has a very limited membership, can be enforced unless such a decision is vetoed. At that time the USA, Britain, France, China (until 1971 represented by Nationalist China or Taiwan) and the USSR were permanent members of the Security Council. The UNO's General Assembly was very antagonistic towards South Africa's domestic policies, and South Africa had to take account of this attitude in all its actions, as it could have had a negative impact on the five permanent members of the Security Council. South Africa therefore focused on maintaining good relations with certain states represented in the Security Council, hoping that these countries would use their veto in favour of South Africa, should a crisis present itself. In its attempts to maintain good relations with these countries, South Africa found its freedom of action restricted in certain cases (and rightly so).

South Africa's long-standing dispute with the UNO regarding South-West Africa gained momentum when the chairpersons of the newly established Committee for South-West Africa, Dr Victorio Carpio of the Philippines, and Dr Salvador Martinez de Alva of Mexico, were sent to the area to investigate various complaints concerning the management and administration of South-West Africa. At a later stage a Council for South-West Africa/Namibia was also appointed to lead the territory towards independence.

The first six insurgents slipped across the border into Ovamboland from Angola in September 1965. At that stage this border, which really existed only on paper, was patrolled by only a handful of policemen. The insurgents were instructed to concentrate on fostering political activism and to provide supporters with some elementary training. A second group crossed in February 1966, and a third in July 1966. The armed struggle began in earnest when shots were fired at a number of Ovambo chiefs and a farmer near his homestead in the Grootfontein district. Shots were also fired at the border post at Oshikango on 16 August 1966.

The Minister of Defence at that time, P.W. Botha, shortly afterwards issued a clear warning to the liberation movements that South Africa was determined to protect the area, and that it had the military capability to do so successfully.

The Security Council ratified the suspension of the South-West African Mandate in 1969, and in 1970 declared South Africa's presence in the area illegal. In that year, too, the Security Council asked the International Court of Justice to give an advisory opinion on South-West Africa/Namibia. The 1971 ruling by the International Court of Justice read that: "… South Africa's continued presence is illegal, and that country should immediately end its occupation of that territory." South Africa had no hesitation in rejecting this ruling and declaring: The government will continue ruling South-West Africa/Namibia in order to promote the welfare and development of all its inhabitants.[6]

Henceforth the South-West Africa question would offer South Africa's opponents a convenient platform for exerting greater pressure on it, and isolating the country diplomatically. Since 1960 the UNO had been dominated by a bloc of South American, Asian and African countries, some of them tiny.

Up to this point the Vorster government had shied away from military action on South Africa's borders, and had mainly deployed the police to combat unrest-related incidents. In future, however, border security would be the task of the SA Defence Force. SWAPO was determined to employ force to conduct its military struggle against South-West Africa/Namibia vigorously inside the country.

SWAPO's military wing, PLAN, had in the meantime gathered 900 recruits who had been trained in Tanzania. After completing basic training, they were sent to Algeria, Cuba, Egypt, the Soviet Union and Red China for advanced courses. Initially SWAPO also co-operated with the Angolan liberation movement, União Nacional para a Independência Total de Angola (UNITA or the National Union for the Complete Independence of Angola), under Dr Jonas Savimbi, and the Caprivian African National Union (CANU), an insurgency movement from that area.

PLAN intensified its campaign of political activism, intimidation and terrorism in 1973, and began to deploy land mines, which cost many civilians their lives.

PORTUGUESE TERRITORIES IN SOUTHERN AFRICA: ANGOLA AND MOZAMBIQUE

Dr António Salazar, the Portuguese Prime Minister from 1932 to 1968, ruled Portugal and its overseas provinces with an iron fist. In the early 1960s Angola was a hotbed of socio-economic and political grievances. These grievances, allied with the independence of colonial territories, and the campaign waged by the communist and Afro-Asian Bloc in the UNO, created a good climate for revolution. Although Portugal is a small country, at that stage it had the third largest colonial empire in the world.

Pressure from Portugal's colonies became almost unbearable from about 1960 onwards. In the early 1970s Defence Force Chiefs reported on Angola in the following terms: "... judged by the degree in which terrorists are presently operating in the territories, Portugal has lost the struggle."[7] Terrorist organisations already controlled certain geographical areas, and were rapidly gaining the upper hand in Angola. According to this report, Portugal had 65 000 soldiers in Angola, and 60 000 in Mozambique. In Angola, large parts of the south had been activated by the insurgents. (In addition Portugal deployed approximately 60 000 troops in Guinea during this period as well.)

Up to about 1970 the support of the Portuguese regime in Angola had been very valuable to South Africa in countering the insurgency campaign in South-West Africa. Up until that stage PLAN could not use southern Angola as a training ground and base for insurgency operations in Ovamboland.

The liberation wars in Portugal's colonial territories resulted in its complete economic exhaustion. In the early 1970s Portugal spent 50% of its national budget on wars in Africa, and inflation was 23%.[8]

The Portuguese forces in Angola and Mozambique were mainly national servicemen who initially served for two years, and after 1967 were compelled to serve for four years in order to satisfy ever-increasing manpower requirements. Many of the junior officers were graduates who did not support the government, and there were too few professional officers to satisfy all the training needs.[9]

The mobilisation of Portugal's population to provide manpower for its African wars brought about one of the longest and most exhausting forms of military conscription in the world. It is estimated that 11 000 Portuguese were killed and 30 000 were wounded over a period of thirteen years. As a result some 50% of those eligible for national service never reported for duty. Emigration soared, and about 1,5 million people left the country – a significant number of them potential national servicemen. This is quite understandable if one takes into account that in proportion to the population, the constant force level of 150 000 men in Africa since 1970 was five times higher than that maintained by the USA in Vietnam.[10]

The turning point in Portugal's destiny occurred when Dr Marcello

Caetano succeeded the dictatorial Dr António Salazar. Caetano was well disposed towards South Africa, but before he was able to complete his socio-economic reforms, his regime was overthrown in a military coup.

Gen. António de Spínola, Deputy Chief of the Armed Forces, had lit the fuse for the subsequent political and military explosion with his book *Portugal e o futuro (Portugal and the future)*, which was published in 1974. He was seeking a political solution through negotiation rather than through military means. In September of that year, Marxist-orientated leftists forced moderate Spínola to resign as Portugal's political leader, and he was succeeded by Gen. Francisco da Costa Gomes, who instituted a drastic political course correction. One could clearly see the Soviet Union's hand in the country's colonial policy towards Mozambique and especially Angola.

There were three rebel movements in Angola which, apart from their joint opposition to the Portuguese, differed from each other in most important matters. They also enjoyed support in different geographical areas in Angola.

Of the three movements, the Movimento Popular de Libertação de Angola (MPLA, or People's Movement for the Liberation of Angola) was later to prove dominant. In typical communist fashion this movement sought the support of the intellectuals, but also of the poorer classes. This movement, with the seasoned Marxist and intellectual Dr Agostinho Neto as its leader, commenced its armed struggle in February 1961. Neto was succeeded by José Eduardo dos Santos, who was later to become President of Angola.

In the north and east the Frente Nacional de Libertação de Angola (FNLA, or National Front for the Liberation of Angola) held sway. Its leader was Holden Roberto, a brother-in-law of Pres. Mobuto Sese Seko of Zaire (Democratic Republic of Congo – DRC). Roberto had his power base amongst the Bakongo tribe living on both sides of the border between Angola and Zaire. This movement was strongly tribe-orientated, anti-Portuguese, anti-communist and anti-MPLA. Roberto enjoyed strong support from the Zairian president right to the end of the struggle.

The third liberation movement was UNITA (União Nacional para a Independéncia Total de Angola or National Union for the Total Independence of Angola), and its leader was Dr Jonas Malheiro Savimbi. Its main support base was the Ovimbundu tribe of eastern, central and southern Angola – blood brothers to the Ovambo of South-West Africa, and the largest ethnic group in Angola. Savimbi had been educated in Portugal and Switzerland and initially joined Roberto's grouping. Savimbi was a committed revolutionary dedicated to the overthrow of Portuguese rule, but a pragmatist as well. He had a disagreement with Roberto in 1964, and then broke away to form UNITA. Although he initially leaned towards Red China, he later associated himself with the West.

In Mozambique, on South Africa's eastern border, the revolutionary movement Frelimo (Frente de Libertação de Moçambique) was engaged in a bitter battle with Portugal, the colonial power. On gaining independence, Mozambique became a socialist one-party state with a totalitarian government headed by the Marxist leader of Frelimo, Samora Machel. It was therefore to be expected that this government, as soon as it had established itself, would support the ANC Alliance. After all, its battle cry was "The colonial yoke must be thrown off!" If decolonisation succeeded in the Portuguese territories, then Rhodesia and South-West Africa were sure to follow, and then it would be South Africa's turn.

At that time communism all over the world used what was know as salami tactics. Just as the well-known sausage is sliced piece by piece, to be chewed and swallowed in bits, the tactic was to carve up and incorporate a geographical area bit by bit, rather than trying to attack the entire territory in one go. This had to be done as inconspicuously as possible.

BUFFER STATES TO SOUTH AFRICA'S NORTH

The former Central African Federation, which consisted of Northern Rhodesia (Zambia), Southern Rhodesia (Zimbabwe) and Nyassaland (Malawi), fell apart in December 1963. The creation of newly independent states meant the end of South Africa's buffer area to the north. These states had now become a bridge along which revolutionary theories could stream southward.

Premier Ian Smith unilaterally declared Southern Rhodesia independent from Britain on 11 November 1965. This marked the start of a drawn-out civil war involving the Zimbabwe African People's Union (ZAPU) and the Zimbabwe African National Union (ZANU), that was supported by China. ZAPU and ZANU were movements or fronts, not disciplined political parties, but jointly acted as "the Patriotic Front" under Marxist leadership. In 1980, at the Lancaster House Summit in London, the Rhodesian Front Party headed by Bishop Abel Muzorewa and Ian Smith was forced to abandon the unilaterally declared independence and to hold elections under British supervision. The elections of 4 March 1980 saw Robert Mugabe (ZANU) and Joshua Nkomo (ZAPU) elected Zimbabwean President and Vice-President respectively. Shortly after these elections, during a session of the OAU in Freetown, Sierra Leone, Mugabe declared: "Now that the question of independence in Zimbabwe has been settled ... must the Organization of African Unity (OAU) not come to the aid of the Frontline States with substantial military support so that these states are enabled both to defend their territorial integrity and to effectively give support to the national struggle in South Africa? Now that we have only South Africa and Namibia to rid of colonialism."[11]

SOUTH AFRICA

The Soviet Union had always regarded Southern Africa in general, and South Africa with its strategic minerals in particular, as an important intermediate goal. In a time of increasing demand, South Africa was happy to supply the West with strategic raw minerals. South Africa had by far the largest reserves of strategic minerals such as manganese, chrome, platinum and vanadium outside the communist world. If the Soviet Union were to control these reserves, it would be able to exert a stranglehold on the Free World.[12]

At that time South Africa occupied a key position on the important trade and oil supply route between Europe and the East. The Cape sea route was protected by strategically important military facilities such as the SA Navy's Joint Maritime Operations Centre at Silvermine near Muizenberg, the largest naval base in Africa at Simon's Town, and the sub-bases at Durban and Walvis Bay, as well as excellent air bases. In the early 1980s some 6000 to 7000 vessels from Western countries used this route, which passed about 30 km south of Cape Point. At that time about 80% of all oil destined for Europe, as well as food and other important supplies, was carried on this route.

About 74% of Africa's total railways are found in South Africa. If the Marxist liberation movements were to conquer South Africa, they would have control over the best infrastructure in Africa, including excellent airports and five deep-sea harbours. Furthermore South Africa was one of only seven countries in the world classified as a net exporter of food, and the only one in Africa.[13]

One should keep in mind that at this time the Cold War was by no means over, and that South Africa was of great strategic value to the West. Gen. Sir Walter Walker, former Commander-in-Chief of the Allied Forces Northern Europe of the North Atlantic Treaty Organisation (NATO), said the following with regard to the Soviet Union's goals: "The first thing to get clear is that the Soviet Union, whether by blackmail, revolutionary war, by proxy or by brute force, intends to absorb the whole of Southern Africa, and then deprive the West of vital minerals and control of Europe's lifeline round the Cape. Southern Africa holds key bases of fundamental strategic importance to the control of sea-lanes and trade routes in the South Atlantic and Indian Oceans. The possession of these bases would give the Soviet Union overwhelming superiority in global strategy."[14]

Communism and terrorism are closely allied in the history of subversion in South Africa. The Communist Party of South Africa, together with other organisations with communist goals, was declared an illegal organisation in terms of the Suppression of Communism Act, No. 44 of 1950. The party dissolved itself to comply with the Act, but was reconstituted in 1953 with a new name – the South African Communist Party (SACP). It then decided to work both overtly and clandestinely. It worked openly by infiltrating legitimate organisations such as the ANC and trade unions in order to promote communism. In this way the SACP became a member of the so-called ANC Alliance.

Members of the ANC Alliance were sent to the Soviet Union and Communist Bloc countries to receive training in politics, administration and revolutionary warfare. The courses also included training in the management of the mechanisms required to run an underground organisation, and communications and intelligence services. The creation of a network in which the identities of members would remain secret, even from one another, was emphasised.

As early as 1972 an ambitious plot to land Alliance members trained in the USSR on the coast of South Africa was uncovered. The operation involved a ship that set sail from Mogadishu in East Africa, but failed due to a radar error.

Furthermore an extensive network of terrorist training camps was established in Africa and elsewhere where basic skills in weapons handling were taught under the supervision of USSR and Soviet Bloc instructors. One of these camps was Kongwa, an extensive training camp west of Dar es Salaam, mainly used by the ANC Alliance, SWAPO and Rhodesian terrorists. The most important Alliance command camp and headquarters was situated in Morogoro. There were other training camps in Lusaka, among others Lapu, as well as the Nkomo Camp of the Pan Africanist Congress (PAC). After Mozambique and Angola became independent, training camps were erected in these countries as well.[15]

Worldwide pressure was exerted on South Africa aimed at creating problems for the Defence Force. As early as 17 November 1964 the British Prime Minister, Harold Wilson, announced an arms embargo against South Africa. In the 1970s the British Communist Party urged the British government to institute a complete boycott against South Africa, and to end all direct and indirect military aid to the white-controlled countries of Southern Africa. Furthermore it was suggested that British labour and progressive movements should show solidarity with the national liberation movements by providing financial support, and by organising industrial action against British military and economic support for the "racist regimes".[16]

In the USA, too, the Communist Party waged a campaign against South Africa. A journalist wrote the following in the 27 February 1976 edition of the American publication *The Guardian*: "If the watershed of history was Vietnam, the fatal blow to imperialism and Western capital at home itself could very well be in South Africa."[17]

The USSR made extensive use of radio as a tool of propaganda and incitement, and broadcast to South Africa in African languages. Between

1955 and the early 1970s possession of radios increased from 875 000 to 4,8 million, and the radio propaganda campaign against South Africa increased by about 50%.[18]

Broadcasts to Africa mainly centred on allegations of aggression against neighbouring countries, attempts at destabilisation and aid for resistance movements. The role played by the South African Defence Force in quelling internal unrest became an issue, and a smear campaign was launched with allegations of atrocities committed against the local population. Civil disobedience, including avoiding national service, was strongly advocated.[19]

It went further than mere propaganda. In the military field, the international Communist Bloc supplied Africa with weapons, which were off-loaded mainly in Zanzibar and Dar es Salaam and distributed from there. Many of these weapons were amongst the most well-known and most advanced in the world. There was the universally known Kalashnikov 7,62 mm automatic assault rifle or AK-47, with a magazine containing 30 rounds, and with an effective range of up to 400 metres; the Degtyarev 12,7 mm heavy machine gun, often used as an anti-aircraft weapon; the 122 mm rocket launcher with a reach of 29 km, serviced by a three-man team, which enabled small terrorist units to do severe damage over a long distance and then disappear. In Angola this weapon was transported on trucks or other vehicles. The weapon with the greatest impact on the campaigns in Angola and Mozambique proved to be the SAM-7 or Strella. This missile was shoulder-fired by one man, homed in on an aircraft's engine heat, and had a range of two to three km. Apart from these hand-held weapons, the USSR also supplied a vast number of anti-tank and anti-personnel mines. Even fishing trawlers were used to deliver mines to their destinations in Africa.[20]

It was very clear to me that the former British and Portuguese buffer areas around South Africa were turning into bridgeheads along which South Africa could be penetrated on all sides, and eventually be overwhelmed. I observed conditions in neighbouring countries where communist one-party dictatorships became entrenched, and where starvation, poverty, misery and internal conflict reigned supreme. It was necessary to take preventive measures against such developments at home. I have always been of the same opinion as former US President

Theodore Roosevelt: "Speak softly and carry a big stick; you will go far."

Having had access to the sources of information available at Army Headquarters, it was clear to me that the struggle being waged by the ANC Alliance and the PAC corresponded with the formulae and methods they had gleaned from studies of and training in revolutionary actions and campaigns from all over the world.

Their actions were predictable from a revolutionary point of view, so the SA Defence Force was able to plan counter-revolutionary strategies and actions. These strategies and actions were endorsed by international military experts.

Furthermore the available information made it quite clear that South Africa had already been involved in a revolutionary campaign from the 1960s onwards. An important factor to keep in mind was that this war was aimed at a legally elected government in South Africa, a government that was recognised by the international community. The international community may have strongly condemned South Africa's apartheid policies, but it also condemned the revolutionary terrorist struggle.

It was also encouraging to find that as far as morale was concerned, the Security Forces were well prepared for the onslaught. They were prepared to allow evolutionary political change in South Africa, but not revolutionary change.[21] Even if the enemy were to use violent means to ensure success during the conflict, it would not succeed easily. To a large degree this attitude explained why the revolutionaries were eventually forced to agree to political negotiations.

Mao Zedong, the main exponent of revolutionary warfare, believed that weapons, however important they may be, are not the decisive factor in warfare. People are most important. A power struggle rests as much on moral force and morale as it does on military and economic power.

Even at that stage the Army's top management and I used every possible opportunity to emphasise the role of the population during a revolutionary onslaught. Good relations between the state and its population were of cardinal importance, and had to be pursued. In addition to this, efficient administration had to be the watchword of all government institutions.

Chapter 5

THE NATIONAL SERVICE SYSTEM

The submissions regarding national servicemen I had made as Officer Commanding Western Province Command kept nagging at me. I owed people answers, either because they had come to me with their problems because they trusted me, or because they had criticised me. Furthermore my proposals were quite reasonable, I thought. As soon as I had found my feet at Army Headquarters, I started making enquiries, and this time I did get answers.

Aspects of my submissions, for example the matter of hitchhiking, not only affected Army servicemen, but also the servicemen of the Air Force, Navy and Medical Services. The answers had to come from Defence Force Headquarters, but a decision on this matter of common interest was still outstanding.

At about the same time that I made enquiries, I was unexpectedly informed that I had been appointed as a one-man committee to examine the present national service system (NS system), at that time comprising nine months service, and to make recommendations. Some years earlier the Defence Force had launched an inquiry to determine the most efficient method of providing manpower for the Defence Force – one that would best serve the national interest. The previous inquiry had determined that economic and financial implications precluded the country from affording an entirely professional defence force (with regard to manpower). That inquiry had therefore recommended that the South African Defence Force (SADF) should consist of a professional Permanent Force (PF), Citizen Force (CF) and Commandos, and a national service force.

During my 12 years as Cabinet Minister I ordered two inquiries similar to the one that had already been completed. I required each Chief of the SA Defence Force (CSADF) to determine whether he was still in agreement with the national formula for the provision of manpower. Leading businessmen were also included in these two inquiries, because I wanted to know whether the private sector agreed. Both inquiries came to the same conclusion as the one that had been completed before I began my examination of the NS system.[1]

The provision of manpower was therefore excluded from the new inquiry. I needed to investigate the need for and functioning of the NS system, and make recommendations. At that stage I was not fully conversant with the NS system as a whole – it was a fairly complicated one. I was thrown in at the deep end as far as this appointment was concerned, but when the inquiry was completed, I was fully up to date with the NS system, and was able to make decisions based on sound judgment. Among other things, recommendations were made that simplified the NS system and made it easier to understand.[2]

Some of the most important questions to be studied pertained to the extent of the manpower demand that had to be met, and the functioning of the system: How flexible and streamlined was the system, and was it able to meet the various demands made on it? Were there always enough national servicemen (NSM) available, either in training or already trained, to guarantee the country's safety at any stage during the year? Should there be one or two intakes per year? Are certain NSM manipulating the system? Are there equal opportunities for all, or do some enjoy preferential treatment? How long should the initial phase of National Service last, and what should the optimum duration of subsequent camps be? Is the system flexible enough to handle an increase or decrease in the threat it may have to face? Does the training take into account both conventional and revolutionary warfare? Are the facilities in the various Defence Force components of an equivalent standard?

The NS system was instituted by the Government of the Republic of South Africa. National service was compulsory for white South African men of 18 years and older. The age restriction meant that people under 18 could not join the Defence Force. There was no cut-off age for completing national service.[3]

Individuals could annually apply for postponement of their national service duties, for example if they wished to first qualify for a trade or complete a tertiary education. A civilian exemption board handled the granting of exemptions. This board operated independently of the Defence Force, and was part of the Department of Labour, which was responsible for national manpower. At the age of 65 a person had no further statutory military duties, and was taken off the reserve list. Each potential national serviceman was given a brochure containing all this information. (There were additional prescriptions, such as a medical examination, and NS medical classifications, which could result in an exemption from national service for medical reasons, etc.) South African white women, and men from other population groups, could volunteer for national service, but the underlying principle was that only enfranchised white male citizens were eligible for compulsory national service. Enfranchised white women who volunteered for military service were never considered for combat duty. I had to accept these guidelines, and any recommendations resulting from the new inquiry would have to fit into this statutory framework.

Col. George Gravett, an excellent officer and expert on the NS system, was appointed the Committee's Secretary. We approached the inquiry carefully and with open minds. Oral and written evidence and submissions were received; inspections and discussions were held, and enquiries addressed to the Committee, as well as interaction with servicemen, parents, SADF personnel managers, large employers' organisations and representatives of professional bodies, were considered. The inquiry received a good deal of publicity, and we welcomed the input of every individual or organisation that wished to make a contribution. Varied reactions were received from the public, and even foreigners and disenfranchised persons responded to the invitation.

The Committee was overwhelmed by the contributions. Most of the submissions came from employers' organisations and potential servicemen who looked at the system from their particular points of view and suggested changes. Some of the suggestions were viable, and were considered and implemented where possible, but it was clear that it would be impossible to satisfy everybody, as there was such a great diversity of views, solutions and suggestions. However, it was fruitful to study all the submissions, because even those that were not viable improved communication between the Defence Force and interested parties.

It was abundantly clear that the Defence Force and the servicemen were the main role players. The duties and responsibilities of both parties were at stake, and both had to ensure that the NS system functioned effectively, as nothing less than South Africa's security was at stake.

The suggestions submitted to the Committee included the following:
- All NSM should be treated equally.
- Posting to the various arms of the SADF (i.e. Army, Air Force, Navy or Medical Service), to the approximately 60 professional divisions within the SADF, or to other state departments and bodies should, wherever possible, take account of the serviceman's qualifications, achievements, personal choice, skills and talents.
- The period of service should be extended from the initial nine months to one year. Any future expansion or contraction of service obligations should be effected in "building blocks", depending on the intensity of the threat to the country. The duration of the building blocks should be six months.
- NSM should preferably be taken in twice a year. Operational circumstances necessitated the availability of trained combat units ready for immediate employment at all times.
- Servicemen needed to be trained for both conventional and revolutionary warfare.
- NSM should be given the choice of voluntarily extending their period of service, with the permission of the Defence Force. They should then receive financial remuneration, or the number of follow-up camps should be reduced.
- NSM should be able to choose what they want to do first: either completing their service, or qualifying for a profession or trade. Certain professions and activities were specified, for example where key posts in the Defence Force were affected. With regard to other professions and activities, the exemption board, after considering input from professional personnel organisations, made its own decisions. Further study was one of the most acceptable reasons for an annual postponement of national service.

- Hitchhiking should be authorised.
- Recognised competitive sport should be accepted as SADF service.

Taken as a whole, the Minister of Defence accepted all the Committee's recommendations, and Parliament subsequently approved them in the form of legislation. The system was later amended or adapted in line with changing circumstances, for example with regard to conscientious objections.

The recommendations brought about visible changes. SADF sport came into its own because sport was officially recognised as duty, so Defence Force members received recognition for their service on the sports fields. Many national sportsmen and sportswomen had the opportunity to practice their sport in the SADF and to improve their skills, for example Frik du Preez, Mannetjies Roux, Peter Kirsten, Kepler Wessels, Ernie Els and Retief Goosen, to name but a few.[4]

As hitchhiking had been approved, certain women's organisations and some local authorities began organising lifts countrywide. Transport was consequently more readily available and better organised. At the same time parents had greater peace of mind, as their children would not have to stand at the side of the road for who knows how long in the hopes of getting a lift.

Some of the women's organisations arranged lifts for NSM countrywide with the help of SABC radio broadcasts and a telephone service. The Ride Safely and the Call and Ride Schemes organising the lifts became quite well known in this regard.[5]

It was no easy task to implement the recommendations. This was due to the fact that I was not dealing with things I had been trained for (i.e. effectively engaging the enemy), but rather with more human circumstances that would affect those who were to be trained for such engagements. I am grateful to all those who made sacrifices during this process, and I express my regrets to those whom I wronged – and I know there were some. If this sounds altruistic, perhaps in this case it is.

In summary, I would like to mention that the Defence Force regarded the availability of and its involvement in the NS system as a great responsibility, especially because it meant that young men were being entrusted to the Defence Force at a very special stage of their lives. The organisation was attuned to determining each man's talents, skills and qualifications, and to utilising these optimally within the restraints of operational requirements, particularly regarding servicemen appointed to leadership positions, combat, administrative and support positions.[6]

In the 1970s and 1980s, more than 500 000 young white men were trained in various positions while undergoing their compulsory military service as NSM. This figure does not include members of the PF, CF, or Commandos.

While these men served in the Defence Force, their spiritual, physical and mental welfare also had to be attended to, and the Defence Force made a great effort to do so.

Naturally the utilisation of this source of manpower covered many fields, but the Security Forces, with the responsibility of deterring the most immediate threat, had the greatest need. This source of manpower was also utilised within the disadvantaged communities, for education and training, medical and veterinary services, aid to and management of local authorities, social services, and in certain approved government departments.

Most of the NSM served in uniform, while some did so in civilian clothing when certain working conditions required this. This concession was granted partly to accommodate those individuals who had no objections to national service as such, but did object to wearing a uniform.

In my capacity as Chief of the SA Defence Force I created a Complaints Office at Defence Force Headquarters in 1979, even though this may have gone against the accepted perception of a defence force. I did this mainly in order to solve problems arising from national service. The Complaints Office was manned by selected personnel-orientated officers and staff, and they had direct access to me and the chiefs of the services. The urgency of the matter dictated to whom it was directed. This Complaints Office served as a management tool, and could rapidly determine trends in incidents within the Defence Force. For example, if a payment or illness problem presented itself at a Defence Force unit, this was soon reported to the Complaints Office. If such events repeated themselves, this information could quickly be followed up, which made it easier to make decisions and take corrective steps.[7]

This facility could also offer urgent help to individual servicemen or their families, as it could quickly deal with any situation that caused a problem for the individual or the Defence Force. Those who made use of the facility always received a reply to their submissions – perhaps not always the reply they would have preferred, but at least an explanation regarding an enquiry or complaint and they did not have to be concerned that they might be discriminated against.

Primarily because of political, religious or other objections a few young men were not prepared to participate in any of the wide variety of military activities. A civil conscientious objectors' committee was established to offer them the opportunity to present their case. However, the majority of these servicemen simply had political objections, and used religion as a cover. Many of them eventually showed their true colours as political activists, and were snapped up by the ANC Alliance as moles or agitators.

There is currently a small but quite vicious group of former servicemen that from time to time tries to create opportunities to spread all manner of evil regarding the Defence Force. The stories relate to their experiences while undergoing national service, and to supposed maltreatment, employment in usuitable positions or victimisation. Their sole aim is to cast a bad light on the former political and NS system.

I wish once again to laud the large, silent majority of servicemen who did their service loyally, with dedication and enthusiasm, under difficult circumstances and with great personal sacrifice. They were part of the winning team that helped to turn challenges into opportunities and carried out their orders with ingenuity. This team tasted great success and helped to create a climate in which South Africa's leaders could peacefully move towards a new political dispensation to make the political transition in 1994 without a hitch. The Defence Force is quite rightly proud and honoured to have had the privilege of training, forming and utilising such men and women into a highly efficient team to which the Citizen Force, Commandos, national servicemen, civilians and Permanent Force all contributed in a unique way.

AN UNEXPECTED PHONE CALL

In June 1973 my family and I were relaxing at the Army Foundation's holiday resort at Umhloti, about 30 km north of Durban. The sea was a bit rough on that particular day, so the whole family was lounging around the swimming pool at the block of flats. One could enjoy a wonderful view from there, watching and listening to the waves crashing on the beach. A summer atmosphere was exuded by the many trees surrounding the holiday resort together with Natal's green winter grass. I was playing games with my children in the swimming pool when an officer arrived with a message from the Command Headquarters in Durban. I had to telephone the office of the Minister of Defence in Pretoria. Cellular telephones did not exist then, and I had never phoned the Minister or his office. In fact, I did not even know where his office in Pretoria was. How was I supposed to know his telephone number? Fortunately Command Headquarters was able to provide it.

I telephoned, and despite a scratchy line I gathered from the Minister's private secretary that the Minister wished to see me at his office at 11h00 the following morning. The secretary also helped me by explaining where the office was located but no, he had no idea what the meeting was about. He did know, however, that Adm. H.H. Biermann, Chief of the SADF, would also be present.

A month or so before, the Chief of the Army had entertained the Minister and a few high-ranking officers; we had spent the weekend at a Defence Force property on the banks of the Limpopo River where the borders of Botswana, Rhodesia and South Africa met. When he was Prime Minister, Gen. Smuts had often used this same farm to escape from the duties of state for a while and to meditate in the quiet of nature. It was a very pleasant weekend. If the Minister had felt the need to talk to me about any serious matter within my area of responsibility, he would surely have touched on it then. I could really think of no reason why he would want to see me the next morning. I took an SAA flight to Johannesburg that afternoon to make sure I would be in time the next morning. I slept uneasily that night, because P.W. Botha would not summon one to his office for a mere bagatelle. Furthermore I felt unprepared should he want to talk about something specific, or ask for more information.

I was at the correct office complex in Pretoria on time, and was escorted to the Minister's office where he and the Admiral were awaiting me.

The Minister ordered something to drink. Tea.

Chapter 6

DIVERSE CHALLENGES FOR THE CHIEF OF THE SA ARMY

The Minister informed me over a cup of tea that he was about to make an announcement about appointments and promotions in the Defence Force; among other things that I had been appointed Chief of the South African Army. He wanted me to hear this news first hand, which explained the urgency to see me before I heard it on the news, or from someone else involved in the appointment.

Still somewhat dumbfounded by the trust being shown in me, I returned to Natal shortly afterwards to complete my vacation. Such an appointment had never even entered my mind when I was trying to think of reasons why the Minister would want to see me. After the Minister had informed me of the appointment, my first thought was: "Will I be able to handle this task, with all the responsibilities that go with it?" Or rather: "Will I be able to execute these responsibilities successfully?" On the flight back to Durban that afternoon, I prayed silently for the wisdom and insight I would need to make a success of this opportunity, with all its challenges.

I assumed command as Chief of the Army without any great ceremony. (The first parade held to transfer command to the Chief of the Army occurred in 1976 when I transferred command to Gen. Constand Viljoen. It then became common practice.) However, moving into the office of the Chief of the Army was a special experience in and of itself, because I became aware of the long tradition I was perpetuating. Army

Headquarters were erected at the time of the Transvaal Republic, between 1895 and 1898. The Headquarters are housed in a handsome, stately building situated in Potgieter Street in Pretoria exuding a sense of history. After moving into my new office in the building, I had to hunt for furniture that would complement my management functions, but would also complement the historical character of the building, and eventually I found suitable furniture in various offices and storerooms. My next task was to meet those staff members I did not yet know, to shake hands and to exchange a few words in order to get to know them a little better.

After a week or so I gathered the staff and told them what I expected of them; we jointly determined the basic office routine, and I made them aware that they could do much to improve the Army's image by their daily behaviour and their telephone etiquette. Efficiency was the watchword.

I then visited the telephone exchange that handled all telephone calls to and from Army Headquarters, and made the telephone operators aware of the importance of their job. I pointed out to them that they had the chance to project a positive image of the Army, and then arranged for each of the ladies to go on a telephone etiquette course. They were to project an image of efficiency, coupled with enthusiasm, and to offer proper service delivery and quick follow-up action.

My next task was to become au fait with the internal situation at Army Headquarters and the South African Army in general. At Army Headquarters I needed to get up to date with personnel and financial matters, operational expectations, etcetera. I also wanted to know from my staff what matters they thought demanded attention, and what matters within their sphere of responsibility I needed to know about. This resulted in many in-depth discussions. With regard to the organisation of the Army in its totality, I needed answers to questions such as: Did we have enough personnel, armaments, ammunition and equipment? Where do we stand with regard to training? How combat-ready is the Army in the face of all contingencies? During these conversations I discovered that the Army had no priority list for the acquisition of armaments and equipment. No clearly formulated requirements with regard to armaments existed, and consequently armaments were purchased rather haphazardly. Information sessions helped us to formulate common objectives, and by pursuing these, the Army's combat-readiness was slowly but surely steered in the right direction. It was a slow process, but at least we had a common goal.

I also wanted to implement a decision to cancel the arrangement that at least 50% of national servicemen were required to be present in Army camps over weekends and holidays. This 50% rule applied only to Army national servicemen, and was introduced by my predecessor. I therefore had to decide for myself whether to continue with it or to abolish it.

I gave the responsible officers certain guidelines for future action. These guidelines worked, because in 30 years of revolutionary warfare the enemy threat never reached such a point that it became necessary to re-implement the restrictions on movement.

However, not everybody was completely happy with this instruction. One of the people who came to see me in this regard was the Chaplain-General, Gen. Koos van Zyl. He argued that by ordering that national servicemen need no longer stay in camps over weekends, the churches would empty, as the 50% NSM restricted to the camp had to attend church parades. I countered by saying that church services should be of such a nature as to induce the servicemen to attend voluntarily, and Gen. Van Zyl regarded this as a challenge. He called the chaplains together and gave instructions for self-examination and additional training. The chaplains then improved their pastoral ministrations and church services to such a degree that after a few months more national servicemen voluntarily attended the services than at the time when attendance had been compulsory! I could rely on the Defence Force chaplains through thick and thin.

REORGANISATION

Another task that needed urgent attention was the matter of finding the most efficient way of ensuring that the Defence Force's new approved staff structure applied to the Army as well, ensuring that the staff accepted it emotionally and then firmly establishing the new organisational culture. Following a thorough investigation, the Chief of the Defence Force,

Adm. Hugo Biermann, approved a new staff structure for the Defence Force based on five functions, and the SA Army was required to implement the corresponding structures. This meant that the new approved staff structure with its five staff functions, namely Personnel Management, Intelligence, Operations, Logistics and Finance, had to be implemented at all headquarters. I liaised with top management to determine the best way to introduce this reorganisation.[1]

The new structure corresponded more closely to the American or French staff structure than to the British system, which had been applied to the entire Defence Force up until this time. Applying this structure to all levels, ensuring that staff bought into it, and establishing it, was one of the biggest and most difficult tasks I had yet attempted. In any organisation, changes of this nature are of necessity introduced from the top down. In such circumstances it is best to use a process that creates an environment and climate in which every member becomes convinced that the organisational structure, and the responsibilities that are determined and assigned, are partly his own creation. This ensures that members accept responsibility for the organisation and its efficiency.

At that time I encountered a fair amount of resistance to the implementation of "sensitivity techniques" during team-building exercises and the organisation development process in and outside the Defence Force. These techniques were regarded as dangerous. However, by exercising the correct control, and using professional management techniques, I ensured excellent results. The end result of this culture change in the Army was that members accepted the new approach and attitude as their own, and that any shortcomings were addressed jointly. The team-building efforts that were attended by the Army's top management, resulted in the organisational changes introduced by Adm. Biermann being experienced very positively on both the intellectual and emotional levels. Subsequently the Army as a whole accepted its future tasks far more efficiently and enthusiastically.

During this intense process of reorganisation and culture change, I received invaluable assistance from the Army's able personnel expert, Gen. Raymond Holtzhausen, and Mr Sep Serfontein. The basis for a new culture was laid with their help.

From military appreciations or estimates available at that time, it was clear that South Africa had to prepare itself for a more intense insurgency and/or conventional assault. The most urgent challenge facing the Army was therefore to undergo a reorganisation process to ensure that its units would be ready for the worst case scenario, namely a simultaneous insurgency and conventional assault.

These challenges meant that the Army had to be divided and reorganised into a reliable and balanced counter-insurgency and conventional force, each with a new command and control and staff structure. At the same time the Army's readiness had to be increased through training.

The counter-insurgency force, responsible for combating terrorism, needed to be able to resist a drawn-out, low-intensity effort aimed at the general population. Personal contact with the local population and the development of good mutual relations, which was crucial to combating any revolutionary war, therefore played a decisive role. On completion of the reorganisation the Army would consist of eleven territorial commands, each of which would take responsibility for a particular area and would therefore be well-positioned to combat insurgency.

The existing conventional units of the Citizen Force were allocated to two separate divisions, each with a number of brigades, which meant that they were in a good position to execute conventional tasks. The divisional headquarters were placed under the direct command of the Chief of the Army. In order to ensure flexible utilisation, the conventional forces were also trained for deployment in a counter-insurgency role.

At the level of national service, provision had already been made for training in conventional and revolutionary warfare, to ensure that national servicemen could be deployed in both areas.

During my term as Chief of the Army I also established the philosophy of decentralised management in the Army. I gave instructions that a detailed explication of the accountabilities, responsibilities and delegations of all the officers and senior non-commissioned officers (NCOs) at Army Headquarters, at the very least, should be provided in writing.[2] These job descriptions meant that management responsibilities were clearly defined, and together with decentralised management, this ensured far greater streamlining of the Army's functioning.

BORDER PROTECTION

Another challenge I had to face as Chief of the Army was to stop unwanted elements from entering the country across South Africa's borders. It would be very difficult to win the conflict if these elements were not stopped.

South Africa has an extremely long international border with very few natural barriers, which is therefore very easy to cross. It was an almost impossible task to guard this border with the available manpower to prevent illegal crossing on foot. Enemy elements could therefore illegally enter South Africa from Botswana, Zimbabwe (Rhodesia), Mozambique and Swaziland with the greatest ease, execute deeds of terrorism here, and slip back again across the border. In time, such border crossings became so sophisticated that enemy elements even used bearers who helped to carry weapons, land mines and ammunition on their backs from the neighbouring countries to our densely populated cities. Caches were created in the interior, from which the "fighters" could replenish their stocks.

In order to find an affordable way of controlling these unwelcome border crossings, I gave the Army's botanists instructions to come up with suggestions for a natural vegetative barrier along certain parts of our international borders. Such a vegetative barrier should give the Army some indication that an illegal border crossing had occurred. Furthermore, anybody trying to get to the other side would have to struggle for some two to three hours to get through the barrier. These crossings should also be easily spotted by regular Army patrols along the barrier. Quick action by trackers and a well-equipped pursuit force would then ensure that the penetration inland was found and neutralised more efficiently.

The botanists came up with various suggestions for such a barrier of about 15 to 20 metres wide. After careful consideration I decided on a sisal barrier, even though there were strong objections from certain quarters that sisal is a noxious weed and that it would lead to undesirable infestation. It was also thought that no animal ate this so-called weed or inhibited its growth.

The sisal was planted, but rain, elephants, porcupines and baboons, each in their own way, undermined the effectiveness of this plant. Too little rain inhibited growth, the elephants pulled up the sisal plants as if they were weeds, the porcupines really enjoyed the roots, and the baboons, perhaps out of curiosity, broke off the sisal's sharp points, which rendered the plants ineffective as a barrier.

The Army then approached farmers living in the areas where the barriers were to be planted and requested their help in the maintenance of the barrier, in particular to water the sisal plants in order to speed up their growth. The barrier was flanked on both sides with a concertina or barbed-wire fence that was about two and a half metres high, and concertina rolls of razor wire were intertwined with the sisal.

The addition of a light electric wire above the sisal barrier, carrying the same current as that used to protect private property, helped to deter the elephants and baboons. The concertina, or barbed wire fence, helped to protect the sisal from porcupines, and in this way the barrier was protected from animals. The baboons and elephants, for example, stayed away from the sisal area after one or two contacts. All these measures at last ensured that the barrier became effective.

The erection of the barrier elicited a debate at the United Nations. The allegation was made that an aircraft sprayed the barrier with poison (with the permission of the South African Government) so that anybody pricked by a sisal thorn would die. The truth was that the barrier was inspected from a light Air Force plane a few times, but was never sprayed. Of course the allegation was deliberately made in an attempt to gauge the real state of affairs from our reaction, and accordingly I ordered that no comment should be made.

I can now categorically state that poisoning was never considered or even suggested at any time, and neither I nor the Defence Force were responsible for the poisoning rumour. However, one thing is clear, namely that the poisoning rumour increased the effectiveness of the barrier, because illegal border crossings suddenly declined quite dramatically.

Experiments with other plants were also conducted. It was not possible to plant sisal barriers everywhere, especially in unpopulated border areas, because such a hedge demanded too much care and attention. It was therefore decided to experiment with swarthaak (*Acacia mellifera*), because it had the potential to form an impenetrable barrier, and required far less maintenance than sisal.

Conditions on other sections of the border compelled the Defence Force to consider technological solutions as well. After careful research and deliberation, permission was granted to seal off certain sections of the international border with an electrified fence.

Access gates were built into the fence in certain areas where families lived on both sides of the international border and were divided by the barrier. This allowed controlled movement to and fro as well as cross-border trade. Nevertheless, there were still people who tried to cross the fence illegally, with fatal results. In general the fence performed so well that it was also used by the ANC Government, when it came to power, in an attempt to prevent illegal crossings.

ESSENTIAL ADAPTATIONS

The rapid evolution from conventional to revolutionary warfare in Southern Africa put the Security Forces, the Army in particular, before new challenges that required adaptations to counter-measures. Actions and factors that were perhaps not essential or taken into consideration before, suddenly became of the utmost importance. A polarisation of South Africa's population into two camps, namely a black group and a white group, had to be prevented at all costs. Within its area of responsibility, and even outside it, the SA Army had to make a positive contribution to actively counter any possibility of such polarisation.

It was also important that sound human relations should be fostered, exemplified and applied by the Army. This meant that the Army's ethos needed to change. The sole purpose of the Army could no longer be making war; it also needed to accept the challenge of fostering good human relations in and outside South Africa.

In the face of these challenges I needed to place the SA Army at the forefront of relational changes that were beginning to take hold in Southern Africa. Because of South Africa's past, the process of relational change, including the creation of appropriate attitudes, the maintenance of human dignity and the acceptance of human rights for all South Africans, would be able to take place only if the Army was sincere in accepting a change in its culture. To ensure that essential adaptations became accepted, the Army initially had to introduce them unobtrusively and over time. Changes in attitude were therefore first tested in the operational area, and then applied in South Africa, without drawing too much attention to the process.

A result of this change in culture and policy was that the Army agreed that all South Africans should enjoy the privilege of voluntarily serving their country in the Army in an honourable way and on an equal footing.

One of the fringe benefits of this process was that a positive spirit of co-operation was achieved, and that the concept of management by objectives (MBO) was accepted. In turn MBO helped South Africans to accept and begin to establish the principle that sound relational changes amongst themselves were of cardinal importance for the country's future.

The Army successfully influenced and created sound relations in many ways, often by using the simplest of methods. One of these methods was to inform civilians of ways in which a revolutionary war could be successfully combated, and then to show them practical examples. Certain agricultural projects in the northern areas of South-West Africa/Namibia are good examples of the way in which the Army tried to foster good human relations.

From the early 1970s onwards, the Army slowly but surely started to remove discrimination on the grounds of colour, religion and sex as part of MBO. Top management, all Army commanders and I removed discrimination wherever we could. This policy was applied everywhere the Army took the lead, in other words, in the Army itself, in the operational area, and wherever the Army was involved in community projects.

The Army also took the lead in creating better relations by becoming involved in countless community projects across the length and breadth of South Africa and South-West Africa. The Defence Force's manpower and other resources were continuously being made available to help communities and local authorities.

As far back as my days at the Physical Training Brigade, it was clear to me that a considerate attitude can engender a very positive spirit in people. For example, Armscor's subsidiary Sonchem, gave its workers a hearty breakfast every morning. This gesture engendered positive attitudes, and at the same time increased productivity quite dramatically.

Poverty, unemployment and a lack of opportunities hit some parts of the country very hard, as they still do today. Because human relations played such a fundamental role in revolutionary warfare, I launched Project Molteno with the Government's approval. This project lay outside the SA Army's direct sphere of responsibility, but I was convinced that the Army would be able to carry it out, over and above its normal duties. It later proved to be of great advantage to the Army.

The aim of Project Molteno was to offer members of the most disadvantaged communities the opportunity of voluntarily acquiring manual skills within a disciplined military atmosphere. A survey conducted at the time revealed that some of the most disadvantaged communities were to be found in the Northern Cape. I therefore decided to launch this project for the inhabitants of the North-Western Cape around Kimberley. We were able to use the site and facilities of the former Physical Training Brigade. The project was comparable to the activities of the Special Service Battalion (SSB), which was created prior to World War II to combat unemployment, and to help with formative training for the youth. From a security point of view, Project Molteno would also help to foster good relations.

In terms of the project, any unmarried South African male between 17 and 23 years of age, preferably with no schooling beyond Grade 4, could voluntarily report for military training as prescribed by the project. Those who were accepted received the same benefits and pay as national servicemen.

Those who were accepted were trained mainly for deployment as security guards. With regard to military administration, medical care, wearing a uniform during training and thereafter, they were subject to the same conditions as those that any other soldier had to adhere to.

After about six months of military and developmental training, the trainees were tested by the Department of Manpower, and then received further training in one of a variety of manual skills. After a few months of manual skills training they qualified as carpenters, bricklayers, painters, welders, etcetra. On completion of their trade training, they could apply for a job work in civilian life, and if they were successful, they could leave the Defence Force without obligations.

Those who were unable to find civilian employment on completion of their manual skills training, were employed by the Defence Force as security guards or artisans if vacancies were available. If they were able to find civilian employment at a later stage, they could leave the service of the Defence Force immediately. Some of these trainees could also transfer to other Army services, for example the auxiliary services, and pursue a career there.

The project was a resounding success. There were so many applications that they overwhelmed the available facilities. The project addressed some of the country's most acute problems, such as unemployment and the lack of persons with elementary technical skills in a unique way and in a disciplined environment. In the years that this project was in operation, it offered refuge to many people in need. The Defence Force enjoyed great benefits from the project, because the communication, flow of intelligence to and acceptability of the Defence Force in the Northern Cape went from strength to strength.

This project, together with many other community projects, had to be abandoned at the end of the 1980s, because of drastic cuts in the Defence Force budget. Purely from a security point of view the projects could no longer be given high financial priority.

Support to civilian communities offered members of the Defence Force, such as national servicemen, many opportunities to help with upliftment and to make a humanitarian contribution in the public interest.

The best examples of upliftment were found in the operational area. Effective communication and the establishment of good relations with local populations suffering because of the conflict, were of cardinal importance, because a great deal depended on winning the hearts and minds of these people. During military training and operations much time and attention was invested in engendering good attitudes towards the local population. Troops and officers were told that they should at all times honour the habits and customs of local populations, particularly those that had had limited opportunities for development, and that they should at all times display a sympathetic attitude. Everything possible had to be done to win the confidence of local populations in order to ensure their support, as this would contribute towards successful operations in the area. These efforts were very successful, as the following examples will illustrate.

In South-West Africa the efforts of the Army's intelligence and liaison teams, known colloquially as "plough and plant", made a particularly good contribution to creating a positive atmosphere. These liaison teams usually consisted of a leader, a medical orderly, a member with basic technical skills and one with an agricultural background. They were usually supplemented with two members trained in intelligence gathering, a signaller to establish radio contact with the local headquarters commanding the liaison team and, depending on the rural area where intelligence was being gathered, interpreters and trackers.

Such teams went to the various rural areas on foot, and helped the local population in various ways. For example, should a water pump in an isolated rural area have broken down, the expertise was immediately available to fix it. If the team could not immediately solve the water problem or any other urgent matter, they could use the radio to call for help from the "outside world", in other words the local headquarters commanding the team, or from a local representative of one of the South-West African/Namibian government departments. If they encountered an elementary health problem such as stomach problems, headaches or flu, it could be treated with the basic medicines they carried with them. They could also help to alleviate serious food shortages, and could also provide seed and plant material for crops, or give advice on stock farming. We tried to arrange that the same team visit the same area for as long as possible, in order to build up mutual trust. This also enabled the team to monitor its own progress.

The Army urged these farming communities to look beyond subsistence farming, and to produce more than was needed for their own use. Whenever their permission could be obtained, the Army helped to prepare and cultivate additional fields at a tariff that was mutually agreed upon in advance. Produce in excess of the inhabitants' needs was offered for sale, and the Defence Force bought this as rations for local consumption.

The SA Army launched extensive agricultural projects in the northern parts of South-West Africa/Namibia in order to transfer skills to the local population for future development. Extensive irrigation farms along the

DIVERSE CHALLENGES

The irrigation farm on the Okavango River in South-West Africa that was initially developed by the SA Defence Force, South African agricultural co-operatives and South African farmers and businessmen in co-operation with local inhabitants and national servicemen. It was later transferred to the First National Development Corporation (FNDC) to be run by the local population to produce crops and foodstuffs for the local inhabitants. (Photo: *South African Panorama*, Aug. 1989.)

Okavango River were developed with the help of South African agricultural co-operatives, farmers and businessmen. On these farms the local population learned to produce vegetables under irrigation, thus creating jobs and income. This project was later transferred to First National Development Corporation (FNDC), South-West Africa/Namibia's agricultural organisation. Assistance was also given to the agricultural college in Ovamboland, particularly with the improvement of a local cattle breed.

I requested the Chief of the Defence Force to amend the tender regulations for this geographical area so that meat and agricultural produce for use by the Defence Force could be purchased north of the Red Line, thereby creating a market for local produce in the immediate vicinity. (The Red Line is an imaginary line that forms the southern border of the area in northern South-West Africa along the border with Angola and Zambia. The area includes Ovamboland, Kavango, and eastern and western Caprivi. The name was derived from the fact that cattle from this area were not allowed to be moved freely south of the line, for fear of spreading foot and mouth disease. The South-West African operational area was actually the area north of the Red Line.) The Government approved the tender request, thus contributing to the generation of income in the area, the transfer of skills and the development of a better quality of life.

The Defence Force helped with teaching in the operational area of the South West Africa/Namibia. Here a national serviceman with teaching qualifications teaches children in the operational area. (Photo: *South African Panorama*, Aug. 1989.)

A large number of national servicemen with teacher training were deployed in the South-West African operational area every year to help with teaching the local children.

Many doctors and medical orderlies were also deployed in hospitals and in sick bays on military bases to help improve the medical welfare of the local inhabitants. Medical specialists were regularly flown in from South Africa to provide medical assistance in special cases, and the local population highly valued this free medical care. Similar medical care was extended into Angola and Zambia during cross-border operations. Because medical care at grassroots level was largely lacking in these countries, the local population was largely dependent on what the South African Defence Force could offer them. Once again such medical assistance engendered positive attitudes amongst local populations on both sides of the border, and this proved to be of immense help in military operations.

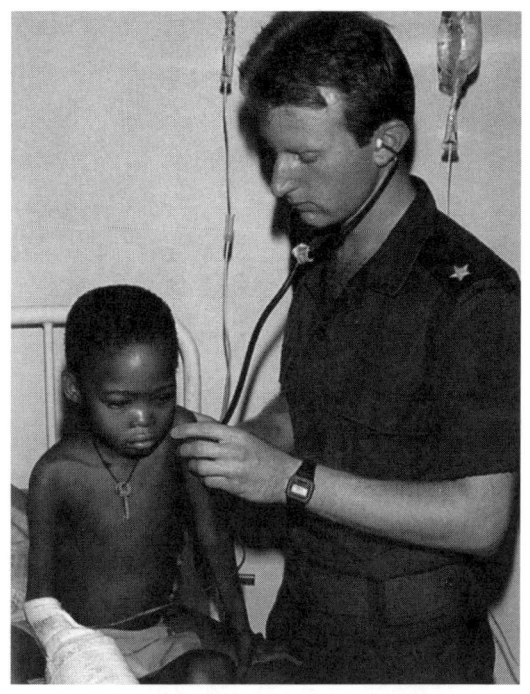

A national service medical officer examines a child in the South-West African operational area. (Photo: *South African Panorama*, Aug. 1989.)

One of the consequences of revolutionary warfare is that the population may become dispirited. The money that the Defence Force and its members regularly spent in the remote operational area of South-West Africa, the new infrastructure created there (for example hydroelectricity at Ruacana), the establishment and availability of medical clinics, the construction of airstrips and roads, the maintenance of services and the success of counter-insurgency methods,

Corporal Moruti in a sick bay pharmacy in the operational area, dispensing free prescription medicines. (Photo: *South African Panorama*, Aug. 1989.)

all contributed towards counteracting feelings of uncertainty amongst the inhabitants.

The assistance given by the Defence Force in South-West Africa/Namibia (which actually fell outside its area of responsibility) was always welcomed, and the Defence Force participated in many governmental projects at the government's request. Due to the remoteness of the area, the aid offered by the Defence Force proved to be of great value to the local population. Co-operation and mutual assistance in South-West Africa/Namibia was always of the highest order. On the other hand, it was not as easy to conduct support activities in South Africa, probably because the conflict was never felt so close to home here.

In my opinion the involvement with the people, and the opportunities for co-operation created by the Defence Force across the length and breadth of South-West Africa/Namibia at the time, made a valuable contribution to the development of sound relations between people in the territory.

In June 1974, during one of my regular visits to the operational area in South-West Africa – this time in the company of Mr P.W. Botha, the Minister of Defence, and a number of journalists as guests – the Minister revealed that Defence Force members had been positioned along the entire border of about 1500 km, from the estuary of the Kunene River to eastern Caprivi. During this visit he stated that the Defence Force had room for people of all races, including black people. A week later, I followed up this statement by the Minister and announced in Pretoria that the SA Army had begun recruiting South African black men to receive fully-fledged infantry training. In the first month more than 300 black volunteers reported, and training of the first coloured officers commenced at the same time. These were major developments, because black and coloured people had not been used as combatants in South African forces since the 19th Century.

Chapter 7

AN INCREASE OF TERRORISM ACROSS THE BORDER OF SOUTH-WEST AFRICA

The South African Defence Force had been involved in counter-insurgency operations in the area south of the Red Line in South-West Africa even prior to 1973. For international reasons, protection of the area north of the Red Line was initially assigned to the SA Police Force. If a country sends its defence force to another country, or if it deploys its forces on the common border with that country, even on request, it could be accused of attempting to invade or take over the other country. These accusations cannot easily be made if police forces are used. The irony was that, in order to determine the extent of the revolutionary threat to Angola, and the development of the threat against South-West Africa, the Defence Force had already deployed a few liaison officers at certain Portuguese military posts in the south of Angola.

However, because cross-border terrorism between Angola and South-West Africa was increasing in intensity, on 1 April 1973 responsibility for the protection of the border and the area north of the Red Line was transferred from a small SA Police anti-terrorist unit to the SA Defence Force. The area south of the Red Line was the responsibility of South-West Africa Command at that stage.

Chapter 4 makes reference of the broader independence struggle in Africa and its influence on events in South-West Africa and the development of civil war in Angola. At that time the three revolutionary movements refused to co-operate, because each wanted to control the entire Angola. There was almost no chance that an interim government of national unity would be launched; national conflict, however, was a certainty.

As a result of its geographical position, its mandate over South-West Africa and political development in that territory, South Africa was sucked into the maelstrom of events. Eventually South Africa would also find itself in the rapids of the Angolan conflict, and would become involved in a military capacity.

In Portugal Gen. António de Spínola, in office for a few brief months, was succeeded by Gen. Francisco da Costa Gomes. Gen. Costa Gomes arranged a ceremony in the Portuguese town of Alvor on 15 January 1975, during which the three main Angolan groups, the MPLA, FNLA and UNITA, concluded an agreement with the Portuguese government. In terms of this agreement the three freedom movements were recognised as the only legitimate representatives of the population of Angola, which would become independent on 11 November 1975. In the interim the four parties were to form a coalition government in Angola, with equal representation, and rule the country jointly until a general election could be held. Internal security would be in the hands of a national army consisting of 24 000 Portuguese military personnel and 8000 men from each of the three Angolan signatories. The Portuguese forces would gradually start withdrawing as from 1 October 1975.[1]

The Alvor agreement was meant to bring the revolutionary struggle between Portugal and the three Angolan factions officially to an end. In actual fact it was a recipe for chaos in view of the enmity between the three warring parties and the weak Portuguese state, which had already capitulated. Because of its domestic problems, Portugal could or would no longer exert its influence in important parts of Angola, and managed the situation in Angola extremely clumsily. A civil war broke out, and the interim or coalition government fell apart. The FNLA, with its constituency largely based in northern Angola, and UNITA, which has established itself predominantly in the south, attacked the MPLA from their traditional support bases. Ideological differences, and years of bitterness between the various Angolan parties, were enough to light the fuse of a civil war that was to last for many years.

Political developments in Angola, the instability that reigned in the country, and the enemy elements that sporadically tried to penetrate South-West Africa from Angola for cross-border operations, all convinced me that South Africa's government would have to take drastic steps to protect the interests of South Africa and South-West Africa on both sides of the international frontier. I had already begun to steel myself psychologically for increased military involvement in the near future.

Angola's mineral riches, including the rich oil fields in Cabinda, simply invited interference by foreign powers. Military power would determine the outcome of the political struggle, and a civil war seemed inevitable. Foreign interference would eventually lead to South African involvement as well.

The Soviet Union, together with its Cuban, Eastern Bloc and other communist henchmen, supported the MPLA. Initially the FNLA was allied to UNITA, and both sought Western help, but had to be satisfied with sympathy and empty promises.

The support in terms of materiel and manpower that the Soviet Union and its communist allies gave to the MPLA lent the Angolan question an international dimension. Portuguese Adm. Antonio Rosa Coutinho, also known as the "Red Admiral" because of his leftist leanings, was Portugal's last Governor General in Luanda. During a secret mission to Havana in 1974, he urged Pres. Fidel Castro of Cuba to intervene in Angola, and to send Cuban troops in support of the MPLA. The suggestion was accepted. In the course of hearings on Angola in the USA, the US Deputy Secretary of State for Africa, William E. Schaufele,[2] pointed to the long-standing connection between the MPLA and Cuba. According to Schaufele, large-scale aid from communist quarters had begun to flow to Angola as early as 1974. The first Russian personnel landed in 1975, and the first Cuban forces entered Angola in August of that year,[3] with orders to support the MPLA in its efforts to gain total military control over Angola.

South Africa's military involvement in Angola followed Soviet, Eastern Bloc and Cuban interference in the area,[4] and was not the cause of Soviet, Eastern Bloc and Cuban interference, as argued by the Colombian writer, Gabriel García Márques, in a series of articles in the *Washington Post* from 10 to 12 January 1976. South Africa was always consistent in its proposals that all foreign forces should withdraw, but this position was opposed by the USSR and her allies: they wanted only South African forces to withdraw.

MAP 3 NORTHERN SOUTH-WEST AFRICA/NAMIBIA AND SOUTHERN ANGOLA.

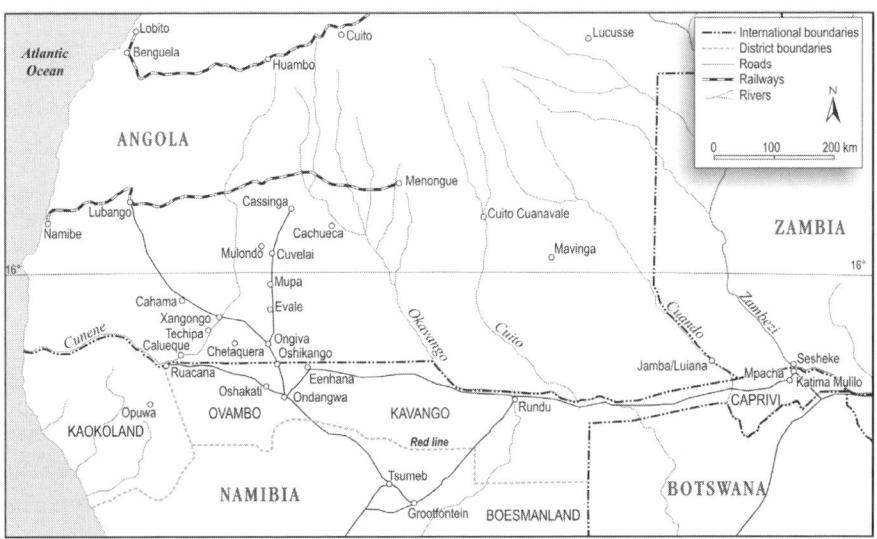

During the period of uncertainty and positioning in Angola, disorder and consequent unrest took hold on the border between Angola and Ovamboland. Ovambos live on both sides of the border between Angola and South-West Africa, and some of the Angolan political movements tried to recruit them for military employment.

The first problem that compelled an unwilling South Africa to become militarily involved in Angola, occurred at the water supply project at Calueque.[5] An agreement on the development of the Kunene River basin water supplies had been concluded between South Africa and Portugal as far back as 1969. Barrages were built at Calueque, and the pump station there supplied large volumes of potable water to Ovamboland through a 300 km long system of canals. Any interruption of the water supply to this area would have had catastrophic consequences for the inhabitants of Ovamboland. The hydroelectric plant at Ruacana in South-West Africa supplied power to the pumps at Calueque, and eventually, after completion of an underground power station, electricity to large areas of South-West Africa/Namibia. South Africa and Portugal were jointly responsible for financing this power station and the development associated with it.

Workers at Calueque were increasingly being intimidated by Angolan groups, and the pump operators were no longer willing to man their posts; they would only return if they were guaranteed protection by the SA Defence Force. This crisis compelled the South African government to make a decision.

The Government's decision to protect Calueque and South Africa's interest there came as no surprise to me or to Army Headquarters. The Chief of the Defence Force, Adm. H.H. Biermann, had already informed me of a Government decision that South Africa had to be ready to implement precautionary measures at Calueque. In any case, the signs of the times made it clear that such measures were essential.

In anticipation of the Chief of the Defence Force receiving instructions from the Government to intervene in order to ensure essential water supplies to the Ovambos, the Army had already received my approval for preparations, including the preparation of contingency plans.

However, because the protective measures would not be a purely Army operation, the Defence Force had already created the necessary structural organisation, and Army Headquarters and Chief of the Defence Force Headquarters had also done joint planning. For example, 1 Military Area had already been created in anticipation of deteriorating circumstances in Angola. At that stage the area comprised the strip from the Angolan border southward to the Red Line, including Ovamboland, Kavango and western and eastern Caprivi. Kaokoland was added later. Earlier I had already given permission for certain Army elements to be deployed in 1 Military Area for purposes of acclimatisation and exposure. They would probably be required to halt illegal border crossings from Angola. On request I had also given permission for other Army elements stationed in Walvis Bay and South-West Africa to be earmarked for this important operation. Apart from Army troops,

Air Force elements were also deployed in 1 Military Area.

Brig. Wally Black, Director of Operations at Defence Headquarters in Pretoria, visited the area on Thursday 7 August 1975. On my instructions the Director of Operations at Army Headquarters gave the green light for the Army's participation. Cmdt Gert van Niekerk, Officer Commanding 1 Military Area, received instructions to send a combat team to the water works of the South-West African Water and Electricity Corporation (SWAWEC) at Ruacana. Furthermore, he had to arrange for a parachute platoon to be flown in from Rundu. A combat team from 2 SA Infantry Battalion at Walvis Bay was ordered to occupy the triangle between Calueque, Ruacana and Beacon 5½. This order was executed by 10 August 1975.

These important military operations were carried out very successfully by 1 Military Area. After the commencement of the operation, 1 Military Area continually kept the Defence and Army Headquarters informed of developments. In turn the Chief of the Defence Force, Admiral Biermann, kept the Minister of Defence informed, and through him the Cabinet was kept updated.

The Portuguese government was immediately informed of these events. They requested South Africa to accept the task of protection until they were once more in a position to do it themselves. That never happened, and the Portuguese government informed the South African Government that in view of its proposed withdrawal from Angola before 11 November 1975, it could make no contribution to the protection of the scheme.

In the meantime communist military and logistical support for the MPLA increased, and there was an ever increasing danger of a military coup in Angola. Some non-communist-leaning African countries, such as Gabon, Ivory Coast, Kenya, Zambia and Zaire (presently the Democratic Republic of the Congo), expressed increasing alarm. To them, the most basic condition was that the future government of Angola should take power following a free election. One group should not be allowed to dominate the others militarily before independence. However, it became clear that the MPLA would attempt to do so with large-scale armaments provision and assistance from the Soviet Union, and with Cuban participation.

South Africa could not permit the development of a situation from the disorder in Angola that could pose a security threat to South-West Africa and South Africa itself.[6] To help create internal stability, South Africa made contact with Dr Jonas Savimbi of UNITA and later also with representatives of the FNLA, through the offices of the Defence Force and the Bureau for State Security.

As a gesture, a small quantity of arms was supplied to these two movements. This was hardly significant, however, and these groups made ever more urgent requests for armaments and military supplies. A trickle of weapons did flow to the FNLA and UNITA from America's Central Intelligence Agency (CIA), and apparently also from French sources. However, there were clear indications that the MPLA would be able to rely on large-scale military support from the Soviet Union and her allies, in particular Cuba.

An early indication that the MPLA would be satisfied with nothing less than exclusive control of the whole of Angola, came when the MPLA began to drive the two other movements from the Luanda area. Fairly large-scale clashes between the MPLA's military wing, FAPLA (Forças Armadas Populares de Libertaçao de Angola or People's Armed Forces for the Liberation of Angola), and the FNLA in and around Luanda had already occurred in August 1975. The Portuguese regime succumbed to MPLA demands that FNLA ministers be forced to withdraw from the interim government. UNITA subsequently also withdrew its ministers and soldiers from Luanda.

Aided by the Cubans, the MPLA then initiated a planned offensive southwards, and thereby signalled an escalation of the conflict. The strategy was to gain control of the country's harbours and airports as quickly as possible, thereby cutting off the other groups from the outside world. During this offensive the MPLA's opponents were soon driven from Luanda and the coastal towns, as far south as Namibe (formerly Moçâmedes).

South African intelligence sources, such as the Department of Foreign Affairs and Military Intelligence, reported that the MPLA's southward drive, with the help of the Cubans, caused concern amongst some states in central Africa. These countries were largely dependent on the Benguela railway line, which connected the Zairian and Zambian mining areas with the coast, and they were concerned that the MPLA could halt all rail transport on this route. They believed that SWAPO would exploit this situation to its own advantage, and therefore they approached South Africa to prevent this.

South Africa's decision on possible military involvement in Angola took the escalating SWAPO assault from Angola and the southern movement of Cuban troops into consideration. The greatest need expressed by the FNLA and UNITA was for weapons, and training in their use. The initial involvement of the SA Defence Force in the conflict consisted of assistance with training and the provision of key leadership elements, followed by logistical support. Defence Force liaison officers (and later liaison teams) who were initially deployed in southern Angola, and officers who specifically assisted UNITA with training, had first-hand experience of the situation on the ground. Reports on their observation of the state of affairs made it clear that training and logistical support alone were no longer enough. Further support with the control and co-ordination of operations followed.

At that stage South Africa had reached a point where further involvement would entail physical participation in the struggle in Angola, aimed at robbing SWAPO of the initiative with regard to action. Furthermore UNITA needed support to survive until at least the proposed date of independence, 11 November 1975.

For the most part, UNITA, which had turned its back on communism, had to be helped to safeguard its traditional area of support in southern Angola, which bordered on South-West Africa/Namibia. South Africa had no goals in Angola other than safeguarding the border between that country and South-West Africa, and ensuring that the Ruacana-Calueque scheme should remain fully functional. South Africa had no desire to extend its territory or to establish a permanent presence in the area. The South African Government had a declared policy on terrorist attacks across its borders, and the borders of its mandated territory, and the Minister of Defence, P.W. Botha, had repeatedly expressed this policy in Parliament. In a speech I delivered to the Council of South Africa, I formulated this policy as follows: "We do not commit any aggression against our neighbours, and we will not permit our territory to be used for aggression against others. We regard this as our very basic principle for any interaction in Southern Africa. We expect our neighbours to conform to this basic principle. If not, they must bear the consequences."[7]

The South African Government's policy was furthermore not to act against a state as such, but to concentrate on those elements that violated the country's borders. If a state was unable to control such elements, South Africa would offer its help at any time.[8]

In view of the southward movement of FAPLA soldiers and Cuban and other Marxist support forces, it began to appear very possible that an aggressive antagonistic state could be established on South-West Africa's northern border. This would give the SWAPO threat far greater momentum.

At this stage the USA encouraged South Africa to become involved in a joint anti-communist holding action in Angola. It was supported by Zambia and Zaire, who were aware of South Africa's views on communism, and the danger the ideology held for Africa. It was anticipated that the Organisation of African Unity (OAU) would try to find an acceptable solution for the situation in Angola at a meeting to be held in December 1975.

With all the available information on Angola in mind, the Defence Force's top management realised that if no swift action was taken to counter the escalating Soviet threat, it would only be a matter of time before South Africa would have to deal with a similar but far more serious situation. Postponing the decision, or trying to sidestep the challenge, would only exacerbate the situation.

However, the Defence Force did not have the authority to take such a decision. The Defence Force realised that a hasty decision could be the wrong one, and that it should rather wait for a properly considered Government decision.

Chapter 8
OPERATION SAVANNAH

South Africa's decision to send its Defence Force into Angola was not taken lightly. Considerable international pressure was exerted on South Africa, particularly because of its domestic policies, and as a result the South African Government found it extremely difficult and risky to make such a decision. The most urgent questions concerned the implications if South Africa were to decide to continue protecting South-West Africa's interests; continue holding out a hand of friendship to the two anti-communist Angolan organisations, namely the FNLA and UNITA, and to accede to the democratic member countries of the Organisation of African Unity (OAU) who requested South Africa to act against foreign forces from outside Africa. Would South Africa create its own Vietnam if it did so? On the other hand the Government also had to consider the consequences for South Africa if it did not react to these matters.

After very carefully considering many factors and consulting with various bodies, the South African Government decided that the interests of South Africa and Southern Africa would be best served if the SA Defence Force were to become temporarily involved in the Angola crisis as soon as possible. The result was an instruction by the South African Government to the Defence Force to embark on Operation Savannah.

On deciding to execute a military operation, a number of very important elements need to be in place. Firstly, permission needs to be obtained and the proper authority for execution must therefore exist. Secondly, there should be a prescribed aim for the operation. All those involved need to know exactly what they have to do, even those working at the lowest levels. Thirdly, proper communication channels need to be in place to ensure that at least all Headquarters are in contact with one another vertically and laterally, or will be able to make contact at any time. Logistical supply and support are of cardinal importance during the operation; adequate and correct units and equipment must be available to complete the task, and reserves for contingencies need to be available. Attention must be paid to the supply of future needs and to lines of communication.

The following happened in order to launch Operation Savannah: The South African Government gave instructions that, due to foreign intervention in Angola, the South African Defence Force had to be ready to protect the interests and people of South Africa and South-West Africa. Furthermore, limited aid had to be given to the two resistance movements, and consideration had to be given to steps that would advance political détente in Africa. There were also restrictions: South Africa was not contemplating any territorial advancement. These instructions were issued to me as Chief of the Army by the Chief of the Defence Force. After analysing them, I provided 1 Military Area (Task Force 101) with the basic objectives (see below). In turn 1 Military Area took these objectives and issued the relevant sections to the various Army units and Task Force Zulu under its command. The separate but narrower goals that followed from the primary goals were issued to combat groups, and further down to the very lowest levels. Each commander involved in Operation Savannah now had a specified goal to reach or a task to perform, and monitoring methods were built in to judge progress. Because the Army had decentralised management, each commander had the responsibility to complete each objective or task successfully.

Acting as security instrument of the Government, Task Force Zulu of the SA Army entered Angola with two combat groups on 14 October 1975, signalling the start of Operation Savannah. The progress of Operation Savannah is comprehensively described in *Operasie Savannah: Angola 1975-1976* (1989) by the historian, F.J. du Toit Spies, that was commissioned by the Defence Force. I will therefore only refer in broad outlines to certain aspects of the operation.

Operation Savannah put the Defence Force before considerable

MAP 4 NORTHERN SOUTH-WEST AFRICA/NAMIBIA AND ANGOLA.

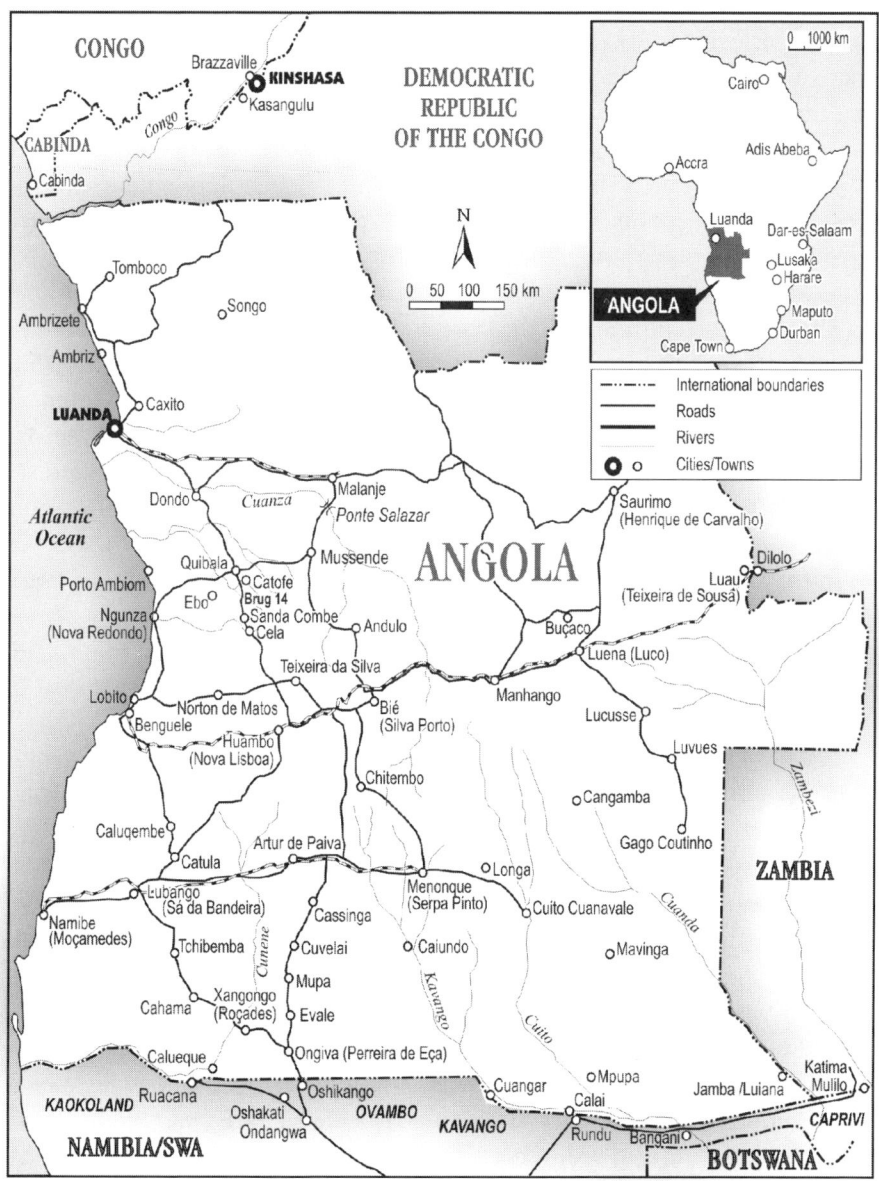

logistical challenges. Northern South-West Africa and Angola are situated at a great distance from the Defence Force's base area in South Africa. For example, it is 2300 km by rail from Bloemfontein to Grootfontein in South-West Africa, which means four or five days' travelling time. Even in a transport aircraft it takes about three to five hours to cover the distance. Yet the Defence Force had to negotiate these vast distances.

The area in which the Defence Force was initially deployed in South-West Africa is equally vast. For example, South-West Africa's northern border with Angola and Zambia is about 1500 km long from west to east, or about the distance from Cape Town to Pretoria.

The Defence Force was deployed along this border, and, at the request of the inhabitants of the area, had to constantly patrol the border to protect them when circumstances demanded it.[1] Initially all Defence Force requirements such as manpower, supplies, building materials, weapons, ammunition, food and medical supplies had to be moved to the front from the base area by road, rail or air links. This enormous task was completed with great success.

In the case of Operation Savannah, the distances involved were even greater, but the Defence Force simply had to cope.

The Defence Force was not an occupation or conquering force, and it had no instructions to establish a particular government, nor was it given any instructions to advance on Luanda.

Initially Operation Savannah was managed by 1 Military Area, but on 12 November 1975 this responsibility was transferred to 101 Task Force, which operated from Rundu and was commanded by Gen. André van Deventer.

The Air Force's 301 Air Component, based at Rundu alongside 101 Task Force, received their instructions from the Chief of the Air Force, and the same applied to the Medical Service and the Surgeon General. Joint decisions were taken on appropriate support for the Army troops. I liaised from Army Headquarters with the Navy, which was not represented in the operational area at that time.

The Defence Force had good radio equipment with equally good encryption equipment. For tactical and security reasons self-imposed restrictions were applied, which meant that radio communications in Angola were sometimes a little more difficult than usual. Radio and telephone communications between Army Headquarters and 101 Task

Force were first rate. Situation reports, from ground level to ministerial level, were provided twice daily. Everybody involved was therefore kept completely up to date with the situation in the operational area at all times. I paid official visits to 101 Task Force and 301 Air Component almost every week in order to meet obligations and to expedite matters.

From the original instruction I received from the Chief of the Defence Force, I deduced a number of detailed basic goals for Operation Savannah, and confirmed these with the Officer Commanding 101 Task Force. These goals were the protection of the Ruacana-Calueque hydro-electric project and water scheme, and the provision of limited aid to the FNLA and UNITA movements. This aid was intended to ensure that these two organisations would be in a position to compete for power in the new Angolan government which was to be established on independence. Operation Savannah also had to help safeguard and develop UNITA's traditional sphere of influence, and if possible also give aid to the FNLA in northern Angola; protect the Benguela railway line; occupy the area up to the Cuanza River; clear SWAPO from along the border with Angola; and safeguard Defence Force personnel and equipment in Angola during the withdrawal.

Col J.S. (Koos) van Heerden commanded Task Force Zulu, comprising two combat groups, Alpha and Bravo. Combat group Foxbat was added later, and combat groups Orange and X-ray even later. Combat group Foxbat moved from South-West Africa to an assembly point at Bié (formerly Silva Porto) on 25 October 1975, charged with the task of meeting the FAPLA threat in central Angola in conjunction with combat groups Alpha and Bravo. Foxbat established its logistical headquarters at Huambo (formerly Nova Lisboa), and its rear link headquarters at Bié.

The two initial combat groups, Alpha and Bravo, raced north at breakneck speed, earning Col Van Heerden, the Task Force Commander, the nickname Rommel. Despite the fact that Cubans were present in large numbers and had far superior weaponry, the Task Force could pride itself on the remarkable achievement of driving the enemy back 300 km in 30 days. In the process large quantities of materiel and piles of clothing were taken at Lubango (formerly Sá da Bandeira). Namibe (formerly Moçâmedes), the most important harbour in southern Angola, also fell to the Task Force, which left a holding force there until UNITA and the FNLA could take over.

Task Force Zulu then continued fighting until it had liberated Lobito and had moved up the West coast to Ngunza (Novo Redondo).

During Operation Savannah troop movements and supplies had to cover a great distance from Grootfontein to the front, but from the base area in South Africa this distance was enormous. Consequently Bié was transformed into a forward base, even though it was still very far from Grootfontein (1500 km by road, three to four days by truck or three to four hours by plane). Even when supplies were established at Bié, they still had to be moved to the front on demand, and in certain cases this amounted to a further 500 to 600 km. Movement from Grootfontein to Bié was through a potentially dangerous area, and the convoys had to be protected. Fuel for vehicles and aircraft had to be transported by road between these bases. Up to a third of the load capacity had to be allocated to fuel. The roads were in poor condition, with heavy going due to wet and muddy conditions, which made great demands on the drivers' abilities.

The military support in southern Angola reached a depth of about 1800 km from Grootfontein (about as far as from Cape Town to Polokwane), and the front was about 1200 km wide (as far as from Durban to Pofadder in Bushmanland).

At the outset the Government had decided to remain involved in Angola only until independence on 11 November 1975, or until the conclusion of the OAU meeting in December 1975. It was thus determined that only 3000 Defence Force members and 600 vehicles of all types could be deployed in Angola at any one time during this operation. This would also ensure that South Africa did not find itself sucked into a situation similar to that of Vietnam. I am not aware of any other country in the world that has ever successfully ventured into such a vast geographical area with such a small force. Much was achieved with very little.

As Chief of the Army I considered it my duty, but also an honour, to pay regular visits to the operational area. The intensity of the working visits depended on the intensity of the activities. Sometimes I visited weekly, sometimes every second week, and eventually once a month. Sometimes I stayed for a week or so. During Operation Savannah in particular, I made many working visits to the operational area.

The purpose of the visits was to get first hand exposure to developments. The further one is removed from the physical fighting, the darker the picture seems, but the closer you get, the clearer the actual situation becomes. During these working visits there were in-depth discussions with the various commanders about the conflict, deficiencies on our side and possible solutions. My presence made it possible to make decisions on support from South Africa far more easily and quickly. I was thus able to make things easier for everybody, and perhaps also ensure that our efforts became more efficient. On many occasions during these visits I took along persons such as the Minister of Defence, the Chief of the SA Defence Force, Members of Parliament from all political parties, and business leaders. Briefings presented during these visits provided ample opportunity for questions and discussions.

Another reason for these regular visits was to make contact with all those involved, no matter their rank. These Defence Force members were prepared to pay the highest price for their country, and it was the least I could do to thank them with my presence. I also regarded it as my duty, responsibility and privilege to be associated with them; it was always a great pleasure. The men there always impressed me; they were inspired, enthusiastic and dedicated, but reluctant to admit that they missed their loved ones. However, if you caught them unawares, they openly admitted their homesickness.

Depending on the number of fellow travellers, I flew in a "flossie", a C-47 Dakota transport aircraft, a C-130 Hercules transport aircraft, a Mercurius or any other available aircraft. Helicopters were normally used in the operational area. When I retired from the Ministry of Defence in 1991, I had more flying hours to my credit than most Air Force pilots!

With every visit to the area I was shocked at the extremely bad state of the roads in Angola. Many of the large rivers were not even indicated on the maps. Almost the entire Operation Savannah took place during the intense rainy season. The Air Force could only use the early morning for flying, because it poured with rain in the afternoons. The aircrews and drivers on the roads who ensured that the troops on the ground got their supplies in time performed magnificently, and deserve honourable mention. The drivers of the heavy vehicles were mainly motivated young NSM who gave their all.

As the fighting progressed and the enemy forces retreated, bridges across the rivers were destroyed to delay our advance and force ground troop movements to a standstill. Fortunately the Army's Sappers (engineers) had the expertise to build bridges fairly quickly.

"THE LIGHTS OF LUANDA"

Over and above the military aid offered by the Defence Force in southern Angola, the leader of the FNLA, Holden Roberto, independently asked the South African Government for help. He had an ambitious plan to attack Luanda on 9 November 1975, in other words just prior to independence on 11 November. His request for supporting fire from South African 140 mm artillery was approved, although the Army opposed this. The request and its approval was handled at the political level. It was a difficult decision, as the provision of South African artillery was only a gesture of goodwill and support. The Army's objection was that it was tactically unwise to deploy military capability in small packages; artillery, in particular, needs adequate protection. Another objection was that the Army itself was experiencing a shortage of guns. This artillery support eventually proved not to be advantageous; nevertheless the three artillery pieces, ammunition and crew were delivered to Ambriz, north of Luanda, in Hercules C-130 transport aircraft.

Brig. Ben de Wet Roos was assigned to Roberto and the FNLA as Defence Force liaison officer. He studied the terrain and concluded that Roberto's plan of attack from the north would amount to suicide. The low-lying terrain – only 10 m above sea level – was dotted with lakes and swamps, which offered the defenders protection against any attack from the north. The road wound between the lakes and marshy ground for 13 km, and this meant that the attacking vehicles needed to stay on the roads.

Roos emphasised the seriousness of the attack to Roberto. To achieve the element of surprise, and therefore success, would require perfect co-ordination, thorough preparation, promptness and good co-operation between the various disciplines. Unfortunately all this advice fell on deaf ears.

The plan was that the three 140 mm guns would first concentrate on certain targets with air-burst rounds, with the aim of softening them up and hopefully persuading the enemy to retreat before the artillery fire. Before the enemy had a chance to recover from this surprise, an infantry attack, supported by troop carriers and a few armoured cars, was to follow. The main force would then be given the opportunity to attack enemy positions in Luanda. Aircraft from the South African Air Force would start the attack with an aerial bombardment.

The circumstances for the attack were far from ideal. Even before the commencement of the attack, it was found that one of the guns was defective. Furthermore, ground fire forced the aircraft to fly very high, which meant that their targets were invisible. To ensure secrecy, they had no radio contact with the ground. The result was that their bombs did not hit the enemy directly, but did induce them to flee from their positions.

The bombardment with the two remaining artillery pieces was due to commence at 05:40, exactly 20 minutes before H-hour. This was the first time since World War II that the Defence Force artillery would be involved in an attack.

However, when H-hour struck, the FNLA infantry force was not at all ready to attack. The commander had not explained the plan of attack to his troops, and an order group had to be held first. As a result, the infantry attack was an hour and forty minutes late. The FNLA's objectives were quite obvious by this time, and FAPLA was forewarned about what was likely to happen during the course of the day.

The FNLA gun crews, who were meant to help the South African crews, made off when the first salvo of enemy Stalin organ rockets fell nearby. The South Africans were then forced to carry on alone, and by all accounts they bravely acquitted themselves of their task.

The FNLA's conventional attack was a colossal failure. With Cuban help, FAPLA dealt the FNLA a heavy defeat. According to Brig. Roos a victory would have been possible if everything had been executed according to plan.[2]

Certain incorrect conclusions were later drawn from the FNLA attack and the night-time preparations for it. Rumours were spread that the Defence Force had approached so close to Luanda that they could see the city's lights, and that they had to withdraw on orders from Pretoria. It is quite correct that the gun crews of the three South African Army artillery pieces that supported the FNLA were as close as that, but neither Task Force Zulu nor any other combat group that was fighting its way north on foot and in vehicles had the privilege of seeing those lights. Nor did Task Force Zulu ever have instructions to move that far north. The nearest of these combat groups was about 200 to 300 km from Luanda. The attack on Luanda on 9 November 1975 did not form any part of the South African Defence Force's objectives, and should be seen as an isolated incident.

The South African gun crews who participated in the attack on Luanda now fell back to Ambriz with their guns. During this retreat they were seriously delayed by FNLA infantrymen who clambered onto the gun barrels for the ride. The gun crews eventually had to threaten to shoot them if they did not get down!

The crumbling of the FNLA front south of Ambriz caused Brig. Roos a great deal of concern, and he was convinced that his men had to be withdrawn for their own safety. The Ambriz airport was too unsafe for this purpose: as Chief of the Army I informed Brig. Roos that he knew the situation, and that he would be in the best position to decide on the way he and his team of 26 were to leave Angola.

Roberto accepted responsibility for the South African guns. They were taken across Angola's northern border to Zaire and eventually handed back to South Africa in 1976.

The frigate *SAS President Steyn* was on patrol off Angola's coast in late November. Navy Headquarters instructed Capt. Sam Davis to pick up Brig. Roos's group at Ambrizete, about 70 km north of Ambriz, on 27 November. All possible identifying marks were removed from the frigate, and a dirty, ragged flag was hoisted to make identification of the frigate even more difficult.

By daybreak the frigate could once again put to sea, with Brig. Roos and his group on board. They were eventually landed at Walvis Bay on 30 November 1975, and the *SAS President Steyn* returned to Simon's Town.

The SA Navy had completed a singular operation in particularly difficult circumstances with great distinction. As Chief of the Army at the

The SA Navy's *SAS President Steyn*. The Navy was closely involved in the fighting in Angola. Without their support, willingness, availability and expertise any victory would have been very difficult. (Photo: Spies, F.J. du T. 1989. *Operasie Savannah: Angola: 1975-1976*)

time, I was informed of their assistance and had great admiration of and appreciation for their efforts. I still am very grateful for the outcome that was achieved.

THE COMBAT GROUPS IN CENTRAL AND EASTERN ANGOLA

Task Force Zulu with Combat Groups Alpha, Bravo and Foxtbat fought hard and bravely in the central part of Angola, which included the provinces of Benguela, Huambo and Bié. Later the southern part of the province of Cuanza Sul also became involved. When the task force was in the vicinity of Cela, and north of Ebo and Quibala, it realised that it was already outside the area that traditionally supported UNITA.

Clearing the Benguela railway line was one of the Defence Force's original instructions. Dr Savimbi also felt strongly about this, because it would support the economy of southern Angola, and as indicated above, be of great help to Zaire and Zambia. UNITA soldiers accompanied most of these combat groups, and were utilised as infantrymen, interpreters, guides, and in various other capacities. Initially the UNITA combat elements had to be shown the ropes, and thereafter they made a worthwhile contribution.

Combat Group X-ray was constituted at Grootfontein in the period 24 to 28 November 1975, and then flown to Bié – this took up to 14 flights per day. This combat group was ordered to fight east along the railway line to Luena (Luso), and then to Luau (Teixeira de Sousa) to the international border with Zaire; and simultaneously also from Luena north in the direction of Saurimo (Henrique de Carvalho). Enemy forces offered strong resistance, but good progress was made.

By early December 1975 the South African Government had a premonition that the outcome of the OAU meeting later that month would not be favourable for South Africa's presence in Angola, and gave instructions that preparations should be made to withdraw from Angola.

Dr Savimbi needed to be informed of the possible withdrawal, and he would have to be urged to withdraw his forces from conventional actions and convert them into a guerrilla force. He also needed to be informed of the nature of future South African aid. The Minister of Defence, Mr P.W. Botha, the General Officer Commanding 1 Military Area, Gen. A.J. van Deventer, and I met Dr Savimbi at Bié on 13 December 1975 to discuss the state of the conflict, as well as the various possible outcomes of the OAU summit and the economic redevelopment of southern Angola.

Combat Group Orange was constituted at Grootfontein at the same time as X-ray. This combat group was ready to attack enemy forces from Bié in a northern direction towards Malanje on 8 December 1975. Combat Group Orange was to protect the eastern flank of Task Force Zulu, and also to help protect the traditional UNITA area. At the same time its presence south of the Cuanza River would offer protection for the Benguela railway line east of Bié.

The combat group progressed quite rapidly to beyond Mussende before any noteworthy enemy resistance was encountered. The enemy was

MAP 5 THE OPERATIONAL MOVEMENTS OF COMBAT GROUP ORANGE TO AND FROM BIÉ DURING OPERATION SAVANNAH.

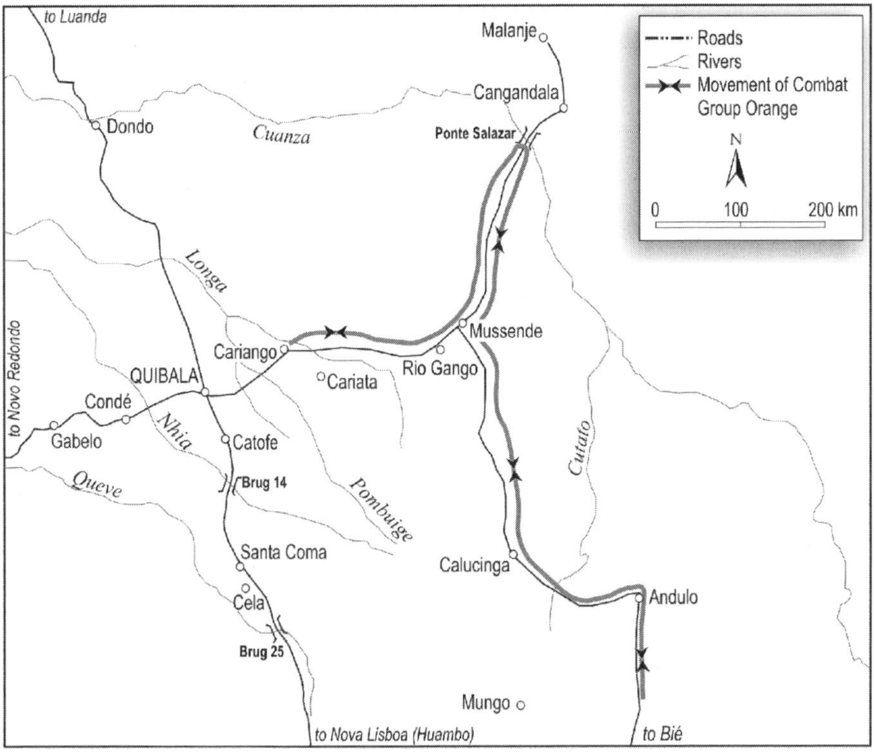

forced to retreat with losses, and escaped across the Cuanza River over the bridge at Ponte Salazar, destroying the bridge before the combat group could prevent them from doing so. The combat group then returned to Mussende and tried to link up with Task Force Zulu by using the road through Cariango to Quibala. At this stage the distance to Quibala was 25 km, but the Pombuige River at Cariango proved to be an obstacle. The bridge across the river had been destroyed, and enemy support fire made it impossible for Combat Group Orange to repair it. The enemy had destroyed most of the bridges in this area. Numerous engagements with the enemy occurred in the vicinity. In order to safeguard its secure base at Mussende, and help prepare the town for a UNITA presence, Combat

Group Orange returned to the town. On receiving orders for the Defence Force's withdrawal from Angola, this combat group joined South African forces at Bié on 21 January 1976.

WITHDRAWAL OF TROOPS

Events elsewhere in the world in the international arena between December 1975 and January 1976 had a far-reaching influence on the course of events in Angola.

The Watergate scandal in the USA had already weakened the authority of Pres. Richard Nixon, and scuppered US support for anti-communist countries and groupings in Africa. He had largely ignored the Democratic Party, which had majorities in both the Senate and the House of Representatives, when they opposed his support for certain African countries. This aid was mostly channelled through the Central Intelligence Agency (CIA), and in Angola the FNLA and UNITA were the main beneficiaries.

Some time after Pres. Nixon's resignation, the US Senate adopted the so-called Clark amendment on 19 December 1975, which blocked any further covert CIA funding for the FNLA and UNITA. Following deliberations, the measure was adopted on 19 January 1976 in the House of Representatives as well. Sen. John Tunney, who was of one mind with Sen. Dick Clark, was delighted by this and declared: "Savimbi has no illusions about how swiftly the end is coming. The war in Angola, beyond guerrilla fighting, is almost over."

On 30 December 1975 Mr John Vorster, the South African Premier, summoned Mr R.F. (Pik) Botha, South Africa's ambassador to the USA and the United Nations, to his holiday home at Oubosstrand. The Ministers of Foreign Affairs and Defence, Dr Hilgard Muller and Mr P.W. Botha respectively; the Chief of the Defence Force, Adm. H.H. Biermann, and the Secretary of Foreign Affairs, Dr Brand Fourie, were present. Gen. Constand Viljoen, at that stage Director of Operations at Defence Force Headquarters, and myself were there to present the military side. Mr Pik Botha was concerned about the political climate in the US. The press had initially been fairly positive, but had lately condemned South Africa's presence in Angola in harsh terms, and in part this induced Mr Vorster's decision to commence the withdrawal from Angola. The Defence Force supported Mr Pik Botha's recommendation of a withdrawal, but thought we should stay at least until the conclusion of the OAU summit in January. Furthermore, we felt that the withdrawal should occur in an orderly and collected manner, but that certain supplies and less essential items could be transported to South-West Africa in the interim.

Gen. Viljoen then flew to Dr Savimbi to inform him that South Africa regarded its task as completed, and would withdraw from Angola. In turn Dr Brand Fourie visited Pres. Kenneth Kaunda of Zambia, the spokesperson for the pro-Western group in the OAU, to inform him of the decision. Zaire, too, was informed, and Pres. Mobuto Sese Seko was very upset. Gen. Brent Scowcroft, Security Adviser to the US President, Mr Gerald Ford, requested Mr Pik Botha not to complete a South African withdrawal from Angola prior to the pending OAU summit, for fear that the Russians and Cubans would overrun the south.

A tragic air crash occurred on 3 January 1976. Brig. J.D. Potgieter, Officer Commanding the Military Area in Angola, had been visiting some of his combat units at the front by helicopter. Due to ground fog and a lack of proper procedures, the helicopter was mistakenly shot down by own forces. Brig. Potgieter was my second in command at the Military Academy at Saldanha in 1971. An outstanding and competent officer with a bright career ahead of him had made the ultimate sacrifice at an early age (he was in his early forties).

The OAU summit in Adis Abeba from 10 to 13 January 1976 did not offer any solutions for the Angolan question. MPLA supporters wanted this movement to be recognised as the only legitimate government of Angola, while the moderates suggested a government of national unity. Despite the efforts of both sides, nobody could ensure a majority vote, and a deadlock ensued, with 22 votes for each side. However, the Chairman, Pres. Idi Amin of Uganda, cast his deciding vote for the supporters of the MPLA.

Following the OAU decision, the South African Cabinet finally decided on 14 January 1976 that South Africa should withdraw from Angola completely, except for the Calueque area, and the USA was immediately informed of this decision. The OAU recognised Angola's MPLA government a month later, and admitted the country as a member of the OAU.

South Africa was of the opinion that the OAU decision should be honoured, but also that she had been left in the lurch by the USA. Min. P.W. Botha reacted as follows in the House of Assembly on 17 April 1976: "They (the Americans) left us in the lurch ... the story must be told of how we went in with their knowledge, how we acted in Angola with their knowledge, and how they encouraged us to act. And when we were close to the climax, they recklessly left us in the lurch by breaking their word."[3] The Premier, Mr Vorster, reacted as follows to the American news magazine *Newsweek* of 17 May 1976: "US Secretary of State Henry Kissinger had urged the SADF incursion into Angola and then failed to provide the necessary back-up."

In view of the fast-changing political situation in the world, South Africa's decision to withdraw from Angola, that is not to carry the burden of Angola and the consequences alone, was the correct one. The entire Western world and the OAU, including moderate African countries, would rightly have condemned South Africa if it had remained in Angola after the OAU had recognised the MPLA as the legitimate rulers of that country. Furthermore, Angola could have drawn South Africa into a Vietnam-like situation, which could have caused the country to bleed to death slowly. From this point onwards the South African Defence Force mainly acted against SWAPO and in support of UNITA in southern Angola, using South-West Africa as its base. Cross-border operations were usually of a short duration, and the policy inside Angola was not to engage Soviet, Cuban or Angolan forces. However, if they interfered with our operations, we did engage them, staging an orderly withdrawal to South-West Africa as soon as the operation was completed.

On 27 March 1976, when the first convoys reached the Kunene River at Ruacana, I shared the podium with Min. P.W. Botha, Gen. Bob Rodgers, Gen. Constand Viljoen, Gen. Neil Webster, Brig. Ben Roos, Cmdt S.W.J. Kotze and Mr Jannie de Wet, the Commissioner General of Ovamboland, while Min. Botha took the salute during the march-past.

On that occasion my thoughts involuntarily went to the troops who were marching past us. They had exceeded my greatest expectations. They displayed courage and faith, perseverance, audacity and enthusiasm, handling all daunting tasks with ease. Above all they had been extremely successful as a team, and they had placed the Defence Force's stamp on the enemy with pride, without sustaining a bloody nose themselves. Do not think for a single moment that they always had things their own way. There were also times of hardship, sacrifice and loneliness. The abilities of our youth, evident to all, filled everyone with confidence in view of the challenges that South Africa was facing at that stage. But I also felt sorrow. We had lost 35 brave, intrepid men during Operation Savannah. In my mind's eye I saw these men's loved ones and prayed that they would find solace and comfort in Him, Father of us all.

My greatest disappointment was that our armaments did not meet our expectations, mainly because of age and a lack of mobility. I realised that the Defence Force and Armscor were facing a great challenge to overcome these shortcomings. The obsolete equipment made me think of a saying by Langenhoven about the cost of peace and disagreement. I have adapted it for this situation: "The price of peace is payable in advance; that of war in arrears."

SA AIR FORCE (SAAF)

1 Air Component of the SA Air Force played an essential role in the success of Operation Savannah. Because Angola and South-West Africa are situated so far from Pretoria, troops, supplies, military equipment and other things had to be transported by airplane over vast distances. The SA Air Force also contributed with air reconnaissance, especially when we were moving into Angola clandestinely. The most important form of tactical air support was spotting enemy positions and directing artillery fire.

Later, when 101 Task Force had been formed, 1 Air Component became 301 Air Component. Even though the SA Air Force was not really employed operationally for air attacks, it sometimes had to operate in very difficult circumstances. Landing strips were often situated in unknown areas, and had to be found without the help of aeronautical maps. Bad weather and night operations meant many hours of flying with instruments only. Due to the clandestine nature of Operation Savannah, road transport was not always possible, and ground forces were largely dependent on the Air Force for provisioning.

In *Operasie Savannah: Angola 1975-1976*, F.J. du T. Spies claims that this operation was more difficult than the Berlin Air Lift in many ways.[4] I fully support this view and would like to give the following reasons for my view: During the Berlin Air Lift the flight took place over developed European territory with every possible air navigation aid. The Air Lift did not take place during wartime. On the other hand, the SA Air Force transport aircraft could often only fly at night due to enemy activities in certain areas. They had to complete each task that same night and fly back to their base of origin. No Air Force transport aircraft was permitted to overnight in Angola.

Operation Savannah took place in the high rainy season, which presented immense challenges to flying, and that in a Third World country with a serious lack of navigation aids. The only available maps were poor, and landing could be accomplished only with the aid of the flight beacons and landing lights that the SA Air Force itself could supply. The landing strips were in very poor shape because of a lack of maintenance, or were simply ground strips. The Air Force itself had to supply and fly in any aids and supplies it required to operate an airfield. Nevertheless the Air Force very successfully completed an immense task in nerve-racking circumstances with limited manpower and equipment.

Using five transport aircraft, the Air Force transported 6500 tons of freight and 5300 passengers to and from the operational area. Additional tasks included evacuating 4093 Angolan refugees who were brought to South Africa. The wounded also needed to be evacuated to South-West Africa and South Africa. Two helicopters were added to 301 Air Component for this purpose, and for the deployment of troops.

Despite the difficult circumstances in which the aircraft operated during Operation Savannah, there was not a single transport aircraft accident – a unique achievement! The SA Air Force lost only two light planes and a helicopter.

THE SA NAVY

By its very nature the SA Navy played a limited but valuable role during Operation Savannah. As Task Force Zulu penetrated deeper into Angola, there was a stronger and stronger possibility that enemy vessels could land between them and Angola's southern border. Lobito and Namibe (Moçamedes), the two harbours already taken by the Task Force, could become the targets for such an attack. If that happened, Task Force Zulu's supply lines – initially to the Rundu headquarters of 1 Military Area, later renamed 101 Task Force Headquarters – could be cut, with dire consequences. This would also mean that Task Force Zulu would have to fight on two fronts simultaneously. Shortly afterwards the SA Navy received the following instructions: to keep guard off Angola's coast (initially clandestinely, and later openly); to stand by for the possible evacuation of Defence Force personnel from Angola; and, if necessary, to provide naval gunfire support; to escort vessels with logistical re-supplies for allied forces to Lobito; and to prevent possible enemy coastal landings.

Two frigates, *SAS President Steyn* and *SAS President Kruger*, were earmarked for these tasks. *SAS Tafelberg* would act as supply ship and provide the frigates with logistical supplies. Everything had to be done in the greatest secrecy, and thorough security measures needed to be applied. For example, when vessels sailed between Walvis Bay and the rendezvous points, decoy routes were followed and radio silence was maintained.

The main function of Naval Intelligence was to monitor all Soviet naval vessels and merchant navy vessels that could possibly supply the MPLA with armaments.

The Navy, too, carried out its tasks with a high sense of duty. The evacuation of Brig. Ben de Wet Roos and his group at night from Ambrizete was a jewel.

SA MEDICAL SERVICE (SAMS)

As always the SA Medical Service performed a vitally important medical and health support service function during Operation Savannah with great success. Apart from excellent medical support, the presence of this Defence Force component, together with the chaplain service, is probably the major source of peace of mind on the battlefield, because every

Defence Force member knows, even if only subconsciously: "Someone will look after me." Medical care of the highest quality would be available should the worst happen.

At the height of the war the Medical Service equipped, opened or manned hospitals at Bié, Cela and Ongiva (Pereira de Eça), over and above the medical services assigned to each combat group. Medical services were primarily offered to the Defence Force, UNITA and civilians, including a mass of refugees. The SA Medical Service treated 20 to 60 local civilians as outpatients at each hospital daily. Wounded prisoners of war also received medical treatment.

Because it is of the utmost important to get wounded soldiers to medical care as soon as possible, the SA Air Force used its helicopters to perform this vital role during Operation Savannah, and succeeded wonderfully.

The SA Medical Service augmented its permanent medical personnel with the Citizen Force Field Ambulance units. This made even more medical doctors, specialists and other medical support and resources available in order to meet the medical challenge successfully.

On one of my regular visits to the operational area I travelled from Rundu across the Okavango River to Calai to acquaint myself with the refugee problem. Thousands of refugees were given shelter at Calai, mostly in Defence Force tents. The Defence Force supplied electricity, water and a hospital with 13 beds. The refugees waited patiently for official permission to enter South-West Africa or South Africa. As there were some teachers amongst the refugees, a school for the refugee children was established at Calai. I also met a member of the SA Medical Service team, Sister Annette Steyn, who was responsible for the medical treatment of the refugees. She was a kind-hearted lady with a sympathetic personality, helpful and caring towards all, to such a degree that she was generally known as "The Angel of Calai".

It was very clear that the refugee problem was mainly caused by the lawlessness, fear of robbery and violence and the economic collapse that was occurring in Angola at that time.[5] For a considerable time the Defence Force was intensively involved in the challenge presented by refugees, particularly in the provision of transport, shelter, rations, medical services and the administration and management of the temporary refugee camps. This responsibility was accepted over and above its main task, and was carried out with care and sympathy, and to the best of the ability of the SA Defence Force.

THE CONSEQUENCES OF OPERATION SAVANNAH

The withdrawal of South African forces from Angola left a military vacuum. This was soon filled by the MPLA and their Cuban allies who tried to take control of southern Angola. The MPLA victory at the OAU summit resulted in great advantages for SWAPO as well, as this organisation had always worked most closely with the MPLA. Initially SWAPO was closest to UNITA, but when South Africa began to support UNITA, SWAPO had little choice but to seek affiliation with the MPLA. It was also clear that the Soviet Union and South Africa would never be good friends. As the communist countries were pumping military aid into Angola, any aid to SWAPO would most probably come from the side of the MPLA. This organisation, thinking back on the beating it took from the Defence Force during Operation Savannah, did not hesitate to give SWAPO its wholehearted support.

Defence Force intelligence reports and intercepted enemy radio communications made it clear that basic facilities would in future be assigned to SWAPO, and that Cuba would support them with weaponry and training. SWAPO was now able to establish itself, and complete the training of the thousands of recruits it had gained in the aftermath of the fall of the Portuguese Government without hindrance. Within months this movement had been transformed from a limping organisation into a powerful, well-trained and well-oiled military machine. Willem Steenkamp sums it up neatly in his book *Suid-Afrika se grensoorlog 1966-1989*, writing: "Swapo now found itself in a stronger military position than ever before. For the first time it had acquired what had become almost a *sine qua non* for any successful insurgency, namely a safe border across which it could fall back. It could openly establish a training, administrative and logistical structure within Angola and infiltrate southwards at will. Everything had changed from the hide and seek years of Portuguese rule [...]. Furthermore Zambia took note of the facts, abandoned her opposition to the MPLA, and not only allowed Plan [People's Liberation Army of Namibia – SWAPO's combat elements – M.M.] to base its attacks on Caprivi on its soil, but also supplied them with food and other necessities."

South Africa's international political position at that time, the limited ability of certain vehicles, the obsolete weaponry and the limited supply of ammunition the country had at that time, offered the communist forces in Angola an opportunity to penetrate South-West Africa. A combined effort by FAPLA, Cuban troops and SWAPO could have seen them challenging the SA Defence Force. This did not happen, however.

One can speculate as to why these groups did not take the obvious step. Perhaps the following circumstances jointly or separately played a role: their experiences during Operation Savannah instilled great respect for the SA Defence Force amongst these groups; they needed to consolidate in the wake of the South African troop withdrawal; the SA Defence Force had earlier caught the communist forces unawares with its rapid action; and lastly the Angolan allies had such an inadequate intelligence system that they were not aware of the actual state of affairs amongst the South African forces. At a later stage East Germans ran the intelligence system, and this resulted in far greater efficiency.

Taking everything into consideration, Operation Savannah proved to be worth the effort. It bought UNITA and the FNLA some valuable time to prepare themselves for attacks by the Soviet Union, Cubans and FAPLA. International communism was at its height, and quick progress in Angola could easily have spurred it on to attempt even greater adventures, with South Africa still its principal target.

South Africa also learnt some important lessons from its military operations during Operation Savannah.

The operation was the first conventional operation under African conditions involving South Africa since World War II. The Defence Force had already moved away from European combat traditions and methods, but it was the first time that the Defence Force was able to test its theories under enemy fire. It was possible to observe the functioning of armaments, tactics, structures and methods under actual combat conditions, and it was possible to test our troops' performance, and indirectly also their training compared to that of their opponents. The results varied from not all that good to outstanding. At one end of the scale the quality

Two captured 122 mm MRLs (multiple rocket launchers), also known as the Stalin Organ or Redeye. At that stage we had no effective counter to this type of weapon with its deadly rockets.

of our men, and their thorough training, far outdid that of our enemies and our allies. At the other end of the scale South Africa displayed an enormous lack of comparable fire power. It was a shock to compare the Defence Force's obsolete weaponry with that of the enemy. These shortcomings needed to be addressed urgently. For example, a plan would soon have to be made to counter the fire power of the Soviet 122 mm multiple rocket launcher (MRL).

It was quite clear that if the communist forces had not been challenged at the time of Operation Savannah, and if the Defence Force had not been so successful, a future clash would have been inevitable. The enemy forces would then have been able to choose the time and place. In view of the state of our armaments, such a clash could possibly have ended in the defeat of the Defence Force, because there would have been no time to rectify the shortcomings in our weaponry. It also became clear that the Russians and Cubans were far less eager to take on the South Africans in the wake of Operation Savannah.

The Defence Force acquired a great deal of experience during the operation that would later stand it in very good stead. Mutual respect between Defence Force members was developed, and this promoted the *esprit de corps*; teamwork improved markedly. However, the operation also took its toll, as the Defence Force lost 35 men during Operation Savannah, of which 18 were national servicemen, and 17 Permanent Force members.

After the withdrawal from Angola, the Defence Force, and myself in particular, on behalf of the Army, insisted on replacing certain armaments and augmenting others. The South African Defence Force was still equipped with British 140 mm guns dating from World War II, with a maximum range of 17 to 18 km. Enemy artillery of comparable calibre manufactured by the Soviet Union, on the other hand, had a range of 20 to 21 km. The reason why our gun crews were superior, even in view of this limited range, was because of their skill and the superb quality of the NSM who acted as forward observation officers.

Yet it must be clearly stated that South Africa did not withdraw from Angola at that stage because it suffered a military defeat, but because of political considerations. If South Africa's actions had been spurred by a desire for territorial expansion, it would have been able to overrun the whole of Angola.

About a month after the 1976 withdrawal from Angola, at the onset of winter, I again invited Mr P.W. Botha to visit the South African forces in South-West Africa. As usual, we visited every military camp and base, where he addressed the Defence Force members and, among other things, thanked them for their personal sacrifices so far away from their loved ones, and for the dedication with which they performed their military service. He was greeted with great enthusiasm wherever he went.

As a conclusion to the tour, we spent the last night with the Commissioner General, Mr Jannie de Wet, at Oshakati. When Mr Botha and I had a moment to ourselves, he announced, out of the blue, that Adm. Hugo Biermann was to retire later that year, and that he was going to appoint me Chief of the Defence Force. This idea came as a shock to me at the time.

It would mean that after three years as Chief of the Army I would have to bid the Army farewell. I had just begun to find my feet in this time, and there was so much I still wished to accomplish in the Army. I had managed to put together a superb top management team, but all the challenges still waiting would have to be abandoned. If it would not have been extremely impolite and ungrateful to do so, I would have asked whether I had the choice of accepting the appointment or not. However, in my heart of hearts I knew I had no choice. During the tour Mr Botha had thanked Defence Force members profusely for their sacrifices, and here I was, immediately afterwards, feeling doubtful about an appointment that would require sacrifices of me. I felt ashamed that I could even have harboured such a thought.

Chapter 9

BASIC REQUIREMENTS FOR A SUCCESSFUL DEFENCE FORCE

ASSUMING COMMAND AS CHIEF OF THE SA DEFENCE FORCE

On 30 July 1976, during a Defence Force parade at Voortrekkerhoogte under the command of Commodore Green, Adm. H.H. Biermann, the retiring Chief, handed over command of the South African Defence Force to me. About a thousand Defence Force members representing all Defence Force components and all South African population groups participated in this impressive parade.

Waiting for the start of the parade, I could sense the excitement and perhaps also the tension amongst all those present, including myself. The colourful flags, with the Republic flag in the place of honour, supported by the flags of the Defence Force, Army, Air Force, Navy and Medical Service, were hoisted and were fluttering in the breeze. The parading Defence Force members with their brown, blue and white uniforms, and the flags and colours of the Defence Force components on parade, created a very handsome military scene. At the same time the military bands entertained the guests and the audience with lively marches while everyone waited for the pomp and splendour of the military spectacle to commence.

After the proper honours had been shown to the Admiral as he stood on the podium, and after he had responded, the Chaplain General was requested to open the proceedings with a reading from Scripture and prayer. The parade was then readied for inspection. I accompanied the Admiral to the area in front of the podium, where the parade commander joined us. Two open vehicles, specially prepared for inspection purposes, slowly moved towards us. Adm. Biermann and Cdre Green mounted the first vehicle and stood side by side on the back. I mounted the rear vehicle and stood on the back all by myself. We slowly moved past the assembled parade for the inspection.

It was a typical Highveld winter afternoon, with a slight movement of cold air. At that moment I longed for my father, who had suddenly passed away the year before. Apart from the thrashing he gave me, he never discussed the distress he must have experienced when I ran away to join the military all those years ago. He had always proved to be a pillar of support during my career, and had always given me great encouragement. I knew he would have felt great pride on this particular occasion.

Alone on the back of that vehicle during this momentous occasion, I felt a bit lonely, and my thoughts wandered between things that had happened in the past and the challenges that lay ahead. At one stage I felt as stripped and alone as the deciduous trees all around the parade ground, leafless and bare on that winter afternoon. Some part of this lonely feeling probably had its origin in the fact that this promotion meant that I had to leave behind most of the Army's top management team, and that I now had to create and develop a new team. Fortunately Gen. Jack Dutton and Gen. André van Deventer, who were well versed in my management philosophy and the ways in which I worked, would go with me to help me introduce the new climate, atmosphere and management style to the other components of the Defence Force.

Following the inspections, and on our return to the saluting base, the Admiral officially transferred command to me. In reply to his most appropriate text addressed to me, I proclaimed the following aloud to all those present at the parade, who represented the entire Defence Force and all its members:

As the office of Chief of the Defence Force has been entrusted to me with effect from 1 September 1976, I, Magnus André de Mérindol Malan, solemnly pledge to serve my country faithfully, courageously and with dignity; to carry out my duties and responsibilities faithfully and diligently, and to set a good example for those placed under me. I herewith officially accept command of the South African Defence Force.

The parade was then concluded with military honours. Leave was taken of Adm. Biermann, and I was welcomed as the new officer commanding.

Adm. Biermann was going to be on leave for a month, and I would be Acting Chief of the Defence Force for the month of August, which is why the parade took place on 30 July, while I accepted my full responsibilities only on 1 September 1976.

BASIC REQUIREMENTS FOR A DEFENCE FORCE

Looking back on the period before I became Chief of the Defence Force, one decisive characteristic of the SA Defence Force stands out very clearly, namely the successful way in which it carried out its primary task in extremely perilous circumstances. This is allied to the adaptability shown by the Defence Force, for example during the very wet and muddy conditions of Operation Savannah.

One of the most urgent needs that became apparent during Operation Savannah was for new vehicles, because some Defence Force vehicles were clearly not suitable for use in the wet Angolan terrain. The experience showed that armoured cars, artillery gun tractors, troop carriers and other vehicles were included in this category. Another shortcoming was a lack of suitable weapons to provide covering fire.

One thing was certain: Armscor and the private sector accepted the challenge of overcoming these shortcomings with enthusiasm and vigour. Teams were formed in conjunction with the Defence Force, and these jointly tried to find solutions as soon as possible.

The primary task of the Defence Force is to ensure national security. However, I also thought it necessary to analyse the efficient functioning, organisational composition and components of the Defence Force for my own purposes. Without a defence force that is able to execute its task of national security successfully, any country plunged into crisis faces a bleak future, in which chaos is inevitable.[1]

To state it simply: in my view a defence force basically consists of manpower, equipment and financial resources, with motivated, enthusiastic, well-trained manpower as the most important element.

One should keep in mind that when South Africa became a republic in 1961, it was the first time that the Defence Force was able to act as an independent entity with regard to its thinking and in determining its needs. At that time, the Defence Force had to be developed and reconstituted almost from afresh. It was an enormous challenge!

After South Africa's withdrawal from the Commonwealth in 1961, it had to create its own military structures in a short time. For the first time South Africa also had to meet its own military needs independently of Britain, and this meant it had to begin acquiring or manufacturing arms for itself. Prior to this political change, South Africa had been almost completely dependent on Britain for determining its organisational military structure, training prescriptions and guidelines, and the manufacture and procurement of arms.

When the established colonial custom of broad armaments prescriptions suddenly fell away in the 1960s, the SA Defence Force was, for the first time, completely independent with regard to task allocations, military thought and actions, and in determining the needs regarding manpower and armaments. South Africa came to realise that its survival, national security and future military challenges would be its exclusive responsibility. Because defence prescriptions from outside its borders were removed, a void in the country's security framework was created. This void meant that the Defence Force would have to adapt its organisation and functions to the new political dispensation, and would have to reorganise and rationalise in order to undertake these tasks.

The battlefield would provide the only practical test for measuring any success. The risk assessments of the time indicated that the SA Defence Force would probably be thoroughly tested by the Soviet Union, the Cubans, the East Germans and Angolan forces on the battlefields of Angola. If South Africa's Defence Force could not perform its primary task with flying colours, the country would face an uncertain future. If it failed, it was quite possible that South Africa would be littered with the ruins of war, and that a foreign communist ideology would form the basis of the system of government.

Against the background of the revolutionary onslaught aimed at the Republic at that time, I stated with conviction that I believed a strong defence force to be our best insurance policy for peace and stability. I would later discover that the South African Government was also able to use this insurance policy to create a suitable climate for a political negotiation process aimed at ensuring peace and stability in South Africa.

It is important to consider some of the factors that had to be taken into account when establishing a successful defence force for South Africa in the circumstances prevalent at the time.

South Africa had never manufactured arms on any significant scale. It developed a limited arms production capability during World War II, when it was cut off from Britain because of circumstances prevailing during the war. Due to the political ties that existed between Britain and South Africa up to the beginning of the 1960s, Britain gave assistance to South Africa regarding military structures and armament requirements. Since World War II until it became a Republic in 1961, South Africa on its side undertook to provide Britain with an armoured division and an air force ground support group for deployment in the Middle East.[2]

Up to 1967 the office of Secretary of Defence still existed, who was inter alia responsible for the production and procurement of arms by the Department of Defence. However, this department employed very few staff members knowledgeable about business and production. One of the first and most important decisions taken in these years concerned the acquisition and/or joint manufacture of certain weapon systems.

The armaments purchases of that time for the first time brought the awareness that poor control within the department could possibly result in errors and therefore financial losses. It was essential that suitable, reliable business people, with enough expertise and experience concerning arms procurement and production, should be available in the Department of Defence.

The initial lack of expertise, and the sanctions that were soon afterwards imposed on South Africa, compelled the Government to create its own, modernised armaments procurement and production organisation. The term of office of the Minister of Defence, Mr P.W. Botha, was therefore characterised by the reorganisation and rationalisation of the Department of Defence, and more extensive liaison with the private sector to increase the production of armaments. Among other things this resulted in the abolishment of the post of Secretary of Defence. The later Armscor was a result of this reorganisation process.[3]

This organisation would develop the necessary expertise and technical ability, and enjoy the required international exposure, to meet the SA Defence Force's armaments needs. A later reorganisation of Armscor led to the establishment of Denel as an independent organisation.

In determining the defence requirements of a country like South Africa, which is situated at the southern extremity of Africa, many interdependent factors must be taken into account. These factors must be based on factual information, and as the facts change, so the determination of needs change as well. A country's initial armament requirements, including its main weaponry, normally require a lengthy manufacturing process. In some cases this also forms the basis of the development of future weapon systems. Immediate requirements also need to be taken into account: The required arms must be supplied in time to trained manpower to enable them to complete the planned military tasks successfully.

However, from experience I want to emphasise that it is also a military prerequisite to consider possible future threats, and the security actions and weaponry that would in future be required to meet these threats. The SA Defence Force calls such an essential predetermination of future threats to South Africa and its neighbours a military appreciation.

The Defence Force's earliest military appreciation of 1960 dealt with the implications of the uncertain political situation in the world, and the increase of territorial threats.[4] Brig. Jan Burger and I used the first appreciation of 1961-1962 to draw up a military needs assessment. Military appreciations or estimates were prepared on an annual basis from 1970 onwards.

Since World War II Africa had become extremely unstable, mainly because of a weakening of former European colonial powers, which impeded their ability to maintain military control over their colonies. Armed insurrections and terrorism by indigenous populations aimed at overthrowing colonial governments were the order of the day. The Soviet Union supplied weapons to many of these movements, and trained them in the use of these weapons.

The 1960 military appreciation indicated that it was essential that South Africa should increase its military capabilities and readiness. To ensure combat-readiness, equipment and manpower needs for the coming years had to be determined and expressed in financial terms.

Another important factor that became clear quite early on was that in the near future, South Africa would no longer be able to rely on the procurement of military equipment, armaments and ammunition from abroad. Neither could the country rely on any form of military alliance with any country in order to form a common front against a security threat in Southern Africa. To survive in a military sense, the country would therefore in the near future have to be completely self-sufficient with regard to its military capabilities.

Unique factors had to be taken into account when determining the need for equipment, manpower and finances. Considerations regarding equipment included affordability, the possibility of local manufacture, how advanced available weapon systems were, and the possible presence and capability of hostile weapon systems.

With regard to manpower, it was important to determine the ideal composition of the Defence Force's manpower from time to time. Other important factors were the numbers of skilled and trained technical personnel as well as academically trained personnel required by the Defence Force. The existing internal manpower situation at the time suggested that it would not be wise to rely solely on a professional or career defence force. In the circumstances that prevailed then, a citizen force, commando force and a national service force, drawn from the civilian population, offered the most efficient solution to the diverse manpower needs.[5]

The military appreciation of the time also predicted with great certainty that the Soviet Union would probably become involved in Southern Africa through the use of surrogate or proxy forces. This emphasised the desirability of access to, or the use of, modern and sophisticated weapons, including nuclear, biological and chemical arms.

The Soviet threat was one of the main reasons why South Africa needed to reconsider its need for a nuclear capability, even if only for peaceful use. The question was: Should South Africa be preparing itself in the field of nuclear weapons? How should South Africa protect its population, and how should it offer resistance should such weapons of mass destruction be used against it? A very long preparation time is needed for manufacturing a nuclear capability, even if it was to be used as a deterrent only, so the decision had to be made early.

The instruction given by the Government of the day that the country needed to become self-sufficient with regard to arms was limited by the country's industrial capacity. This capacity first had to be augmented, and if any weapon system was too sophisticated for local production, other solutions had to be found.[6]

It was clear to me that arms sanctions would definitely play a role in the availability of armaments. South Africa was forced to find ways to decrease its dependence on the outside world with regard to its arms requirements, and to develop the greatest possible self-sufficiency. I, however, always maintained that this should be strategically essential, technically possible, economically viable and therefore affordable. In general it was agreed that if the quantity or volume that could be produced locally was comparable with the quantity that could be imported from abroad, the local prices would have to be competitive or even better, and there had to be other advantages.

In view of the international arms embargo imposed on South Africa at the time, I believed – and I made my thoughts very clear on this – that if we could become self-sufficient in the area of weapon systems, "it would in effect amount to political independence, because it would then not be necessary to have our policy and course determined by anybody else, as we would be largely independent. We would not have to beg anyone for weapons." We were well on the way towards reaching that goal.[7]

I was convinced that it was very important for a country to allocate financial resources towards ensuring the combat-readiness of its defence force, because this has an effect on the country's economic growth. I therefore instructed the Defence Force to very carefully determine and clearly spell out its short-term, medium-term and long-term financial requirements with regard to manpower, armaments, equipment and possible operations. I had to approve these financial requirements annually, and submit them to the Central Government's Treasury.[8]

A defence force's military requirements, with regard to materiel, manpower and its financial needs, are determined by the task it must fulfil.

This task is determined by the Government's strategy or plan, and must constantly be updated and applied. The Government's strategy must be embedded in its policy, decisions and guidelines.

In adapting organisationally and functionally to the new political dispensation after 1961, the most important deficiency that the SA Defence Force had to cope with, was the absence of any real national strategy. What were the State's national goals? What goals had been determined for the various security and welfare departments?

Fortunately Pres. P.W. Botha's government approved such a national strategy with a description of the country's national objectives and interests, in 1980. It was the first time in the country's history that this had been done, and after much toil and sweat it was completed and forwarded to all Government departments.[9]

The Republic of South Africa's "national interests" were derived from the Preamble to the Constitution of the time: "... to safeguard the integrity of the country and the freedom of its people; to maintain law and order; to promote the happiness and spiritual and material welfare of all."[10] In its formulation of national interests, the Government added the following: "to accept our duty and to seek world peace jointly with all peace-loving nations."[11]

From this the Government's national goal was derived, which was aimed at improving the living standards of all peoples and population groups in the Republic of South Africa.[12] In reality this aim formed the heartbeat, the core of the national strategy and was intertwined with the aims and implementation of the departmental strategy and performance of the SA Defence Force.[13]

The Government's national security policy was aimed at protecting all South Africans from any security threat. The Security Policy formulated early in 1980, which was regularly brought up to date thereafter, included the following:
- To defend and safeguard the Government, the Constitution and the political order against any form of foreign aggression or internal revolution, no matter its nature or origin, with all force at its disposal.
- To hold to the firm policy that South Africa does not have aggressive intentions against any state or group; that it does not envisage any territorial expansion, and that it wishes to exist alongside its

neighbours in peace and co-operation. This policy does not mean that aggression by states will be tolerated. South Africa's posture is offensive (i.e. pro-active). It must retain the initiative and ensure its national security by proactive actions.
- To involve all population groups in the maintenance of public law and order and the defence of South Africa, and to complement the manpower requirements of the Security Forces through a system of national service.
- To support the civilian infrastructure by maintaining or preserving lives, health and property and maintaining essential services.
- To make the Republic of South self-sufficient with regard to armaments and the continued production thereof as far as possible in practice.

In addition to this national strategy, and in accordance with the security policy, the Government forwarded the following decisions to the Defence Force: There will be no interference in the domestic affairs of other states; the violation of South Africa's international borders will not be tolerated; and no arms race should be precipitated with any other country.[14]

The SA Defence Force had to analyse this security policy in detail in order to determine its course of action, and to formulate the tasks required to execute these policy prescriptions. Departmental strategy had to be determined accordingly. At the same time the mission contained in the Defence Act had to be complied with.

South Africa found itself in a difficult position; in view of the prevailing political atmosphere it could not rely on open support from any country. The national strategy was also designed to give the Defence Force an indication of which geographical areas were regarded as being politically indispensable in planning any possible future military action. Such an indication was essential for planning the composition, organisation, manpower and armament requirements of the Defence Force. The country's economic ability to execute and sustain military operations in these areas was also very important. The size of and distance to the areas, as well as the intensity or nature of any potential military action, would determine the finances, manpower and armaments required. All military operations outside the country's borders needed to be judged on merit. Economic factors would in such cases be as important as political considerations. Some politicians were reluctant to identify such strategically important areas, but I took it upon myself to determine three areas and to submit these to the Government. The three areas were identified through an analysis of the security situation at the time.

Taking into account the prevailing political situation in South Africa at the time, the Government subdivided the geographical areas regarded as of national importance for the country into three categories: Firstly, there was the South African geographical area, including South-West Africa/Namibia as its area of responsibility, which constituted the heartland. Then there was an area that was regarded as tactically important to South Africa, which broadly included Botswana, southern Angola, Zimbabwe, Lesotho, Swaziland and Mozambique south of the Zambezi River to where this watershed river flows into the Indian Ocean. Thirdly, the area considered to be of strategic importance included the states to the north of the tactical area, more or less as far as the equator.

This Government classification of the areas it regarded as vital for the various types of military actions, was of key importance. Apart from the fact that it enabled the Defence Force to determine the extent and type of manpower and equipment that would possibly be required, it also meant that the availability and condition of resources such as harbours, airfields, railway lines, roads, hospitals, industrial development, etcetera. required for future military use had to be determined and kept up to date. At the time the topography, climatology, soil analyses and so on in the designated areas also revealed very important data, and many new facts were presented for consideration. For example, soil analyses indicated that the Defence Force should move away from the international military use of tracked vehicles, and should rather deploy wheeled vehicles because of their accessibility, speed and so forth. The conclusion regarding wheeled vehicles even applied to the tanks to be used in the area. The results of various investigations had a good effect on two areas in particular: there were financial savings because of employing force-multiplying or multi-purpose equipment, and there was a general increase in the efficiency of military operations.

With regard to meeting the need for main weapon systems, the goal

MAP 6 SUBDIVISION OF SOUTHERN AFRICA INTO OPERATIONAL AREAS.

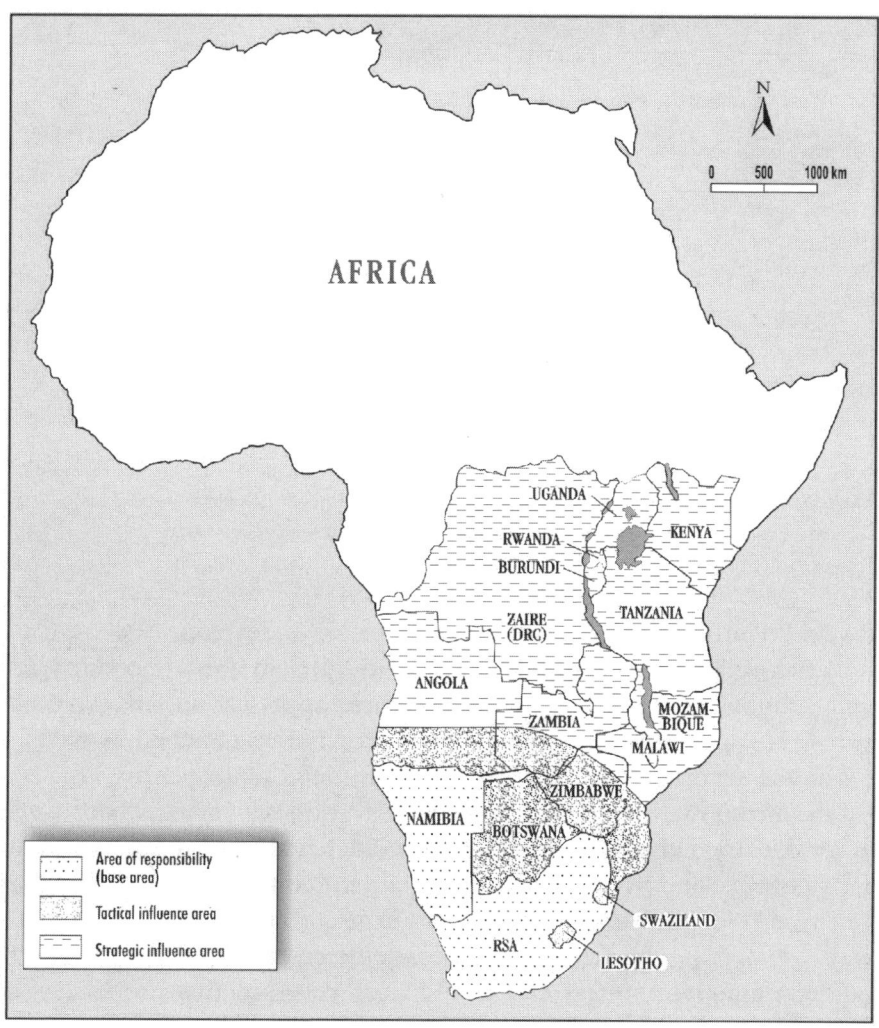

was to create a well-equipped, balanced main weapon system timeously for the Defence Force, a weapon system that was capable of completing security tasks efficiently. The logistic process to achieve these goals

Refuelling Cheetahs by a multi-purpose aircraft. This gave these fighters a far greater operational range, and meant that fewer expensive airfields had to be developed. This multi-purpose aircraft can be used for refuelling, as a freighter or as an electronic intelligence aircraft.

would be intricate and would take a long time to develop.

A focused, properly considered security capacity for any country requires, among other things, a national security appreciation. This can then be used to spell out future threats, with time frames attached, as well as a national security strategy which helps to determine security tasks, finances, manpower and equipment. In this way one can ensure that a well-motivated, trained and properly equipped defence force will be ready at the right time and place to turn challenges into opportunities.

Since 1976, the Defence Force and Armscor had been well on their way to executing this long-term process efficiently. Since 1990, however, political intervention has ended and even reversed this process. As a result of the political advances, the success of F.W. de Klerk's 2 February 1990 speech in Parliament, and the consequent decline in the so-called struggle, I drastically reduced financial allocations for the Defence Force and Armscor with the co-operation of these bodies and with the approval of the Government of the time.

The Defence Force and I were also cheered by the fact that Pres. F.W. de Klerk had clearly revealed, in his well-known speech, that he fully realised that this type of war, while it can be lost on the security front, is primarily fought on, and must be won in the political arena.

In order to show the SA Defence Force's support in this regard, I referred to this welcome change in policy in most of the public speeches that I made in the first half of 1990. One of my pronouncements was reported as follows in the *Cape Argus* of 28 July 1990: "Solutions to the country's challenges were being found through political methods which went hand in hand with economic and social development ... The Defence Force supported the search for political solutions, but had to provide the secure and stable environment that was needed before the political process could succeed."

A CRITICAL EVALUATION

In retrospect it is now accepted locally and internationally that the SA Defence Force of the 1970s and 1980s was probably the most efficient and best-equipped defence force organisation this country has ever had. The men and women who served in it were honourable, loyal and courageous – in a word, superb! At one stage the media lauded this organisation as the best on the African continent.

One can hardly say enough about such a defence force and its people. Hundreds, no thousands, of Defence Force members served their country faithfully and with distinction, made great sacrifices and never refused to play their part. Even today I think back with pride on the highly successful organisation that the Defence Force was in my days.

An appreciation of the Defence Force and the manner in which it executed its duties requires a synthesis of many events, influences and factors. In order to judge yesterday we need to take into consideration yesterday's circumstances. For a proper judgement of the decisions and actions of the past, we need to know which factors were the defining ones at that time. Because prevailing circumstances have changed drastically since then, I have tried to describe events as I experienced them.

People say: "Hindsight is the most exact science in the world", but I wonder if the reverse is not even more true. It is very difficult to take yourself back to the climate and circumstances that prevailed 20 or 30 years ago. We all realise why things look the way they do today, but we do not always know how to answer accusations about past events, or how to describe and explain the circumstances that prevailed then. I am trying to disclose facts so that the truth about the Defence Force will be clearer. Other recent attempts to find the truth have failed miserably.

In peacetime people often look back on events during conflict or war, and are then shocked by the fact that human beings are capable of treating other human beings so cruelly. On looking back, a great many actions that took place then, now seem inexplicable and morally indefensible.

One should never shy away from realities. In South Africa's case the SA Defence Force achieved successes with its cross-border and internal operations. On the other hand the ANC Alliance planted bombs in shopping and entertainment centres. In both cases innocent people were killed, although both parties were convinced that their actions were aimed at creating a better South Africa for future generations.[15]

The ANC Alliance leaders were trained by seasoned leaders of the revolution. These leaders formulated and adapted their battle plans according to those of experienced revolutionaries who had tested the plans in practice. This meant that there was no fixed code or battle plan for actions directed against the State. The plans or actions rather targeted every activity of the State and its citizens, including security and welfare. Individuals were also terrorised simply because they were members of a wider society. All enemy actions were aimed at breaking down and destroying the existing order; the country had to be made ungovernable.[16]

After 1985 the revolutionary forces in South Africa intensively and visibly turned their attention to the cities, and in particular to the townships, with the eventual goal of making the country ungovernable. The ANC's own writings on the subject prove that I am not making this up. I am not debating whether or not the actions were justified; I simply wish to point out that a proper understanding of the realities of that time is essential for an understanding of certain defensive actions. Without this understanding, objectivity is impossible.

The risk scenario of the 1970s and 1980s can be properly interpreted

and judged only if one takes into account the following:
- The external threat of the Marxist communist imperialism led by the Soviet Union, its allies and surrogates in their pursuit of world domination. The interference and increasing aggression of the Soviet Union in potential conflict areas constantly confirmed that its goal was to gain a stranglehold on the free world's supplies of strategic resources and to extend Soviet dominance to strategic foci, at the expense of the West. Events in Poland, Central America, Afghanistan, Iran, Iraq and the Horn of Africa serve as evidence.
- The unremitting continuation and increase in the intensity and extent of actions by the Soviet Union and its surrogate forces in Southern Africa. More and more so-called military advisers from Russia, Cuba, North Korea and the East Bloc were present in Angola, Mozambique and Zimbabwe in this time. The Soviet Union wanted to destabilise Southern Africa by such means, with the eventual goal of conquering South Africa, which was almost the sole obstruction in the way of Soviet imperialist expansionism in Africa, and eventual world domination.
- The countrywide incidence of terrorism, which was aimed at making South Africa ungovernable, and the threat to the South-West African mandated territory posed by the revolutionary forces of SWAPO.
- The establishment of active communist governments in neighbouring countries; foreign pressure and attempts to isolate the Republic of South Africa completely.
- A large-scale propaganda and disinformation campaign to break down the image of the Government and Defence Force of the time, and in so doing to undermine their authority and to increase the public and national servicemen's resistance to these institutions.

To recapitulate: The Defence Force's actions always had to flow from the Government's political will and goals. The SA Defence Force had no standing authority for executing operations inside or outside the Republic of South Africa without receiving a mandate for this from the Government and Parliament. A former Chief of the Defence Force, Gen. Kat Liebenberg, once put it succinctly during a discussion at a staff course of senior officers at the SA Defence College in 1989: "The Defence Force is an instrument of the State or Government, and as such it is one of the most important power bases the Government has to achieve and promote its goals ... the Defence Force served the State, and therefore also the Government of the day. The Defence Force did not serve a political party, nor did it defend apartheid. On the contrary, the Defence Force was the first department to ignore so-called petty apartheid, to such a degree that it was often criticised for this by various politicians."

THE WINNING FORMULA

In view of the prevailing challenges of that era, it was essential for the Defence Force to be able to act in a disciplined, rapid and efficient manner, among other things, by ensuring that the top echelon was familiar with the parameters within which the Defence Force was permitted to operate. Some of the core guidelines were in writing, and others were passed on verbally. The most important were:

- The Government's national strategy had to be adhered to in terms of its prescribed security instructions.
- Proactive action was approved Government policy. The aim was to ensure that the Defence Force could take the initiative and maintain the advantage.
- The Defence Forces' approved, decentralised management had to be adhered to with corresponding identified objectives.
- The Government would not tolerate enemy elements being harboured in our neighbouring states, and acting against the Republic of South Africa from safe havens in those countries. The Government therefore warned those countries that they should not allow such situations to develop, or they would have to face the consequences.
- Cross-border military operations had to be carried out according to an approved written Government policy. South Africa had a policy of non-aggression, and territorial expansion at the cost of other states was not envisaged.
- In the course of cross-border operations against South Africa's

enemies in a foreign country, South African troops were to avoid engaging the forces of that country (or any allies), unless actions by those forces made it necessary to do otherwise.
- The Defence Force always had to treat civilians with dignity, and had to avoid civilian casualties.
- Weapons of mass destruction would be considered only in reaction to extreme situations, i.e. only in cases where the enemy used such weapons against us and conventional methods would not succeed against such attacks.

At a lower tactical level the Defence Force pursued the following:
- Proper physical, mental and moral preparation for the task at hand. It believed in the motto: "Train hard and fight easy".
- Combat-readiness that is not only aimed at daytime operations, but at night-time operations as well.
- Strictly avoiding casualties amongst its own forces. Military operations with fewer combat advantages but potentially lower casualties should be preferred to those with more combat advantages but higher risks and casualties.
- Regarding the handling of casualties during military operations as of the greatest importance. Casualties were often evacuated at very great risk, also by the SA Air Force.
- At all times the attitude needed to be that we are preparing to WIN, that we can win, and that we will win!

One will always be troubled by the question: how good a military machine was the SA Defence Force in actual fact? Up to and including World War II the effectiveness of armed forces was measured in terms of victories over the enemy, territory conquered and the eventual achievement of political control.

The era that followed the introduction of nuclear power rendered conventional wars too dangerous, because the use of nuclear weapons could lead to the extinction of mankind. Nowadays the most popular method of achieving political goals is to use unconventional military means. Military actions do not only take place on the battlefield but simultaneously in the socio-economic, political, sport and security arenas as well, with the political arena as the most important of these.

In the last few decades of the 20th century the Defence Force distinguished itself in fighting a counter-revolutionary war. The purely revolutionary onslaught against South Africa occasionally escalated in Angola into conventional operations. The Defence Force was equally successful in these operations. One only has to think of the Battle of the Lomba River east of Cuito Cuanavale!

Such efficient security actions enabled the Defence Force to contribute towards foiling attempts to make the country ungovernable. This created a suitable climate for negotiations that first took place with regard to South-West Africa/Namibia, and then, also with great success, with regard to South Africa.

Chapter 10

MANAGEMENT AND COMPOSITION OF THE SA DEFENCE FORCE

Up to and including 1957, South Africa's security was entrusted to the Union Defence Force (UDF). The South African Defence Force (SADF) then came into being, and was entrusted with this task. The present Government created the South African National Defence Force (SANDF) in 1994, and entrusted it with the important task of national security. The name of the previous Defence Force was therefore changed in 1994.

When judging the actions of the Defence Force during the period of conflict, one needs to bear in mind that the Defence Force was a service organisation of the State. The Defence Force therefore had to operate in support of the State, and in accordance with the constitution of the day, as the new SANDF has to do today. The instructions the Defence Force received and the orders it issued should therefore be understood against this background. These instructions were received from the legal government of the country, recognised as such internationally, and were bound by a written, approved constitution.[1]

The SA Defence Force was a well-disciplined, professional organisation, not above the law, and apolitical. It had to act in accordance with the laws of the country, and was not permitted to break these laws. Participation in politics was also prescribed by strict regulations, as is the case in most Western democracies.[2]

The Defence Force, like the Army, had a decentralised command structure. The Defence Force also commenced with the removal of dis-

A well-trained mortar section in the operational area of South-West Africa. These South Africans, who were involved in the protection and security of Southern Africa, experienced the ending of discrimination in the Defence Force even at this early stage. (From left to right, in civilian dress: Messrs Punch Barlow, P.W. Botha, then Minister of Defence, and Dr Wim de Villiers, accompanying me on a visit in the mid-1970s. (Photo: *South African Panorama*, Aug. 1989.)

crimination, as did the Army (see Chapter 6).[3]

In the case of the Defence Force the joint military training and actions of all population groups, joint participation in ceremonial military events, the occupation and use of messes by rank, joint participation in Defence Force sport, the joint training and appointment of officers and non-commissioned officers constituted the beginning of the normalisation process that had previously been lacking.[4]

In Chapter 6 I referred to community projects, where the Defence Force assisted developing communities. Defence Force manpower and other means were often utilised to assist local authorities and to offer aid to people in need.

THE ORGANISATIONAL STRUCTURE OF THE SA DEFENCE FORCE

On taking command of the Defence Force, I was aware that I would have to become familiar with a great many facets of the organisation. I would have to become far more comprehensive in my thinking and actions. The Defence Force was not only a large organisation; the tasks it had to perform were quite wide-ranging. The capabilities of the Defence Force were so diversified that its activities can, in their range, be compared to those of the State's civilian activities, albeit on a smaller scale. Furthermore the management styles, points of view and cultures within the four components of the Defence Force differed from one another, for good reasons. Each component also harboured a great sense of independence. In this regard ideas would be exchanged and, if necessary, adjustments would have to be made.

At this stage a large section of the public displayed an unconcerned attitude towards the Defence Force and the challenges facing South Africa. I would have to address this shortcoming in time as well. The support of the public for the Defence Force is absolutely necessary in any country, and in the South Africa of that time there was much room for improvement.

To bring myself up to date and familiarise myself with certain components of the Defence Force, I obtained a brief summary of its organisational composition. I am including a useful organisational overview and some important prescriptions below:

South Africa's defensive force, i.e. the South African Defence Force, was under the military command of the Chief of the SA Defence Force. He was also the accounting officer of the Department of Defence, and was thus financially accountable to Parliament. The Chief of the Defence Force was responsible to the Minister of Defence for executing the defence policy of the South African government. The Minister was therefore responsible for political control over the Defence Force, while the Chief of the Defence Force had to ensure the efficient functioning of the organisation.

In terms of the Constitution, the State President was Commander-in-Chief of the Defence Force, but the Defence Force executed all normal command functions.

As Chief of the Defence Force I was assisted by certain staff divisions. However, whereas the Headquarters of the Army and other Defence Force components consisted of five staff sections, namely Personnel Management, Intelligence, Operations, Logistics and Finance, there was an additional section at the level of Defence Force Headquarters, namely Planning.

The Military Intelligence Division was also a staff division. These staff divisions jointly formed the Chief of the Defence Force's Defence Headquarters. Headquarters have no operational units, and none of the divisions therefore have the capacity to perform any operational tasks. Yet there was a fairly general misconception with regard to the functions and activities of the Military Intelligence Division. In the past certain misinformed writers on military matters have made the mistake of crediting or blaming this Division for physical operational actions that it most certainly could not have executed because it lacked the capability for such actions. Examples of this type of inaccurate blame are those presented during the KwaMakuthu trial, and the investigations into the Webster and Lubowksi murders.[5] Even if the Defence Force could have undertaken unlawful actions such as murder at the time, these could, for various reasons, not be ascribed to Military Intelligence. A staff division simply does not have such capabilities.[6]

Apart from Defence Force Headquarters, the Defence Force additionally consisted of four defence force components, namely the SA Army, the SA Air Force (SAAF), the SA Navy (SAN) and the SA Medical Service (SAMS). In short, the SA Defence Force = SA Army + SAAF + SA Navy + SAMS (the four Defence Force components).

The four Defence components were independent of one another, and could act independently. Usually more than one Defence Force component and even as many as all four could jointly be involved in operational actions. When more than one Defence Force component was involved, the operation was usually conducted under the aegis of the SA Defence Force.

THE SA ARMY

The Chief of the Army commands the SA Army. The Army was organised into Army units that had to execute the physical operational tasks. One component was made up mostly of the so-called Citizen Force units, that were mainly required to serve as part of a conventional task force, and who were responsible for the physical defence of South Africa. Many of the Citizen Force units served in South-West Africa/Namibia and Angola during the war.

The other component comprised mostly the so-called Commando Force, which had to support the SA Police in South Africa when necessary. The Commando Force delivered an essential service on the home front, by, among other things, protecting home and hearth.

The main difference between the Citizen Force and the Commando

The SA Army's G6 155 mm self-propelled gun in action.

Force was that the Citizen Force's activities were largely aimed at conventional military actions that could take place anywhere in or outside South Africa, while the Commandos were largely earmarked for counter-revolutionary actions within their own commando areas.

It is an internationally accepted practice to deploy the defence force in conjunction with the police in order to control unrest. When referring to joint operations by the Defence Force and the SA Police, even when they were operating independently and under their own commands, the term Security Forces (SFs) is applied.

THE SA AIR FORCE (SAAF)

The Chief of the Air Force commands the SA Air Force. The main functions of the SA Air Force were to ensure a favourable air situation; air cover and air support during battle; to undertake coastal patrols and protection in conjunction with the SA Navy; and to provide air support

The SA Air Force's Mirage III in action.

when required by the SA Police. The Air Force also supplied air support in the case of disasters and emergencies, and executed search and rescue operations.

The SA Air Force, which consisted mainly of Permanent Force members, always performed very professionally, and one could rely on them through thick and thin. South Africa had an Air Force that could compare with the best in the world, with extraordinary flying and fighting abilities. The Air Force's Citizen Force component contributed significantly to this outstanding service.[7]

THE SA NAVY

The task of the SA Navy was to protect South Africa from enemy threats and attacks, to support land operations where possible, and to help protect the country's maritime capabilities.

The Navy provided outstanding service during my years as Chief of

SA Navy's strike craft on manoeuvres.

the Defence Force. They volunteered a larger involvement in the conflict, and accordingly I gave them responsibility for the Eastern Caprivi operational area in South-West Africa/Namibia. They thus helped the Army to complete its task on land successfully. The Navy had a Citizen Force component that delivered excellent service, at great sacrifice.[8]

The Navy was commanded by the Chief of the Navy.

THE SA MEDICAL SERVICE (SAMS)

The purpose of the SA Medical Service was to provide medical support to the Defence Force and allied organisations. The SA Medical Service was commanded by the Surgeon General.[9]

This support was of supreme importance to the other three Defence Force components and the local population, especially in South-West Africa and Angola. The medical services were of the highest possible professional standard, and were often provided in very difficult or life-threatening circumstances. Without the support of the SA Medical Service, the

The SAMS practising the evacuation of casualties.

SA Defence Force would not have been able to carry out its tasks nearly as efficiently as it did. The SAMS Citizen Force also contributed a lion's share of delivery in this medical service of superb quality.

SPECIFIC MANAGEMENT MATTERS

For more efficient management of the Defence Force, I created a Command Council. The Defence Force's Command Council, consisting of the Chiefs of the four Defence Force components, the Army, the Air Force, the Navy and the Medical Service, drew up rules of engagement during the various revolutionary onslaughts, and made the necessary adjustments to management, human resources development and security matters.

Continuous vigilance against deliberate attacks on the populace, and in particular on the Security Forces, was especially necessary. These attacks were mainly aimed at promoting the denigration of, negativity towards and resistance against the prevailing order of the time. There was constant negative criticism of and rumours about the Security Forces, aimed at breaking down morale. The terrorist attacks on civilian targets in the 1980s, for example the attack on the Silverton branch of Volkskas on 15 January 1980, the car bomb explosion on Durban's Marine Parade on 14 June 1986, and limpet mine explosions at various shops, represented but a minor aspect of the onslaught.[10]

It took a huge effort on my part to establish in the Defence Force as a whole, the new state of mind and management requirements that had already been introduced in the SA Army. The Chiefs of the Army, Air Force, Navy and Medical Service, namely Gen. Constand Viljoen, Gen. Bob Rodgers, Adm. Flam Johnson and Gen. Cockie Cockroft respectively, the six Chiefs of Staff of Defence Force Headquarters staff divisions, the Chaplain General, Gen. Koos van Zyl, the Quartermaster General, Adm. Burt Bekker, and Adm. Ronnie Edwards and Gen. Neil Webster as observers, were involved in these intense sessions, which fell outside our official duties, and were therefore conducted over weekends. The culture change was also effected by means of team-building activities and an organisation development process, which at the time was regarded as sensitivity techniques by some. I launched team-building activities as soon as I had found my feet after my appointment as Chief of the Defence Force.

The effort was a huge success. Among other things we discussed the following aspects: unity and efficient functioning within the organisation, as well as military management practices; service to the country and all its people, and improved interpersonal relations within and outside of the organisation, including the management of conflict situations.

The decisions about efficient management methods or requirements that emanated from the team-building efforts made it clear that the location of SA Navy Headquarters at Simon's Town was one of the Defence Force's management weaknesses. In intense consultation with the Navy, I decided to relocate Navy Headquarters to Pretoria. This brought about that joint Defence Force planning, co-ordination and actions could take place more efficiently. Thus the Defence Force could do its future short-term, medium-term and long-term planning more efficiently and successfully. Such planning was important because it would continuously and jointly determine future manpower, armaments and financial requirements. This added capacity improved co-operation with the Government and Government departments. In this way the Navy also became an integral part of the Defence Force's planning and internal workings, and were able to contribute significantly to the efficiency of the greater organisation.

The team-building activities revealed the need for a national strategy. Once this need was identified, I first had to convince the Minister of Defence that such a deficiency existed. He initially gave permission for the Defence Force to draw up a national strategy for its own use and for ministerial purposes.[11] When he became Prime Minister in 1978 Mr Botha attended to this need and it resulted in the National Strategy of 1980, referred to in Chapter 9.

Other uncertainties that emerged from team-building activities involving the Government and the Defence Force also needed to be cleared up.

RE-EXAMINATION OF GOVERNMENT POLICY

By 1976, when I took over as Chief of the SA Defence Force, the Government prescribed to the Defence Force that its security actions had to guarantee the Government enough time to bring to fruition its party-political policies. In brief this meant that the Government wanted enough time for the full deployment of the policy known at the time as separate development.[12]

I pointed out to the Minister of Defence, Mr P.W. Botha, that this prescription was unacceptable, because it placed the Defence Force squarely in the political arena. Fortunately he realised this and agreed to amend the instruction to read: "The SA Defence Force must ensure that the Constitution of South Africa is maintained." The present Government requires the same of the South African National Defence Force.[13]

This Government resolution was very important, because in brief it meant that it was not the task of the SA Defence Force to protect or defend apartheid, but only to maintain the country's approved Constitution. It also clearly exposes the absurdity of the allegation that in those days the Defence Force was merely the handmaiden of the ruling party in carrying out its policy.[14]

The concept of the new Government instruction sprang from this amended instruction – one that I often repeated in public, and that the Defence Force established at military training units. Briefly it meant that the Defence Force would countenance no revolutionary political changes, because these militated against the spirit of the Constitution. On the other hand, evolutionary changes, for example those effected through the ballot box, were constitutionally acceptable changes that had to be supported by the Defence Force. The Defence Force therefore ensured a climate for negotiation that could bring about evolutionary political changes, and submitted to the results of the 1994 general election that followed.[15]

The escalation of hostilities and the involvement of the Soviet Union, which employed African and Cuban proxy forces, necessitated the amendment of another Government instruction, namely that the South African Defence Force had to maintain a defensive profile. In view of the extent of the revolutionary assault, it was unwise to limit South Africa's approach to defensive or counter-actions only.[16] In order to retain the initiative, prevention had to be the watchword. One could not wait until the enemy launched an attack on South Africa on its own soil; proactive offensives or pre-emptive security actions were required. (In this context offensive should not be understood in the sense that has become current, i.e. as synonymous with aggression, but rather as action aimed at gaining the initiative.) The Government acceded to my request to change the profile from defensive to proactive, as it was in the national interest to approve proactive actions to maintain national security.[17] This change to a proactive posture was one of the main reasons why no war ruins are to be found in South Africa, why the current ideology in South Africa is not totalitarian, and why the ANC Alliance could never succeed in making South Africa ungovernable.[18]

Another limitation, which often handicapped military operations, in my opinion, was the Government's established procedures for approving such operations. At that stage a very cumbersome process had to be followed to get approval to cross the border. The section or platoon leader, or the company commander on the border between South-West Africa and Angola, first had to go through his chain of command to the area commander, a general, and then via Army Headquarters and Defence Force Headquarters to the Minister of Defence for approval. The decision to grant or not grant approval then had to follow the same route back. This was a time-consuming process, particularly if one or more of the links in the chain happened not be immediately available. In theory the enemy could fire a few rounds at the local population from across the border, and then the indicated route would have to be followed before the people in the area could be protected against the attack. Such situations could develop very quickly, and success depended on an equally quick response. Apart from the elaborate approval procedure, the level of responsibility for a rapid cross-border operation also had to be established. For example, a lieutenant and his platoon could attack SWAPO terrorists across the border between South-West Africa and Angola, and cause an international embarrassment. Who would have to accept responsibility for this? Such an embarrassment could very easily result in more international sanctions, and in particular economic sanctions.

In August 1977 the Prime Minister at the time, John Vorster, visited troops in South-West Africa's operational area in order to gain first-hand experience of the situation there. A typical scenario was discussed with him in detail, and he was able to personally acquaint himself with the circumstances, problems and challenges that prevailed on the border.

When the then Ministers of Defence, Foreign Affairs and I, as Chief of the Defence Force, subsequently visited the Prime Minister during his holiday at Oubosstrand, he had had enough personal experience for a proper consideration of the matter.

It was agreed that if any serious threats to South Africa were to develop across the border in Angola, and a lack of time made it impossible to get prior ministerial or cabinet approval for an urgent military action, the enemy could be engaged with military approval only. In such a case the military authority would accept responsibility for the military actions, and the Government would accept responsibility for any international consequences. One should add, however, that certain conditions would apply, among other things that the State authority had to be informed of such a military action as soon as possible after the event.

After a thorough consideration of the question of responsibility for cross-border operations in general, it was decided that if the Defence Force had carried out the action, it would be responsible for its military success or failure. On the other hand, the South African Government still accepted the political and international responsibility. Determining these responsibilities in my opinion created a workable situation, which would contribute to the Defence Force being able to perform its task even more efficiently.

The responsibilities for cross-border operations were spelled out in more detail at a later stage. The Government extended and defined the area inside Angola where quick military actions could be undertaken without its permission. It was decided that the Chief of the Defence Force could grant permission for rapid military action up to a distance of 150 km across the Angolan border without Government authorisation. He could also grant permission to the Chiefs of the Army and Air Force for decisions to cross the Angolan border to a depth of 100 km for the purpose of rapid military operations if the military situation required this. The normal proviso that the Government had to be informed of the operation as soon as possible, still held. This formulation of the authorisation process for cross-border operations ensured efficient action. At the same time it confirmed the principle of decentralised management, which was essential during revolutionary warfare, and also determined the responsibility for action in and outside South-West Africa/Namibia. It also ensured trust between the Government and the Defence Force.

With regard to considered military actions within Angola, the authority for approval was still vested solely with the Government. Considered actions meant actions involving large forces that take time to plan, assemble, prepare and move.

Later, in my capacity as Minister of Defence, I compiled a written policy document concerning cross-border operations for consideration by the Government. This document was approved by a resolution of the Cabinet under the chairmanship of the Prime Minister, P.W. Botha. Various policy prescriptions applicable to possible cross-border operations from South Africa and South-West Africa, and aimed at various neighbouring countries, were formulated and updated regularly. The following was taken into account in formulating each policy prescription for action against each neighbouring state: its political and military attitude; probable actions; the attitude of the neighbouring country concerned towards South Africa; aid to, protection and support of enemy elements; and covert or overt approval of the use of its territory by enemy elements.

The policy prescription set out the procedures, responsibility parameters and approving authority for cross-border operations individually. This Cabinet resolution was reconsidered on a continual basis, taking into account changing circumstances, and was then confirmed or amended.[19]

RELATIONS WITH THE LOCAL POPULATION IN OPERATIONAL AREAS

During my term as Chief of the Army I issued an instruction that the Army was to treat all civilians with dignity. Furthermore the presence of civilians had to be taken into account in combat, and injured civilians had to be cared for. This instruction was made applicable to the entire Defence Force when I was appointed Chief of the Defence Force.

If it was necessary to operate against terrorist forces who had insinuated themselves into a civilian population, the Defence Force, consequently, would go out of its way to prevent or limit civilian loss of life. This was made possible by accurate intelligence and by taking into account the presence of civilians during operational planning. The thrust of an attack was thus planned in such a way as to present a minimum risk for the civilian population.

The Cuban and Angolan forces followed the usual revolutionary practice and often established their headquarters within civilian communities. This increased the risk for the civilian population, and reduced the risk for their own forces. In some cases where this scenario was encountered, for example during Operation Protea, the Defence Force even scattered pamphlets over the target area from aircraft, using pictures and text to request the local population to evacuate the area and remove themselves to a good distance.

It was also policy that the Defence Force should provide the population with direct medical support if civilian casualties occurred, no matter which side caused these casualties.

THE REMOVAL OF RACIAL AND GENDER DISCRIMINATION

Thinking back on the circumstances prevailing at the Physical Training Brigade and what happened there, I always remembered the way individual human dignity was violated. It is a pity that it happened. Instead of young people enjoying an uplifting experience, it was, in some cases, probably experienced as something negative that left a permanent scar.

This is why I heartily subscribe to the author C.J. Langenhoven's saying: "Treat your superior courteously, because it is your duty, your equal because it is your pleasure, and your inferior because it is your privilege." The Defence Force pursued this as its policy.

The SA Cape Corps was established as a component of the Permanent Force (PF) in 1968. With the agreement of the Coloured Representative Council, coloureds could voluntarily undergo military training from 1973 onwards. An infantry company of the SA Cape Corps first served in the operational area during military operations in South-West Africa in 1976, and did so outstandingly. A similar service battalion for Indians was established in 1975, when the SA Indian Corps was established in the PF. Many more applications for this voluntary service in the Navy were received than there were vacancies available. Those who completed the training offered by the Navy rendered outstanding service. Since 1975, black male citizens could put on an Army uniform with the establishment of a combat unit, 21 Batallion, at Lenz.[20]

A women's college for training white women in defence techniques was established in 1971. By 1977 there were already 971 women serving in the PF under conditions of service similar to that of their male counterparts. They were not, however, permitted to participate in combat situations.[21]

So many people wanted to volunteer for the Cape Corps, the Indian Corps, the Support Services Corps, 21 Batallion, and the Women's College that even after a thorough sifting process they could not be accommodated. They literally queued, and many, regrettably, had to be turned away because there were not sufficient finances, training or utilisation facilities.

Against this background I was able in 1981 to insist as Minister of Defence in Parliament that all population groups should be treated with dignity and should be involved in the defence of South Africa. However, the Cabinet and Parliament had to amend all discriminatory sections in existing legislation before the Defence Force could openly apply this policy in public. The Defence Force could nevertheless apply internal prescriptions to end discrimination in areas under military control, and in fact started to implement this gradually from the 1970s onwards.[22]

The Citizen Force and Commandos already had my permission as Chief of the Defence Force to train black soldiers in 1976, and were encouraged to do so.[23] Terrorist operations at the same time were not aimed only at whites, but most often at the other population groups. Instructions made it clear that all Defence Force members, irrespective of gender or colour, were to be treated with dignity. It was thought that a professional defence force could only achieve its goals if it treated its people on merit alone. Some malicious persons condemned this Defence Force policy as integration of the population groups.[24]

Some units recruited many black volunteers, and others fewer. These members were issued with equipment and were fully-fledged Defence Force members. As usual, each case was judged on its merits.

Concerning the removal of discrimination and the way other population groups (and women) were treated, the Defence Force was far ahead of certain sections of the private sector, and most other government departments. The removal of discrimination occurred in all areas of Defence Force responsibility, and areas over which it had control, for example Defence Force housing, status determination, the creation of equal opportunities and conditions of service. Merit, not skin colour, slowly became the determining factor in the mid-1970s and throughout the 1980s. With these positive steps the Defence Force established the principle of human dignity within its area of responsibility. For example, more than 20% of the South African forces that served voluntarily in the South-West African/Namibian operational area in 1977 were black people who acquitted themselves admirably of their task.[25]

As Chief of the Defence Force I publicly stated the following view at the beginning of 1978: "... if black and white are trained together and fight together ... then there can be no question of differentiating between them – equal or nothing!"[26]

ADULT EDUCATION

Initially the purpose of adult education was to offer all members of the Defence Force the opportunity to develop to their full potential, according to their desires and needs. When other population groups entered the Defence Force, it was clear that there was a great need for better educational qualifications amongst adult Defence Force members. A programme for adult education up to Matric (Grade 12) existed from 1980, and the spouses of Defence Force members were also included in the programme.[27]

CHAPLAIN SERVICE

When people are exposed to great danger in times of conflict, they experience their vulnerability and dependence on the Creator in a very unique way. This is when they feel the greatest need for spiritual guidance.[28]

A church parade of the type that had a chaplain in the field saying that they would never forget the sense of God's presence and power at services held when battle was imminent, or over. (Photo: Spies, F.J. du T. 1989. *Operasie Savannah: Angola 1975-1976.*)

Since the earliest settlement at the Cape, chaplains had accompanied the soldiers (on the battlefield too), and this led to the designation of chaplains to the forces.

Freedom of religion reigned in the SA Defence Force. Each member of the Defence Force had the right to belong to the church of his or her choice, and, while always taking urgent service requirements into account, was given the opportunity to practice his or her religion.

Thousands of chaplains served in the permanent force, the Citizen Force and the Commandos during the operations in Angola and South-West Africa from 1974 onward, and later during the unrest situation in South Africa. Each was responsible for the spiritual welfare of the members of his denomination.

The chaplains played an important role, especially during operations. They were an essential element of support in military hospitals. They also had to give support whenever there was loss of life and soldiers were unsettled by emotional trauma. Those who were wounded during military operations and suffered a disability thereafter also needed their support.

Because most of our troops were young and inexperienced national servicemen, the chaplains had to spend a good deal of time handling tension and fear before operations and again following their involvement in operations.

LIAISON WITH OPINION-MAKERS

In order to create communication and interaction between the Defence Force and political, business, media and youth groups, foreign visitors, parents and other interest groups, the Defence Force regularly issued invitations for structured area and base visits, where such groups were given Defence Force briefings in a Defence Force environment.

These regular visits, particularly those to the operational area, gave the visitors an opportunity to become better acquainted with the Defence Force and Armscor through their own observations, and by means of the briefings. They were encouraged to ask probing questions or to offer criticism. This also gave the Defence Force an opportunity to come to grips with the public's perceptions of it. Senior Defence Force officers and Armscor officials gave the visitors and observers important background information during these visits.

State presidents, representatives of all Houses of Parliament and all political parties in and outside of Parliament, important foreign visitors,

Politicians, journalists, businessmen, Armscor officials and defence force officers visited the

South African businessmen, church leaders, university heads, editors and members of the media, representatives of various professions and academics, members of women's organisations, trade union leaders, agricultural, welfare, cultural, youth and community leaders were amongst the visitors to the operational area. The opinion-makers represented all population groups, both genders and all beliefs. This exposure was initially on a small scale, but later there were more visitors, and they were managed much better. As early as 1975 I took identified key persons

operational area in South-West Africa/Namibia to gain first-hand operational knowledge.

on tours of this nature to help me develop agricultural projects in the South-West African operational area.

Thousands of visitors used these opportunities to gain first-hand knowledge of the assault on South Africa, and to inform themselves about Defence Force operations.

OTHER ACTIVITIES

A variety of other, minor tasks were purposively managed within the Defence Force and played an extremely important role in rounding off the organisation and helping to increase its standards of efficiency and interactions between members. Some of these activities were aimed at improving the morale of the Defence Force members. Others helped to support a sense of caring and well-being. Good management ensured the proper standard for these essential minor activities. I will refer to only a few.

Mail

The regular and prompt receipt of mail and food parcels from family and friends was very important to all Defence Force members, especially on operational service. It was easy to use the postal service in South Africa itself, but what was to be done in an operational area as vast as South-West Africa/Namibia? From east to west this area stretched as far as from Cape Town to Pretoria, and in depth it varied from 50 to 250 km along the Angolan border. Units were widely scattered within this enormous area, and were constantly moved from one temporary base to the next. And of course we have not even mentioned the operational area in Angola, where there were no postal services whatsoever.

The Defence Force's existing Citizen Force unit that was earmarked, trained and responsible for this task was called up for service. It made short work of the challenge, and created an efficient postal system. There was even an instruction to reserve space on Defence Force aircraft especially for mail to and from the operational area. Mail and parcels were delivered to an individual's unit within a very short space of time after having been posted, and mail from the operational area was transported to South Africa in the same way. It must however be acknowledged that at times mail had to give priority to operational necessities such as ammunition.

Evacuation of the wounded and fallen

The highest priority was given to the recovery and/or evacuation of the wounded and fallen to designated Defence Force facilities by air or road, with South Africa as the final destination. It is of cardinal importance to ensure that the wounded reach suitable medical care as soon as possible. The SA Medical Service was very successful in executing this task. Two newly equipped military hospitals were established in Pretoria and Cape Town to provide this essential medical care.

Public relations

During any conflict, but particularly during a revolutionary war where the attitude of the population towards the authorities is crucial, it is important to ensure that government bodies have a good image, worthy of emulation. A sound, energetic, helpful government administration is essential. In order to create sound relations, the government administration should function so efficiently that it is a pleasure for the man in the street to do business with it. The authorities have to make a concerted effort to build and maintain all instruments of government and authority, because the public's active support and positive attitude towards the authorities was of vital importance in such an exhausting and merciless war.

On the other hand the enemy is intent on continuously breaking down, belittling and ridiculing the esteem of the authorities by means of propaganda. Should the enemy succeed in these efforts, it would largely have won the battle. Psychological warfare is just as important to warfare nowadays as the operational areas are.

It is therefore vitally important that the authorities should be fully aware of all the aspects that can have a direct influence on the success of a revolutionary struggle. The focus should not be on violence only.

From the late 1980s to the early 1990s the propaganda war and creation of perceptions aimed at belittling and breaking down authority increased sharply. These efforts were particularly aimed at the security forces, with the goal of driving a wedge between the Government and the Security Forces in order to cast suspicion on Security Force operations, and make them less efficient. These efforts were very successful in the 1990s.

An example of the creation of perceptions was the many allegations and accusations of human rights violations supposedly perpetrated by the Defence Force in the early 1990s. These accusations against the Defence Force never let up, and their constant repetition caused the Government of the time and the general public to lose confidence in the Defence Force. The public, in particular, found it very difficult to distinguish between the truth and fabrication.[29]

Particularly during a revolutionary war, it is most important for the State to protect its departments from denigration and accusations, even if this would mean that a judicial enquiry is instituted to examine every accusation, and that the results and any consequent actions should be made public immediately. The State must have full confidence in its institutions until proven wrong. If not, the State may lose efficiency and lose the revolutionary war.

I take my hat off to and salute all the members of the SA Defence Force, men and women, who continued to carry out their tasks efficiently and dutifully, despite a crisis of trust. They are the co-creators of a peaceful "New South Africa".

I want to dedicate this extract from Ralph Waldo Emerson's poem "A nation's strength" to these men and women:

Not gold, but only men can make
A nation great and strong
Men who for truth and honor's sake
Stand fast and suffer long.
Brave men who work while others sleep
Who dare while other shy
They build a nation's pillars deep
And lift them to the sky.

Chapter 11

OPERATIONAL AND RELATED MATTERS

TOTAL WAR: THE TOTAL ONSLAUGHT OR TOTAL RESPONSE

As Chief of the Defence Force I had an interview on the above subject with a Sunday newspaper in March 1977. For various reasons the international concept of total war or total onslaught became controversial in South Africa some months later. In the course of time more and more speculation on the concept appeared in the media, and more and more people became involved. The Defence Force and I therefore became entangled in this net as well.[1]

One should bear in mind that physical conflicts or war have been a feature of the world for a very long time. Much has been said about war, and in the future as many thoughts on conflict (war and strife) will probably be offered. For example, the following quotation shows that the realisation that the art of war does not consist solely of action on the battlefield, has been around for a very long time. In other fields there are actions that are just as important, if not more important, that can ensure your victory over your enemies: "All wars are primarily based on misleading an enemy. Actions on the battlefield are the most primitive way of waging war. There is no higher art than destroying your enemy without a battle – by reversing everything of value in the enemy's country." (Sun Tzu, Chinese strategist, 500 B.C.)

Since World War II, the evolution of physical conflict or war has produced other, more popular forms of waging war, rather than the usual declaration of war followed by conventional warfare. The most common of these is revolutionary war. This meant that during conflict, certain responsibilities would remain vested in the political leaders because they could no longer be devolved onto military commanders, as was previously the case.

Up to the 1950s South Africa's security was managed and run according to the framework of an internationally established pattern, namely that the political order moved in stages from peace towards a declaration of hostilities and a state of war. This transition to a state of war was effected by means of certain tasks as prescribed in a government war book. The government's war book was compiled and regularly updated to ensure that in the run-up to a declaration of war, government and semi-government institutions executed important predetermined actions, tasks and instructions individually and/or in a co-ordinated manner.

One of the most important responsibilities that was no longer delegated to the military leaders, due to recent developments in the nature of conflict, was the right to decide where action may be taken against the enemy in a geographical sense. A very good example of this type of clash, and the dissatisfaction that resulted from the refusal to delegate decisions regarding geographical actions to the military authority, is found in the dismissal of Gen. Douglas MacArthur by Pres. Harry S. Truman of the USA. During the Korean War (1950-1953) MacArthur had chafed at his political leader's refusal to delegate the usual decision to him regarding the geographical extent of military action in Korea. He was restricted by his political leader, and was forbidden from any military operations and movement north of a certain area without the permission of his President.

In contrast, Gen. Eisenhower, the Supreme Commander of Allied Forces at the time of the invasion of Europe during World War II, was given the instruction to conquer Europe! The political leaders of the time did not attach any limitations to this instruction. Gen. MacArthur was probably still used to that management style.

Later, during the Vietnam War (1961-1973), this refusal to delegate political responsibility to the military authority was accepted as a fact.

Due to the evolution of conflict, political leaders therefore no longer delegated all their responsibilities to the military leaders as they had done before, but retained some of the major high-risk responsibilities. During our own period of revolutionary conflict, the South African government, too, retained a great deal of responsibility.

In this same period the communist order took the evolution of conflict much further. The intended victim of communist aggression was deprived of the luxury of preparing for the conflict, right from the stage of mobilisation up to the declaration of a formal state of war. The USSR was a past master at this procedure: its actions were aimed at every activity of the community in the target country, with the intention of destroying the building blocks of national power. Military power, in particular, had to be neutralised, for example, by elusive terrorist bands that hit widely dispersed key points in an attempt to damage the economy. The final goal was to make the country ungovernable, and to rob the population of its will to resist.

In order to launch an effective counter against a total onslaught, the target country has to initiate, at the highest level, measures that are managed in accordance with that country's total national strategy. In time this has developed into an internationally accepted, broadened way of management, planning and action to halt the "total onslaught".[2]

In both cases it briefly means that all the resources or capacities of the country or parties concerned need to be utilised in a co-ordinated manner in order to win the struggle. This means that action cannot and should not take place only in the field of security, but that the country must utilise its entire capacity strategically and in a co-ordinated and orchestrated manner, with varying intensity. Capacities such as politics, diplomacy, the economy and propaganda must form part of the strategy, and all of these factors play a major role.[3]

The need for an organisation with the capacity to resist the total onslaught in a co-ordinated and efficient manner led to the creation of the National Management System (NMS), which consisted of the National Security Management System (NSMS) and the National Prosperity Management System (NPMS).[4]

It seems that the leader of the Progressive Party at the time, Dr F. van Zyl Slabbert, understood the development of the concept "total onslaught", and certainly supported it. Peter Stiff quotes Slabbert as follows: "Therefore, the very institutions – political, economic and social – which could serve as instruments of peaceful change had to be defended against attack and violence from the outside."[5]

Institutional counter-revolutionary action must still take place within certain parameters, and there are limits to the utilisation of the state's capabilities. Government institutions can therefore not be permitted to act illegally and do as they wish. Any action must take place within the laws of the land, and within clearly defined and universally accepted norms as determined by conventions, international protocol or usage. In South Africa any actions by government departments had to take place within the terms of the Constitution, and had to be legally justified and therefore capable of being tested in court.

In *The last trek – a new beginning* (1998), F.W. de Klerk says: "It has become fashionable to mock P.W. Botha's opinion that there was a total onslaught against South Africa. But in the mid-1980s, the information we received in the State Security Council every two weeks, time and again indicated a very serious situation facing us. We were not only faced with a joint campaign to make South Africa ungovernable, as a preliminary to revolution, we also had to deal with a particular threat from outside the country. Seldom was such an extended, unrelenting international campaign waged over such a long period of time against a single country as the one that the anti-apartheid alliance launched against us.

"The sanctions net surrounding South Africa began to tighten in virtually every sphere of its international relations. The USSR and its Cuban allies adopted a threatening stance in some of our neighbouring countries. We were involved in a low-intensity war in northern Namibia and southern Angola that placed the South African Defence Force in direct conflict with forces under Cuban and Russian command. Guerrilla and terrorist groups, based in neighbouring countries, began launching attacks against South Africa. If all these things, taken together, did not constitute a total onslaught, I can hardly imagine a situation which does deserve this label."[6]

Furthermore, F.W. de Klerk says: "The total strategy required the greatest emphasis rather be placed on the efficient provision of government and social services and the promotion of all-encompassing constitutional solutions ... It was a question of winning the people's hearts and minds. Everything was aimed at gaining and retaining the population's support in this way."[7]

The concepts "total strategy", "total onslaught" or "total war" are recognised at advanced defence force training institutions the world over, and are also applied in practice in the Western world. A recent example is a reference by President George W. Bush of the USA to the "total onslaught" in his radio address of 11 September 2001, in the context of his country's battle against international terrorism. Special reference was made to the aircraft attack on the World Trade Center and the Pentagon by Osama bin Laden and his Al-Qaeda terrorist organisation. The daily *Beeld* of 25 September 2001 referred to this as follows: "Dit was die eerste sarsie skote waarin finansiële, militêre, tegnologiese en diplomatieke metodes gebruik gaan word in die Bush-administrasie se 'onkonvensionele oorlog' teen internasionale terrorisme."[8]

BACK TO THE OPERATIONAL FRONT

After the Defence Force's voluntary withdrawal from Angola, on conclusion of Operation Savannah on 27 March 1976, it was relatively quiet in South-West Africa's northern area. However, the Defence Force did have to carry out limited cross-border operations in southern Angola from time to time to restrain SWAPO.

At the end of 1976 and the beginning of 1977, SWAPO insurgents began liquidating local political leaders in the area. In February and March 1977 Toivo Shiyagaya, Minister of Health in the Ovambo government, as well as Clemens Kapuuo, the wise leader of the Herero tribe, were murdered. Various tribal members were also killed.

At the end of 1977 SWAPO began infiltrating South-West Africa in larger groups. The groups had previously consisted of only a few members, but now they numbered between 80 and 100. This almost conventional assault using larger numbers required a different approach by the Security Forces.[9]

Notwithstanding the SWAPO build-up, the period from the withdrawal from Angola in March 1976 to the beginning of 1978 was an important one for the Defence Force. It had taken due note of the lessons learned from aiding the FNLA and UNITA during Operation Savannah. Preventative and corrective measures could be effected in case the military conflict was to flare up again.

In April 1978 the Security Forces made contact with at least 100 SWAPO insurgents moving together as a group. Fortunately this group did not do much damage. However, the event did confirm intelligence warnings that SWAPO was extending its semi-conventional capacity, and was operating in larger groups. The Defence Force was compelled to react to this, and the result was a series of military operations that did not entirely meet with my expectations.[10]

In the meantime the Soviet Union continued landing more and more conventional weaponry near the borders of South Africa and South-West Africa. This included: aircraft, attack helicopters, anti-aircraft systems, tanks and armoured vehicles. This created an umbrella of safety for the revolutionaries, which gave the ANC Alliance and SWAPO a greater freedom of movement in the neighbouring countries. Later even more sophisticated arms would be supplied.

In the period after 1978 the threat posed by the Soviet Union and international Marxism to South Africa increased – not only from the north west (Angola and South-West Africa), but now also from the north east (Mozambique) and the north (Zimbabwe). The Soviet Union and its allies would now provide help to revolutionary organisations from these countries, with the eventual aim of helping the communists to conquer South Africa as well.

From public pronouncements and the daily propaganda broadcasts aimed at South Africa at the time, it was clear that the leaders of the Soviet Union and their henchmen pulled no punches in their references to South Africa. South Africa was the ultimate goal in Africa.[11] The other areas were interim objectives only. The efficiency of the Security Forces, however, was demonstrated by the fact that for the entire duration of the struggle SWAPO was never able to establish any base within the vast and sparsely populated South-West Africa/Namibia.

Western proposals for a settlement in South-West Africa, the Draft Settlement Plan that would eventually become known as the United Nations' Security Council Resolution 435, was accepted by the South African government under Premier John Vorster on 25 April 1978. (This resolution would result in the independence of Namibia on 31 March 1990, 12 years later.)

Shortly after the acceptance of the settlement plan for South-West Africa/Namibia, I approached the Minister of Defence, P.W. Botha, in my capacity as Chief of the Defence Force, for permission to launch a daring air and paratroop attack on Cassinga. The Cabinet approved my request, and gave permission for the attack. Internationally, this type of military operation – especially in view of the prevailing circumstances, such as the long distance between the South-West African border and Cassinga – is regarded as a very high-risk operation. This is particularly so because paratroopers descending from aircraft are very vulnerable to ground fire, and also because there is a strong possibility that it could be difficult to find an escape mode or route should the troops be pinned down at some distance from their supporting ground forces.

Operation Reindeer was launched on 4 May 1978. It basically involved an attack on two targets. The first was Cassinga, or Moscow, as it was known in SWAPO ranks. This base was situated about 250 km north of the border inside Angola. Cassinga was SWAPO's main operational headquarters, with training and logistical support facilities. SWAPO had deployed anti-aircraft guns at this well-entrenched target. The fire power available to the enemy increased the vulnerability of the paratroopers. In view of the potential enemy fire, it was of the utmost importance that the element of surprise had to be maintained.

At that stage some Defence Force intelligence sources in the operational area had begun to report that the take-off of conspicuous numbers of SA Air Force attack aircraft from South Africa or South-West Africa – especially at night or in the early hours of the morning – caused a marked uneasiness within only an hour or so amongst enemy elements in the Angolan operational area. In other words, there was a distinct possibility that enemy observers near or in the vicinity of the SA Air Force's airfields were able to report these movements of aircraft, probably by telephone. These reports were most probably forwarded directly to a central point (i.e. a SWAPO or an Angolan, Cuban or Soviet headquarters in Angola) via an overseas country. A radio warning could then immediately be given to all potential targets, and this gave SWAPO time to react.

The Defence Force knew about this, and took steps to thwart such actions, among other things by scrambling enemy radio communications in northern South-West Africa and southern Angola, and making sure that the Air Force operated from different airfields.

At the same time the other target, namely Vietnam – the name given to it by SWAPO – would be attacked by a mechanised force of the Defence Force. Vietnam was an extensive complex, which included a network of transit facilities. SWAPO members on their way to the "front" in South-West Africa, or returning to the "home front" in Angola, were received at such a transit facility. They were cared for and equipped here, and could recuperate and enjoy life before they moved on. This target was spread over a large area of Chetequera, and was situated about 30 km north of the international border.

The air and paratrooper attack on Cassinga would have to be carried out in the early hours of the morning with accurate timing and good co-ordination in order to ensure surprise and therefore a greater possibility of success.

SWAPO spokespersons later tried to deny that Cassinga was an armed position, and described it as a camp for South African expatriates, with only 300 men as the defensive unit. However, aerial photographs tell a different story. The base also included a network of trenches on the Soviet pattern.

The Defence Force's task was made more difficult by the deployment of tanks and armoured personnel carriers in the area, at Techamutete. This force was situated about 16 km south of Cassinga, and consisted of five Russian T-34 tanks and about twenty armoured personnel carriers.

In order to neutralise and soften up Cassinga as a target for the airborne attack, the Defence Force first carried out an air attack with the Air Force's Mirage and Buccaneer aircraft. The air attack would immediately be followed by C-130 cargo aircraft with 250 paratroopers. As soon as these soldiers touched ground, it was their task to neutralise the target's anti-aircraft capability as quickly as possible in order to pave the way for the further clearing of the area.

The paratroopers were given instructions to destroy all enemy ammunition, equipment and weapons, and to confiscate documents and intelligence material – in particular any pointing to a link with the Soviet Union. On conclusion of the operation the paratroopers would be picked up by helicopters and transported back to South-West Africa.[12]

The operation was extremely successful, and the element of surprise paid off. We lost one man as the result of a parachute mishap.[13]

During the operation Gen. Constand Viljoen, then Chief of the Army, was taken to Cassinga by helicopter. Just before his helicopter – the last to leave – took off for the return flight, one of officers asked whether prisoners of war were to be taken along. His answer was: "No, we are not taking prisoners of war!" The implications were clear: there was no room on the overloaded helicopters for prisoners of war. Normally prisoners of war are a very valuable source of intelligence, but unfortunately there was simply no room for even one.

During its investigation the Truth and Reconciliation Commission (TRC) insinuated that Viljoen's words implied that the prisoners of war were to be shot. Anyone who knows Gen. Viljoen will know that he would be the last person to give such a despicable order.

On leaving Cassinga, Gen. Viljoen had a narrow escape. While his helicopter was preparing for take-off, a Cuban tank unexpectedly arrived on the scene. The helicopter was directly in the way of this advancing Cuban tank. Fortunately there were Air Force fighter planes over the target at the time, and they saw what was happening. They immediately attacked the tank, and in so doing saved the helicopter and its precious cargo from falling into enemy hands.

After the attack on Cassinga, SWAPO still maintained that nearly all the victims were women and children. It cannot be denied that there may possibly have been civilian adults and children at this camp. Terrorists often used civilians as human shields in their military camps. Some of the women fought more intensely than the men. Terrorists rarely wore uniforms, and therefore easily melted into the general population. Dead comrades who were not wearing uniforms could therefore easily be presented as refugees.

In his book, *A general's story from an era of war and peace* (1995), Jannie Geldenhuys says: "After more than a decade, in some circles Cassinga is held up as a gross massacre of innocents. Apart from accusations and counter-accusations, the South African claim that it was indeed a military target is supported by aerial photographs that cannot be forged and that show extensive fortifications. Furthermore there is the stiff resistance shown by the defenders, to the extent that the paratroopers stayed far longer than planned, and had to leave part of the town in the hands of the garrison."[14]

Col Jan Breytenbach says he found, to his alarm, that all the "refugees" were very well armed with a variety of weapons, including AK-47s, 12.7 and 14.5 mm anti-aircraft guns, 82 mm mortars and RPG-7s. There was a magazine packed to the rafters with weapons of almost every calibre, including land mines, mortars, bombs and rockets. Excellent protection for so-called refugees![15]

The second attack, in the Chetequera area, was conducted by a mechanised force of the Defence Force, which consisted mainly of national servicemen with little combat experience, and which was equally successful.

In his book on the border war, Willem Steenkamp says: "Operation Reindeer was a complete success."[16] PLAN (SWAPO's fighting arm) suffered about 1000 casualties and 200 prisoners, its insurgency was seriously disrupted, and large numbers of valuable documents were captured. The well-known military analyst Helmoed-Römer Heitman[17] also claims that PLAN never really recovered from its loss of trained and partly trained manpower. PLAN was compelled to use its remaining experienced fighters as instructors, and to deploy green recruits. The experienced fighters now had to lead large groups of newly trained infiltrators; this made SWAPO more vulnerable, and resulted in heavy losses on its side.

Although the Defence Force had withdrawn its troops from Angola after Operation Savannah, it was compelled to carry out periodic operations on a limited scale against PLAN forces, because SWAPO attacks from Angola across the border of South-West Africa/Namibia occurred with increasing intensity and venom.

Some other cross-border operations that followed Reindeer while I was Chief of the Defence Force included Operation Safraan, Rekstok and Sceptic or Smokeshell. These operations were all concluded successfully.

During Rekstok, the military bases of PLAN, SWAPO's military wing, were attacked. One of our aircraft was hit by enemy ground fire during the joint air attack; the plane crashed and the crew were killed. However, the PLAN bases were destroyed, and the enemy found its cross-border infiltration to be more difficult as a result of the operation.

Operation Safraan – an attack in the south of Zambia – was executed jointly with Operation Rekstok, and was the result of a treacherous SWAPO attack on the town of Katima Mulilo with 122 mm rockets on the night of 23 August 1978. One rocket hit the military sleeping quarters, killing ten national servicemen and wounding ten more. The attack came from Zambia, so the attack on a SWAPO camp some 30 km north of the international border with Zambia was ordered. The counter-attack was executed by a small combat team as well as Buccaneer and Canberra aircraft, and virtually wiped out the insurgency in the Caprivi.

Operation Sceptic, also known as Smokeshell, started with a lightning attack by mechanised infantry on PLAN bases in Angola in June 1980. The object of the operation was to destroy PLAN's command and control centre situated at Chifufua (code name Smokeshell). It was from this centre that sub-bases and many PLAN arms caches spread over at least 45 km were controlled. This centre was situated about 180 km north of the South-West African/Namibian border, and was camouflaged and dug in so well that it could only be destroyed by means of a large-scale ground attack. The operation grew in scope as more and more sub-bases and PLAN caches were discovered in the area.

During this operation there was a large-scale clash with Angolan forces – the first since Operation Savannah – and the South African Defence Force for the first time also had to deal with SWAPO's mechanised elements. PLAN's bases and caches were destroyed, and a very large quantity of enemy weapons, equipment, stores and vehicles was captured. It is estimated that about 400 of the enemy were killed. The Defence Force, and indeed the whole of South Africa, paid a great price, because we lost 17 heroes. During this semi-conventional clash the Defence Force gained valuable experience and excellent intelligence.[18]

SWAPO moved its bases further north as a result of this operation, even to within the MPLA and FAPLA areas.

A very interesting incident had occurred in the meantime, which indicated that not only the ANC Alliance, SWAPO and the Soviet Union were interested in South Africa, but that we had a spy plane in our midst.

In the winter of 1978, a well-know ophthalmic surgeon and a good friend of mine, Dr Hennie Meyer, invited me one weekend to hunt on

Various types of Soviet weaponry, vehicles and equipment captured during operations were concentrated in the Defence Force's depots in the operational area. Most of these weapons, including T-34 tanks, were repaired and issued to UNITA for their use.

his farm in the Eastern Transvaal Lowveld. At the same time he informed me that he had also invited the US military attaché, and that the attaché would arrive by plane on Saturday. He arranged that I could fly with the attaché, and this is how it turned out.

We took off from the SA Air Force Base Waterkloof, and landed on the farm's landing strip in the vicinity of Hoedspruit. We enjoyed a very pleasant and successful day in the company of our host and his wife, and returned to Waterkloof late that afternoon.

It was the first time I had flown in an aircraft of this type, and I was impressed by its sophistication, and all the technology it had available. A little later I requested the Military Intelligence Division to give me details about who had given permission for the aircraft to be stationed on a South African Air Force base, and also what the plane was being used for, its capability, etcetera.

It transpired that the USA had received permission from the South African Government in the 1970s to operate a twin-engined light aircraft in South Africa from the Waterkloof Air Force Base in Pretoria. As a gesture of goodwill the Defence Force had gone further and had also given the aircraft landing and parking rights on this partly sensitive fighter base. The plane was mainly used to provide staff at the USA's embassy – the Ambassador and his military attachés in particular – with air transport to enable them to do their work in Southern Africa more efficiently and comfortably.

At the time, relations between South Africa and the USA were somewhat strained at governmental level. This was a result of the way the USA had initially requested South Africa to help it halt the communist influence and presence in Angola, only to turn its back on South Africa a few months later at the end of 1975 with the Clark amendment in the US Congress, and to abandon South Africa in Angola. Furthermore the USA applied the arms embargo policy against South Africa very strictly in the late 1970s, which further soured relations and caused tensions to move towards boiling point. No wonder that my enquiries did nothing to lower the temperature.

The tension almost reached breaking point when the Military Intelligence Division unexpectedly and secretly inspected the USA aircraft at the Waterkloof Air Base in April 1979, and found a hidden 70 mm aerial survey camera on board. This camera was used to photograph various sensitive South African installations. A large number of aerial photographs were also found, among others of the Atomic Energy Corporation and its uranium enrichment plant at the Pelindaba complex near Pretoria. Aerial photographs can reveal a great many details from which deductions can be made and conclusions can be drawn. Aerial photographs of the Pelindaba uranium enrichment plant would partly help to determine the extent to which South Africa was able to enrich uranium or not. It is probably not far-fetched to deduce from this case of espionage that the USA, just as the USSR did through Dieter Gerhardt, tried to determine whether South Africa had the ability to develop weapons of mass destruction – in this case, of course, nuclear weapons. The aerial photographs made up only a part of the incriminating evidence that was found. The troubled relations between South Africa and the USA only serve to prove that countries do not have friends, only interests.

The end result was that South Africa requested the USA's military attachés in the country to leave because of their illegal spying activities, and to take their airplane with them. The USA reacted by kicking out the South African Defence Force attaché in the USA, Brig. Jerry Coetzee, who was then stationed in Washington. This counter-action was their attempt to try to divert attention from the fact that we had caught them red-handed.[19]

I would like to repeat: there are no friendships between countries, only self-interest! It would be good if all South Africans could accept this truth, particularly as we have now seriously become involved in African affairs.

EXPERIENCE WITH NEGOTIATIONS

In 1978 some of the Western countries constituted a so-called Western Contact Group to negotiate with South Africa about the future of South-West Africa/Namibia. This Contact Group consisted of the ministers of foreign affairs of the USA, Britain, West Germany, France and Canada, and included such internationally well-known people as Cyrus Vance, David Owen and Hans-Dietrich Genscher. The Prime Minister at the time, P.W. Botha, gave Mr Pik Botha, the Minister of Foreign Affairs, Dr Brand Fourie, the Secretary of Foreign Affairs, and me, as Chief of the Defence Force, instructions to undertake the negotiations on behalf of South Africa in October 1978. His instruction to us was almost impossible, and it would therefore require very nimble footwork to succeed.

Our instruction was that the envisaged elections in South-West Africa/Namibia had to proceed, despite the objections of the Contact Group, and that the settlement proposals were not to be implemented immediately, but preferably much later. Furthermore the withdrawal of Cuban soldiers from Angola had to be linked to this implementation plan.[20]

A month before the start of the negotiations, on 29 September 1978, the United Nations Organisation (UNO) accepted Resolution 435, which would in effect determine the future of South-West Africa/Namibia. This international resolution could only make matters more difficult for us.

Pik Botha took the lead in determining the strategy and tactics for the negotiations. He would talk, reason and argue on behalf of the three of us. From our side there would be only one point of view – we would not allow them to detect any differences between us. However, if something was unclear, or if any difference became apparent between the three of us, or if there were aspects that should be taken further, we would clear them up amongst ourselves during breaks in the official negotiations.

The Contact Group was made up of five VIPs of different nationalities. Such a composition inevitably meant that differences of emphasis or nuance would appear, especially if they were placed under pressure concerning a delicate subject. This proved to be the case, and we exploited the differences to the full.

Furthermore some of these members clearly had views of their own individual importance, as if they wished to convey that they were their country's representatives, and that they could maintain that country's, or their own individualism by stating an individual opinion. It was clear that the members would have difficulty melding some of these different points of view into one workable solution. At times their contributions were individual, rather than the opinion of a team.

The five main members' secretarial support group, headed by Mr Don McHenry of the USA, was far better acquainted with the situation in South-West Africa/Namibia than their "masters", the ministers. However, with their permission it was arranged that this secretarial support group would have an opportunity to visit local tourist attractions while we were negotiating. As a result this secretarial group could not always be contacted, and so its members were not always available to cast light on problem areas that became apparent to the Contact Group. This meant that situations sometimes developed during the negotiations where we three South Africans were the only ones who had intimate knowledge of the circumstances in South-West Africa/Namibia. With only our first-hand knowledge available, the Contact Group was often inclined to accept our views.

As was usual with any negotiations at this level, our team referred any complications that occurred to the Prime Minister, P.W. Botha, for his decision and advice. He was always available during the negotiations, and did not hesitate to make decisions or to take a stand.

The negotiations were tough. We differed from the start, and sometimes the talks came close to collapsing. Yet, despite the odds, we succeeded in our goal and in fulfilling the mission given to us, mainly thanks to Pik Botha's negotiation skills.

In the wake of these negotiations, I was present – in my capacity as Chief of the Defence Force, and later as Minister of Defence – at nearly all the negotiations we conducted on the security situation of Southern Africa with representatives of various countries, such as the USA, Soviet Union, Cuba, Angola, Mozambique, Zambia and other African countries. However, I think that the negotiations with the Western Contact Group still stand out most clearly in my memory.

Together with Pik Botha I was also involved in the successful negotiations on South-West Africa's future and the application of Resolution 435 of the UNO, and in the negotiations with representatives of the Government of Mozambique regarding the acceptance of the Treaty of Nkomati, also known as the Nkomati Accord. I therefore knew Pik Botha very well in his capacity as a negotiator, and was very surprised when Pres. F.W. de Klerk at a later stage did not give Pik Botha an opportunity to negotiate directly with the ANC Alliance on behalf of the Government of the time during the Convention for a Democratic South Africa (CODESA). Those familiar with Pik Botha's negotiation abilities and techniques are of the opinion that this decision may have been an error of judgment on the part of Pres. De Klerk. Pik's absence created the generally incorrect impression amongst the public that he was incapable of such an important task, which would determine South Africa's political future. My experience of Pik Botha and the Department of Foreign Affairs was that they always achieved excellent results, and that there was a good understanding and co-operation with the Defence Force in this regard.

On one occasion the Secretary of Foreign Affairs, Dr Brand Fourie, and Gen. Viljoen as Chief of the SA Army, had to negotiate with the Cubans on behalf of South Africa with regard to certain aspects of the conflict in Angola. The three of us flew to the Ruacana Waterfalls by helicopter, where I would leave them and continue with inspections in the operational area. After we had landed and they had alighted and walked away to meet the Cubans, I looked at our team, analysing the situation. What did I, or the average Defence Force officer, know about negotiation techniques? There was no formal training on this subject in the Defence Force, and up to that stage members of the military had had few opportunities to gain any practical experience. My intuition told me that there would be many negotiation challenges ahead, and that it was my responsibility to ensure that the Defence Force and its members were prepared for this.

I decided there and then to instruct the Defence Force's Chief of Staff responsible for Personnel to study this glaring deficiency. The officer in charge of this enquiry was Adm. Edwards. On conclusion of the enquiry he reported that very little theoretical knowledge or expertise regarding existing techniques for formal negotiations was available in South Africa. Even the large private companies had little expertise, but he undertook to come up with a plan.

A year or so later, Adm. Edwards and two professors from the University of South Africa (UNISA) visited me in my office. UNISA had sent these two academics to the USA for wide-ranging studies on negotiation. They had recently completed a university course in negotiation for UNISA, and were ready to lecture on this as a future university subject. They gave me the course notes and prescribed books as a token of their appreciation because I had noticed the deficiency and had presented them with the challenge.

A month or so after this visit by the two professors the Defence Force decided to offer Defence Force members the opportunity to gain the necessary expertise in the field of negotiation.

In 1991/1992 I was instructed to attend a three-day seminar on negotiation at the Union Buildings in Pretoria. I received this instruction so late that I could not reschedule my programme without causing the Government some embarrassment. However, in order to prove my willingness and support, I undertook to attend the seminar whenever I was able to. When I did so, I was very surprised to hear that the presenters of the seminar were British citizens from England, in other words a foreign team. I only hoped that the organisers of the event could guarantee this team's loyalty and integrity, particularly because the Government's negotiating strategy and minimum requirements would be discussed during the seminar. I could not help but be somewhat surprised that South Africans who did have the knowledge and practical experience of negotiations were not involved in this seminar.

Chapter 12

THE NATIONAL SECURITY MANAGEMENT SYSTEM

Due to the wide-ranging responsibilities of the Defence Force during the hostile onslaught on South Africa, and the many tasks it had to fulfil, it was almost inevitable that many additional, important management activities had to be developed. This took place together with interaction between various organisations and the Defence Force. Most of these activities occurred during my term as Chief of the Defence Force and as Minister of Defence, and were indirectly and sometimes directly part of my responsibilities, with the Defence Force involved in some way or another. One of these tasks was the extension of the State Security Council (SSC) by creating a secretariat and a working committee, and creating the National Security Management System (NSMS), which was closely involved in the broader security situation in South Africa.

As discussed above, the classic concepts of warfare changed after World War II. Events in the former colonies in Africa brought the South African government to the realisation that the principles and changing nuances of warfare should be studied in depth. Accordingly there was a need for Defence Force officers with a thorough schooling in military science who would be able to take the lead in future. An academic institution would have to meet this need, and this prompted the establishment of the Military Academy in Pretoria, which later moved to Saldanha.

Officers who were trained at the Military Academy began occupying senior posts in the Defence Force just as the military struggle was developing in the country. They became convinced that innovative action was required in the struggle, because it was clear that it could not be conducted and won by force of arms only. The revolutionary struggle brought to the fore other important factors, such as the creation of sound human relations, positive attitudes, human dignity and so on.

P.W. Botha became the Minister of Defence in 1966. He had a good deal of experience as an organiser within the National Party, and became known as someone who would not tolerate sloppy or inefficient administration. He had an open mind when I began to tell him about the philosophy of total and revolutionary warfare, and how to combat it. The essence was that the State needed the structures, strategies and plans for the co-ordinated, orchestrated and efficient employment of all available resources to combat this type of assault.

Using this view of security matters as a point of departure, Mr Botha persuaded the Government of the day to create a National Management System (NMS), consisting of the National Prosperity Management System (NPMS) and the NSMS. The particular purpose of the NSMS was to withstand the internal assault efficiently and in a co-ordinated way.

The SSC, a Cabinet committee, controlled the NSMS. The other three Cabinet committees, namely Political, Economic and Welfare, were responsible for the NPMS. Each minister and/or head of a government department was therefore part of the NMS, and had a responsibility or could offer a contribution towards national security. This allowed the State to utilise its resources in a co-ordinated way through the NMS.[1]

Decisions of the SSC first had to be ratified by the Cabinet before they could be executed. The State President was chairman of the State Security Council, and certain Cabinet ministers and their heads of department served on it in terms of legislation. The State Security Council was created in an attempt to optimise the State's social welfare and security function, and to ensure integrated management. A working committee of the State Security Council was created to support the SSC's decision-making, with co-ordinated inputs by officials.

For security purposes the country was further subdivided into various geographical areas, and these areas corresponded roughly with the provincial boundaries we have today. A joint management centre (JMC) was created within each of these areas. Each JMC was responsible for co-ordinating security management within its geographical area. Depending on the circumstances within an area, a JMC could be further subdivided.

In view of the prevalent circumstances in South Africa, security was closely allied to social welfare and social upliftment, and therefore many departments, authorities, bodies and organisations were involved in the JMCs at various levels. The members of a local JMC appointed a chairperson from amongst themselves.

The JMC delegated the execution of decisions taken at the regional or local level to the appropriate department, authority or body within whose sphere or authority this fell. The JMC was there to co-ordinate functions and to ensure that needs were satisfied. It could not enforce any decision, and could not cancel any decision by a department. In broad terms the JMCs therefore had a co-ordinating function within their areas.

If a department or organisation did not have the necessary funds to meet a security need identified by the JMC, it could request additional funds via the State Security Council. If a minister or the Head of Department did not agree with the JMC regarding a particular need, the issue could even be referred to the State Security Council for a decision. This system gave national security a new status. The Security Forces were no longer responsible for the state's security in isolation, but would henceforth act in co-operation with the political, economic and socio-psychological power bases.

As Chief of the Defence Force and later as Minister of Defence, I was automatically a member of the SSC and the working committee, and was consequently closely involved in the NSMS. The functioning of this Security Management System was the one government activity that really impressed me. Various departments took part in this system at various levels and in a properly co-ordinated manner.[2]

The system did initially have teething problems, but soon operated smoothly and efficiently. Most members came to realise, through their participation in the system, what national or state security actually encompassed, and what role their departments or organisations played. Co-ordinated action was possible across the security spectrum for the first time, and security was no longer the sole responsibility of the Defence Force and the SA Police Force.

The NSMS must be given credit for stabilising internal unrest following the setbacks that were experienced from 1985 onwards. The system operated smoothly, and served as an early warning system. For the first time the state had its finger on the pulse of internal problem areas, could identify problems proactively, and could meet them in a co-ordinated manner. At the same time the system proved a thorn in the flesh of the revolutionary forces.

Thanks to this system, the functioning of state systems in the social field could, for the first time, be determined in a co-ordinated manner and, where necessary, dealt with – to the benefit of all population groups. Examples of this are the lack of facilities and housing, poverty, inadequate job opportunities and so forth. These social inadequacies provided a barometer which could point to the intensity of the underlying factors in the revolutionary onslaught on South Africa's society and national security.

The system was a major responsibility of the State Security Council. I received permission from the SSC Chairman, Pres. P.W. Botha, to visit the various JMCs to make sure that they were functioning efficiently. I visited all management centres at least once, and those in larger population centres three or four times, within a short space of time. When I had satisfied myself that they were functioning efficiently, I invited Mr Botha and a few of his colleagues who had an interest in the matter, to visit the Eastern Province JMC, under the Chairmanship of Brig. (later Gen.) Joffel van der Westhuizen.

This area presented the most serious threat to national security. It was an area with a great many poor people, inadequate housing and facilities, and widespread unemployment. The result: many agitators and antagonistic elements in action!

The JMC had to deal with various challenges, all with some or other effect on security. Fortunately this organisation was geared for quick and efficient action.

For example, there was the case of large-scale unrest, riots and shop boycotts in Aliwal North, a fairly large town in the Eastern Cape rural area. The JMC members immediately tried to determine the cause of the violence, and found that there were inadequate toilet facilities for the residents of the nearby township. The residents were sick and tired of the situation, and this led to the unrest. According to the representative of the department responsible for sanitation, that year's budget made no provision for something to be done about the situation.

Previously the SA Police and the Defence Force would have suppressed this justified protest action with violence, and with some danger to their own lives. Such actions are counter-productive in a revolutionary struggle because they turn the population against the authorities, and promote resistance. The JMC realised this, and persuaded the government department concerned to try to get additional funding, which it did with the help of the SSC. The facilities were erected in a trice, and the unrest and violence subsided.

Thanks to similar experiences with JMC involvement, government departments soon realised the important role and responsibility they had with regard to national security.

In the 1980s a well-known oil company offered the SABC a series of educational television programmes free of charge. The SABC was very willing to broadcast the daily programmes, which were aimed at helping pupils with their school subjects, free of charge. The request to broadcast was directed at the government departments with the suitable responsibility, who summarily denied the request. However, educationists who were well aware of the educational worth of the programmes approached the Johannesburg JMC. Because these programmes would be of particular value to black pupils, this Management Centre took co-ordinated steps to obtain the permission of the department concerned for the programmes to be broadcast daily and nationally. This permission can be described as a preventative security operation, particularly if one takes into account the climate of unrest in the wake of the pupil riots in Soweto in 1976. The television series was very successful, and was used by SABC-TV until recently.

One of the success stories is that of Alexandra, one of Johannesburg's northern townships, bordering on Sandton. This was one of the most challenging and complex areas in the country – the only area the ANC could at one stage declare a "liberated area". Archbishop Desmond Tutu once addressed a rally there under a communist banner complete with hammer and sickle.

As in many townships, the housing in this area was in a very bad state, and services were inadequate. There were about 4500 houses, and if these are added to the various squatter shacks and other shelters, there were probably some 8000 to 9000 housing units, with an estimated 110 000 residents. Originally only 2500 plots were allocated, which meant these had to provide living, playing and learning space for an average of 44 people per plot.[3]

When a local authority was established for the township in the 1980s, a well-known black cleric was elected as one of the first black mayors in the country. Because this black authority did not receive adequate government assistance, it could not make any socio-economic progress. The community consequently withdrew its co-operation, and the cleric and his councillors decided to disband the council.

At this stage criminal and hostile elements in Alexandra drove resident members of the SA Police and their families from the area. These families were forced to live in Defence Force tents in a neighbouring township, Wynberg. The hostile elements took control of Alexandra and barriers were erected to prevent non-residents from entering the area. The township, situated only a few kilometres from the Johannesburg CBD, was also made inaccessible to the authorities. Car hijackers, of whom there were many in the area, felt that they were safe there. Crime and lawlessness ruled.

Some of the residents of the area protested and came to speak to me about the matter. It transpired that Alexandra had been declared a white area in 1963. Black homeowners had been bought out with cash, and would be required to move from the area at a later stage, but then everything came to a halt, with the sword of Damocles hanging over their heads for years. They did not know if they would in fact be moved, or where they would be moved to, or when they would be moved. The residents were very unhappy with the situation. Some had saved the money from their expropriation so that if the Government were to change its mind, as they hoped it would, they would be able to buy back their houses.

On 4 May 1986, Pres. Botha, my colleague, Mr Louis le Grange, the

Minister of Law and Order, a number of officials and I discussed the Alexandra situation, and then the Security Forces decided to intercede. Alexandra was freed of the criminal elements, the barriers were removed, and the residents could once more move freely and go about their daily tasks.

However, Alexandra was in a shocking condition. The pavements and open spaces were littered with rubbish, refuse, wrecked vehicles and anything the residents wanted to get rid of. This state of affairs continued for some time.

The houses did not have water or flushing toilets. The brick and jerry-built houses and squatter huts were crammed with people. Single men in the large, overcrowded hostels were a danger to married people in the vicinity. Roads, if one could call them that, were in a very poor condition. They turned into quagmires when it rained, because no proper storm water drainage existed, and Alexandra is situated in a hollow alongside the badly polluted Jukskei River. The local authority was not functioning, and there was no law and order. Nobody's safety was assured. The message I got from a visit to the people was one of despondency, despair and desperation.

Because I was of the opinion that Alexandra could serve as an excellent example of how the authorities should not deal with the population, I decided to introduce representatives of the authorities, prominent businessmen and members of the South African media at different occasions to this rebellious area. Those invited met at the Defence College in Pretoria for a visit to the township. On occasion a cross-section of the media, amongst others people such as Tertius Myburgh of the *Sunday Times* and Alf Ries of *Die Burger*, came along. The programme provided a briefing and a description of revolutionary warfare, and then the group accompanied me in a helicopter to gain a general impression of Alexandra from the air, before visiting it at ground level.

Following the discussion and the visit, it was clear to all that if a dramatic change could not be brought about in Alexandra, we would lose the area in our counter-revolutionary efforts. Furthermore there was a real danger that the situation could spill over into Tembisa, Sandton and Johannesburg. What was happening in practice went absolutely against everything that was supposed to happen in a counter-revolutionary struggle. The situation was so unacceptable that I felt compelled to confess to the group that if I had been born in Alexandra I would surely have been the leader of the terrorist group there. The select group did not challenge my statement at all.

A mini-JMC was established for Alexandra. The West Rand Development Board appointed Mr Steve Burger, one of its excellent employees, and someone with the gift of getting along with people, as administrator for the area. They drew up a plan for upgrading the area and, thanks to their enthusiasm, made good progress with it. Among other things, the following was taken on: provision of Escom power, the erection of a post office with telephone links, four primary schools, one secondary school, a medical clinic and crèches, the provision of storm water and sewage systems, the establishment of a boxing club, the upgrading of houses and roads, the removal of rubbish from the streets, and the development of flats and an elite suburb. The management centre established under Steve Burger functioned so well that some of the local residents participated with enthusiasm. Initially Alexandra's youth did sterling work in clearing up refuse, and cleaning up their living environment. This laid the foundation for creating good relations between the mini-management centre and the local residents.

In the meantime the expropriations and removal of the residents by the Government were thrown into reverse. The Minister of Finance, Barend du Plessis, voted about R12 million to implement the improvement or upgrading plan for Alexandra. With the mediation of Mr Oberholzer (Oom Obie), the Regional Services Council and the Johannesburg City Council donated the eastern bank of the Jukskei River for extension of the township. This area of about 400 hectares was very suitable for meeting future housing needs. The private sector immediately started building houses in this new area, and residents moved into the completed houses very quickly. The police members and their families moved back to Alexandra, and law and order were restored. The Defence Force established a facility for medical services in Alexandra to provide the residents with free medical services in the interim.

The Johannesburg City Council conducted an opinion poll to determine the attitude of the residents of Alexandra towards the presence of the Security Forces in the area. The results showed that 92,7% of the residents were satisfied with their presence, and 87% indicated that there had been a reduction in intimidation.

Alexandra was once more able to breathe freely, and residents could go about their daily lives unhindered.

Pres. Botha had an excellent grasp of the revolutionary struggle: I am convinced this was one of the main reasons why he introduced his essential political reforms in the 1980s.

He tried to get rid of laws that clouded attitudes amongst South Africa's population, and repealed discriminatory legislation.

During a revolutionary onslaught it is essential that 20% of the State's actions should be concentrated on security issues, but 80% of its actions should be concentrated on other matters, particularly political and socio-economic issues.[4]

In view of my account of the success of the National Security Management System, it is surprising that F.W. de Klerk, shortly after he became President in September 1989, announced drastic revisions to the system on 28 November 1989, on the grounds of "a personal impression". He had previously regarded himself as a "passenger" in the State Security Council, and therefore perhaps did not really have a "clear picture" of the activities of the "securocrat system", nor a good understanding of it.[5]

The thorough investigation of the National Security Management System ordered by F.W. de Klerk could not find any solid grounds to justify his later drastic changes to the system. The main reason he gave for his action was that the system had possibly intruded on the area of responsibility, in other words the line functions, of certain government departments. He appointed an Investigating Team, which found that the system worked very well, a finding that was confirmed by most Heads of Department. Only a few Heads of Department felt that the management system possibly intruded on their authority. Pres. De Klerk's emotional decision to change the system resulted in this extremely important system ceasing to function efficiently. In view of certain variables such as the security situation at the time, and continuing conflict, this was a high-risk decision. The conflict situation could possibly worsen, with uncertain results. At that stage political negotiations with the ANC Alliance were only a vague possibility. Was the real reason for his decision that he wanted to placate the ANC by removing this thorn in their flesh?

In his book *Gister se dade, vandag se oordeel* (2000), the Director General of Justice at the time, Adv. J.P.J. Coetzer, who served in the State Security Council and the Working Committee *ex officio*, and whose department was part of the NSMS, says: "I always had a great regard for F.W. de Klerk's opinions, but unfortunately I must confess that I cannot agree with his critical remarks regarding the State Security Council and the National Security Management System that appear in his book *Die laaste trek -'n nuwe begin*. As someone intimately involved in the country's security since 1953, who could see the errors made during Vorster's period in office (and to a degree also during Verwoerd's period in office), I can attest without any hesitation to the fact that the State Security Council and its structures (such as the National Security Management System) saved the country in the periods concerned." [My translation]

These drastic changes actually meant that the system had to be eradicated. In May 1990, I convened a meeting of top Defence Force managers who had practical experience of the system. We discussed the possibility of erecting a similar system within the Defence Force only in order to assist with the co-ordination of measures regarding the security challenges of the country. The unanimous view of these senior officers was that the President's decision regarding the NSMS proscribed the creation of a similar organisation within the Defence Force.

An acknowledged expert on revolutionary war and member of the National Security Management System, Gen. André van Deventer, said the following in this regard during the abovementioned meeting: "Looking back in hindsight, the biggest mistake the military made in managing this system was the fact that it brought its own specific management style to bear on their sister departments: a style of, results must be achieved irrespective of what it takes – a style which is foreign to the civilian departments and although, I am sure, it never really was the intention of the military to 'take over' from the civilians, the intensity with which they tackled a problem was perceived by the civilians as just that. Was the management style then not the reason for the unnecessary demise of the Joint Management Centres and the National Security Management System as a whole? Was the main reason for F.W. de Klerk to change the system maybe not the fact that he did not understand the system but rather the fact that he disliked the manner in which the military was involved in identifying the problems, and suggesting the solutions and in so doing showing up certain other departments and cabinet ministers? Who knows?

"However, the system proved itself over the period it existed. Although negative reports were made by ill-informed and sometimes hostile people. It was ultimately destroyed in 1989, by the stroke of the State President's pen."

Chapter 13

NUCLEAR AND RELATED TECHNOLOGICAL DEVELOPMENT

The development of South Africa's nuclear capability did not initially involve the Defence Force or the Defence family, but at a later stage it did become involved. When I retired from public life in 1993 and it became known that South Africa indeed had a nuclear capability at its disposal, most of the enquiries and requests for interviews I received from diplomats, foreign intelligence agencies, students at various universities in the Western World and journalists, centred on nuclear weapons.

The Atomic Energy Board (AEB) started with approved South African uranium enrichment experiments, and a programme of enrichment, in the 1960s. The uranium enrichment programme was very successful, and the first highly enriched uranium was produced in 1978.[1]

The development of South Africa's own nuclear explosive capability dates back to the 1960s. In turn this nuclear explosive capability led to an inquiry in 1969 to determine how this development could be utilised for peaceful purposes. The AEB tried to determine whether it was economically and technologically feasible to employ controlled nuclear explosives to help the mining industry. Furthermore there was speculation about the use of nuclear power to help with the preparation of underground oil storage facilities and with the dredging of harbours. The result of this inquiry was very positive, and the Minister of Mines at the time gave the AEB permission to proceed with research into and development of the use of nuclear energy for peaceful purposes.[2]

The Prime Minister, Adv. B.J. Vorster, gave the initial permission for the development of a limited nuclear explosive capability in 1974, and for the creation of an underground test area. The rapid progress made with the development of an underground nuclear device meant that the development of a suitable testing site became a matter of urgency. To this end the Vastrap area about 100 km north of Upington was identified as a testing area, and preparations were made at the site.[3]

The nuclear power development team made very good progress. Because of the escalation of the physical military threat to South Africa, the Government was compelled to re-evaluate the need for and production of nuclear devices. At the same time incisive attention was paid to the active Soviet presence on the African continent. The initial purpose of the development of a non-military nuclear capability had to be re-evaluated in view of the increasing hostile threat.[4] It was realised that it was necessary to possess nuclear explosive devices, and their development was approved at the highest Governmental level. (Authors Hannes Steyn, Richard van der Walt and Jan van Loggerenberg provide an excellent report on South Africa's experience with the development of nuclear weapons in *Armament and disarmament*.)

In developing South Africa's nuclear capability, the purpose was not to use nuclear bombs in a war situation, but rather to use them as a credible deterrent against the possible deployment of nuclear weapons in a war situation by the enemy. In other words, South Africa would consider using a nuclear weapon only in such circumstances. This strategy could only become a reality if any success with regard to the development, production and availability of the weapon could be kept secret, at least initially. South Africa therefore needed to maintain strict control over the infrastructure, development and production of this nuclear capability, and would have to keep it strictly secret.[5]

Furthermore a nuclear capability to be employed as a deterrent had to be developed in such a way that it would be in proportion to the threat. It also had to remain within the limits of the country's scientific and industrial capabilities.[6]

The Vastrap nuclear test site with its two test shafts was completed by 1977. These shafts were 90 cm in diameter, and were drilled to a depth of 385 m and 216 m respectively. The facilities were completed to enable South Africa to consider underground nuclear explosions for experimental purposes; or possibly to use them as a warning signal to the outside world.[7]

In 1977 a Soviet spy satellite – one of many satellites belonging to the great powers that moved over South Africa almost daily – noticed the activities at Vastrap. The information was given to the media, to be used to create a climate intended to harm South Africa. Internationally there was no certainty as to whether South Africa already had a nuclear capability, or what progress had been made with the development of such a capability. If the resultant uncertainty and speculation could be utilised effectively, it would be to the country's advantage.[8]

However, the speculation resulted in more international pressure on South Africa, with the great powers making certain demands. For example, the USA insisted that South Africa should immediately cease all proposed nuclear tests and development, and that South Africa should sign the Nuclear Non-Proliferation Treaty (NPT).

In essence the Nuclear NPT means that a signatory country makes an agreement with the International Atomic Energy Agency (IAEA) and undertakes to honour the terms of the contract with regard to nuclear development. At the same time the country undertakes to ensure that all its nuclear plants are subject to international guarantees, and to open them to inspection, at any time, by this international nuclear agency. The IAEA is the international watchdog which tries to limit the proliferation of nuclear weapons.[9]

The Koeberg nuclear power station in the Western Cape was built with French assistance, and France was obliged to supply the nuclear fuel required for the nuclear plant to operate. In the circumstances that reigned at the time, no other country was prepared to supply South Africa with nuclear fuel unless it signed the nuclear NPT. This power station, which had cost the country billions of rands in taxpayers' money, therefore was in danger of becoming a white elephant.[10]

In the meantime it became quite clear that the USA was no longer prepared to supply South Africa with nuclear fuel, as it was contractually obliged to do. Furthermore, on the insistence of the USA, France also decided not to supply South Africa with nuclear fuel, unless the USA were to supply the enriched uranium for this purpose, or give France permission to supply it. France also demanded that South Africa should sign the Nuclear NPT. As a result the country decided in 1978 to become self-sufficient in the field of fuel supplies to Koeberg, which involved both the enrichment and the manufacture of fuel. At the time there even was talk of cancelling the Koeberg nuclear contracts.[11]

The pressure – mainly from the United States, and specifically with regard to the signing of the Nuclear NPT – increased when the USA claimed in September 1979 and December 1980 that there were indications of a South African nuclear test in the southern Indian Ocean. South Africa denied these allegations, but the pressure on the country simply mounted as far as its nuclear development and testing, and the signing of the Nuclear NPT were concerned.[12]

At the time South Africa was unwilling to sign the Nuclear NPT unconditionally for various strategic reasons. Among other things it would have to open its nuclear installations to IAEA inspectors, after which it would be simple to determine whether the country was able to enrich uranium, and therefore would be able to manufacture nuclear warheads. Still, South Africa administered the situation in accordance with the spirit and aims of the Nuclear NPT, and made its policy known to the USA and other interested parties.[13]

In order to co-operate in the matter of responsibility for and management of the nuclear weapons question and the nuclear NPT, the so-called Witvlei Committee was created in 1978 under the chairmanship of the Prime Minister at the time, P.W. Botha.[14]

The committee officially approved the continued development of a nuclear bomb, and indicated that its use as a weapon should be avoided. However, if it had to be used in exceptional circumstances, the Head of State, together with his most senior ministers, would have the final say in the matter. The committee was, however, unanimous that this technological and scientific feat should be used mainly to place South Africa in a position of power and authority, particularly in any future political or other major international negotiations.[15]

Initially the locally developed underground nuclear device was temporarily stored in a disused coal mine near Witbank. It was then transferred to the Circle Complex that had been erected on an Armscor site in 1980-1981. A special vault for storing the device was built. This underground device was designed mainly for demonstration purposes, should such a need arise in the future.[16]

The Circle Complex or workshop was renamed the Advena Central Research and Development Laboratory – a subsidiary of Armscor – in 1987, and was situated about 15 km west of Pretoria. The exclusive development, control, care, security and storage of South Africa's nuclear warheads were entrusted to Advena, with the help and support of the AEB and the Atomic Energy Corporation.[17]

The Uranium Enrichment Corporation and the AEB merged as the Atomic Energy Corporation in 1982.[18]

The first nuclear device manufactured by Armscor in 1982 would be delivered by aircraft should its use be required. The SA Air Force would carry the nuclear bomb in one of its Buccaneer attack planes or one of its fighter-bombers in the Mirage stable. When the nuclear weapons programme was cancelled, there was one underground device, that is a nuclear bomb or nuclear device that could be used for an underground test, and a further five completed and approved nuclear devices, ready for use. The highly enriched uranium components and non-nuclear components for a seventh device or bomb had already been completed.[19]

For safety and security reasons each nuclear device was made up of two components, namely a front and rear part. For safety reasons the two sections were stored separately in different vaults. No simultaneous maintenance or handling of the two sections was ever permitted, therefore from a practical point of view, it was almost impossible to activate a device accidentally.[20]

The collapse of the Soviet Bloc and world-wide communism, symbolised by the tearing down of the Berlin Wall at the end of 1989, resulted in the Soviet Union withdrawing its nuclear war potential from Southern Africa. The physical military threat against South Africa diminished markedly thereafter, and consequently an ad hoc Cabinet committee could reassess the ending of South Africa's nuclear weapons programme in 1990. Following an inquiry, this committee recommended, among other things, that South Africa should declare its willingness to sign the Nuclear NPT, dismantle all existing nuclear warheads as soon as possible, melt the fissionable material used in the warheads, and store it at the Atomic Energy Corporation under strict supervision.[21]

Because of the danger of international terrorism and the unpredictable behaviour of certain governments regarding the use of nuclear weapons, international control of nuclear weapons is very important. At that time it was accepted that any country with a nuclear capability possessed a very powerful bargaining chip. Should pressure be brought to bear on such a country to dispose of its own nuclear weapons, it could insist that the entire region of which it is a part should become a nuclear-free zone.[22]

Apart from the increasing international pressure on South Africa, the USA at that time seemed most concerned about the possibility that South Africa's nuclear capability could fall into the hands of an irresponsible government or an international terrorist group. The USA was therefore intensely preoccupied with the local situation and placed a great deal of pressure on South Africa to dispose of this nuclear war capability and to sign the nuclear NPT.

While the Cabinet committee was considering the future of South Africa's nuclear capability, Pres. De Klerk's attention was drawn in particular to the possible advantage of such a negotiating lever, and the desirability of South Africa at least gaining as much advantage as possible from the destruction of its precious expertise.

He agreed only to South Africa's doing away with its nuclear capability. From a security and negotiating point of view, the most advantageous result of such a step would be to, at the same time, have the whole of Southern Africa declared a nuclear-free zone. This would mean that no nuclear warheads could be manufactured in or brought to the region. He thought that this would be a great advantage to this geographic region in the future, and that it would simultaneously serve as an example to the international community, encouraging it to create nuclear-free geographic zones all over the world.

South Africa agreed to the Nuclear NPT in July 1991. However, no political announcements were made in this regard, and therefore one must conclude that the very good bargaining chip was never used to its full advantage, and that South Africa succumbed under international pressure without achieving any quid pro quo to its own advantage or that perhaps the country simply caved in. I am of the opinion that South Africa should have negotiated an advantageous agreement. This could, for example, have included the following: participation in a programme for defence exports; a participative programme to ensure that the "new South African Defence Force" be brought up to par with developed countries with regard to technological weapon systems and joint training programmes; a technological exchange programme to bring South Africa up to date with information technology, etcetera.

The nuclear devices and installations were dismantled under strict supervision over a period of 18 months. All the documentation created during the development and production process was collected and destroyed on instructions from the government.[23] As a result, the Nuclear NPT was only signed in March 1993, and F.W. de Klerk could make an announcement on South Africa's nuclear weapons technology and material on 24 March 1993.[24]

At the same time as the development of South Africa's nuclear weapons capability, other technological research and development projects were carried out as well. Some of these projects concerned nuclear development, while others were independent of the nuclear project, but made it possible for the country to acquire new and advanced technology, thanks to the capabilities developed during the nuclear project.

Research into and the development of alternative nuclear delivery systems was directly linked to the nuclear project. Research into the first nuclear device for delivery by artillery was done in 1987. More attention was then given to a missile delivery system for nuclear warheads. This missile delivery system was far advanced, and included, among other things, specifications for firing the missile from a prepared static platform as well as from a mobile platform.

The development of a missile capability would have enabled South Africa to place a satellite in a low orbit around the earth. Using such a satellite would have made it possible to gain credible intelligence far more quickly by means of television cameras and other equipment. At the time, South Africa had the technological capacity for the local development of such an intelligence satellite. Such a development would have cleared the way to manufacture and place in orbit other, more advanced satellites, for purposes such as communication and navigation.

An example of a locally manufactured prototype missile (RSA-3). It was the precursor to the manufacture of a missile developed to place a satellite in an orbit around the earth. (Photo: Steyn, Hannes, Van der Walt, Richard, Van Loggerenberg, Jan. 2003. *Armament and disarmament: South Africa's nuclear weapons experience.*)

South Africa was indeed on the threshold of the exploitation of space to its own advantage.

The development of sensitive missile delivery systems emphasised the importance of suitable missile test sites. In choosing such a site, the following considerations were important: security; the possibility of launching the missile safely in an easterly direction; the development potential and ecology of the terrain, and the impact area where the missile would re-enter the atmosphere.

A terrain which allows for the missile to be launched in an easterly direction is necessary to permit the missile to move in the direction of the earth's spin, which makes it possible to carry a greater payload. Payload is of great importance, because the rough calculation is that an additional 1300 kg of fuel is required for every additional 500 g of payload.

Following intensive inspections of and research into a number of sites in various South African regions, the choice fell on the coastal area southeast of Bredasdorp between Waenhuiskrans and Cape Infanta, south of Potberg. Property in the area was then expropriated.

Bredasdorp was a prosperous rural town situated close to the pro-

The control or operations centre for space flights at the Overberg Test Site near Bredasdorp. (Photo: Steyn, Hannes, Van der Walt, Richard, Van Loggerenberg, Jan. 2003. *Armament and disarmament: South Africa's nuclear weapons experience.*)

posed site. The town had good educational facilities and lent itself to accommodating the families of the experts who would be working at the Overberg Test Site. Furthermore there were enough inhabitants in the Bredasdorp area to take advantage of the job opportunities that the test site would create.[25]

The test site could be divided into two parts. The Air Force and Armscor would use the smaller part for possible day-to-day activities, and a very large runway was built on this section, which is situated to the west of the De Hoop Nature Reserve. The second part was far larger, was used only periodically by Armscor for firing missiles, and was situated to the east of De Hoop.

I appointed a committee to determine whether the proposed Armscor military activities there would be environmentally friendly. Amongst others the committee consisted of Dr Douglas Heys as chairperson – someone who was internationally accepted as a leading nature conservationist – and representatives of organised agriculture and Armscor. I reassured the committee that no explosives would be deployed on the site; that no tracked vehicles would be tested there or indeed driven on the site; and that invasive alien plants would be destroyed, and wildlife that was not endemic to the area would be relocated. After a thorough examination the committee unanimously recommended that the designated site could be used as missile test site.

With this missile development effort Armscor managed to bring together a remarkable team of experts consisting, amongst others, of technicians, systems experts and engineers. These experts achieved extraordinary results in extremely difficult circumstances, and placed South Africa at the forefront of international technological development. However, these teams were disbanded when the Nuclear NPT was signed. It will be difficult to ever equal or improve on the standards that they set.[26]

To sum up: South Africa was compelled to go down the path of nuclear armaments because sanctions made it impossible to approach the traditional arms suppliers in the West to satisfy the Defence Force's needs. In the meantime the Soviet Union was building up a formidable arsenal of weaponry on the continent. It was incidental that South Africa's nuclear programme for peaceful use was so far advanced when the decision to develop a nuclear bomb had to be taken. When the political decision was made, it became the responsibility of the Defence family to ensure the development of the nuclear weapons systems and the execution of the nuclear strategy in the most responsible manner possible.

Looking back on the East-West confrontation in the 1970s and 1980s, one wonders why the conflict was so intense. The ideological struggle for "world dominance" has sometimes even been expressed in terms of religious differences. Judging the remnants of the once mighty Soviet Union today, it is difficult to understand how the earlier imperialistic ambitions of that mighty military machine and its striving towards communist world domination could actually exist.[27] Yet that previously feared regime cold-bloodedly murdered 20 million of its own citizens in the time of Stalin and later kindred spirits such as Brezhnev, and no one took any notice. The impact of the Cold War on Africa is probably no longer appreciated properly, but it was a reality which had an impact on South Africa as well. It should be remembered that our Defence Force met the

Soviet Union's warriors in Angola. Given that country's criminal record and ambitions of world dominance, a decision to use a nuclear bomb or two in Angola would probably not have troubled its conscience too much.

Considering all that had taken place, South Africa therefore had to prepare itself for the possible use of Soviet nuclear weapons during the military struggle for Southern Africa. If this possibility had been ignored, the results of an unexpected nuclear assault could have had unpredictable consequences for the SA Defence Force and the inhabitants of the region.

I am still of the opinion that, given the circumstances of the time, and in view of the undesirable presence of the unpredictable and highhanded Soviet Union in this geographic region, the decision made by the South African government with regard to the development of nuclear weapons for defensive purposes was the correct one. The decision was also made at the right time.

I have already mentioned that after I retired from public life, I received countless enquiries and requests for interviews regarding South Africa's nuclear weapons programme. In order not to impact on the credibility of the Defence Force in this regard, I accepted requests for interviews and answered these questions. The information regarding the development of arms by South Africa and its nuclear programme that I provided at that stage, is repeated in this book.

In such interviews I usually left it to the person concerned to state his or her requests. Usually they wanted to know why South Africa felt it necessary to have a nuclear capability, and why South Africa developed the capability completely on its own.

In order to understand the interviewer's life experience and to gauge his or her exposure to the determination of a country's arms requirements and needs, I usually asked a counter-question, more or less in the following vein: "Have you ever been involved in the decision-making process where the defence requirements or needs of your country, or any other country, was determined?" Predictably the answer is always no, because nobody who has ever been involved in such a complex process would seek information about weapons from somebody else!

I would then ask what value one can attach to the judgement, pronouncements or views of such a person who has no practical knowledge, experience or exposure with regard to the intricate process for determining a country's defence requirements or survival needs.

The conversation then usually ends with me explaining that determining a developing country's defence requirements or national security needs is the result of intense and complex research by experts. It certainly is not a simplistic process of hit and miss.

A balanced, flexible end-product requires a co-ordinated effort, in which various factors need to be taken into account. The country's national strategy is included; the analysis of the threat to the country, including the nature and probability of this threat, measured in time-scales; the country's technological development; the quality and quantity of the available manpower; the funds available for national security; affordability; the available production and maintenance facilities; defence treaties, etcetera. After a discussion of the factors that relate to South Africa in particular, the interviewer usually would be satisfied, and I received many letters of appreciation for the interview.

Chapter 14

ARMSCOR, THE OTHER MEMBER OF THE DEFENCE FAMILY

THE ARMAMENTS CORPORATION (ARMSCOR)

Because of their close co-operation and mutual support, the Defence Force and Armscor were collectively known as the "Defence Family". In difficult circumstances these two organisations depended on each other to function well, and together they made a formidable combination. It is therefore appropriate to devote a chapter to Armscor too, because without Armscor's support the Defence Force would not have been able to fulfil its role so successfully.

My first actual direct contact with Armscor occurred when I, as a member of the Defence Force, was appointed *ex officio* to the Board of Armscor. This was just before Armscor was reorganised in order to achieve greater efficiency. My appointment gave me a good opportunity to become acquainted with Armscor's staff and functioning.

Later, when I was Minister of Defence, Armscor became one of my responsibilities. Armscor, in turn, was responsible for acquiring, delivering and developing arms for the Defence Force. The international arms embargo imposed on South Africa meant that Armscor was the Defence Force's main source of weaponry. Armscor carried out this responsibility successfully and with passion, innovative thinking and action, with dedication and boldness – usually in difficult circumstances.[1]

Resolution 418 of the Security Council of the former United Nations

Organisation (UNO – today known as the United Nations or UN) was adopted on 4 November 1977. It compelled member countries to cease all exports and deliveries of arms and other military equipment to South Africa. This was the beginning of mandatory arms sanctions against South Africa.[2]

Although various countries had previously imposed voluntary arms sanctions, these sanctions could in most cases be regarded as a political pretence. With a few exceptions, it had still been possible to obtain arms freely from certain Western countries. However, the UNO resolution changed this situation drastically, and the international community now conscientiously tried to apply this mandatory international arms boycott.

The mandatory arms boycott was imposed to prevent South Africa from importing any weapons and ammunition from abroad, in other words to create a situation in which the government of the day would not have the necessary weapons and ammunition to defend the country. It would therefore also not be able to defend its citizens against a possible bloodbath.

However, in the long term the international arms sanctions held advantages rather than disadvantages for South Africa, as it forced the country to become almost completely self-sufficient with regard to arms. This progress was not limited to the development and manufacture of arms, as other areas also benefited from these developments.

The achievement of self-sufficiency in arms provision and the concomitant development of the technological skills required to do so, places a country on a different level when it is judged internationally in a military sense. The outside world cannot easily prescribe to or blackmail a country with such abilities. It is not possible to apply political pressure by means of possible arms sanctions or security threats on such a country. Self-sufficiency therefore guarantees internal political independence, and negates any coercion. This technological development had positive as well as negative implications for South Africa's international relations. For example, one of the negative implications was that if only a small number of items were required, it was usually far more expensive and time-consuming to manufacture them than buying an existing product.[3]

Many interesting incidents regarding the import and export of arms to and from South Africa occurred during the years of the arms embargo. However, because the sword of amnesty and punitive economic measures still hangs over the heads of those who helped South Africa in its struggle, these stories cannot be told. One also needs to take into account the effect such revelations could have on international relations with certain other countries. In order to give the reader an idea of the challenges and problems of those times, I will therefore mention only a few well-known cases that cannot cause further damage.

By the mid-1970s international pressure was increasingly being applied to certain countries to impose arms sanctions against South Africa. After a thorough investigation it was decided that the two arms organisations that had supplied the Security Forces with weapons up to that time should be amalgamated into one organisation. This resulted in the creation of the Armaments Corporation of South Africa, or Armscor. From 1977 onwards the arms procurement and manufacturing functions would be combined.[4]

This reorganisation was aimed at giving the private sector a more active role, and ensuring that South Africa would become self-sufficient with regard to arms as soon as possible. In order to accomplish this task according to a wide variety of arms requirements, 800 private contractors were involved in supporting arms manufacture – apart from the eight Armscor subsidiaries.[5]

In order to perform this huge task successfully, energetic and formidable people were utilised in various capacities in Armscor. We still owe these top businessmen and businesswomen our thanks for their selfless service. These persons included some who may not necessarily have agreed with the Government's policies, but were of the opinion that political change in South Africa should be evolutionary, not revolutionary, and for this reason wanted to help.

Following the Armscor reorganisation, "Commandant" Piet Marais was appointed as Chairman of the corporation. "Commandant" was actually a nickname dating back to his early commando days in De Aar. His actual rank in the Commando Force was colonel. Incidentally, he was such a fine commando commander that when I was in charge of South-West Africa Command I always used his commando as a role model.

Commandant Piet Marais, Chairman of Armscor.

The uninitiated may find it strange that a farmer was appointed as chairman of a corporation that required so much military expertise and business acumen. Piet Marais was a rare phenomenon, much like Gen. Christiaan de Wet or Louis Botha: a farmer with a natural military talent, coupled with business acumen, a sharp mind and sophistication – a completely bilingual farmer's son. South Africa owes him much gratitude for his wonderful contribution.[6]

Thanks to sound relations between the Defence Force and Armscor, I began referring to these two organisations as the "Defence Family", and the term soon gained currency. Armscor turned all Defence Force requirements into specifications, and these were handed over to the suppliers who had to develop and manufacture the particular products. Armscor then controlled the quality of the products.[7]

After the official approval of the arms sanctions against South Africa, it was our highest priority to make sure that local arms production would succeed. Much progress had already been made in this regard, but no country on earth is completely self-sufficient and completely independent with regard to arms. The second priority, namely to procure any weapons that we could not manufacture ourselves from some other source, was thankfully also on track by this time, and led to some interesting but nail-biting incidents.[8]

During the struggle period members of Armscor and its subsidiaries were active abroad, trying to find ways around the embargo. At times they were exposed to nerve-wracking and even life-threatening situations that was often comparable to those of spies. For example, four Armscor employees, the so-called "Coventry Four", were arrested by the

Commander Viljoen and his officers ready to take command of the first corvette, *SAS Good Hope*, after the corvette had been taken into service on 17 September 1977. The French were actually guilty of breach of contract when they decided not to complete this naval order, and declared South Africa's deposit forfeited

British police while they were trying to circumvent the arms boycott, and ended up in a British jail.

In the early 1970s the SA Navy wanted to augment their vessels with French products. To this end Armscor had - long before the UNO arms embargo - placed orders for two French Agosta submarines and four corvettes. The French demanded a prepayment of about R120 million; the money was paid, shipbuilding commenced and was far advanced by 1977.

Even though UNO arms sanctions were in the air, the French indicated in July 1977 that they would still complete this naval order, but a few months later they announced that they would no longer deliver the vessels, and that the money that had already been paid would be declared forfeited. The reason for this only became apparent later: they had incorrectly translated a UNO resolution, and only discovered this after the decision to cancel had been taken and made public.

At this stage more than a hundred South African crew members were in France, becoming acquainted with the vessels. In fact the first corvette was already undergoing sea trials under the command of Cmdr Flip Viljoen.

However, the French feared that the South African crew, on learning that the French would no longer honour their contract, would seize the corvette, and therefore told the crew that South Africa had cancelled the contract. The French went even further and gave orders for a blockade of the entrance to the Toulon harbour to prevent the South Africans from manning the ships and slipping out to sea. Israel had recently had a similar experience with France but the Israelis took possession of the vessels which they had bought, slipped out of the harbour and caused the French acute international embarrassment.

What was to be done to prevent the loss of these millions of rands? Our international standing was so low that nobody wanted to help us. Dr Brand Fourie, the then Secretary of Foreign Affairs, was the doyen of the State's heads of department, and was also very wise and helpful, so I went to see him. He listened attentively and immediately suggested that we call in Dr Kobus Loubser, head of the erstwhile South African Railways and Harbours, and Mr Louis Rive, head of the Postal Service, for advice. These heavyweights in Government administration were willing to listen to my story, and equally willing to do all in their power to help solve the problem.

Both bodies which these gentlemen headed, were about to place large orders worth hundreds of millions of rands abroad, and France and Germany were the two contending countries. They undertook to inform the French very cordially that no future transactions with that country would be considered unless Armscor's prepayment was reimbursed. Of course the French hastily paid up. (Because the French franc appreciated strongly against the rand in this period, South Africa even showed a profit on the deal.)

This incident gained even more importance when the heads of various Government departments suddenly realised that, due to the prevailing circumstances, they had to act in greater concert. I therefore launched a team-building plan. The departments that helped to increase the efficiency of the Defence Force and Armscor and with which we needed to liaise closely, were invited on annual visits to remote Defence Force areas in order to improve communication and mutual understanding. Dr Piet Rautenbach, then Chairman of the Public Service Commission, and various auditors-general, gave these efforts their strong support, and it was quite clear that management benefited from them.

The foreign embargos not only thrusted South Africa in the direction of its own arms industry, but practical experience, as shown in this example, pointed to shortcomings in the Government's management style, and it was necessary to take action and make plans with regard to both the management style and the manufacture of weapons.[9]

One of the greatest deficiencies that was demonstrated to the artillery corps in military operations was the lack of a suitable artillery piece and an inefficient artillery system.

The Defence Force was equipped with British 140 mm (5.5 inch) towed guns, dating back to World War II. The enemy forces (Cubans in this case) had Soviet guns of similar calibre. The big difference was that the South African guns had a shorter range than those of the enemy. This was a serious disadvantage, because in certain circumstances the enemy could rain their gun fire on us, while we could not reach them with ours.

Despite this weakness, the greater skills of our artillerymen gave them the upper hand over the enemy in life-threatening circumstances, thanks to the excellent service provided at all times by the gun crews and forward observation officers. Despite their lack of experience, the young national service gun crews displayed excellent skills and dedication.

Another deficiency in our equipment revealed by the artillery support fire, was our lack of a rocket system. The enemy had the top Russian Katyusha 122 mm mobile rocket launcher (Stalin Organ or Red Eye), but thankfully they employed these systems badly. We did not have an efficient counter to the world-renowned Stalin Organ, and this created an untenable situation. It was difficult to neutralise this rocket capability by concentrating fire on the enemy in a short period of time.

After Operation Savannah, the Defence Force urgently requested Armscor to find a solution for the lack of suitable artillery pieces and rocket systems.

Within a relatively short time the manufacturers rectified our lack of

The Bateleur rocket system. Armscor developed the Valkiri 127 mm artillery rocket system as a counter for the Russian Stalin organ that the Cubans used in Angola. The Bateleur rocket system was then developed from the Valkiri. This gave the SA Army the upper hand against the enemy with regard to rockets.

rockets, with the result that our rocket capability matched or even exceeded the capabilities of the Russian Stalin Organ. The Valkiri 127 mm rocket system developed by Armscor more than held its own against the Stalin Organ. This system was later upgraded and developed into the Bateleur rocket system, probably one of Armscor's most successful weapon systems.

In order to meet the short-term challenge of the artillery, it was decided to buy a number of guns and the required ammunition abroad. However, it was somewhat more difficult to meet the need for long-range artillery.

We then investigated the possibilities of developing a capability that would meet the long-term need locally. Such an undertaking would take a great deal of time, as many factors would have to be taken into account. First, one would have to determine whether South Africa had the technological capability, equipment and skills to take on such an exacting task, taking into account that South Africa had never attempted something like this before.

By using existing intelligence channels (and with considerable luck and innovation), feelers were put out to certain Western weapons experts, and our efforts were rewarded: we found sympathetic ears and a willingness to help South Africa.

After further intensive research, extensive discussions and deliberations, it was decided to approach a certain private company represented in various countries, amongst others the United States, Canada, Belgium and the West Indies. This company, Space Research Corporation (SRC), headed by Dr G.V. Bull, was involved in the development of a so-called "space gun", a very large artillery piece. The company was a direct outcome of the American Space Research Programme. The giant gun's barrel was 52 m in length and it had a diameter of 40 cm. It could reportedly fire a projectile to a height of 185 km and the American and Canadian defence forces reportedly showed great interest in this development.

As an interesting footnote, there were rumours that during preparations for the USA's "Desert Storm" war against Iraq, this giant "space gun" was actually being manufactured for Iraq, to be used against Israel, and Dr Bull was killed by an assassin in Brussels at this time. The guilty party was never found, and one can only speculate about which secret service was responsible.

There were discussions between SRC and a representative Defence Force/Armscor team in South Africa in February 1976. During these negotiations it was agreed that the South African team would buy ten used M2 155 mm Long Tom guns with sufficient ammunition from SRC. The deal would at the same time open up research opportunities for Armscor. At that stage SRC was concentrating on research into and the development of ammunition.

The successful negotiations and the agreement reached subsequently resulted in an excellent long-term commitment between the two parties. South Africa also profited considerably in the technological field.

Furthermore SRC indicated that they could deliver a projectile with a range of more than 25 km within nine months. The ten Long Toms would be delivered in various calibres: a 155 mm calibre with a firing range of about 27 km, and a 175 mm calibre with a firing range of about 43 km.

In view of the danger of transporting filled projectiles, and as Sonchem, a subsidiary of Armscor in South Africa, manufactured excellent projectile propellants, the projectiles were transported to South Africa as empty shells. Because of the sensitivity of the project, and in order to avoid the media bloodhounds, this consignment of artillery pieces and empty projectiles was disassembled, painted yellow, packed and marked as road building plant and tractor parts, and transported by ship via the West Indies.

The transfer operation almost foundered because an SRC employee who spoke Flemish overheard two people talking about the ruse used to cover up this consignment to South Africa. Fortunately we suspected the leak, and arrangements were quickly made for a South African shipping line to accept the transportation in one of our own vessels.

The SRC employee did however inform the Canadian police of the clandestine operation aimed at circumventing the arms sanctions. The police did their duty conscientiously, arrived at the harbour of St John and opened one of the crates. Seeing only yellow metal parts, and assuming that they were destined for road construction, they accepted that the informant had misled them, and allowed the consignment to continue on its way to South Africa. Eventually this "road construction equipment" would become known in the Defence Force as the G3 gun.

A few months later we accepted SRC's generous offer of help with the development and modification of a certain American medium gun. The end product would be used to mount another type of American medium gun. By taking part in this process, South Africa would reach parity with artillery development in the Western world. The experiment would be undertaken with the full co-operation of the Defence Force and Armscor, and on completion, 32 of the modified guns would be delivered to South Africa within twelve months.

It was an extraordinary offer by SRC, which paved the way for exceptional advances by the South African arms industry. Participation in the initial development of a modified gun laid the groundwork for the local development and manufacture of the South African G5 gun.

Initially SRC was principally interested in research, and not so much in the military application of the product in various circumstances. It was therefore essential to place a South African team with SRC on a full-time basis in order to ensure that the proposed projects would be conducted strictly according to our needs. To be placed in this unique position was a great compliment to our arms industry, and as far as the development of the end product was concerned, it meant that we were able to ensure delivery of only the best to meet our needs.

Exposure and training also gave us the opportunity to gain extensive knowledge with regard to the following: artillery designs, qualification of ammunition and the development of ballistic systems, including modern artillery projectiles, artillery fuses and control systems.

SRC even indicated that they were willing to develop a new gun up to the prototype level in co-operation with South Africa. Of course Armscor accepted the offer willingly, because direct involvement in the development of such a gun was urgently required at that stage. Such an agreement meant that South Africa could attempt to include locally manufactured components in the final design. In terms of the co-operation agreement, SRC would take responsibility for providing a package of technical data, a prototype and a manufacturing plan.

The agreement also provided for the establishment of production facilities in South Africa, and delivery of a prototype before March 1978.

The entire development process significantly increased the risk of security breaches. A large number of increased range projectiles had to be transported by ship, and this involved extensive handling activities; among other things, there had to be quality control testing on the firing of these projectiles before they reached the end-user destination.

Foreign politicians hostile to South Africa eagerly sniffed out any information regarding possible boycott circumventions. The publication of sensational allegations of illicit arms transactions meant that South Africa was constantly in the crossfire. Many of these reports were frighteningly close to the mark.

The shipping routes used for transporting this type of equipment were changed regularly. Diversionary relations were formed with other countries - at great cost - in order to limit the possibility of security leaks. A great deal of time and money was spent on this aspect, but it was definitely worth it. If the mutual agreements were to become public, the countries and persons concerned would have encountered enormous problems.

In order to limit such problems, a decision was made in 1977 to test artillery ammunition in South Africa. The country's technological expertise and production capacity had developed so rapidly that it was decided to develop and manufacture the ammunition and the gun locally.

The development of this G5 155 mm gun put South Africa at the forefront of international astillery technology. This is a towed gun-howitzer with an auxiliary engine which enables it to move more easily if required, and to take up its position quickly. The gun can go into action in less than two minutes. The technological expertise gained from manufacturing the G6 gun in South Africa led to the local development and manufacture of the G6 gun.

The highly mobile, self-propelled G6 155 mm gun can be in action 60 seconds after it has come to a standstill, and move again 30 seconds after having fired. It carries 45 projectiles, and has a firing range of up to 53 km. The G6 has a maximum speed of 85 km/h.

In 1978 the project was taken further with the decision to start local production of the self-propelled or motorised G6 155 mm gun. Both the G5 and G6 were great successes, and are now offered for sale worldwide. In this unique way South Africa was able to progress to the forefront of artillery development. These guns are exceptional because they were tested in battle, and clearly proved their superiority.

The first 15 production models were completed in 1979, and the first G5 artillery battery was battle-ready in 1980. Initially the gun had a firing range of only about 28 km, but subsequent refinements and development of the ammunition increased this distance to about 40 km, and even 50 km, depending on the type of projectile.

Some of the Armscor members who were active in various countries with different customs and value systems often had to learn how to approach situations and circumstances outside the limits of normal South

African patterns of thinking and behaviour. For example, they had to find a market for locally manufactured G5 and G6 guns, but in the target country it was customary to provide backhanders at the various levels of the approval process to ensure a smooth purchasing process. Such an approach would immediately have been branded as bribery in South Africa.

Armscor had approached me beforehand to make a decision, and after thinking it through thoroughly, I said "yes". This approval applied only to countries where such fees were customary, but my authorisation was always required, and Armscor still had the accounting responsibility. Defence Force members abroad who found themselves in similar circumstances were also given permission – with the same conditions.

Other locally manufactured equipment that made an important contribution to the conflict include the following: the Ratel fighting vehicle, the *Drakensberg* replenishment vessel, the Seeker reconnaissance aircraft, the Cheetah multi-purpose fighter plane, the Namacurra, the Rooikat armoured car and the Olifant tank. (Armscor actually manufactured many other weapons, equipment and ammunition locally that are not mentioned in this book.)[10]

SAS *Drakensberg* was the SA Navy's high-technology replenishment vessel launched on 24 April 1986. It is the largest vessel yet developed and built for the Navy in South Africa, using local expertise.

The "Seeker". This unmanned locally manufactured reconnaissance aircraft can operate up to 250 km from its base. It can carry out reconnaissance tasks directly by means of television cameras, or be utilised for directing artillery fire.

The Cheetah was a complete upgrade of the SA Air Force's obsolete fleet of Mirage III aircraft. These aircraft were introduced in 1986. The deployment of the MiG-23 in Angola overshadowed the 20-year old Mirage III, and consequently the Cheetah – an upgraded Mirage III which had reached half of its life expectancy – was developed. In actual fact the Cheetah was a new multi-purpose fighter more than capable of meeting the MiG-23 threat. The Cheetah represented a milestone in the development of the South African aircraft industry, as it not only created an opportunity for this industry to upgrade aircraft, but also to develop completely new ones.

ARMSCOR

The SA Navy's Namacurras on harbour patrol.

The Rooikat is South Africa's high-mobility armoured car, equipped with a 76 mm anti-tank gun. It has a top road speed of 120 km/h, and a top cross-country speed of 50 km/h.

Missile technology was not the only field in which South Africa's electronic industry excelled; it also proved its worth in telecommunications. As South Africa's defence electronic industry grew, it developed from the ability to manufacture radio sets, including the design, development and manufacture of the entire range of electronic equipment required by modern combat forces. This included electronic counter-measures and counter-counter-measures, radar sets, artillery computers, combat information systems, navigation systems, command and control centres, avionics systems and even meteorological equipment. It is quite remarkable that the successes of this industry depended on a relatively small group of enthusiastic and hard-working people who laid the foundations for an industry that stood at the forefront of high technology in South Africa.

These locally manufactured South African arms were used to great effect in Angola to halt and reverse the thrust and aggression of the communist forces against the SA Defence Force. To quote Commandant Piet Marais: "South Africa can be proud of the weapons it tested during recent attacks in Angola. They were superb!"

The fall of the Berlin Wall at the end of 1989, and the withdrawal of the Soviet Union and Cuban troops from Africa, brought about the prospect of a peace agreement between the South African Government and the ANC Alliance. This meant that the SA Defence Force's demand for arms and finances would begin to decline. This coincided with an international decline in military needs, because the end of the Cold War meant that a surplus of arms began to appear on the world markets.

Taking into account the above-mentioned events and the new era of international politics in the wake of the capitulation of international communism, I was compelled to recommend to the Cabinet that funds earmarked for the Department of Defence should be cut. The Cabinet approved these recommendations.[11]

Together with the approved cuts, which would have a decisive influence on the future Defence Force and Armscor, the Cabinet also accepted the following deductions:
- It was highly unlikely that South Africa would be exposed to a conventional military onslaught in the next 25 years.
- It should be accepted that arms sanctions against South Africa would be lifted within four years, which meant that South Africa

would then have access to the world's arms markets. If sanctions were to continue after this period, Armscor would have to increase its rate of weapons production, and the Government would have to approve additional finances for this purpose.
- Due to the current situation, arms projects and delivery would be scaled back, but not ended abruptly. The scaling back or closure of certain activities would have to be executed in the national interest, and in such a way that it would not cost the country more in the long term than the temporary savings. This would mean that each project and congruent expenditure would have to be analysed individually in order to make the best decision in the circumstances.

Due to the decline in the local military threat and other factors, I decided in 1990-1991, after thorough consultation and planning, that Armscor would have to undergo certain structural changes. This was necessary in order to ensure that this organisation would be able to keep pace with rapidly changing international conditions which created new arms needs.

The changes at Armscor were meant to ensure that South Africa would retain its technological advantage in certain fields and in so doing help to stimulate the national economy. At the same time arms exports to certain markets had to be expanded in order to limit local job losses to the minimum.

The main goal was to convert the arms industry from a manufacturer of military products only into a manufacturer of all types of equip-ment. This would enable Armscor to use technology and innovation to increase its share of the international market. In 1991 I therefore gave instructions that Armscor should be split into two independent organisations. The industrial company, Denel, was therefore erected in 1992. This company would be able to manufacture both military and commercial products.

The acquisition function would remain Armscor's responsibility. Armscor retained its name and would continue providing the Defence Force with weapons and equipment according to agreed specifications. It would also be responsible for administering contracts, and applying quality control.

This new division of work or responsibility was aimed at retaining certain technological knowledge and skills for the country, and making

The Rooivalk, which can compete with the best in the world.

the expertise previously built up by Armscor available for application by the private sector. At the same time it would ensure that the Security Forces received adequate arms and equipment.

Early on during the war in Angola the SA Air Force identified the need for a sophisticated combat-support helicopter. The Rooivalk is certainly one of the most challenging projects ever undertaken by Armscor, the SA Air Force and the private sector. This highly mobile attack helicopter was introduced in 1990. Its armament consists of two types of missiles and two types of rockets, and it has three different types of night vision sensors, which means that all its weapons can be used at night.

One of the greatest challenges facing Armscor and the Defence Force, prior to and during the mandatory United Nations Organisation arms sanctions, was secretly transferring funds from South Africa abroad. These funds also had to be shuffled about abroad to make sure that they could not be traced back to South Africa.

The development of modern methods, techniques and aids has made it easy to trace the origin of funds, and their foreign destination. It took much thinking to circumvent this tracing ability.

In the military world it is of great importance to prevent other countries, intelligence agencies and hostile elements from knowing when and where a country is satisfying its arms needs abroad. Should this information be made public, enemy elements could ascertain certain weaknesses in such purchases, and use this knowledge to their own advantage on the battlefield. If it had become general knowledge that South Africa was developing an artillery system, everybody would know that the Defence Force was vulnerable with regard to supporting fire.

In South Africa's case, it could also undermine all future arms purchases and sales, as various techniques for circumventing normal purchasing channels would also be revealed. This could seriously damage international relations in other areas, such as the economy, politics and diplomacy.

Hostile countries and elements therefore regarded it as of prime importance to know how and for what purpose funds left the country, and where these were headed. Armscor and the Defence Force therefore had to be very cautious, and make sure that this information did not leak out.

I measure the success of Armscor's work against the resolutions taken by an outside body such as the UN. The first mandatory international UN resolution was aimed at preventing South Africa from importing any arms or ammunition from abroad. However, as the war raged on, and Armscor and the private sector used their ingenuity to ensure greater arms independence for the country, South Africa was actually able to export arms to foreign countries. The result was that the UN warned the international community that because of Armscor's successes, the situation in South Africa had changed. Now countries had to be certain not to buy or import arms from South Africa. This success by Armscor brought about the adoption of Resolution 558 by the Security Council of UNO on 13 December 1984, preventing member countries from importing arms from South Africa. This really is an indirect feather in Armscor's cap!

Chapter 15

ADAPTING TO MY NEW POSITION AS MINISTER OF DEFENCE

PARTY POLITICS

I was appointed as Minister of Defence in 1980 in somewhat unusual circumstances. Some time after Mr P.W. Botha, who had been the Minister of Defence, succeeded Mr B.J. Vorster as Prime Minister in 1978, he gave me a list of the names of three people he was considering as successors to his previous position. He asked me who would be acceptable to both the Defence Force and Armscor, but I looked at the list and said I did not think any one of the three would fit the organisation like a glove. His reaction was: "In that case you will have to do the job." I never had an ambition or longing for any involvement in party politics in the country. The good news was that this appointment would give me the opportunity to remain in touch with the Defence Force and national security. I would not have considered accepting a position in the Cabinet if it did not involve the Defence Force.

Another reason why I was willing to consider the appointment favourably was the clear indication of dissatisfaction among certain rightist elements within the National Party at the time, who would not recognise that political reform was essential. From experience I knew that South Africa could not afford or permit this type of political dissatisfaction to penetrate its Defence Force. Strong convictions and leadership were therefore still necessary in this regard. Given this potential source

My wife and I positively and gladly accept the new responsibility assigned to me.

of conflict or dissatisfaction, I was not certain that a new Minister of Defence, while trying to make his mark in party politics, would or could maintain the accepted principle that the main aim of the Defence Force was to protect the constitution. This aim was of prime importance to me, and I was convinced that there was a high probability that the opposite could occur. If I were to accept this position, I would have the opportunity to ensure that the Defence Force remained detached from politics, not allowing itself to be drawn into politics as had been the case in the 1950s. This is why I was willing to accept the appointment, and the challenges associated with it, as a special privilege.[1]

Personally I wanted to maintain the culture, thought, methods of working and conduct of the Defence Force. P.W. Botha had been an excellent Minister of Defence, and I would have to do my very utmost to fill his shoes, but I resolved that the appointment should not change me as a person.

I also resolved not to take the easy route of becoming a nominated Member of Parliament without a constituency. I wanted to represent a constituency in Parliament, so that I could fulfil my duties towards the voters in a practical way. This would also afford me the opportunity of establishing how the voters, who played an important role in Defence Force matters, felt about issues.[2]

The constituency of Modderfontein on the East Rand asked me to represent them, and I accepted. Mr Ben Smith chaired the District Divisional Council, and the two of us organised and intensively canvassed the constituency. As a result this constituency was awarded most of the trophies at the annual Transvaal Provincial Congress of the National Party year after year. Trophies for the best-organised constituency; the constituency with the most paid-up members; the constituency that collected the most funds for the National Party; and many other awards were won.

Fortunately I had already experienced many stormy years in the field of security before my appointment as the new Minister of Defence on 7 October 1980, so I was thoroughly prepared for the many stormy years that were likely to lie ahead!

However, there was another field of responsibility that I would quickly have to master, and that was Parliamentary responsibilities and public political appearances. After much deliberation I wisely decided to go against the generally accepted practice, and to prepare notes for all speeches I delivered in public. Preparing for speeches in this way was intended to prevent me from falling into a political or security trap, and it helped a great deal. For example when murder charges were pending against me in the KwaMakutha case, the Attorney General officially warned me to be ready to answer or elucidate, in cross-examination, any questions or statements regarding the contents of any speech I may have made during my career as member of the Defence Force or as Minister. At that moment I was very pleased that I decided all those years ago to prepare my speeches in a way that would prevent me from making emotionally loose, irresponsible or rash statements in public that could later land me in hot water.

It is difficult for me to judge objectively how well I adapted to Parliamentary duties. I would rather present a quotation from a comment made by a sympathetic newspaper soon after the commencement of my Parliamentary career: "It was an impressive debut ... As a seasoned military man he has probably experienced far more dangerous situations than a defence debate, so he was in full control from the start ... his approach was calm and explanatory. Members of the House of Assembly listened in absolute silence as he sketched the extent of the onslaught" (Willie Kühn, *Die Burger,* 25 September 1981) [my translation]. This more or less reflected the opinion of most of the media at the time.

AN EVENT THAT SHOULD NEVER HAVE HAPPENED

The process of finding my feet in my new capacity had hardly started when there was a controversial, what could almost be called a "James Bond"-like event which involved the government of the Seychelles and eventually the Defence Force as well.

A group of mercenaries assembled in Johannesburg on 24 November 1981 and departed from the Matsapa Airport in Swaziland on 25 November in a 60-seater F28 Fokker aircraft of Royal Swazi National Airways. The leader of this group was "Mad Mike" Hoare, who had awarded himself the rank of "Colonel". At that stage he was apparently employed as accountant in Hilton near Pietermaritzburg in Natal. The mission's goal was to overthrow Pres. Albert René of the Seychelles in a coup d'etat.

The 92 islands making up the Seychelles are situated in the Indian Ocean east of Kenya and Tanzania. The islands situated furthest from one another are about 1000 km apart, and the main island of Mahé is only about 40 km long and 12 km wide. The island group formed part of the British Empire from about the 17th century, and was granted independence only in 1976. Its first President was James Mancham, and its Prime Minister was Albert René. Mancham wished to retain close relations with Britain, while René was a proponent of communistic African socialism.

Eleven months after independence, while he was on a visit to England, Mancham was overthrown by René in a coup d'etat. Mancham and his Cabinet members were banished from the country, and all their properties and possessions were confiscated. A new Cabinet consisting of Marxist Soviet sympathisers was constituted.

René instituted martial law in 1979 because he was expecting former Seychelles residents to attempt an overthrow of his regime from Durban, and more than 50 islanders were arrested.

Hoare attempted a coup d'etat at midnight on 25 November 1981 but failed, and the Hoare mercenaries then hijacked an Air India aircraft that had landed after dark on Mahé. The pilot was forced to fly to Durban, and this fuelled rumours that the South African government had been involved in the attempted coup. The Government, however, immediately denied having been a part of it, or having given permission for the attempt.

With regard to any involvement of the Defence Force in this affair, the following should be noted: In about July 1981 a high-level member of the National Intelligence Service (NI) contacted the SA Defence Force's Military Intelligence Division (MID). Apparently the idea existed that if the Marxist government of the Seychelles could be overthrown successfully, South Africa's landing rights there would be restored, it could be used as a listening post for monitoring Soviet fleet movements in the Indian Ocean, and South Africa could possibly win the support of anti-communist governments in the Organisation of African Unity (OAU). The NI member was apparently instructed by his employer to hand over to the Defence Force an operation they were planning in the Seychelles in co-operation with Mike Hoare. Written permission for the operation had apparently already been received at the political level.

Documentary evidence of approval for the operation was requested, and the NI member undertook to bring this along on his next visit to the MID. The NI furthermore requested the Defence Force to supply weapons that would be needed for the coup as soon as possible. The Seychelles resistance movement would supply the money needed for the operation.

Hoare, who had been waiting outside the office while the discussions were taking place, was then called in to explain in broad terms the planning he and his group had done. The plan was to bring the arms required for the operation to South Africa. These would have to be smuggled in from elsewhere, or otherwise acquired in South Africa. The NI could not supply the weapons, so the Defence Force's help was needed. The plan was to send the weapons to the Seychelles as soon as possible aboard a yacht that was being purchased. The resistance movement would take possession of the weapons and equipment in the Seychelles and store them until the Hoare mercenaries could assist in staging the coup. As soon as the weapons and equipment had been transported to the Seychelles in the yacht, the Hoare group of mercenaries would travel there by air in smaller groups.

The Defence Force listened to this plan and set the following conditions: the NI had to supply the document of approval; no Defence Force members were to be involved in the operation; and the weapons would be supplied when the yacht had been bought and was available. Hoare and the NI member then left.

Shortly after the initial visit, Hoare and the NI member informed the MID that the yacht had been purchased and was ready, and that it was essential that the requested weapons should be supplied as soon as possible, so that the yacht could depart. Hoare was then visited in Hilton in order to inspect the facilities at his disposal, and to go through the rest of the plans with him in greater detail. In order to give members of his expedition the opportunity to shoot in the weapons and to ready accoutrements before packing them for transport by yacht, they were delivered to Hoare's house shortly after this visit.

Not long after the delivery of the weapons and equipment, the MID was informed that the purchase of the yacht had not been concluded, and that another plan had to be devised. Hoare subsequently submitted various plans to the MID, but none of them were regarded as likely to succeed. On each occasion Hoare was asked to change these plans and to come up with a workable plan for the operation.

In the meantime the MID made contact with the Seychelles resistance movement, as the MID doubted that Hoare was capable of executing his planned task. It was then suggested that a more suitable and capable person should be found, and a Frenchman was suggested, but the MID later heard that this person's fees were evidently unaffordable.

The plan to fly to the Seychelles as members of one or other "Order of the Froth Blowers" (beer drinkers) was not approved, and at this stage

Hoare was informed that the whole idea of a coup may have to be called off. Documentary evidence of the NI's approval for the attempt had not been received yet either. It was also learnt that the original NI member who had suggested that the MID should support the Seychelles coup had in the meantime been dismissed from the NI.

At this stage Hoare slipped away without the permission or support of either the MID or the NI, and went ahead with the coup attempt, followed by the hijacking of the Air India aircraft. Subsequent to Hoare's failed coup, contact was made with the Seychelles resistance movement, and it was established that they, too, were completely unaware that such an attempt was planned, with or without the support of the MID. It has been suggested that the NI member had become impatient with the MID's dragging its feet and had given Hoare the green light to go ahead with the attempt.

News of the failed coup d'etat and the hijacking of an Air India aircraft first came when Jan Smuts Airport (Johannesburg) informed Louis Botha Airport (Durban) that an Air India aircraft had deviated towards Durban because of mechanical problems. It was suspected that there were hijackers on board.

The flight landed in Durban just after 05:00. Hoare and his men – about 40 in number – were arrested and taken to the Waterkloof Air Force Base in a Hercules C-130 of the SA Air Force, and from there were taken to the Zonderwater prison.

The case was heard in the Natal Supreme Court on 10 March 1982 before Mr Justice James and two assessors. Judgement was given on 27 July 1982. Judge James found that the manner in which the defendants had reached the Seychelles and had left it again formed the main issue, and that all other charges were only peripheral.[3]

The court dismissed all allegations of involvement by the South African Government and determined that most of Hoare's evidence regarding individuals and Government departments was unfounded. In general he was also not found to be a reliable witness. He had been supplied with weapons by MID officers, but the court found that they had not been aware of his plans, and that they had not offered him any active support or help.

I can only state that this attempted coup d'etat had never been discussed in or approved by the Cabinet or State Security Council prior to the attempt.[4] The entire incident occurred quite suddenly, and had cost a great deal of effort and sweat. Following a thorough Defence Force inquiry, certain adjustments were made to prevent anything similar from occurring in future.

DEFENCE FORCE OPERATIONS, 1981-1984

Military operations in South-West Africa/Namibia and Angola from 1981 to 1984 presented the Defence Force with the most varied and intense challenges, as it found itself fighting conventional enemy forces, guerrilla groups and terrorists bands. Various operations were launched, severally and jointly, mainly against the forces and capabilities of the Soviet Union, Cuba, East Germany, the MPLA and SWAPO. The best way to assess how well the Defence Force executed its primary responsibilities up to the conclusion of the "Peace of Namibia", is to look at the outcome of the Defence Force actions and battles in this period.

Perhaps we should therefore return to the challenge faced by the Defence Force in South-West Africa/Namibia, with a new but extremely competent Chief of the Defence Force, Gen. Constand Viljoen, and myself, as a novice, the new Minister of Defence.

I will discuss only one or two of the many military operations, and name the others merely for the sake of completeness. They were Operation Carnation (July 1981), Operation Protea (August 1981), Operation Daisy (October-November 1981), Operation Super (May 1982), Operation Meebos (July 1982), Operation Phoenix (February 1983) and Operation Askari (December 1983-January 1984). During each of these operations the Defence Force, without exception, gave SWAPO's military wing (People's Liberation Army of Namibia or PLAN) a thorough beating. (Willem Steenkamp offers an excellent overview of the military operations in South-West Africa/Namibia in his publications *Borderstrike* (1983) and *South Africa's Border War 1966-1989* (1989).

Terrorist activities in South-West Africa/Namibia increased in 1981, and consequently Operation Carnation was launched in the area immediately north of the Ovambo border in Angola on July 1981; about

200 terrorists were killed. Operation Carnation provided a solid base for launching Operation Protea a month later.

Operation Protea was mainly aimed at destroying the large quantities of heavy weapons and arms at Ongiva (Pereira de Eça), a stone's throw from the border, where PLAN was in the process of setting up an extensive network of radar and missile sites which posed a serious threat to the Air Force's aircraft.

On 23 August 1981 Air Force planes caused a great deal of damage to radar installations at Cahama, 130 km inside Angola. A South African mechanised column crossed the border north of Ondangwa, overwhelmed PLAN forces at Xangongo and captured Ongiva on 26 August in the face of a strong FAPLA force consisting of infantry, tanks and large-calibre guns.

A strong semi-permanent garrison was left at Xangongo and Ongiva, but was withdrawn across the border by 1 September. More than 1000 SWAPO infiltrators were killed during this operation, while 3000 to 4000 tons of the most modern Soviet arms were captured, including tanks. A Soviet officer was counted amongst the casualties, and another Soviet officer was taken prisoner by South African forces. The MPLA's FAPLA was very much at the receiving end of this operation – apart from large numbers of soldiers wounded or killed, large quantities of weapons and equipment were captured, which severely hampered further operations against Jonas Savimbi (leader of UNITA). They also got the message: expect to be punished if you support SWAPO insurgents.

In these operations against SWAPO, South Africans were confronted by numerous well-armed FAPLA forces. It became clear that the Defence Force would need better arms for future cross-border operations.

In Operation Protea the new 127 mm multiple rocket launcher (MRL), designed to counter the famed 122 mm MRL (Stalin Organ), was taken into service. Armscor had researched, developed and manufactured this weapon system in a very short time. With its superb support for the Defence Force, Armscor was already beginning to satisfy the need for more modern arms.

I regularly invited Members of Parliament from the various political parties to visit the front in South-West Africa and Angola as my guests,

MAGNUS MALAN

A SMALL PART OF THE IMMENSE QUANTITY OF ENEMY WEAPONRY CAPTURED BY THE DEFENCE FORCE DURING OPERATION PROTEA.

Captured BRDM-2 Soviet armoured vehicles. Some are in good condition, while others are somewhat battered but repairable.

These captured but efficient enemy anti-aircraft guns were refurbished and put to our own use. These weapons supplemented our lack of adequate anti-aircraft capabilities very well. Capture of undamaged enemy anti-aircraft guns is usually a sign that the enemy has been defeated and has abandoned his position to beat a hasty retreat.

There were many captured T-35 tanks, like these three, which were still in good condition and which were recovered to the Defence Force depots in the northern South-West Africa/Namibia. UNITA took over these tanks and other weapons from us after training in their use.

and one such occasion occurred in the wake of Operation Protea. At that stage all the captured modern Soviet arms had been collected at the military depot in Ovambo, and the quantity, variety, numbers and technological sophistication of the weapons and equipment simply left those present breathless. Such a loss must have been a cruel blow even to so large a power as the Soviet Union.[5]

Operation Phoenix – a counter-operation aimed at PLAN's cross-border operations from Angola – took place in February 1983. PLAN had infiltrated South-West Africa/Namibia with approximately 1700 of its members, but the Defence Force combined brilliantly with the South-West African Territorial Force and killed 309 SWAPO members, suffering a loss of 27 of its own. SWAPO was forced to retreat across the border with its tail between its legs.

The Defence Force and the South-West African Territorial Force launched Operation Askari across the border into Angola on 6 December 1983. This operation was aimed at preventing a build-up of certain PLAN elements. It gave the border war a new dimension, however, because it became clear that Cuban forces were ready to play a far greater role in the offensive. Furthermore, FAPLA forces were protecting PLAN units to a far greater degree. Following good ground reconnaissance, four combat groups consisting of about 500 mechanised infantrymen and smaller motorised infantry groupings led the attack.

The combat groups were confronted by two Cuban battalions near Cuvelai, and this resulted in the destruction of eleven Russian T-54 tanks, and 324 of the enemy were killed. Because of increasingly joint Cuban, FAPLA and PLAN forces, the Defence Force was compelled to act more conventionally, and would have to be prepared for armoured and air attacks whenever it crossed the border.

At the conclusion of Operation Protea the Defence Force did not withdraw all its forces from Angola, but left a light, mobile search-and-destroy unit in Angola on a semi-permanent basis to continually disrupt SWAPO's military capability.

While the South African teams were still clandestinely present in Angola, the South African Government invited the Angolans to take part in discussions on the conflict. There were intensive discussions between South Africa, Angola and the USA in Lusaka in February 1984. The meeting ended with an agreement on a seven-point plan for South Africa's withdrawal from Angola. In terms of the agreement Angola would ensure that no SWAPO or Cuban forces would move into the areas that South Africa was vacating. The Joint Monitoring Commission (JMC), of which South Africa and Angola were members, was also born of this meeting. The JMC was given the task of determining the manner in which the Defence Force was to withdraw from Angola in phases and according to a set time-scale. The JMC furthermore had to ensure that SWAPO and the Cubans did not occupy the vacated areas.

Right from the start it was quite clear that SWAPO was not going to keep to the agreement. On 16 May South Africa withdrew from the Commission after several fruitless attempts to rectify this situation. Seen from a South African military point of view, this first attempt at a withdrawal from Angola was not a success, because the Commission was able to reach only one of its goals, namely South Africa's withdrawal from the area; it certainly did not succeed in preventing SWAPO from exploiting the situation. Any expectations that the JMC would succeed in ending the regional conflict and ensuring an internationally acceptable independence for South-West Africa did not materialise.

From mid-1985 SWAPO also had to transfer a third of their combat forces to the MPLA for deployment against UNITA, in exchange for their base facilities and other privileges in Angola.

Dr Jonas Malheiro Savimbi, leader of UNITA, was a member of a prominent Ovimbundu family of Manhango. He obtained a Ph.D. in Political Studies at a Swiss university and was fluent in English, Portuguese, French, German and Italian. In the meantime he had built up a well-disciplined force which acted everywhere in Angola with success against the MPLA's FAPLA. I regularly arranged visits to his main base at Jamba in south-east Angola for South African politicians, business leaders, media and other opinion-makers. He managed his forces operationally and continuously gathered information in an admirable manner.

A welcoming military parade was usually held during such visits and tours, which included visits to the schools and dormitories Dr Jonas Savimbi had had built for thousands of UNITA orphans; demonstrations of how UNITA technicians were able to maintain and repair vehicles in Angola's sand; and the clothing factory where UNITA made women's clothing for the local population. The visit was usually concluded in the evening with an insightful cultural programme. Because Savimbi faced a challenge similar to that of South Africa with regard to people of various languages and backgrounds, the cultural evening was only one way of bringing the various language groups closer together. It had been the custom to use only one language, namely Portuguese, in the vicinity of Jamba, but since Savimbi made contact with the SA Defence Force, it became his policy that his headquarters officers should learn to speak English in order to facilitate communications with the Defence Force, and very soon his officers in the Jamba region conducted all briefings and conversations in English. (A full report on such a media visit to Jamba appeared in *The Star* of 25 July 1984.)

Because Cubans and Russians were becoming more involved in the border conflict, more Cubans were dying every year, and the USSR was losing more and more arms. The Soviet Union was therefore forced to supply more arms, and the Cubans were forced to bring more troops. These reinforcements were essential in order to counter the growing UNITA attacks and the devastating Defence Force operations. These events certainly did nothing to help them realise their dream of a communist revolution across the length and breadth of Southern Africa.

FACTORS CONTRIBUTING TO SUCCESS

It was not always easy to determine which military standards were used to measure operational successes. People involved in an operation usually use their own criteria to determine success.

During the border conflict I always emphasised the following important goals for successful actions: "We cannot afford to lose our men; look after your weapons and equipment well; ensure that the mission is achieved."

It was of cardinal importance to safely bring back those for whom one is responsible; their safety is one's prime responsibility. Weapons and equipment had to be maintained and handled with care, because a Defence Force member's life, and those of his comrades, often depended on it. Assigned tasks had to be carried out faithfully, and objectives had to be reached, because this determined success or failure.

I believe that the Defence Force succeeded wonderfully in carrying out its operations and in meeting the demands for success made of it, and that in the process the enemy was mortified time and again. Once thing is certain: the Defence Force had leadership - officers and non-commissioned officers - of top quality.

The three Chiefs of the SA Defence Force who were in command during my time as Minister were superb. The Defence Force was privileged to have men of the calibre of Generals Constand Viljoen, Jannie Geldenhuys and Kat Liebenberg in its midst. Their expertise ensured the success of the Defence Force. All three were leaders of distinction, even though each had his own leadership style. They were not leaders who issued orders from a distance, instead they were visibly present whenever an operation was in progress. South Africa owes them a great debt of gratitude.

The Defence Force's successes can be attributed to various factors, among which leadership, the quality of the Defence Force members and their equipment, the support of loved ones and the general public played an important role.

The support and hospitality of the inhabitants of the Karoo town of De Aar serves as an example of the type of support which yielded very positive results for members of the Defence Force. Food, shower and sleeping facilities were offered free of charge to each crowded troop train on the way to the operational area or back. There were many such trains in this very long period, but each Defence Force member was received with Karoo hospitality at a centre specially created for this purpose. This was an enormous community effort which hugely increased the morale of the men.

Furthermore many communities and local authorities committed themselves to the military units from their area. For example they offered financial support, created administrative and other facilities, and organised official farewells for military units before they departed to commence their operational duties, and officially welcomed them again on their return. Such communities even sent delegations to visit the units in the operational area and to report back on their findings.

There was also huge support from various charitable organisations. For example, the Southern Cross Fund expressed its gratitude towards the soldiers in the form of regular food parcels, creating facilities and providing essentials to the value of millions of rands for which there were no state funds. The Defence Force's Women's Association, at the time probably one of the largest women's association in the country, collected funds for the care of wounded, injured and disabled Defence Force members. This organisation also cared for the families of Defence Force members on operational duty. One must also mention the SABC, and the various women who broadcast programmes with messages for the troops. All these actions gave the Defence Force members and their families a very important message: "We care!"[6]

These tokens of compassion, combined with the spiritual support offered by the chaplains, particularly on the battlefield, provided excellent support for the Defence Force's morale, and in turn this contributed towards successful operations.

All the national servicemen, the Citizen Force, the Commandos with their volunteer elements, and the members of the South-West African Territorial Force also deserve honour. They faced an enemy of far superior numbers but never wavered, protested or complained. There were times when individuals did complain, and this is normal. The men in these Defence Force units should at that stage of their lives have enjoyed innocent adventure, love and family ties, coupled with peacetime excitement. Yet they were prepared to defend their country, the constitution and their fellow South Africans in sacrificial, often wearisome and difficult circumstances. We are grateful to them, and enormously proud of them!

Chapter 16

THE GREATEST BATTLEFIELD VICTORY OF THE SA DEFENCE FORCE

DEFENCE FORCE OPERATIONS 1985-1987

By the mid-1980s the Angolan conflict was being waged on a large scale. At that stage there were more than 30 000 Cubans troops in Angola, in comparison to the 10 000 in the mid-1970s. More and more Cuban troops were sent to Angola and eventually the numbers stabilised at about 52 000. The Cubans were supported by at least 3000 East German and Soviet specialists, who were mainly commanders and operational planners involved in training, radar and anti-aircraft systems, and gathering and applying intelligence. (A very good account of the events in Angola, and Operations Modular, Hooper and Packer in particular, can be found in Fred Bridgland's book, *The war for Africa* (1990.))

The MPLA "masters" decided to launch the greatest offensive yet against UNITA on 2 September 1985. It was planned to coincide with a six-day meeting of the ministers of the Non-Aligned States in Angola. International attention would be focused on Luanda in this period, and media coverage of events in Angola offered the MPLA and its allies an opportunity to regain lost prestige through the military victory that was envisaged.

The plan was for FAPLA, the MPLA's combat organisation, to conquer and occupy with Cuban and Soviet support the sparsely populated south-eastern region of Angola that was controlled by UNITA since the

1970s. The attacking force would consist of about 20 army brigades, supported by a modernised and re-equipped Angolan air force, which included more than 30 advanced MiG-23 and 50 MiG-21 aircraft. At least 100 helicopters of various classes were also available.

From 1984 to mid-1985, FAPLA had been receiving brand new Soviet arms and equipment. Its tank strength alone amounted to some 325 T-55s, 175 T-34s and 50 amphibious PT-76s.[1]

In the meantime Gen. Jannie Geldenhuys had taken over as Chief of the Defence Force from Gen. Constand Viljoen, who had retired.

When the Non-Aligned States conference in Luanda was concluded after a few days in September 1985, the FAPLA brigades had not really picked up steam, and had only advanced to the vicinity of the Lomba River, still a few hundred kilometres from the UNITA Headquarters at Jamba. Mavinga, on the road to Jamba, had been chosen as an intermediate objective with Jamba the final objective in this operation aimed at destroying UNITA.

As the FAPLA brigades neared Mavinga, UNITA with limited support from the SA Air Force and SA Army artillery mercilessly attacked its enemy, causing FAPLA to halt and retreat with heavy losses. FAPLA used the convenient excuse that the coming rainy season made it important not to be trapped in this remote area.

Considered in retrospect, it was fortunate for FAPLA, the Soviet Union and the Cubans that the summit had ended early and the delegates had already left, or they would have been seriously embarrassed, as had happened many times before.

Despite the political changes in the Soviet Union and the more liberal views of Mikhael Gorbachov, the reformer who had been chosen as leader of the USSR in 1985, the country was still hugely committed to the MPLA in Angola. The Soviet Union once again made the decision, difficult as it is to comprehend, to attack UNITA's headquarters and to destroy it once and for all. The Soviet general who had to accomplish this task, Constantin Shaganovich, therefore arrived in Angola in December 1985 to take control of all forces and military operations. He was regarded as an expert in counter-insurgency, and was a specialist in chemical warfare.

At the same time "Comandante" Arnaldo Ochoa Sanchez, who had a truly impressive military career, was appointed as officer commanding all Cuban forces in Angola. He was a member of the small group that had originally invaded and taken over Cuba with Fidel Castro by overthrowing the Batista regime, and had been in command of, or had served in, Cuban forces in Ethiopia, Somalia, Nicaragua, Grenada, Syria and Afghanistan. He was very popular in Cuba and amongst members of the Cuban armed forces, and had been awarded the Cuban Order of Maximo Gomes. I will refer to this well-known and popular Cuban officer again at a later stage.[2]

Information pointed to Shaganovich having at his disposal some 1000 fellow Soviet officers in command and training posts, as well as some 2000 East German military personnel deployed with FAPLA's intelligence and communication services. Great expectations were therefore created by the Soviet and Cuban side with regard to the pending battle.

Soviet replenishments for the coming battle occurred on a formidable scale. Even aircraft kept in reserve for strategic purposes in case of a major military conflict in Europe were made available for this operation, including a number of Ilyushin 76 cargo planes and giant Antonov 22 long-range transport aircraft. At that stage the Soviet Union only had a total of 50 of the latter. These aircraft transported tanks and other armoured combat vehicles directly from the Soviet Union and the harbours of Luanda, Lobito and Namibe to destinations such as Menongue (Serpa Pinto), Cuito Cuanavale and Luena (Luso). More new helicopters and MiG-23 fighters were delivered than had been lost during the 1985 operations.[3]

The Shaganovich offensive was planned for 1986, but floundered for a number of reasons. For example, elements of the Defence Force's Special Forces launched early surprise attacks on Cuito Cuanavale and destroyed essential radar and artillery installations and bomb caches. The planned offensive was further hampered when Special Forces and UNITA sank one Soviet vessel in the harbour of Namibe and badly damaged two others that were carrying essential materiel for the attack. At the same time some of the oil reservoirs at the harbour were also destroyed.[4]

At about this time differences between Cuba and the Cubans in Angola reached a climax. One of the reasons for this disunity was that the remains of Cubans who had died in Angola were to be kept there until the conclusion of the war, when they would be transported to Cuba for mass burials. Another reason was that the Cuban forces, as was the case in other communist countries, did not really cater for personal wellbeing and the survival of the individual. The availability of medical services and casualty evacuation, for example, were not high priorities. Individual Cuban fighters began to realise that if they were wounded, they stood a slim chance of survival because of the poor medical services, and if they died, the chances of a speedy burial were also unlikely. The clumsy and sometimes unpredictable manner in which the wounded were treated, and the indifferent manner in which the remains of the Cuban dead were handled, particularly in view of a lack of refrigeration facilities, had a seriously demoralising effect on the Cuban soldiers. It was quite clear that a communist fighter was simply regarded as a number.

It was also known in Cuba that their soldiers were beginning to experience more difficult times on the battlefield than before. As a result greater dissatisfaction with and unwillingness to undertake periods of service in Angola began to develop. The perception started to develop that service in Angola was akin to punishment. There was also great dissatisfaction because Cuban soldiers who had contracted AIDS-related diseases in Angola – and there were many – were apparently isolated in a prison on their return to Cuba.

As a result of these dissatisfactions inferior, undisciplined elements were earmarked for service in Angola, and of course this had a direct influence on service delivery on the battlefield.

These factors that negatively affected the morale of Cuban fighters also visibly affected their attitude towards and co-operation with the Angolans and representatives of other countries. Tension developed, and this had a further negative effect on operational efficiency.[5]

OPERATIONS MODULAR, HOOPER AND PACKER, 1987-1988

Very early in 1987 a visible build-up of FAPLA, Cuban and Soviet forces made it clear that large-scale military operations were being planned. It was also noticeable that these forces were planning a joint attack on Jamba via Mavinga along two access routes.

THE GREATEST BATTLEFIELD VICTORY

The first front was opened from Lucusse in a southerly direction against Mavinga in April–May 1987. UNITA had to defend this front with its own forces, which it did with strong resistance, and by cutting the enemy's logistical lines of communication with the front. The enemy was driven back to Lucusse in humiliating fashion and would play no further role in the attack on Mavinga or Jamba.[6]

The enemy opened its second front on 14 August 1987, with its attack route aimed at Jamba. This was considered their principal effort. The

MAP 7 THE ENEMY OPENED TWO FRONTS, ONE FRONT FROM THE NORTH VIA LUCUSSE, AND THE OTHER FRONT FROM CUITO CUANAVALE, BOTH AIMED AT MAVINGA AND EVENTUALLY JAMBA.

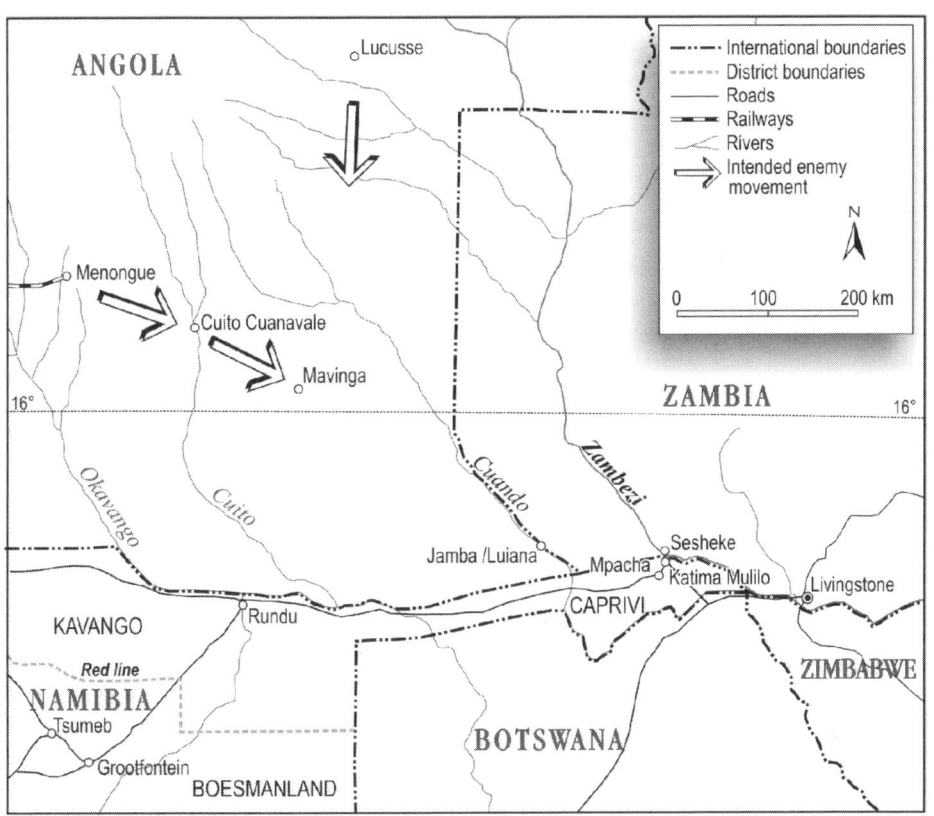

front stretched from the Cuito River at Cuito Cuanavale east to Mavinga, and from there to the south-eastern corner of Angola, with Jamba as its final objective. The forward enemy forces consisted of the 16th, 21st, 47th and 59th Brigades, while the 25th Brigade was already deployed in the area east of the Cuito River.[7]

The combined strength of the enemy forces amounted to at least 50 000 to 60 000 men armed with the most modern Soviet weapons, and was supported by excellent air cover and aerial combat capability.[8]

The nature, quantity and sophistication of the arms made it quite clear that UNITA would not be able to take on this enemy force successfully on its own. On the recommendation of the Chief of the Defence Force, Gen. Jannie Geldenhuys, the South African Government gave heed to UNITA's request and gave permission for limited military aid to be given during the coming operation. Furthermore I gave Gen. Geldenhuys a clear message: he had to ensure that the enemy's offensive did not succeed. This time UNITA had to be helped in such a way that it would no longer be necessary for Savimbi to ask for military aid every year.

On analysing the mission, the Defence Force decided the following goals were important: prevent the enemy offensive from succeeding; at the same time maul the enemy to such an extent that it would not be able to launch an offensive against UNITA every year; create an effective barrier by using the Cuito River in a way that would make it difficult to launch an annual offensive in future; give usable captured enemy equipment to UNITA, and train UNITA so that it will be able to employ this equipment in future.

This mission should make it clear that the allied forces' campaign or counter against the enemy's second front was not planned and aimed at achieving a regime change in Angola, and neither was it planned to attack or occupy the town of Cuito Cuanavale. It was not even envisaged that our forces would cross the Cuito River.[9]

Following extensive discussions and briefings, Gen. Geldenhuys and I decided to give as many Defence Force members as possible combat experience by regularly rotating them during operations. This would create the maximum opportunity for Defence Force members to become involved in the very important battle east of the Cuito River. It was of cardinal importance to expose as many Defence Force members as possible to physical combat.

The Defence Force used the same deployment pattern in regard to the latest arms that had been developed, that is, as soon as weapons and equipment had been issued to the Defence Force, they had to be tested on the battlefield to determine whether they satisfied the Defence Force's needs. There was always a greater demand for battle-tested weapons that had been deployed successfully. In this way we were helping Armscor to establish its arms and ammunition export market.

Our ground forces assigned to halt this enemy offensive were dubbed 20th Brigade.

For the second time the enemy made the error of judgement of launching an offensive to coincide with a major political event, in an attempt to give the event greater publicity and political importance. This time the focus was an official visit by Pres. Dos Santos of Angola to Portugal in September 1987. The plan was that the fall of Mavinga would be announced at the same time as Pres. Dos Santos' arrival in Portugal.

Once you know your enemy, it is easier to fathom what he is planning. The challenge lies in preventing him from achieving his aims. In both instances when FAPLA (the military arm of MPLA) launched a major offensive, the Defence Force immediately realised what was afoot, and then, metaphorically speaking, kicked them in the teeth. Not only did FAPLA and its cohorts fail in both their efforts, but the failure also had a serious demoralising effect on their own forces.

The combined forces of the Defence Force, South-West African Territorial Force (SWATF) and UNITA were divided into two artillery-supported combat groups. Combat Group Alpha consisted mainly of the 61st Mechanised Batallion Group, with support from elements of 32 Batallion and UNITA's 5th Battalion. Their task was to halt FAPLA's 47th Batallion and prevent this enemy task force from moving east along the southern bank of the Lomba River and eventually linking up with the 59th and 21st Brigade north of the Lomba River. It would be easier for them to establish a bridgehead across the Lomba River if they acted as a combined force.

MAP 8 OPERATIONS MODULAR, HOOPER AND PACKER: DEPLOYMENT OF ENEMY TROOPS EAST OF THE CUITO RIVER AND THE COMMENCEMENT OF THEIR MARCH ON JAMBA THROUGH MAVINGA.

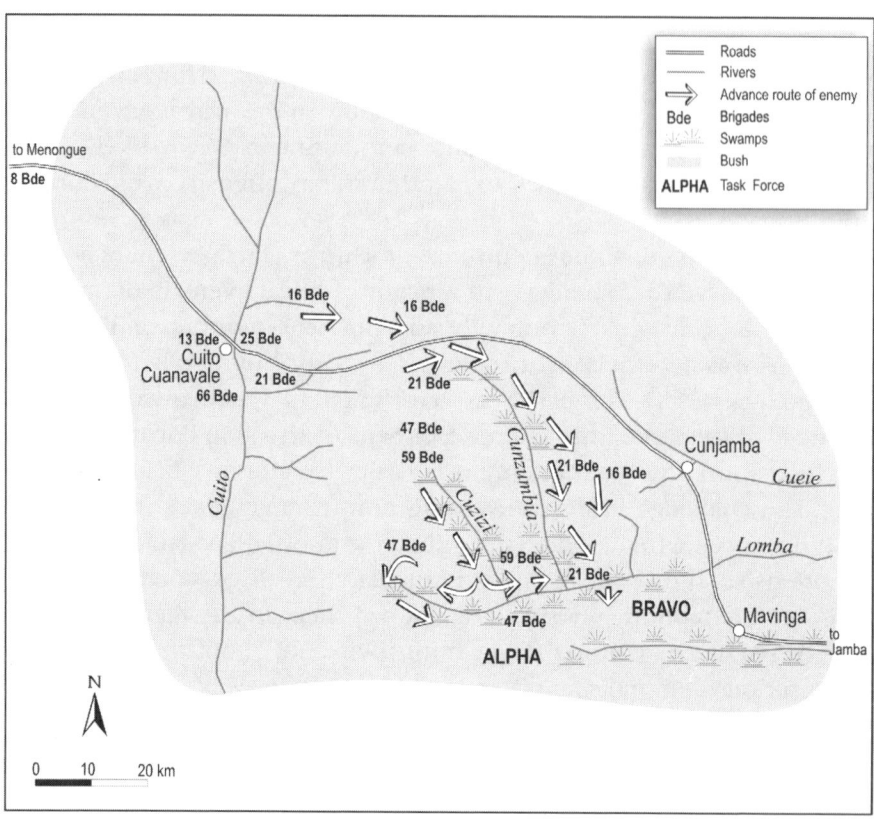

Combat Group Bravo consisted mainly of 32 Battalion, 101 Battalion and UNITA's 3rd Battalion. Its area of responsibility was south of the Lomba River and east from its confluence with the Cunzumbia River. Their task was to prevent the 21st and 59th Brigade, and possibly the 16th Brigade, of the enemy's task force from crossing the Lomba River from the north, and in so doing threatening Mavinga. The two enemy brigades, namely the 21st and 47th, were accompanied by a tactical armoured group with tanks. Both brigades were particularly strong, and had had a great deal of combat experience.

By intercepting the enemy's operational communications, for example by listening in on enemy radio communications, the Defence Force at this stage confirmed that the enemy's 21st Brigade was in possession of chemical weapons. Experts in chemical warfare were immediately despatched to the front from South Africa, and a limited quantity of protective chemical warfare gear was issued to UNITA and certain units. The rest was centrally stored, to be issued as the situation demanded.[10]

The Defence Force was seriously concerned about the possibility of the enemy deploying chemical means during the conflict. At this stage the Defence Force, through Project Coast, was engaged in research into and the development of new counter-measures for chemical warfare, as well as refining existing counter-measures. The great powers such as the Soviet Union had chemical weapons at that time, and were quite prepared to experiment with them and to employ them. In this respect the Defence Force therefore had a great disadvantage which it had to make up for.

At that stage international protocols forbade the use of chemical agents in warfare. South Africa could only hope and pray that they would not be used in Southern Africa, because the country could not afford to equip the entire Defence Force with protective gear. The majority of the mass of combatants on our side could therefore not be protected against chemical weapons.

It was furthermore determined, from intercepted enemy radio communications, that the artillery of their 21st Brigade already possessed projectiles filled with chemical substances. These interceptions also provided the unsettling information that chemical rounds had already been fired at UNITA and the Defence Force; fortunately the wind had changed direction, and the chemical gas was blown back towards the 21st Brigade's own positions, with unpleasant results. Using the Defence Force's interception capability, we were able to intercept the explanation given to members of his unit by the commander of 21st Brigade – he tried to put the blame on UNITA. The Luanda broadcasting service then publicly spread the accusations made by 21st Brigade.[11]

One needs to bear in mind that there are great differences in testing conventional, nuclear, chemical and biological weapons. One can test conventional weapons and determine their efficiency on the battlefield in normal combat conditions. Nuclear weapons may be tested in controlled circumstances, for example by limited underground explosions. Chemical and biological weapons are different, because their effect is usually tested on animals, and then certain assumptions are made about their effect on people. The effects of wind and weather on the battlefield cannot be judged in a laboratory, and therefore it is necessary to determine the effects of changing climatological conditions on these weapons. The best way of doing this is to test them on human enemy targets in combat conditions in remote or isolated areas.

Proof of the use of chemical weapons by FAPLA and the Cubans against UNITA was found in the remote south-eastern part of Angola. In this regard one can refer to the lengthy and intensive investigations conducted in Angola by Prof. B. Hendrickx, Head of the Department of Toxicology at the University of Ghent in Belgium. He found that the Cubans and Angolans had used cheaply manufactured bombs containing a lethal mixture of calcium and cyanide mixed with gas and dust. His findings were supported by academics at other European institutions.

Chemical weapons need not necessarily be lethal. Some simply produce a sense of pacifism, and inhibit any fighting spirit. However, the international community shows revulsion at experiments with and the employment of chemical weapons, and as a result totalitarian or dictatorial regimes test these weapons in areas and circumstances where it is difficult to trace such use.

The SA Air Force became increasingly involved in operations in Angola. In modern conventional warfare it is not possible to carry out operations only on the ground, and air cover is essential during any military conflict. It also became clear that sufficient air cover would be required in south-east Angola. The designated battlefield was some 500 km from Grootfontein, the base from which the SA Air Force aircraft operated. It takes a Mirage F1AZ fighter-bomber (used for ground attacks) some 40 minutes to cover this distance at treetop level, and as long again to return. Aircraft had to fly low to avoid enemy radar and anti-aircraft measures. The result was that they had only a few minutes' fuel left to complete their designated tasks over the target areas. Normally this was very difficult, if not impossible: what would happen if an enemy aircraft with a 45-minute fuel reserve were to appear on the scene?

The Mirage F1CZ (air to air fighters) operating from Rundu were closer to the target area, but still almost twice as far as enemy aircraft operating from Menongue, which was situated about 160 km west of Cuito Cuanavale. The more than 30 MiG-23 and MiG-21 fighter-bombers stationed there were only 10 minutes from the battlefield. Time was a determining factor that always gave the enemy a marked advantage. Furthermore, the MiG-23 and MiG-21 aircraft of the enemy were larger in numbers and technologically more advanced than the Mirages of the SA Air Force.

The Air Force soon realised that it would have to rely on the exceptionally high quality of its pilots. This high quality could be attributed to their dedication, excellent training, discipline and expertise. In their combat mission the Air Force could also rely on a large amount of valuable intelligence coming from their mobile air operations teams, forward observation personnel and Special Forces. Ground maintenance crews performed an enormous task with great self-sacrifice. The Air Force and Armscor equipped the fighter and bomber aircraft with important electronic improvements.[12]

Radar plays a determining role in modern warfare with regard to the deployment of the air force and in air defence. Both the distance of the radar from the target and the radar quality are very important. In this case the enemy radar had a great advantage, thanks to their closer proximity to the battlefield, which helped them in their task of co-ordinating their extensive ground-to-air missile system and quickly aiming it at aerial targets. The enemy could also fire missiles and adjust the missiles tracks in flight.

There were many and various types of enemy radar and missile systems. For example, there were seven different types of radar systems, duplicating and supporting one another. These static and mobile radar stations were guarded and electronically maintained by units of the East German Army.

The missile systems available to the enemy included SAM-8s, SAM-9s and SAM-13s, and various shoulder-fired missiles. They also had the SAM-6 (a computer-controlled missile with a range of 30 km), which could successfully be deployed to lock onto aircraft and then automatically follow them from as close as 100 m above the ground to as high as 18 000 m. Over and above the SAM-6 missile system various radar and missile systems were deployed in the vicinity of the Cuito River. The radar systems could follow the movement of aircraft on screens from 50 m above the ground to as high as 7500 m. Above this height there were other missile systems and MiG-23 aircraft to do further damage. The closer Defence Force aircraft were to these radar and missile systems, the more dangerous it became. SA Air Force aircraft could only operate safely in this area by flying below the radar umbrella, that is at a height of about 50 m.[13]

Radar also plays an important role in guiding sophisticated aircraft to their targets. In this field the enemy therefore had the advantage, while the SA Air Force had a limited capability because of its distance from the target area. The pendulum of control of the airspace above the front had moved in favour of the enemy, but the SA Air Force air crews moved it back in our favour thanks to their excellent training and dedication.

The further an aircraft flies from a radar station at a low height, the more difficult it becomes for that radar station to follow it, until it entirely disappears from the radar screen. This means that it is difficult to track a departing or approaching aircraft flying at a low height until it is close to the radar station. The higher an aircraft flies, the greater the range at which and the greater the ease with which the radar station can track it.

The distance from or place where the battlefield or target is in relation to one's own air force bases or radar systems is an important factor. In oversimplified terms it can be explained as follows: a radar station can track an aircraft that is 10 km away if it is 200 m or more above the ground. An aircraft that is 30 km from the same radar station can be tracked only if it is 1000 m or higher. The further a target is from a radar station, the more difficult for the radar to track it, due to the curvature of the earth, distance and other factors, and therefore the radar becomes less useful. SA Air Force aircraft moving away from Cuito Cuanavale with its sophisticated radar system would initially be observed on all the radar systems there, but the further the aircraft moved away, the higher they would need to fly to be observed, in other words the band of high-altitude observation becomes less and eventually vanishes.

As the aircraft arrive at Grootfontein, they would no longer be visible on radar screens at Cuito Cuanavale at any height. The shorter the distance between the radar system and the battlefield, the greater the advantage; and the longer the distance, the less useful the radar station may be. In this case the positioning of the Defence Force radar stations was greatly to its detriment, and the positioning of the enemy's radars stations of great advantage to them.

Sophisticated fighter planes can be brought on target only by radar; without radar these aircraft are blind to any enemy aircraft. In this regard the enemy also had the advantage of radar while the Air Force had to do without it.

In the important field of air defence the scale once again tipped firmly in favour of the enemy. The distance from the target, sophistication, variety and number of radar and missile systems controlling the air space over the target were all in favour of the enemy.

The Defence Force relied mainly on American Stinger shoulderlaunched missiles for ground-to-air defence on the battlefield or in the target area. These were missiles that the USA supplied to UNITA only under strict conditions. Enemy aircraft were perhaps overly afraid of these relatively feeble missiles, but with the help of the Special Forces they were deployed far more efficiently than would normally have been the case.

The heaviest anti-aircraft guns in the Defence Force's arsenal in the field were its own 20 mm guns, and 23 mm guns taken from the enemy. This was better than nothing, and forced the enemy aircraft to fly higher than 6000 or 7500 m. As a result the enemy aircraft recorded very poor results: they launched an average of 50 sorties per day and rained rockets, phosphorous bombs and delayed-action bombs on the Defence Force and its allies, but with hopeless results. Measured by economic standards, these efforts were very far from cost-effective. The enemy bombarded its own positions far more often than it hit those of the Defence Force.[14]

The facts given above with regard to enemy air superiority in the vicinity of the battlefield east of the Cuito River explains why the SA Air Force decided to deviate from the old principle of gaining and maintaining a favourable air situation before undertaking any other air force tasks. From an early stage it was clear that air-to-air dogfights were completely out of the question in the air space above the target area, and particularly near Cuito. This was the case because of the advantage enjoyed by enemy aircraft in terms of speed, range, radar capabilities and anti-aircraft missiles; and also because of the many nearby airfields that the enemy could divert to. One also needs to take into account that the enemy air force was inflicting only minimal damage to our allied ground forces. There was no loss of life as a result of enemy air strikes during the campaign in south-eastern Angola.

It was jointly decided that the SA Air Force would provide the required air cover when the SA Army requested this. The SA Air Force produced well thought-out plans that took account of all the technological possibilities, and executed these plans very well. An example is the way in which the Air Force neutralised the danger of enemy attack helicopters. These helicopters began to pose an increasing threat to our ground troops, not only because of their heavy armaments, but also because of the flight profile they adopted, which made it almost impossible to issue early warnings of their arrival. The Air Force then went to immense trouble to draw up a plan that resulted in our Impala aircraft intercepting and shooting down six enemy attack helicopters in the area south-east of the bridge across the Cuito River. This successful operation was not made public, because we did not wish to say anything that could possibly compromise the methodology used. However, the result was exactly what the Air Force had envisaged, because the enemy's uncertainty about what had happened to the helicopters caused them to cancel all attack helicopter sorties immediately.

This must have been a bitter pill for the enemy to swallow, because they sent out six attack helicopters that disappeared without a trace. Heavily armed helicopters that were quite capable of ensuring their own safety had mysteriously vanished. Even worse was the fact that the Air Force maintained absolute silence regarding the incident. All of this ensured that the Defence Force achieved the desired results: the enemy decided not to use its dangerous attack helicopters again.

In order to ensure efficient Air Force support for the Army, mobile air operations teams were deployed in the target area together with the Army. These mobile air operation teams guided SA Air Force aircraft to feasible targets. Using this method the Air Force caused the enemy heavy losses at the Lomba River. The Lomba turning point would have been difficult without the support of the SA Air Force.[15]

A particular feature of this front was the repeated, failed efforts the enemy made to cross the Lomba River at the same spot. The enemy's 21st Brigade tried to cross the river on 10 September 1987, but suffered heavy losses. One of the two battalions they used was virtually wiped out, and three tanks were destroyed.

On 12-13 September two battalions of the enemy's 59th Brigade braved the river, while a small section of T-55 tanks tried to cross the river with the aid of a bridging vehicle. Approximately 300 FAPLA soldiers were killed, and three tanks were destroyed.

Attempts to cross the river continued; 21st Brigade tried to do so almost daily. They were unsuccessful, and were driven back with heavy losses on every occasion. It was clear that this Brigade, despite its setbacks, was still trying to implement the usual Soviet tactics; the repetition of the same failed methods could not but have taken place under Soviet leadership and instructions.[16]

While these attempts to cross the river were taking place, I brought various South African Cabinet ministers, amongst others, P.W. Botha, F.W. de Klerk, Pik Botha and Barend du Plessis, to visit the operational area in relays. During these visits they showed intense interest in the Defence Force's command and control structure during combat operations, and in the protective gear bought as a defence against chemical warfare. Some of the Cabinet members donned the gear and could see for themselves how these suits restricted the wearer's movements and made breathing difficult, thereby seriously hampering any effective action. A combat force that simulated a chemical attack by using coloured artillery smoke, or some other means, could seriously hamper the enemy's movements by forcing it to put on the protective gear.[17]

The decisive battle of this offensive took place on 3 October 1987. The Defence Force was aware that the enemy's 47th Brigade wanted to cross the Lomba River from south to north in order to join the remnants of its 59th Brigade. When the 47th Brigade moved into the open to attempt the river crossing, our Task Force attacked. The Task Force consisted of 61 Mechanised Battalions Group, 32 Battalion and companies

While I was on a working visit to the operational area, the enemy under the command of Russian commanders instructed 21st Brigade to attempt crossing the Lomba River once again.

of 101 Battalion with artillery support from G5s and MRLs, including a tank squadron. The Brigade was destroyed, despite the fact that it could depend on air support as well as fire support from 59th Brigade and was about four times as strong as our Task Force. The Task Force, on the other hand, could not be sure of close air support and tank support at that stage.

The Defence Force/UNITA Task Force won this conventional battle by deceiving the enemy's air force; thanks to accurate timing, for example by allowing 47th Brigade to move into the open before attacking; and thanks to accurate support fire given at the right time and place. Good timing was therefore a decisive factor. The men of the Task Force also

From left to right my guests at this occasion were Barend du Plessis, Danie de Jager, Jonas Savimbi, F.W. de Klerk.

fought with incredible bravery. As a result, the enemy offensive launched on 14 August fell apart, and in the wake of this beating the envisaged enemy offensive was replaced by a hasty and poorly controlled retreat to Cuito Cuanavale by the remnants of the various Brigades. They realised that their only salvation lay in fleeing from the Lomba River area.

The Defence Force had therefore executed its main mission very successfully, namely to halt the enemy offensive in a very short time and with a limited force of fewer than 3000 men.

During Operation Modular the enemy tried its best to locate our G5 artillery positions, as these guns hit them with deadly accuracy. They could not succeed in this during the entire campaign, much less destroy

G5 155 mm guns deployed in the bush near the Lomba River to play havoc with the enemy targets.

a single gun. The Defence Force's success can be attributed to many factors. Needless to say, the gun crews were superb. Less well known was the role of deception forces, particularly the employment of 81 mm mortars used in conjunction with the guns. As soon as the Defence Force became aware that MiGs were flying around inconspicuously in an attempt to spot G5 and G6 positions, 81 mm mortars were used to fire a few special mortar bombs from positions situated at some distance from the guns and in a direction away from the guns. The explosions of these special mortar bombs caused a column of flame and smoke that look very much like the flashes of the G5 and G6 guns. This alerted the Stinger teams with their anti-aircraft missiles to try and hit the enemy aircraft. When the enemy pilots accepted that the mortar bomb explosions were G5 and G6 gun positions and, to the great delight of the Stinger teams, attacked them, the Stinger teams used the opportunity to get the enemy aircraft in their sights.[18]

Special Forces, or the Reconnaissance Commandos, also played a key role. They hid themselves as close as possible to the runways of enemy airfields such as Menongue and Cuito Cuanavale in order to be able to transmit radio reports of enemy aircraft movements as soon as possible.

This gave the guns and other vulnerable Defence Force elements enough time to evade enemy aircraft attacks.[19]

On other occasions Reconnaissance Commandos operated as forward observation officers for G5 guns bombarding the Cuito Cuanavale airbase. This enabled G5 guns to hit enemy MiGs on the ground, and to destroy two Hind-24 helicopters during take-off. Thanks to more such G5 gun fire, the Cuito airbase became unusable by enemy jet and transport aircraft, which meant that the enemy had to operate from further away, namely the airfield at Menongue. They were therefore able to inflict even less damage on the battlefield and they could spend less time above it. Even though they flew more than a thousand sorties to the battlefield at one stage, they were able to hit only one gun, one logistical vehicle and a water bowser. The Defence Force suffered no loss of life.[20]

Another, very important early task undertaken by the Special Forces at the beginning of September 1987 during Operation Modular, which certainly was another nail in the enemy's coffin, was their daring action against the well-guarded bridge across the Cuito River. The bridge was the easiest way of crossing the river from the east or west – without it, the river could only be crossed on foot, by helicopter or by ferry. These methods were slow and impractical, particularly when heavy loads had to be transported across, or when logistical support and replenishments were required. The bridge therefore formed a very important key target in any operation.

Enemy brigades were already positioned to the east of the Cuito River in August 1987, but they relied on logistical support, including supplies of ammunition, from across the river, to the west. The Defence Force therefore decided to create an extra dilemma for them: Special Forces supplied a seven-man demolition team that made its way, with the help of UNITA guides, through enemy-occupied territory to the Cuito River, to a spot some 30 km north of the Cuito Bridge. From there the frogmen, supplied with compressed air cylinders and the necessary explosives, left their guides behind and made their way underwater downstream towards the bridge.

At the bridge they encountered sand banks in the stream that caused a rapid flow of water between the bridge's supports. The water near the sandbanks was very shallow, and this forced the team towards the deeper but faster flowing part of the stream. The bridge was well guarded, and the enemy guards noticed the movements of the frogmen away from the sandbanks towards the deeper water; they directed fierce small-arms fire at the frogmen, and hurled hand grenades at them.

The shooting and the fast-flowing river made things very difficult for the frogmen. It was not possible to secure the explosives against all the bridge supports. However, some of the supports did give way as a result of the explosions, and the bridge was badly damaged. Matters became very serious for the frogmen, however. They moved as a group about 20 to 30 km in an extended formation before emerging one by one from the river at more or less the same place.

As the commander was lifting his foot from the water, a giant crocodile grabbed his flipper, which he hastily kicked loose, thereby saving his life. Fortunately the rest of the seven-man team reached the rendezvous safely, apart from the last two, who had accompanied each other from the bridge as a rear guard.

Just before emerging at the agreed point, a crocodile grabbed the lower body of one frogman between his legs, and began dragging him to deeper water. Quite possibly it was the same crocodile that had earlier lunged at the leader. Fortunately this Reconnaissance Commando kept his head, took out his knife, felt for the crocodile's eye in the muddy water and then stabbed it. The jaws opened immediately, and the Commando and his comrade quickly scrambled onto dry land. The crocodile left some serious wounds on his upper thigh, but fortunately his private parts were unhurt.

The enemy was furious at the damage to the bridge, and pursued the audacious team mercilessly, so that they were compelled to hide in shallow mud in the vicinity of the place where they had emerged. They were covered in mud from head to toe, and had to breathe from beneath the mud through straws. They lay under cover of the mud for a day or two.

The enemy used light aircraft, helicopters and trackers to find the men, but eventually gave up the chase. The team was only able to move to the next rendezvous under cover of darkness some days later. Here the UNITA guides who were waiting for them took them back to the safety of the Defence Force.

The frogmen had damaged the Cuito Bridge so badly that it could carry only a limited traffic load, and could not be used as regularly as before, which negatively influenced logistical support for the enemy east of the Cuito River. This Special Forces operation was to handicap the enemy forces severely in days to come. By early September it was clear that the enemy formations were insufficiently supplied as a result of the damaged bridge. (At van Wyk provides excellent descriptions of other examples of heroism by members of the Defence Force in *Honoris Crux. Ons dapperes* (1982) and in *Honoris Crux. Ons dapperes II* (1985).)

On another occasion the Defence Force once again used the Special Forces as forward observation officers in an attempt to inflict more damage on the Cuito River bridge with artillery fire. This did not succeed, and FAPLA was still able to make limited use of the bridge.

The second part of the mission given to the Defence Force was that it should ensure that UNITA did not need to ask for help every year. This would entail strengthening the Cuito River as a barrier in order to gain enough time for the Defence Force to train UNITA soldiers in the use of the captured equipment.

The setbacks suffered by the enemy's 47th Brigade at the hands of the Defence Force and UNITA early in October 1987, the large quantities of materiel captured, and the defeats suffered by the other enemy brigades in the latest operations, forced them to make a hasty retreat to the Cuito River.

The Defence Force hastened the retreat of Cuban and FAPLA forces east of the Cuito River by successfully attacking them on 9, 11, 13 and 17 November 1987. More than 500 enemy soldiers fell during these clashes, and at least 33 tanks were captured. As a result of these battles all the enemy's offensive elements were driven to within 24 km of the eastern bank of the Cuito River. Despite the enemy setbacks, or because of it, reinforcements were still being despatched to Angola, and more Cuban soldiers and Soviet T-62 tanks were deployed in the vicinity of the Cuito River.[21]

Col (later Gen.) Deon Ferreira, the commander who planned and executed this unbelievable defeat of the enemy, was – with the help of his successful allied forces – responsible for the turning point in the Angolan war. The tremendous loss of enemy life and equipment resulted in a marked lack of appetite for violence from that point onwards.

War is cruel and relentless, and should preferably be avoided. Everything suffers – even fauna and flora. This is a part of the battlefield after the SADF and its allies defeated the aggressive Soviet Union, Cubans and FAPLA at the confluence of the Cunzumbia River with the Lomba River and in so doing changed their perception of the situation.

UNITA played its part at all times, and made a good contribution. It supplied the majority of the infantry for most of the operations, and also provided troops to protect captured objectives and artillery positions.

The campaign reached its final phase with successful attacks by UNITA, the South-West African Territorial Force and the SA Defence Force on the enemy on 13 and 14 January, and again on 25 February 1988, during which all enemy offensive forces, apart from a FAPLA presence east of the Cuito River, were driven back across the river.

The very last clashes took place at Tumpo on 23 March 1988, without changing the position. The enemy suffered many fatalities and the Defence Force none, but unfortunately three Defence Force tanks had to be abandoned in a minefield.

Certain FAPLA elements had successfully entrenched themselves east of the Cuito River. If the Defence Force had to dig out these enemy elements and force them back across the river, it would have resulted in unnecessary loss of life, with few advantages. The presence of these elements east of the river was of little importance, because they had no real influence on the laying of mines in support of UNITA. A minefield was required east of the Cuito River in order to create a future barrier against Cuban and FAPLA forces. Defence Force sappers also continued laying mine fields at possible future crossing points on the Cuito River.

In the meantime UNITA forces were trained in the use of serviceable captured enemy weapons, because it was important for the future that they should have the ability to fight the enemy with a more balanced and more powerful force.

In the book *Dié wat wen* (1993: 177) Gen. Geldenhuys provided the following outcome of the battles between September 1987 and April 1988. (This publication contains a very good overview of Defence Force activities in an era of war and peace.)

SADF/UNITA/SWA Territorial Force losses		Combined Soviet/Cuban/MPLA losses	
Tanks	3	Tanks	94
Ratels	5	Armoured troop carriers	100
Casspirs	3	BM-21/BM-14 MRLs	34
Rinkhals (vehicle)	1	D30/M216 guns	9
Withings (vehicle)	1	Mobile bridges	7
Kwêvoël (vehicle)	1	Logistical vehicles	389
Bosbok (aircraft)	1	MiG-21 and MiG-23 aircraft	9
Mirage F1 aircraft	2	Helicopters	9
(1 because of enemy action;		Artillery, rockets, missiles	15
1 because of an accident)		Radar sets	5

During the campaign in south-eastern Angola that lasted six to eight months, the Defence Force lost 31 heroes. The enemy forces lost between 7000 and 10 000 men, and thousands were wounded. It is estimated that enemy materiel worth about one billion US dollars was destroyed or captured. These were large losses, even for a major power.[22]

During the operations FAPLA launched a large-scale propaganda campaign and used disinformation to make themselves look good. For example, it was claimed that more than 3000 SADF troops were present in Angola at the same time. An even higher figure of 7000 troops who were simultaneously supposed to have taken part in operations was mentioned. On another occasion it was claimed that the Defence Force had lost more than 40 aircraft as the result of enemy actions. Propaganda was furthermore used to convince the world that it was the aim of the Defence Force to take the town of Cuito Cuanavale, but that this had failed.

If the media had initiated the propaganda, one could understand all of this, but the Angolan President and some of his ministers participated actively as well. On the other hand one should have sympathy for a government that had received so much military support – even from a world power – but then had to explain to its supporters and the international community that it had been humiliatingly defeated. In such circumstances it is more convenient to inflate the strength and losses of those against you, and to ascribe goals to them that they had never been interested in. To put it bluntly: even though the MPLA was constantly compelled to reinforce and enlarge its forces, it claimed that its enemy (the SADF) had lost the battle, and by implication that FAPLA had won it. Fortunately the facts speak for themselves.

The 1987–1988 campaign in south-eastern Angola, and in particular the clash between allied and enemy forces at the Lomba River, undoubtedly constituted the turning point of the Angolan war. South Africa and UNITA tasted the success of a conventional military victory over Cuba, the Soviet Union, East Germany and FAPLA (MPLA); a victory that was probably the biggest military clash on the continent of Africa since El Alamein (1943) in North Africa during World War II.

This victory was one of the most important factors that contributed to bringing to an end Soviet military intervention in Africa, Cuban military involvement in Africa, and to put a stop to the hateful and aggressive speeches by leadership elements in Zambia, Zimbabwe and Mozambique aimed at South Africa. It also marked the beginning of the run-up to negotiations in South-West Africa/Namibia and South Africa.[23]

I realise that even today there is still fierce speculation and argument about who had actually won that battle. Of course propaganda still plays a leading role in perceptions about who had won and who had lost. At the time of the battle, South Africa was decried as a "polecat", and the Defence Force would scarcely have been given any credit for its efforts.[24]

According to Sir Robert Renwick, a former British ambassador to South Africa, a South African force, which never amounted to more than a brigade, had defeated a large Soviet and Cuban assisted FAPLA force. This happened because of military efficiency![25]

One need only look at the numbers of enemy personnel who took part: about 50 000 to 60 000 men, equipped with 500 tanks, 100 MiG and Sukhoi Su-22 jet fighters and bombers, 30 Mi-24 Hind and 30 Alouette-type attack helicopters and 70 Mi-8 and Mi-17 transport helicopters.

The fact is that the South African allied forces reached their goal thanks to the Battle of the Lomba, because it halted and reversed the enemy's attack on Jamba, Savimbi's UNITA headquarters. This kept the communist enemy from South Africa's borders. At the same time UNITA was equipped with captured enemy materiel, and was trained to enable it to defend itself against future enemy attacks without any outside help. This in fact happened during the next attack on Jamba.

One doubts very much whether South Africa will in future be able to produce such a military triumph as the one in Angola. It was always clear that the quality of the Defence Force members and their equipment was the decisive factor that ensured success.

To return to the Cuban forces and that popular Cuban officer, "Comandante" Arnaldo Ochoa Sanchez, who was in command of Cuban forces in Angola at the time: In *The war for Africa* (1990: 375) Fred Bridgland writes the following: "… General Arnaldo Ochoa Sanchez, the soldier chosen by Castro to pull his chestnuts out of the fire in the War for Africa. For his efforts in Angola and elsewhere over the years Ochoa was one of only five officers to have been made a Hero of the Republic of Cuba. But scarcely a year after the Cubans and the South Africans fought their last battle in Angola, Ochoa was put to death in 1989, by a firing squad, ostensibly for drug smuggling offences of which he was found guilty at a bogus show trial."

This remarkable Cuban warrior's sentence was ratified on 9 July 1989, and Fidel Castro gave his version of what happened during the war in Angola. Reports appeared in our local newspapers, and one carried headlines that read as follows: "Why Cuba's scapegoat general died at dawn

– Fidel's fight not to lose face – Castro explains why Angola lost battle against the SADF" (*Business Day,* 27 July 1989).

This is how the communists treat their most ardent supporters. If they do not succeed in an imposed task or mission, or should they become too popular and become a threat to the leader (Fidel Castro himself in this case), they are eliminated. Back in Cuba in 1989, Ochoa quite rightly said, with regard to the Angolan campaign: "I was sent to a war that had already been lost so that I could take the blame for the defeat."[26]

Seen from a military point of view, this victory achieved by the SA Defence Force, UNITA and the South-West African Territorial Force in south-eastern Angola was not limited only to Africa; it resounded as far as Moscow and Havana, and finally quenched the Cubans' thirst for any further confrontations. At a later stage it also resulted in a serious relationship crisis between the Soviet Union and Cuba, to the extent that the aid and support that Cuba received from the Soviet Union was drastically reduced.

Gen. Jannie Geldenhuys reported as follows in *Dié wat wen* (1993:185) on the Battle of the Lomba River: "Our forces achieved the one incontrovertible success after the other. They achieved a combat performance that will, in the history of war, be regarded as unique military art. They did this in a manner that speaks of enormous character, that speaks of commanders displaying stratagems and a warlike spirit; of men on the ground and in the air who showed courage, as one expects of South Africans; of black, white, brown and yellow members of the South African Defence Force and the South-West African Territorial Force who did not stand back."

I support the General's words without reserve, namely that 3000 members of the SA Defence Force and SWATF, supported by about 8000 UNITA troops, performed extraordinarily well on the battlefield. The enemy force, consisting of troops from the Soviet Union, Eastern European countries, Cubans and the Angolan FAPLA was in the order of 50 000 strong. This remarkable success played a decisive role in the international change of course that occurred in Africa and it also made a contribution to the fall of international communism in 1989.

Chapter 17

DESPERATE ATTEMPTS TO TRUMP THE SA DEFENCE FORCE

COMPLETION OF MILITARY OPERATIONS 1988-1989

The Cubans in the meantime continued to move their military units south, toward the border of Namibia, opposite Kaokoland and Ovamboland. It has been estimated that 3500 Cuban troops were deployed in the south-western part of Angola at the beginning of February 1988. The Cuban troop strength increased slowly but surely, and in April-May Cuban troops had been positioned from Namibe, Cahama, Xangongo (Roçadas) and Cuvelai to Cassinga.[1]

During April 1988, the situation deteriorated for the Defence Force in the area where the Cubans were deployed. SWAPO activities increased under the protection of the Cubans that were moving south-westwards, and Cuban units began interfering with Defence Force cross-border operations against SWAPO's PLAN concentrations in Angola. As a result there was a clash between the Defence Force and the Cubans about 50 km inside Angola. The Defence Force was compelled to deal with this situation, and to determine the reason for the Cuban presence and movements.

During the advance on Mavinga and its aftermath, Pres. Fidel Castro of Cuba directed day-to-day actions in Angola by telephone.[2] As far as the Defence Force was concerned he was still an unknown presence in military terms, and therefore it was difficult to predict his intentions. Were

MAP 9 CUBAN UNITS IN POSITION IN SOUTH-WESTERN ANGOLA AT CAHAMA, XANGONGO, TECHIPA, CUVELAI AND CASSINGA.

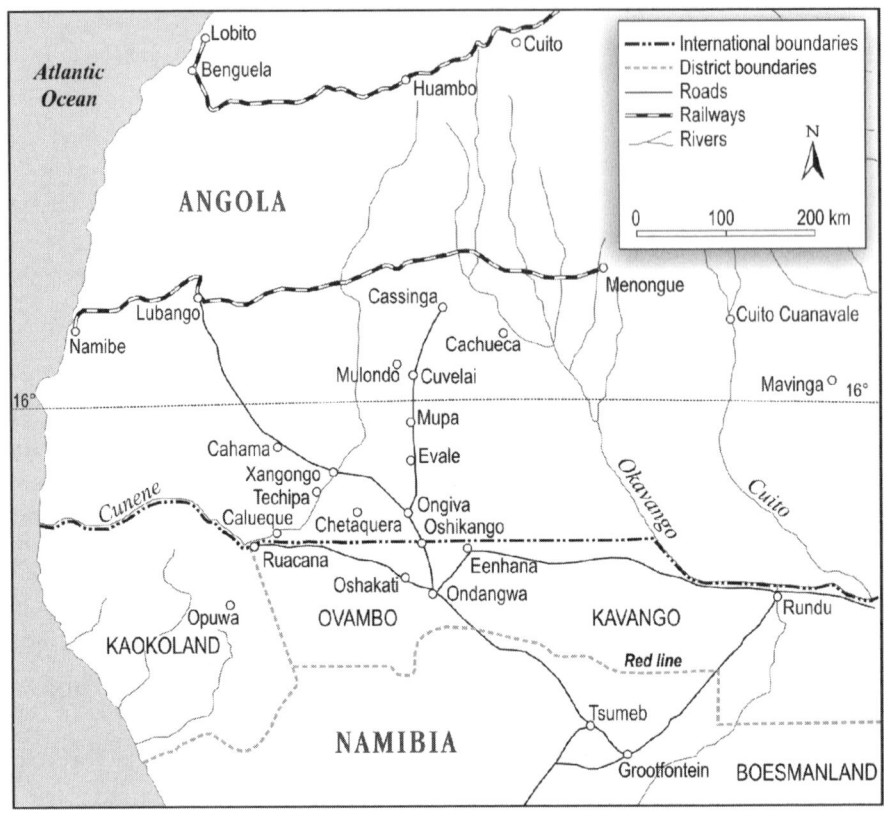

the Cuban military activities in the south-western part of Angola near the South-West African/Namibian border a sign of Castro's military bravery or bravado? What was he trying to prove in the wake of the beating his troops had taken at the Lomba River?

It was also possible that this south-western Cuban movement was aimed at dividing the Defence Force's efforts between the south-eastern front at Cuito and the south-western front. The Defence Force's military capabilities would diminish on both fronts if it tried to handle both simultaneously. In turn this could create an opportunity for a SWAPO supported incursion into South-West Africa/Namibia. This could serve as revenge for the humiliation at the Lomba River, and could possibly restore their image locally, in Cuba and internationally. On the other hand the operation could be a deception operation to dilute the Defence Force's strength at Cuito while they once again attempted to capture Mavinga and Jamba in an effort to turn a military defeat into a political victory.[3]

The most acceptable conclusion was that the Cubans wanted to threaten targets inside South-West Africa/Namibia from south-western Angola, with the intention of attacking at the slightest provocation. These attacks would afford SWAPO the opportunity to operate actively in South-West Africa/Namibia and to declare the country liberated. Of course this would lend SWAPO much more stature in any future peace negotiations.

The Cubans deployed even more troops in the region and upgraded airfields. The destroyed bridge over the Cunene at Xangongo (Roçadas), which was more than 200 m in length, was rebuilt for future use. This was the kind of action one would expect of a military force readying itself for an offensive.[4]

The runway at Xangongo was also improved to the extent that heavy cargo planes would be able to land there in the future. Furthermore MiG-23s would be able to take off from Cahama, the most southerly fighter airfield only 300 km north of the border, instead of from Lubango. This would mean that they would be able to fly to within 20 km of Oshakati and Ondangwa, the SA Air Force bases in Ovamboland. These aircraft could fly higher than the reach of our Cactus ground-to-air missiles.[5]

Cuban brigades were dug in at Xangongo and Techipa. Both places could serve as strong bases for offensive operations aimed at the Calueque waterworks. With masterly expertise and improvisation the SA Defence Force laid a dummy minefield (without any actual mines) at Calueque. This dummy minefield had all the usual fences and markers, as well as a so-called "lane" leading through it, and it was backed by tank positions containing dummy tanks made of plastic. The local population was led through the minefields with great pretence. Information regarding the "minefield" spread quickly, and this achieved the desired result.[6]

Intelligence now suggested that the Cubans were preparing to move aggressively towards the South-West Africa/Namibia border. It was quite probable that an attack by Soviet-Cuban and SWAPO's PLAN forces via

Calueque was imminent. The Defence Force and the South-West African Territorial Force (SWATF) would therefore be wise to be prepared for such an attack or any similar events.

As Chief of the Defence Force, Gen. Jannie Geldenhuys had announced in a press statement of 8 June 1988 that additional Citizen Force units would be called up for duty in South-West Africa/Namibia. This call-up would ensure that the required strength would be available should additional operations be necessary, or should the expected enemy attack on South-West Africa/Namibia take place. At the same time it would serve to discourage or mislead the enemy forces.

Once again it was quite clear that the enemy was instantly aware of anything announced in South Africa. South Africa therefore lost the element of surprise, which is so necessary in military actions. Enemy movements and military preparations clearly demonstrated that the enemy wanted to pre-empt this Citizen Force call-up. They wanted to act before Citizen Force elements reached South-West Africa/Namibia.

In view of the tension that was building up on both sides of the border, the Defence Force then decided to do something that would force the enemy to show its hand. On the afternoon of 26 June 1988, a number of Impala aircraft were ordered to take off from Ondangwa in combat formation in order to activate the enemy anti-aircraft positions. When this formation reached the border just before nightfall, a number of meteorological balloons with tinfoil tails were sent up into the sky. As the balloons rose, so the Air Force planes also gained height, as if preparing for an air attack, but then peeled away in a southerly direction.[7]

The movements of the aircraft and radar reflections from the tinfoil must have made the enemy believe that an air attack was imminent. The Cubans quickly activated their anti-aircraft system and launched six SAM-6 ground-to-air missiles at the balloons. This gave the Defence Force's radar operators and other observation officers the opportunity to determine precisely where these positions were. By this time it was totally dark and no enemy aircraft could take off to threaten ours.

The Defence Force replied to this anti-aircraft barrage with G5 and G2 artillery, multiple rocket launchers and 120 mm mortars. The first artillery salvo destroyed the enemy's artillery command post, and this

The early hours of 27 June 1988. Our mechanised infantry in Ratels are ready for action, while observing columns of smoke rising from the vicinity of Techipa.

eliminated any counter-bombardment. The Cubans were bombarded for six hours without cessation, particularly at Techipa, and suffered great losses. Enemy radio communications were knocked out, and at daybreak great columns of smoke were observed at Techipa and other targets in the area.

Despite these heavy losses, the enemy commenced an advance on Calueque, and in the process they clashed with a Defence Force Task Group that had been deployed to halt such an action; once more our men acquitted themselves admirably, and the Cubans were compelled to break off contact within half an hour and retreat to Techipa.

After breaking the back of the Cuban force in south-western Angola, the Defence Force and SWA Territorial Force, which had provided valued support for every operation, decided to withdraw from Angola. However, it would be necessary to keep a careful eye on Calueque because it was still the source of essential water supplies to Ovamboland.

Up to this point the Defence Force and its support elements had always given the Cubans a thorough beating in any military confrontation. Peace negotiations had already commenced, and the Cubans could certainly perceive that the Angolan/South-West African/Namibian question was rapidly moving towards a conclusion. However, they wanted to throw a last punch at the Defence Force with minimal risk to themselves, perhaps also as revenge for the defeat of 26 June 1988, when they were really caught napping.

On the afternoon of 27 June eight of their aircraft attacked the Calueque Dam wall; one of them then peeled off and bombarded the water pipeline to Ovamboland. Another's bombs missed the target, but fell amongst our military vehicles, close to a Buffel (Buffalo) personnel carrier that was parked some distance from the target, and the explosion killed ten Defence Force members. Defence Force anti-aircraft fire hit two MiGs, and one crashed on the way back to Angola.[8]

As was the case with all Defence Force, SWA Territorial Force and other allied heroes in this extended struggle, our hearts still go out to the next of kin of the ten warriors who were taken from us in such a tragic manner. However, we think back with great gratitude on the sacrifices they were prepared to make. We know that if not for them, there would not have been a peaceful resolution in South-West Africa/Namibia and South Africa.[9]

The confrontations on 26 and 27 June, and the great losses suffered by the enemy, halted the Cubans' southward movement, and also put a stop to any plans to execute further military operations in Southern Africa.

These victories, and in particular those at the Lomba River and in the vicinity of Techipa and Xangongo, constituted a bitter pill to swallow for FAPLA, but also for the Cubans and the Soviet Union. One could measure their defeats by their losses of arms and international prestige.

This takes one back to the truth expressed by Gen. Omar Bradley of the US Army: "In war there is no second prize for the runner-up."

INTERNATIONAL NEGOTIATIONS TAKE PLACE IN ALL EARNEST

The serious nature of the negotiations between South Africa, Cuba, the MPLA, and the USA that took place in Cairo just prior to the June clashes in Angola must have brought the Cubans to other insights, because from then on only the redeployments and a phased total withdrawal of Cubans from Angola were at issue.[10]

In his book *The war for Africa* (1990: 374-375), Bridgland reports on this as follows:" [T]he Cuban failure in Angola added to the collapse of the Marxist Leninist creed in Eastern Europe, left Castro much exposed ... The real pinch was due in January 1991 when the Soviet Union planned to begin cutting off all trade subsidies to socialist states, such as Cuba ... Some 400 000 Cuban troops were rotated through Angola over a period of 15 years, bolstering Castro's pet project. Every Cuban family in a

The successful South African negotiation team in Cairo (from left to right): Dr Niel Barnard (National Intelligence), Gen. Jannie Geldenhuys, myself, Pik Botha, Neil van Heerden and Derek Auret (both of Foreign Affairs).

population of only 10 million must have been affected directly or indirectly by the war ... In Cuba now the veterans of Angola are commonly referred to as the generation of disenchantment. They regard themselves in much the same way as the veterans of Vietnam did in the USA in the 1970s. The sad thing for Castro is that while everyone else seemed to have learnt lessons from the Angolan War and the extraordinary historic events of 1989 in Eastern Europe ... He tried to dress up political, economic and military failures in Angola as glorious triumphs."[11]

At a subsequent round of negotiations in Geneva, a timetable for withdrawal was agreed to, and South Africa Cuba and Angola formally ratified this on 22 December 1988. In brief it amounted to an agreement on a Cuban withdrawal northwards, and on the number of troops to be evacuated from Angola by certain dates.[12]

The Defence Force's military successes gave the South African negotiating team the high ground and psychological advantage during the negotiations on the future of South-West Africa/Namibia. They made the best possible use of this advantage, and in masterly fashion ensured that South Africa and Namibia reached their predetermined negotiation goals successfully. In this regard one must give full credit to former Pres. P.W. Botha and his colleague, Pik Botha, and the negotiation teams who made all this possible through their exhausting perseverance and good footwork.

The trilateral agreement between South Africa, Angola and Cuba was signed in New York on 22 December 1988, and the implementation date for Resolution 435 was fixed as 1 April 1989.

In the meantime, however, information was pouring in that SWAPO (PLAN) was executing manoeuvres that were not in accord with the agreement. According to the Geneva Protocol of August 1988, the withdrawal of South African troops from Angola was to coincide with the withdrawal of all PLAN members from the border area to north of the 16th parallel. The SWAPO withdrawal was to be completed by 1 September 1988. But this did not happen and despite serious objections by the South African Department of Foreign Affairs regarding this breach of contract, SWAPO took no notice.[13]

Signing of the Trilateral Agreement about Angola and Namibia at the UN Headquarters in New York on 22 December 1988. From left to right: myself, Mr Pik Botha, Mr Javier Pérez de Cuéllar (UN Secretary General) and Mr George Schultz (US Secretary of State). Behind Mr Botha is Mr Martti Ahtisaari, the UN's Special Representative for Namibia. (Acknowledgement: *South African Panorama*, Aug. 1989)

SWAPO IN VIOLATION OF GENEVA PROTOCOL 435

In the early hours of 1 April 1989 the first 1600 heavily armed SWAPO terrorists crossed the border between Angola and South-West Africa/Namibia at various places and penetrated South-West Africa.

A small group of SA Police, Air Force and other Defence Force and SWA Territorial Force members had to act quickly to save the situation. They killed 300 PLAN members, but lost 26 of their own.

The USA issued a legal statement on the matter and condemned SWAPO's flagrant breach of the agreement.

Peter Stiff describes the events in *Nine days of war* (1991): "The 1st of April 1989 marked the first day of peace in Namibia. After seemingly endless years of dispute between SA and the UN, after 23 years of bush warfare between the Marxist orientated SWAPO and the SA forces, which had spread from Namibia into Angola and, at times in Zambia, and after eight months of American brokered talks between SA, Cuba and Angola, Namibia was finally on course for UN supervised 'free and fair elections' in November 1989, which would lead to independence in 1990. The South Africans had stuck strictly to the letter of the agreements and even more. By the 1st of April they had demobilised the powerful SWA Territory Force, drastically reduced the strength of the SA Defence Force and confined the residue still remaining in Namibia to bases.

"When the sun rose on that fateful day, it would catch the shadows of only five SA Air Force Alouette helicopter gunships, emasculated of their deadly cannons and dispersed along 400 km of Namibian border with Angola. SWAPO leader Nujoma knew it, for the news was international property via the UN. Nujoma had transmitted his written agreement to a ceasefire to the UN Secretary General in late March. More than 1600 of his PLAN fighters, who should have long been removed to camps north of the 16th parallel by the Angolans and Cubans, under UN supervision, were massing in Angola along the Namibian border, heavily armed.

"On the night of 31st March–1 April, they surged over in what they obviously believed was an unstoppable wave. A wave, which once it broke into pools, they believed, would be allowed by a weak UN to remain in Namibia and subvert the elections by means of a brutal intimidation campaign.

"For nine days until the Mount Etjo Agreement was signed they [the Security Forces] fought the SWAPO infiltrators to a grim standstill, beating them hands down."[14]

In the wake of the incident of 1 April 1989, additional intelligence was received which indicated that SWAPO had freedom of movement in Angola and was not being monitored in accordance with the settlement plan and agreement. Furthermore, SWAPO had not handed in all its weapons and materiel, and even the armoured cars of their mechanised force were still under their control. This was another breach of the agreement, and the SA Defence Force and Ministry of Foreign Affairs lodged objections to this state of affairs. Neither did PLAN enter South-West Africa/Namibia at the predetermined points, as was agreed in the Resolution and Settlement Plan.

The Settlement Plan was eventually implemented on 19 May 1989 after these gross violations were corrected.[15]

The extremes to which the Truth and Reconciliation Commission (TRC) has selectively reported on the SA Defence Force's external operations is quite startling. These operations are viewed only from the enemy's point of view, and the other half of the truth, to which the TRC had access and which they were supposed to have taken into account, was ignored. There are many examples of this, but the one that cannot simply be ignored concerns the breach of the ceasefire in South-West Africa/Namibia as reported by the TRC.[16]

The TRC Report refers to the New York Accord which was signed on 22 December 1988 and which instituted UN Resolution 435, which had been accepted ten years before. This envisaged the Accord to commence on 1 April 1989 and would culminate in a general election seven months later.

According to the TRC's first public report, which was literally distributed globally, the fighting that broke out on 1 April 1989 as a series of military clashes across a front of 320 km in Ovamboland must be laid at the door of the South African regime of the time. According to the TRC this was a method used by the Government of the day to "get at SWAPO and disrupt its election campaign by breaking the ceasefire agreement". The TRC deliberately creates the impression that South Africa, and, by implication, the SA Defence Force, initiated this series of clashes. This is complete nonsense, and factually incorrect.[17]

The actual facts, which were probably deliberately omitted from the first report, are as follows: The Geneva Protocol was signed by South Africa, Angola and Cuba on 5 August 1988. It recommended that Resolution 435 should be implemented on 1 November 1988. (This protocol was suggested by the military component of the South African delegates to the negotiations.)

This resolution provided for a cessation of hostilities between the parties (including SWAPO). It also provided for the withdrawal of South African troops from Angola and the redeployment of SWAPO north of the 16th parallel.

In a letter to the UN Secretary General on 18 March 1989, Mr Sam Nujoma confirmed "SWAPO's acceptance of the de facto cessation of armed hostilities in and around Namibia between SA and SWAPO, in accordance with the Geneva Protocol of 5 August 1988".

A Joint Military Monitoring Commission was established to monitor the period between 1 November 1988 (cessation of hostilities) and 1 April 1989 (implementation of Resolution 435). During these meetings the attention of the Angolan and Cuban delegations was constantly drawn to the fact that SWAPO was not keeping to the agreement. There were combat indications that SWAPO was planning a large-scale infiltration of Namibia on 1 April 1989 (the implementation date for Resolution 435). Despite the fact that the officer commanding Sector 10 was aware of SWAPO's intentions, he went ahead with the implementation of Resolution 435, which involved the disbanding of Namibian "ethnic" units, and confining South African forces to their bases. In order to cope with SWAPO's intentions, the South African forces were reinforced with two combat groups at short notice.[18]

Contrary to Mr Sam Nujoma's undertaking to the UN Secretary General, SWAPO invaded Ovamboland and Kaokoland with 1629 fighters on 1 April 1989. These SWAPO members were heavily armed with automatic weapons, mortars, SAM missiles and an unusual number of antitank weapons. There is no doubt, therefore, that they were the transgressors. The counter-attack force deployed to halt this SWAPO invasion force consisted of the South-West African Police's counter-insurgency force. Initially they suffered a large number of casualties, and it therefore became essential that the SA Defence Force should become involved. They were deployed at 14:00 on 1 April 1989.[19]

Gen. Prem Chand, officer commanding the UN Task Force, Mr Thornberry of the UN and the officers commanding South-West African forces visited Sector 10 and were briefed on the local situation. The UN then gave formal permission for the revocation of the official instruction confining the Defence Force to its bases. This enabled Sector 10 to execute full-scale operations under the UN flag, and in so doing to restore the situation. As a result of its breach of the ceasefire agreement, SWAPO suffered heavy losses.

The Joint Monitoring Commission then held an emergency meeting on 8 and 9 April, in accordance with the Brazzaville Protocol. In co-operation with United Nations Transitional Assistance Group (UNTAG) the Commission drew up a plan that would bring about a cessation of hostilities. This was implemented on 23 April 1989, when SWAPO's invasion was already something of the past.

The factual situation as sketched above makes it crystal clear that SWAPO must be held accountable for the situation created in northern Namibia on 1 April 1989. It was reported as such in his report to the Security Council by Mr Pérez de Cuéllar, the UN Secretary General. He confirmed that the large-scale invasion of Namibia was perpetrated by SWAPO forces from Angola. This SWAPO action was a serious challenge to both UN authority and the international agreement. The opinion expressed by the Secretary General was based on a legal opinion issued by the US Department of State and accepted by the UN. The US document concluded that if Angola and Cuba had permitted the infiltration of insurgents into Namibia, they too were guilty of a "flagrant breach" of the Geneva Protocol.

Simon Barber's "Washington Letter" in the *Cape Times* of 18 April 1989 provided the correct perspective and interpretation: "A determined effort is underway to shift the blame. Already, we are being told that South Africa's response to the incursion was too vicious, that South Africa is hampering the intruder's return to Angola by placing menacing forces next to UN assembly points and demanding the right to interrogate those who do come in; that therefore, by some spectacular leap of logic, South Africa has no interest in free and fair elections."

The burning question remains why the TRC would include untruths in its most important report, and why this report refers only negatively to the Defence Force's external operations while ignoring positive aspects or refusing to refer to them at all. This Commission owes the country and Defence Force members an answer!

DEFENCE FORCE RESPONSIBILITY VERSUS POLITICAL ACCOUNTABILITY

Time and again the Defence Force has been accused of insufficient transparency and information given to the public and the media especially when operations were being executed. I acknowledge that there was such a deficiency, but there were very good reasons for it. Whenever I had an opportunity to raise the matter in Parliament, I used it because I hoped that this would give it a greater impact, and therefore engender a greater understanding amongst the public.

Von Clausewitz is regarded as one of the founders of the theory of warfare, and one of the most honoured experts in this regard. He stated that warfare was simply the continuation of politics at another level – a violent level. Warfare should be regarded as an attempt to reach one's political goals through violence rather than negotiations. He also formulated and laid the foundations for internationally accepted principles of warfare. To ensure success, it is important to apply these principles, which are to this day recognised and applied all over the world. The military institutions of most countries, including South Africa, teach their defence force members these principles. There may be shifts of emphasis in various countries, but in general they are the same. In South Africa we had always accepted these principles, and had applied them to military operations with great success. I would even say that this was one of the reasons why the Defence Force had so much success in its actions.

For the purposes of this discussion, which is really only about secrecy and the practical application of the military concept of "need to know", I will refer to only two principles of warfare, namely security and surprise.

Security: One must never allow the enemy to gain an unexpected advantage. Given proper security, the freedom of action enjoyed by one's forces is increased in order to neutralise their vulnerability to enemy actions, influence and surprise.

If one has insight into the enemy's plans while one's own remain hidden, the chances of success increase immeasurably.

Surprise: One attacks the enemy at a time and place and in a manner for which it is not prepared. This is much safer, and increases one's chances of success if one can attack the enemy at a time when and in a place where it least expects it. Factors that contribute to surprise include rapid action and the unexpected employment of certain forces as well as efficient intelligence, various diversionary operations, changes in tactics and operational employment, and above all operational security. To a large degree the element of surprise depends on the principle of security.

It is not always easy to ensure strategic surprise, yet time and again the Defence Force was able to catch enemy forces in Angola with their pants down, thanks to unexpected actions as well as strategic and tactical surprise.

The consistent and unyielding application of security in order to ensure surprise meant that the Defence Force was at some stages extremely unpopular amongst the next-of-kin of Defence Force members and some media representatives. This was particularly the case when national servicemen, Citizen Force or Commando members were called up for service on the border, or for service across the international border in Angola or in other countries. In cases where the Defence Force had to be deployed operationally far from home, the risk of security breaches and the consequent undermining of the element of surprise were greatest because those who were called up had to make arrangements at work and at home to be absent from South Africa for some time.

In such cases the Defence Force usually maintained a stony silence when enquiries were made, or used deception tactics. This was not done in order to deny the persons and bodies making the enquiries the necessary information. It was done only to withhold the information from the enemy, and to deny the enemy the opportunity to reach conclusions about future actions. If this were to happen, there was a far greater chance of a defeat with great loss of life on our part. In any case, all loss of life on the part of the Defence Force was unacceptable!

Fortunately Defence Force security worked well and the enemy was operationally surprised. This was one of the most important reasons why the Defence Force was undefeated during the 30 years of the struggle. To achieve this, and to consequently protect its members, demanded security. One had to play one's cards, out of necessity, close to one's chest.

Providing the media with information on military matters has also been a contentious matter internationally. I do not believe that the various parties involved in this issue will ever completely agree. The parties have real differences when it comes to their approaches and interests, and at times these differences clash head on. The media will always claim that they are given insufficient information, and the military will always say that the media is insensitive to the military's need for secrecy.

Of course both of these arguments are very subjective, with strong elements of self-interest.[20]

Because of the situation where the media, on the one hand, insists on news, and the military, on the other hand, insists on sensitivity, the media often and quite rightly complain that they do not know what is going on. This complaint has been heard in every war.

In order to promote better co-operation between the media (and especially the press) and the Defence Force, Mr P.W. Botha created a Liaison Committee between the SA Press Union and the SA Defence Force in the early 1970s. The Press Union was represented by members of the various press groups in the country, and acted as a forum that addressed common points of view, interests and uncertainties on behalf of the media. The regular meetings of the Liaison Committee resulted in some success, among other things through the accreditation of military correspondents to the various press groups, and the appointment of media liaison officers in the Defence Force. This improved co-operation, and the contact points that came into being on both sides improved communication and helped to clear up uncertainties quite quickly.

Rightly or wrongly, the initial phases of the Angolan conflict were completely dominated by secrecy. The international news media was silenced by all the parties involved. The aid given by the USA was clandestine, and the extent of this aid only came to light when the US Congress discussed it in January and February 1976, a year after the commencement of this aid. The aid and weapons that the Soviet Union and other communist countries provided to the MPLA has to this day been kept as secret as possible by those countries.

Cuba's part in the war was only made known to the world in January 1977 by a Colombian journalist. The first extensive press statement on the role of the SA Defence Force in Angola was issued only in February 1977. African countries such as Zaire, Zambia and others which were involved also maintained secrecy. The MPLA, FNLA, and UNITA too, did not disclose the aid they received from elsewhere.

Of course not all events could be kept secret. There was no shortage of journalists in Angola willing to supply the world's press with reports. However, they could not find all the available information, and not all their questions were answered. Politicians and military who were involved in the military sense applied the principle of secrecy for various reasons, and even now the border war is surrounded by a haze of uncertainty. Some journalists wrote fascinating descriptions, while others are still concocting fabrications and perceptions that the uninformed readily accept.

Another reason why the Defence Force tried to keep these sensitive operational actions and movements as quiet as possible, was to prevent the international community from hearing about them too soon. The Defence Force attitude was normally that the essential things had to be done as quietly and as efficiently as possible. As soon as military intentions regarding movements and operations, for example those in Angola, became public, the political pressure on the South African government would noticeably increase. Such pressure was usually accompanied by threats and messages to "withdraw from Angola immediately!" The underlying message was that if the Defence Force did not immediately withdraw from Angola, South Africa would not be able to rely on a particular country's veto in the UN Security Council, and this would mean a very strong possibility of general economic sanctions against South Africa.

The political pressure did not come from the United Nations only. Many great powers had their own agenda, pursued their own interests, and therefore applied pressure on South Africa.

Thanks to first-rate security, disinformation and surprise the Defence Force was adept at penetrating Angola and completing the necessary tasks rapidly and efficiently before its presence was detected. For example, the Defence Force had been busy with successful military operations for a month or two prior to the Battle of the Lomba River in south-eastern Angola before their presence became known to the international community. Not only did secrecy help ensure a greater element of surprise, it also provided an extended period of grace in which to complete the proposed military tasks.

When it became known that the Defence Force was engaged in military operations in south-eastern Angola, a major power suddenly sent word on a particular Friday (using the channels of the South African Department of Foreign Affairs) that if the Defence Force did not withdraw from Angola by the following Monday, South Africa would not be able to depend on that power's veto during the UN Security Council's next discussions on Angola. These discussions of the Defence Force's actions in Angola were to take place in New York in the coming week. Such threatening instructions at short notice usually came from sources with no inkling of the time-scales involved in carefully considered military operations. With the best will in the world it would have been impossible to accommodate such threats without withdrawing our forces from Angola in life-threatening circumstances, and creating an impression of military spinelessness.

At that time Pres. P.W. Botha was not one to succumb to pressure, and he had strong feelings on this matter. He would also not permit any bullying of South Africa, so his instructions were that the threat was to be ignored. When Monday arrived, this power was dead quiet, so the Defence Force could complete its military operations quite unperturbed. It was always difficult to judge which political pressures would really hold consequences for us, and which were simply a result of that country's own agenda, and therefore a matter of self-interest.

The military concept known as "need to know" was subject to heavy public criticism on many occasions. As soon as the concept was explained, however, emotions cooled down, and the idea was accepted. The use of the "need to know" principle is not aimed at hiding information from certain persons or organisations, but to prevent all and sundry from freely accessing and misusing information that does not concern them. If this were to happen, the possibility of a security breach is far greater, which then makes it easier for the enemy to obtain information that may be detrimental to the Defence Force.[21]

In reply to criticisms about secrecy at that time, I said the following in Parliament on 11 February 1986: "The activities of the SA Defence Force are not above Parliamentary discussions, nor are they a closed book to the public. However, when we are dealing with sensitive projects and operations, we must never lose sight of the "need to know" principle. This is an internationally acknowledged practice that is maintained even at the highest level within the Defence Force. The more so when a country is engaged in an unconventional armed conflict with an enemy that operates from its neighbouring countries. Naturally any actions against such an enemy are sensitive. One should furthermore guard against certain organisations that wish to exploit the disclosure of information regarding sensitive projects and operations for their own profit, and not always in the public interest."[22]

The so-called "moles", such as Dieter Gerhardt, who will be discussed later, would have caused the country far less damage had the "need to know" principle also been applied strictly and consistently in his case. He would subsequently not have been in a position to give the Soviet Union information regarding the SA Air Force's television-guided glider bomb that had the potential to deliver a nuclear device, also information regarding the envisaged tests that were to have been conducted by the Council for Scientific and Industrial Research (CSIR) at the nuclear testing site in the Kalahari.[23]

The above makes it clear that secrecy and the "need to know" principle were of prime importance to the Defence Force in the execution of its duties, particularly in times of war. During any conflict the Defence Force needs to control the application of these two principles carefully and with sound judgement. In peacetime these requirements need to be weighed against the principle of greater transparency, and therefore greater flexibility should be shown towards the media. The media can play an extremely important role for any defence force, provided that sound mutual relationships are fostered and maintained.

Chapter 18

TWO CONTROVERSIAL MATTERS: DIETER GERHARDT AND THE DEATH OF PRESIDENT SAMORA MACHEL

DIETER GERHARDT, A RUSSIAN SPY

If one considers the course of Dieter Gerhardt's life up to and including his act of treason against his country, it soon becomes clear that from his very early youth his entire mental make-up made him ripe for it. He later admitted that his whole life consisted of rebellion. As a member of a German-speaking family, he was opposed to the English; he rebelled against his father; as a declared agnostic he rebelled against the church; and eventually he also rebelled against the political dispensation.

Gerhardt was a difficult character since early childhood. Cdre (later Rear-Admiral) S.C. Biermann told of how Dieter's father, Alfred, pleaded with him to accept his son in the Navy and to take him under his wing so that Gerhardt could learn discipline. As a youth Gerhardt was constantly in trouble at school. The request was acceded to, and Gerhardt ended up in the Navy.

Gerhardt was in his late twenties when he commenced his spying activities. He was then still married to Janet Loggin, a very wealthy woman of Irish descent. Perhaps this contributed toward his becoming used to a "la dolce vita" way of life. After years of separation, he and Loggin were divorced in 1967, and she eventually wrote a book about her life with him.

The communist spy, Dieter Gerhardt, and his Soviet controller, Gregori Shirobokov.

The Navy trained Gerhardt in a technical direction, and he did well. In 1963 he was sent to the United Kingdom on an 18-month advanced weapons course. He claims that he had already developed an antipathy towards the Government's apartheid policy at that early stage, but as a Naval officer he could not openly oppose it. For him the next logical step was to contact senior members of the SA Communist Party and to offer to spy for the USSR, an offer that was eagerly accepted. Shortly thereafter he was placed under the direct supervision of Soviet Military Intelligence (GRU) and was informed that he was to continue his career in the SA Defence Force. He was given the code name "Felix" and became a full-blooded spy.[1]

In the years 1963–1964 he was regarded as one of the GRU's most valuable spies. The British completely trusted the young officer during his course, and gave him access to some of their most sensitive systems; he passed on information he gained there to the Soviet Union.[2]

While undergoing the course in England, he flew to Moscow via Vienna and Budapest, using a supposed skiing holiday in Europe as a cover. In Moscow he received intensive training in espionage techniques, among other things in the use of miniature photographic equipment, observation and evasion methods, disguise, the manufacture of false passports, and many other techniques. He was also trained in emergency procedures should his employers become suspicious and should he need to cover up his tracks.[3]

On completion of his course in the United Kingdom, Gerhardt was appointed as the Navy's liaison officer to the precursor of the Armaments Development Corporation (Armscor) in the early 1970s. He therefore had access to all information on Navy arms requirements, which were forwarded to Armscor for provision and/or manufacture. Together with a member of the SA Army and the SA Air Force he was one of three people to serve in this sensitive post. These three officers occupied positions that enabled any one of them to determine – simply by asking – in general terms what the other was occupied with.

Unfortunately the "need to know" principle was not applied strictly enough to the activities of these three men. Gerhardt was therefore in a very favourable position to acquire an extensive knowledge of Armscor's activities, and in so doing, to determine the Defence Force's requirements with regard to arms. He could also determine its progress in this regard. If he needed more particulars on any Army or Air Force projects, he had indirect access to it by virtue of his work situation. The Navy regarded him as an extremely reliable senior officer. In those days we blindly and absolutely believed in the loyalty of all fellow officers.

In the meantime, Gerhardt had married Ruth Johr in 1969; she was a Swiss citizen he had met at Klosters, a Swiss ski resort. In consultation with GRU he decided to inform her of his spying activities in pre-planned stages. Eventually she was asked to help her husband with his spying activities, and also received training in all the necessary techniques in Moscow.

When I was transferred to Pretoria in 1973, and later, when I was appointed as Chief of the SA Army, my attention was drawn to the possibility of a security breach due to the reigning circumstances at Armscor.

My only reasons for having any doubts about Gerhardt were that he had been married twice, the second time to a Swiss citizen who worked in the Swiss embassy in Pretoria. He was exposed to extremely sensitive military projects. Given these facts, and the circumstances, the warning lights should have been flashing quite brightly.

I therefore requested the Military Intelligence section to determine whether Gerhardt could possibly be a spy.

Some time later it was reported to me that there were no indications of espionage. What was to be done? A high security risk persisted.

In the meantime Gerhardt had passed on information about weaponry to the Soviet Union, in particular information concerning maritime weapons and the areas where these were to be deployed. Some documents of the North Atlantic Treaty Organisation (NATO) contained information about Russian naval weapons, as well as the names of the officers who had gained access to documents of the Warsaw Treaty countries. As a result a large number of British spies in Czechoslovakia were exposed by the Soviet Union, and paid the price.

Gerhard was particularly interested in South Africa's nuclear developments. He organised a visit to the Kalahari nuclear test site at Vastrap, and he passed information about what he saw there on to the USSR. The information troubled them so much that their ambassador in the USA requested Pres. Jimmy Carter, on behalf of Pres. Brezhnev, to pressure South Africa to terminate the tests.[4]

Gerhardt had managed to get the keys and combinations of the safes used by his fellow officers, and even gained access to their offices, using copies of skeleton keys in order to gather the information he wanted.

On becoming Chief of the Defence Force, I wanted to be absolutely certain that strict security would be maintained at Armscor, and so I changed the set-up with regard to the three liaison officers. They were replaced, and their stations, working methods and delegated responsibilities were altered. These changes had to be made very tactfully, because there was no evidence of possible espionage.

As the Chief of the Navy was also the Navy's personnel management officer, the Chief of the Defence Force actually had no direct jurisdiction over the employment of Naval officers. As a result the Navy was unhappy at my direct intervention, which could possibly harm Gerhardt's naval career. Without giving any reasons, I insisted that the Chief of the Navy transfer Gerhardt from Armscor; this was done, and he was sent to the Naval Dockyard at Simon's Town, where the Chief of the Navy appointed him as Officer Commanding.

However, Gerhardt tried to keep his contacts at Armscor intact. It is fortunate that this transfer took place, or he would have been able to do far greater damage through his spying activities. He was an intimate friend of his GRU handler, Gregori Shirobokov, one of Russia's most experienced agent handlers, with whom he worked for 18 years. Gerhardt even named his son Gregory, after his Russian friend. The USSR demanded more and more information from Gerhardt.

Gerhardt was sent to the USA at the end of 1982 to attend an advanced course. On landing at Kennedy Airport in the USA, he noticed with some alarm that the passport control officer had made a note after checking his passport. (Among other things the Soviet Union insisted that he should be able to read upside-down, so he saw the control officer noting that he was problematic.)

He was arrested in his hotel room shortly afterwards. The door burst open, and agents of the Central Intelligence Agency (CIA), the Federal Bureau of Investigation (FBI) and Britain's MI6 stormed into the room. They addressed him with his codename "Felix", and he knew immediately that the game was over.[5]

South Africa was notified within hours of his arrest, and Ruth Gerhardt was arrested at their South African home that same night.

Two weeks after the Americans had started interrogating him, he was transferred to Pretoria.

The South African Prime Minister, P.W. Botha, announced Gerhardt's sensational arrest on 26 January 1983. Gerhardt and his wife were interrogated for six months; the court case that followed lasted months, and was held *in camera*. Only a few facts were made public, among other things that he had been spying for the USSR since 1962, and that he had already visited Moscow five times.[6]

The State Prosecutor demanded the death sentence, and Gerhardt was expecting this. However, he received a life sentence while his wife was sentenced to ten years' imprisonment. The judge made it quite clear that had Gerhardt caused the death of even a single soldier, he would have paid for it with his life.[7]

Ruth Gerhardt was released in 1990, after having served eight years in prison, and after various representations by the Swiss government; Gerhardt was released in 1992 after having served nine and a half years in prison.

Pres. F.W. de Klerk visited the Soviet Union in 1992, and during a visit to Pres. Boris Yeltsin it was stated that the immediate release of Gerhardt was a condition for the restoration of diplomatic ties between the two countries and the signing of a trade agreement. Gerhardt was therefore released on 28 August 1992, and was immediately placed in the care of two KGB generals; he was reunited with Ruth in Zurich, and then taken to Moscow as part of a USA-USSR spy exchange programme.[8]

Gerhardt's conviction as a spy was declared invalid during a TRC sitting, and he was fully acquitted, despite the fact that he had transmitted more than 400 000 pages of the most secret information of the USA and NATO to the USSR, and that he had admitted that he was a communist spy.[9]

In summary it seems to me that Cdre Dieter Gerhardt, a senior officer of the Defence Force who should have known better, had sold his soul for 30 pieces of silver. His actions show that he sold his country and its people out of avidity and greed, and not to promote a foreign ideology. Of course he could later twist the reasons for his high treason to suit himself.[10]

THE SAMORA MACHEL AIRCRAFT CRASH, 1986

The plane disaster in which Pres. Samora Machel of Mozambique was killed, caused an international sensation in the media. This crash was in actual fact not a military matter, although the Defence Force became embroiled in it, but I still want to broach the incident in this book.

One can understand that the death of a head of state in an aircraft disaster, such as that of Pres. Samora Machel of our neighbouring state, Mozambique, in October 1986, would be given wide coverage in the local and international media.

Because there had been conflict between South Africa and Mozambique at some stages (the latter harboured enemy terrorists who were acting against South Africa), accusations regarding the air disaster were immediately levelled against South Africa, and the Defence Force in particular. It was said that the Defence Force had deliberately caused the crash.[11]

Despite a thorough investigation by an international board of experts, which found that South Africa was in no way involved in the disaster, all manner of rumours will simply not die down.[12] As recently as 2002 some of Machel's relatives publicly threatened that they would ensure that those responsible would be brought to book. It was also said that the South African investigating agency, the Scorpions, would investigate the matter anew. As recently as June 2003, representatives from the office of the Public Prosecutor visited me with regard to the crash. Once again I conveyed the facts at my disposal; the facts on which the description of the accident given below are based.

The few times I personally met Pres. Samora Machel, he made a particular impression on me – he seemed a competent and friendly leader, and a man with his feet planted firmly on the ground. I am still convinced that Machel's untimely death was a setback for Mozambique and Southern Africa as a whole. Historically Mozambique, to the east of Mpumalanga and north of KwaZulu-Natal, has always played a large role in South Africa's existence; in the future it is likely to develop into one of our most important neighbours.

At the commencement of the revolutionary war, the ANC Alliance regularly made illegal border crossings from Mozambique, and there were constant mutual accusations and actions in this regard between the two neighbouring countries. However, the Nkomati Accord was signed between the two countries on 16 March 1984, and as a result the enmity abated. In brief, it was decided that South Africa and Mozambique would mutually recognise the independence of the other, and neither would in future permit its territory to be used as a jumping-off point or sanctuary for the other's enemy elements.

Despite the Nkomati Accord, both sides continued to make accusations of alleged violations.[13] For example, Mozambique alleged that South Africa was digging a tunnel beneath the international border to gain access to Mozambique in order to support RENAMO, the freedom movement fighting the Mozambique government at that stage, and which South Africa had supported prior to the signing of the Nkomati

Accord. RENAMO has become the official opposition in Mozambique since then.

I found it difficult to accept the far-fetched allegation that someone was digging a tunnel, while it would be far simpler simply to flatten the border fence and drive over. I requested the co-ordinates of the position of the so-called tunnel, and that Mozambican guides should lead us to the tunnel. Needless to say, there was no reaction to these requests.

There were also many allegations of violations of Mozambican airspace by South African aircraft across Mozambique's western border. I discussed these alleged violations with the SA Air Force and was given the assurance that the Air Force was not guilty, and had in fact tried its level best to avoid such border violations. The Air Force maintained a radar capability at Mariepskop, and a base for supersonic aircraft at Hoedspruit close to the Mozambican border. They would therefore be able to determine who was guilty of these violations.

In brief the result was that there were no deliberate violations: they were mostly the result of civil aviation and small private aircraft moving between Mozambique and South Africa, Swaziland, Zimbabwe, Malawi, Zambia and Kenya. These border violations were apparently accidental, and most probably caused by navigation errors; there were no malicious intentions.

On occasion such a violation by a C-47 Dakota (also known as the DC-3) was reported. This aircraft was intercepted by SA Air Force fighters and forced to land. It was then determined that it was carrying a legitimate Zimbabwean soccer team; the aircraft had strayed from its flight path on its way to participating in a football match in Swaziland, but there was no malicious intent. Mozambique accepted the facts of this apparent violation.

The border fence between Mozambique and Mpumalanga and KwaZulu-Natal was very closely watched and patrolled daily by Defence Force elements. Parts of the border consisted of electrified fencing and sisal, which made violations difficult.

Before sunrise on 20 October 1986, my colleague Louis le Grange, the Minister of Law and Order, telephoned me unexpectedly and wanted to know whether I was aware of the Machel air crash in the then Eastern Transvaal. My first question on conclusion of his brief description was: In which direction had the aircraft been moving? He wanted to know what the point of such a question was. I answered that if the aircraft had been flying from Mozambique to South Africa, it was possible that Machel was fleeing from Mozambique in the wake of a coup d'etat, and was trying to seek asylum in South Africa. If the aircraft was flying in an opposite direction, it had possibly strayed off course, as so many had before.

The Soviet Union had given Pres. Machel a luxury Tupolev Tu-134A-3 passenger aircraft for his personal use. At that stage he was the one African statesman not too easily influenced by the Soviet Union. The aircraft could have been a Soviet courting present.

Pres. Machel left Zambia en route to his capital, Maputo, on board this Russian-designed and Russian-built aircraft on 19 October 1986. He had just concluded a very successful official visit to Zambia, and was in a jovial mood.[14]

At 39 seconds after 19:21 the Tupolev with its Russian crew flew into the ground at Mbuzini in the Komatipoort district, and only 10 of the 44 persons on board survived the crash.

The wreck of the aircraft was found approximately 35 nautical miles from Maputo Airport, in hilly terrain at a height of 666 m above sea level, and about 150 m from the Mozambican border on South African territory.

It was confirmed that all relevant equipment and instruments were fully serviceable and airworthy immediately prior to the aircraft's impact with the ground. After an analysis of the information shown by the aircraft's instruments, the South African Government appointed a Board of Enquiry at the beginning of 1987 to determine what could have caused the accident and who might have been responsible for it. The Board consisted of experts from South Africa, the USA and the United Kingdom (UK).

Mr Justice Cecil Margo, the Chairperson of the Board of Enquiry, was a former test pilot and participant in the aerial warfare of World War II. At that time he had already taken part in investigations into 30 national and international air crashes. He was assisted by Col Frank Borman, an astronaut, flight engineer and former chief test pilot in the USA; the Right Honourable Sir Edward Walter Eveleigh, former Judge-President of the

British Appeal Court and an internationally acknowledged expert with regard to the investigation of air accidents; and Mr Geoffrey Wilkenson, a member of the Ministry of Transport in the UK, who at that stage had a valid licence to fly the Concorde, the Boeing 747 and the Tupolev. On the South African side there were Messrs Jacques Geldenhuys, the former Commissioner of Civil Aviation, and Piet van Hoven, an aviation expert closely involved in the aviation industry in South Africa.[15]

The Board commenced its work by visiting and inspecting the scene of the crash, the wreck of the aircraft and the vicinity of the accident. The South African Government invited Mozambique and the Soviet Union (as interested parties) and other stakeholders to participate in the investigation by attending proceedings and presenting evidence, or having it presented. They would also have the right to cross-examine witnesses and make representations to the Board.

The Board was convinced of the reliability of details of the flight, as gathered from the cockpit voice recorder, the digital flight data recorder, flight control's tape-recording, the radar record of the SA Air Force, inspection of the crash site and wreckage, as well as oral and written evidence.

The cockpit voice recorder is a device that registers and captures all sounds above a minimum range on the flight deck. The digital flight data recorder is a device that records certain flight parameters such as height, speed, speed of ascent or descent, the performance of every engine, the position of the control surfaces and other relevant data at appropriate times. These two devices are usually known as an aircraft's "black boxes".

Of course all the information presented cannot be dealt with in the limited space available to me, but brief reference is made below to the summary of the Board's findings.

The findings of the Board of Enquiry were based on the incontrovertible evidence of the digital flight data recorder, the cockpit voice recorder and the specialist reconstruction of the flight path, as well as data recovered at the point of impact. The main findings were as follows: the crew was qualified and licensed to fly the Tupolev Tu-134A-3, and had enough experience to land at Maputo Airport at night; the aircraft was airworthy and properly loaded, and there was no malfunction during flight prior to impact; the status of the radio navigation aids on the ground and in the aircraft was adequate for an approach and landing using the instrument landing system; the digital flight data recorder and cockpit voice recorder both functioned properly and had provided vital information for the purposes of the investigation; the weather at Maputo was not a factor; the crew had not submitted a flight plan as required by Mozambican regulations; the crew was not aware of the exact number of passengers on board; the aircraft had too little fuel on board to enable it to divert to another suitable airport; during its descent the aircraft made a turn of 37 degrees to the right too early. The navigator signalled the turn to the right because the VHF omni-directional radio range (VOR) signal indicated that this was required. The only VOR signal which could have indicated this was the one at Matsapa in Swaziland; the required procedure and verbal confirmation that should have been executed in accordance with the final let down procedure was not followed. The crew did not use the secondary navigation aids that were available, for example the Maputo broadcasting station and the aircraft's onboard radar. At the critical stage the co-pilot was listening to music and a news broadcast; the captain continued with the aircraft's descent below 3000 feet even though no runway lights or other visible reference points were available; the crew ignored the alarm of the ground proximity warning system. There was no confirmation of the malicious allegations that the aircraft was lured from its course by means of a false VOR signal or by any other method. On discovery of the crash, medical and rescue aid was provided as soon as possible.[16]

The Board concluded that the cause of the accident was that the flight crew did not follow the required procedure for an instrument let down, but continued the descent and followed the procedure for a visual flight, even though it was dark and cloudy. The flight crew therefore did not take into account the inadequate visual contact with the ground below the minimum safe height, or the minimum allocated height for it, and also ignored the ground proximity warning system.[17]

The Russian Board of Enquiry and the USA's Federal Board of Aviation Administration concurred with the findings.

The Mozambican and Soviet media, however, kicked up a fuss about the accident that simply would not die down. In their opinion the Defence Force must have received instructions to erect a false VOR beacon in order to lure the Machel aircraft from its flight path towards Maputo Airport into the hilly area west of Maputo near Mbuzini.

None of the other aircraft that were in the air and on their way to Maputo at the same time were influenced by any strong VOR signal, which would have had to be even stronger than the one of the Maputo VOR.

The expert opinion was that it would have been easier to switch off the Maputo VOR signal than to use a false beacon that was stronger than the one in Maputo. However, at the time of the accident the Maputo VOR was not switched off, and was functioning normally.

It was possible to deduce from the transcription of the cockpit voice recorder, the simple fact that for several minutes during the descent the aircraft did not follow any VOR signal, despite the fact that a selector was tuned to a VOR on the Maputo frequency, and should have been receiving the signal.

There was evidence that the SA Air Force had no prior knowledge of the flight to Maputo, the time of the flight or the identity of the aircraft when it appeared on the radar screen. Neither was it aware of Machel's presence on board, as no flight plan had been filed.

Allegations were made about a camping site near the scene of the crash, but the evidence pointing to the presence of a tent or tents at the camping site made no mention of the presence of a 4,5 m high antenna or other equipment required for erecting a VOR beacon. The investigating team's inspection of the camp site made it clear that the entire site was visible from Mozambican territory, and that it would have been difficult to erect a VOR beacon without it being seen from that country.[18]

All the evidence regarding the possible use of such a radio beacon by the SA Defence Force refutes such a possibility. The unanimous conclusion reached by the experts who gave evidence before the Board was that the rumour of a false beacon must be rejected.[19]

The reaction to the report by the Soviet Union and Mozambique was that the navigator could not have selected the Matsapa beacon in error, because there is a large mountain between the aircraft's route and the Matsapa beacon; the mountain would have made it impossible for the signal to reach the aircraft.

When the Board of Enquiry received this reaction, both the USSR team and the Mozambican authorities were in turn asked to test the theory that the mountain would have blocked the signal from Matsapa. In both cases they declined, as they thought it unnecessary. The Board then requested permission from Mozambique for South Africa to carry out the test, but once again they thought that such a test was unnecessary. This presented the Board with a dilemma, as the USSR/Mozambican theory had not been examined adequately.

The former Chief of the Air Force, Gen. Dennis Earp, received permission from me as representative of the South African authority, and despatched two Air Force officers to confirm or refute the USSR/Mozambican theory. They followed the flight path of the Machel aircraft in SA Air Force aircraft, and determined that the Matsapa signal came through loud and clear on every occasion; these tests were conducted in the immediate vicinity of the crash site.

Mr Piet van Hoven, a member of the Board of Enquiry, who knew of the dispute regarding the Matsapa signal, requested a Kenyan airfreight company operating a freight service between Nairobi and Maputo twice a week, to do a similar test. They conducted two tests in the flight path taken by the Machel aircraft, and in both cases the Matsapa signal came through loud and clear; the test was positive, and was confirmed adequately.

In the case of both these independent tests – the one conducted by the SA Air Force and the other by the Kenyan company – the pilots submitted affidavits, which provided sworn support for the Board's findings.

It is inexcusable that the Soviet Union and Mozambique refused to give permission to conduct the tests.

About eight years after the crash, Pres. Mandela unveiled a memorial at the site of the aircraft crash. He promised Samora Machel's widow, Graça, that the South African Government would leave no stone unturned in its search for the criminal elements who were responsible for the accident. It is strange that the President could contend that Pres. Machel had possibly been murdered, with no reference to the findings of the Board of Enquiry.

I am concerned that the continued blackening of the good name of the Defence Force, including false accusations concerning the accident, may have occurred in a calculated manner in order to score strategic points long after the conclusion of the game. What is the purpose of this continued sowing of suspicion?

A few years ago the Chairperson of the Board of Enquiry informally heard that a committee had been appointed to investigate the crash anew. This committee consisted of an attorney-general, a so-called forensics expert and a reporter, Deborah Patta. They "investigated" the accident without the help of any aviation expert or technologist. The entire process was conducted in secret and was based on hearsay evidence.

Ms Patta conducted an interview with the Chairperson of the original Board of Enquiry, Mr Justice Margo, but concealed the existence of the committee and her membership of it. It was soon clear to him that she was hopelessly unqualified for her role as member of the committee; that she had no expertise or experience, and that she had no knowledge of the practical side of aviation.[20]

The appointment of the committee had eventually been announced publicly, but no further details were provided; everything reflected a lack of expertise. There was no attempt to declare invalid the findings of the original Board of Enquiry. It would serve a good purpose if the current authorities were to make public the findings of both the Board of Enquiry led by Mr Justice Margo and those of the most recent committee.

I have no doubt whatsoever that the findings of the 1987 Board of Enquiry, which was made up of internationally acknowledged aviation experts, did penetrate to the heart of the matter.

One thing is certain: As in many other cases, the SA Defence Force was made the target of undeserved accusations, reproaches and allegations concerning something it was never guilty of. I hope this perception of the SA Defence Force from the side of the ANC Alliance will now be abandoned.[21]

Chapter 19

THE EMINENT PERSON'S GROUP AND THE CIVIL CO-OPERATION BUREAU

THE EMINENT PERSON'S GROUP (EPG) INCIDENT IN 1986

Because cross-border operations always have to be conducted clandestinely and in the greatest of secrecy, it is not normal practice to make public any facts concerning such operations from which correct deductions can immediately be made. At the same time a great many perceptions are normally formed, and rumours concerning such operations are spread, while intense speculation is rife. One such operation – regarded as quite sensational at the time – is known as the EPG incident.

Cabinet and Defence Force members were subpoenaed to testify under oath at Truth and Reconciliation Commission (TRC) sittings in 1997 about a military cross-border operation that was launched simultaneously into Zambia, Zimbabwe and Botswana on 19 May 1986. My account of this important incident follows below.

According to Margaret Thatcher, the British Prime Minister at the time, discussions during the meeting of the British Commonwealth (from which South Africa withdrew in 1961) at Nassau in the Bahamas in 1985 were dominated by South African politics and military operations. Among other things, there were speculations about how pressure could be applied to South Africa, particularly with a view to economic sanctions. The Conference condemned apartheid, called on the South African Government to commence political dialogue, and requested a simultaneous termination of violence. The Conference also decided that a group of dignitaries, the so-called Eminent Persons Group (EPG), should be constituted under the chairmanship of Gen. Olusegun Obasanjo of Nigeria to institute political dialogue with South Africa. The EPG was to investigate and find ways to bring about a peaceful resolution of the escalating conflict in Southern and South Africa.[1]

The main objection to such an investigation brought by the South African Government was that the EPG had been established and tasked without any consultation with South Africa, and that this inevitably amounted to uninvited interference in our domestic affairs. It was also pointed out that the process of reform and negotiations between the various parties in South Africa was the responsibility of the South African Government.[2]

Another objection voiced by the Government was that some of the countries represented in the EPG themselves had no democratic government. How could one expect members of such countries to investigate South Africa's internal political situation and come up with suggestions to bring about a democratic political system in South Africa?

Primarily the EPG was supposed to make suggestions aimed at dismantling apartheid; the withdrawal of Security Forces from black townships; the release of Nelson Mandela and other political prisoners; and the lifting of the ban on the ANC and PAC.[3]

At this stage – in the mid-1980s – terrorist attacks inside South Africa increased markedly. In 1985 they increased by 300% in comparison to the previous year. This, together with unrest in certain parts of the country, compelled the Government to declare a partial state of emergency in 36 magisterial districts in July 1985.[4]

The declaration of the partial state of emergency and the security operations that followed did not have the expected results. Hundreds of South Africans were killed in terrorism-related incidents within the first three months, thousands were injured and even more were detained by the Security Forces on charges of public violence.

The Government initially refused to co-operate with the EPG, but in view of South Africa's deteriorating international standing, it was decided in December 1985 to accept the EPG, and to allow the group to conduct its investigation.[5]

The EPG's terms of reference entailed visits by air to South Africa and other countries in the region. In view of the conflict situation in South Africa in 1985 and 1986, it was a difficult but very important mission. The group envisaged visiting South Africa a number of times to talk to members of the public with a variety of political and economic viewpoints.

With regard to the revolutionary situation at that stage, the ANC and PAC cadres no longer operated against South Africa from isolated bases in the bush across the border; they were already making use of houses, camps and similar facilities in our neighbouring countries. These facilities were mainly situated in the suburbs of cities such as Maputo, Lusaka, Gaborone and Harare. At that time it was the Alliance's tactic to hide themselves amongst civilians in these places.[6] This meant there was a greater risk of civilian casualties during Defence Force operations than before. In order to limit civilian casualties, accurate information, surprise, favourable weather conditions and other factors played a very important role. The Defence Force always tried to avoid civilian casualties, but this was very difficult where the ANC lived amongst civilians.

Because of the increase in unrest-related incidents, the employment of the Defence Force in support of the Police became inevitable. This was necessary to create and consolidate peace and order, and in so doing to give the Government an opportunity to fully develop its initiatives. The Government was therefore compelled to deploy the Defence Force internally in 1985. This occurred in co-operation with the Police. Deployment of the Defence Force in support of the Police did not only take place in South Africa. Such a deployment of a defence force in conjunction with the police to combat unrest is an internationally acknowledged principle.

At an extraordinary meeting of the State Security Council in December 1985, the members discussed the current security situation. After thorough reflection the State Security Council gave certain instructions regarding the illegal provisioning of terrorists from neighbouring countries, which the security departments had to prevent in future. In view of the increase in the number of unrest-related incidents, the Defence Force's executive powers were extended, in that all South African territory was declared an operational area.

At no stage, from the formation of the important EPG to any time thereafter, was the SA Defence Force informed of its itinerary or discussions with the Government; the Defence Force therefore had no knowledge of these activities at all. However, during the December meeting of the State Security Council, note was taken of the important task with which the EPG had been charged.[7]

Complicating matters on the psychological-propagandistic front, Mr Oliver Tambo, the leader of the ANC, dedicated the year 1986 to Umkhonto we Sizwe (MK – the ANC's armed wing).[8] Pres. Robert Mugabe of Zimbabwe also made a public prediction at the beginning of 1986 that the ANC/SACP would govern South Africa from the Union Buildings by the end of that year.[9]

On 4 February 1986 I warned Parliament that if the assault on South Africa did not abate, cross-border actions were inevitable. A few days later, on 11 February, I once again spoke in Parliament about cross-border operations and about the essential, internationally recognised "need to know" principle applicable in such a case. As mentioned before, this principle is applied to certain sensitive military operations to help guarantee the element of surprise, and the safety of forces.[10]

In view of the prevailing circumstances, the State President, P.W. Botha, requested the security departments to contain the terrorist attacks. This would have to be preceded by the collection of intelligence and target identification. These preparations for operations took place in February and March 1986.[11]

Despite the deteriorating internal situation, the Government decided in March 1986 to end the partial state of emergency, which applied only to certain geographical areas in the country. From a security point of view this partial state of emergency had not functioned efficiently.

The State President made a comprehensive statement on the deteriorating security situation in the country in Parliament on 17 April 1986, and referred to the sharp increase in unrest.

At the same time the public began to place great pressure on the Government. Black leaders were increasingly demanding intervention from the State to protect the lives and property of black South Africans.

In the meantime the Defence Force had, after thorough planning, formulated its own operational tasks aimed at executing the specific instructions of the State Security Council, and stood ready to execute these. In brief, these operational plans involved an attack on certain external ANC/SACP headquarters and facilities. These capabilities needed to be disrupted, put out of order or even destroyed by the Defence Force. This would destroy or disrupt the ANC's supply lines and means of communication as well as the terrorists' accommodation and their transit and training capability. Stores, including weapons and ammunition in transit, would be intercepted. It would take time to repair the disruption caused by the Defence Force, and this would result in a temporary discontinuation of the ANC's external support for internal terrorism and unrest. In turn this would have a direct influence on the intensity of internal terrorism and unrest activities, and help to abate it. It would also send a strong message that the Defence Force knew where the ANC's external bases were, and that it would find and destroy them. It was a message with strong psychological content in these particular circumstances.

As a certain level of liaison and interdependence existed between the various external ANC headquarters, it would be better to eliminate too many rather than too few of these headquarters. This would reduce the possibility of alternative communication and supply routes being established in support of the internal effort. South Africa had on numerous occasions warned that it would not stand by passively while ANC and PAC members were accommodated in neighbouring countries and were allowed to perpetrate cross-border acts of terrorism from those countries. Those countries would have to bear the consequences of South African actions.

The envisaged military attack was provisionally planned for the second half of April 1986. After careful consideration and thorough discussions, the State President gave approval in principle for action during this period. As the actual time of the operation depended on a number of variables, the exact date had not yet been determined. This meant that the normal procedure for the approval of cross-border operations, including the State President's approval for an exact date of execution, was not followed at that stage. The danger of a security breach and the consequent probability of heavy Defence Force losses was too serious.

At this stage the State Security Council was also warned once again about the possible penetration of government departments by ANC/

SACP supporters. The results of such a situation, and the dangers of state intelligence being leaked, meant a dramatic increase in the possibility of loss of life amongst members of the Defence Force participating in the planned military operations. It could in fact mean that enemy elements in the target areas would be expecting such an attack, with disastrous results for the Defence Force.[12]

As a result of these circumstances, the military operations planned for April were put on ice, and the State President was accordingly informed of this.

In the middle of May 1986 circumstances for an attack on ANC targets in foreign countries had improved, and the Defence Force once again sought permission for the planned operation. After thorough discussion, the State President once again gave his permission. Aspects taken into account during the discussions included the following: security surrounding the operation; the possibility of intelligence leaks; the vital element of surprise; the safety of Defence Force members who would have to operate in life-threatening situations; probable weather conditions at the time that could lead to the operation being postponed. Once again all these uncertain factors meant that no precise date could be determined.

On this occasion the State President emphasised the vital importance of security regarding the operation, and that the prescribed procedures for cross-border operations would not have to be followed in this case. He also gave his approval for the execution of the operation, provided that nothing unforeseen occurred and that the Defence Force was of the opinion that the circumstances for success were favourable.

The simultaneous military attacks were executed successfully on the identified targets in Harare, Lusaka and Gaborone in the early morning hours of 19 May 1986. The Defence Force was not aware that this was the very day that the EPG was to visit South Africa again. Fortunately the attack did not put the EPG off its stride, and on a later occasion the Minister of Foreign Affairs was able to comment: "They [the EPG - M.M.]... stated categorically that the raids were not the reason for their decision to discontinue the discussions."[13]

In their discussions with several South African Cabinet ministers and government leaders, the EPG had made proposals with regard to the problem of violence in Southern Africa, and decided not to continue with its investigation into the problem. Without any further discussions, the members then decided to return to their respective countries.

It is a well-known international tactic of terrorist movements to use refugee camps as a smokescreen to hide behind. In such cases terrorists pretend to be refugees, and a day or so after an attack such camps are cunningly rearranged for effect; the media are then welcomed to the target area with much fanfare and shown the so-called aftermath of Defence Force atrocities.[14]

However, it was of primary importance that the military operation was a great success, and that the Defence Force suffered no casualties.

An analysis of the casualty statistics for the mid-1980s shows that there was a marked increase in terrorism attacks in South Africa. Of course the decision by the ANC Alliance at their Kawbe Conference on 21 June 1985, namely that there should no longer be a distinction between "hard" and "soft" targets, contributed to the increase in deaths of South African citizens in political violence.

The following casualties were noted in the period September 1985 to February 1987:

Sept. 1985–Feb. 1986:   565 persons killed
March 1986–Aug. 1986:   955 persons killed
Sept. 1986–Feb. 1987:   187 persons killed

The National Security Management System (NSMS) and its Joint Management Centres (JMCs), the general state of emergency declared in the whole of South Africa on 12 June 1986, and the Defence Force attacks on those three enemy targets in Harare, Lusaka and Gaberone, contributed greatly to the reduction in the number of casualties from September 1986 to February 1987 by more than 80%, in comparison with the previous period. This attack on the three targets was therefore worth it, because it prevented an even greater loss of life amongst innocent South African citizens (soft targets).

In *The last trek - a new beginning*, former Pres. F.W. de Klerk says: "In the anarchistic months prior to June 1986, many of them believed that the tide of internal unrest was unstoppable, and that further action would quickly result in the government's revolutionary downfall. By

1988 this perception had changed drastically. The more realistic leaders of the ANC and the internal revolt realised that a quick or easy victory was not possible. They also began to accept that a lengthy struggle between themselves and the government would be so bitter and destructive that there would be little left as anybody's legacy. This perception was an essential prerequisite for the start of true negotiations."[15]

In 1986 South Africa's state intelligence agencies reported that the so-called frontline states made their most aggressive speeches yet aimed at South Africa during that year, in anticipation of the ANC Alliance's takeover of South Africa. When this takeover did not happen, these so-called frontline states reconsidered their strategy. They did not want to experience any more of South African cross-border operations in their respective countries. This resulted in Zambia putting pressure on the Alliance to use the opportunity to begin talks with the South African government.

The effect of cross-border operations, such as the one during the EPG visit, together with the Alliance's failure to force South Africa to its knees by means of unrest, therefore played an important role in promoting talks and negotiation politics in Southern Africa.

THE SPECIAL FORCES, INCLUDING THE CIVIL CO-OPERATION BUREAU (CCB)

Apart from the SA Army, Air Force, Navy and Medical Service, Special Forces were the only other operational component of the SA Defence Force. Special Forces included all the reconnaissance commandos (RCs or Recces) and the Civil Co-operation Bureau (CCB). The Reconnaissance Commando and Civil Co-operation Bureau's joint General Officer Commanding was under the direct command of the Chief of the SA Defence Force.[16]

Any conflict, but particularly a revolutionary war involving terrorists on a large scale, is characterised by the use of unconventional means. Internationally it is quite normal for a defence force to use clandestine or covert counter-measures in such circumstances. The Defence Force also followed this pattern with the Government's permission.[17]

The Special Forces was the organisation destined to carry out covert operations. Special Forces was later subdivided into five reconnaissance units and the CCB.

The CCB grew out of the covert D-4O. It was later renamed Project Barnacle, then 3VR, and by 1986 it became known as the Civil Co-operation Bureau or simply CCB.[18]

In 1985-1986, in the wake of the Kabwe Conference, the ANC Alliance drastically changed its tactics and increased its underground, unconventional methods, both internally and externally. This resulted in the Defence Force being forced to create the CCB in 1986 as a subdivision of Special Forces.[19]

I approved the CCB as a component of Special Forces in principle at that time. The CCB had the task of penetrating enemy organisations, gathering intelligence concerning them, and disrupting them. The CCB consisted of ten divisions or regions.[20]

The establishment of the CCB had my approval, but I personally insisted on one condition: Region 6 (namely the interior of South Africa), one of the ten regions, would not be manned and activated without my permission. In other words, I only approved the organisational structure for this region. The reason for this limited approval was a result of the Government's geographical allocation of primary security responsibilities, which determined that the SA Police were responsible for the interior of South Africa. This was also the reason why Region 6 was only approved structurally – if the internal security situation were to deteriorate, this region could be manned and activated with the approval of the Minister of Defence.[21]

The internal conflict in South Africa entered its cruellest and most uncompromising phase in 1984-1985. There was a clear shift from "hard" to "soft" targets by the ANC Alliance. This shift brought about a lowering of the standards of the armed struggle, and was accompanied by the destruction of property and the death of civilians. In the next five years about 400 people were killed by "necklacing" them with burning tyres. Another 372 died when they or their houses were doused with petrol and set alight. More than 7000 private dwellings and 1700 schools were badly damaged or totally destroyed during unrest situations. In 1986-1987 alone, about R90 million's worth of damage was done during unrest incidents.[22]

The Government's policy remained rock-steady during this period: Halt the perpetrators of violence at all costs. Those who tried to bring car bombs, landmines, limpet mines and other mines to South Africa from across the country's borders, should be stopped outside the borders. If they managed to enter the country, they had to be prevented from perpetrating their outrages. Government policy stated that it was the task of every member of the Defence Force to destroy the terrorists, their bases and their capabilities. This was the only way to prevent the slaughter of civilians.[23]

The morale of the entire civil society, especially in the black townships, was very low at this time. The combat-readiness of and quick actions by the Security Forces played a large part in raising morale, but it entailed great sacrifices and tremendous risks for these forces. The standards that the Security Forces set for themselves in those times entailed determining the dangers that members of the public would be exposed to should the ANC manage to break through their protection. If these dangers could be stopped in time, that possibility would be averted. Both MK and the Security Forces went all out at that time.[24]

Unconventional action in a time of conflict is nothing new or unusual in modern times, and occurs the world over. Organisations such as the CIA, Delta Force and Seals in the USA, Britain's MI5, MI6 and SAS, and Russia's KGB all have their own special ways of acting to counter threats.[25]

Governments act according to their view of circumstances. Pres. Ronald Reagan of the USA ordered and launched an air strike aimed directly at Pres. Gaddafi of Lybia. Mrs Margaret Thatcher, the British Prime Minister, at one time ordered that the Irish Republican Army (IRA) should be attacked in Gibraltar, and accepted personal responsibility for her decision because she was convinced that she had saved the lives of innocent people by doing so.[26] Pres. George W. Bush of the USA attacked Afghanistan in the wake of the contemptible terrorist attacks on the World Trade Center in New York and the Pentagon in Washington on 11 September 2001, in order to retaliate against Osama bin Laden's Al-Qaeda terrorist organisation.

War is now waged in the international community on many levels, without it ever having been declared. One cannot condone many of these actions without qualification, but they are understandable in certain circumstances. It is always difficult to judge such occurrences objectively in hindsight, and one is usually inclined to condemn them as done in *mala fides*.[27]

In the nature of things, members of the CCB, as could other members of the security departments, deduced from public speeches made by myself and some of my colleagues, that in the terrorist conflict they need not always react according to established military principles. Circumstances that threatened national security were the determining factor. For example, I said in the House of Assembly: "Once more I wish to place it on record that the ANC and its followers continuously threaten the security of this country ... my colleague, the Minister of Law and Order, spelled this out recently, and I want to again state clearly – and I make no apologies for this – that we will use all means at our disposal to find and winkle out the ANC and act against them wherever they may be ... I also wish to give the assurance that this Government will not allow these murderous gangs to execute their planning, their training and their preparations in the safety and protection of neighbouring states and to act against South Africa from there. The Security Forces will punish them wherever they are. What I am saying here is Government policy. We cannot allow these terrorist organisations to decide where they are going to commit these foul deeds inside or outside of South Africa ... in order to efficiently meet the threat of revolution, it may happen that we, as do other countries, may have to employ unconventional means ... As in other governments, we do not talk about it."[28]

Pronouncements made by the Alliance at the time did not exactly pour oil on troubled waters. For example: "This ANC conference at Kabwe from 16 to 23 June 1985 which took the form of a council of war decided that the distinction between 'hard' and 'soft' targets should disappear."[29] However, even before this official decision was made public, it was clear that the so-called "new" strategy had already been put in place, because there were four bombing attacks in East London and Durban between 15 and 21 June 1985, and an hotel, a tea-room, a garage and a city hall suffered.[30]

Mrs Winnie Mandela's declaration is well known: "Together, hand in hand, with our boxes of matches and our necklaces, we shall liberate this country. We have no guns – we have only stones, boxes of matches and petrol."[31]

Tim Ngubane, the ANC representative in the USA, made the following declaration in a speech to students of the California State University: "We want to make the death of a collaborator so grotesque that people will never think of it (i.e. collaboration)."[32]

Mr Chris Hani wrote: "The necklace was a weapon ... to remove this cancer (collaboration) from our society ... to cleanse the townships from the very destructive and even lethal activities of the puppets and collaborators."[33]

Not only members of the CCB, but also all members of the Defence Force, had to operate against this background and in these circumstances. They regarded themselves as a shield that protected civilians, and that had to prevent the violence and the death of civilians.[34]

I met Pres. De Klerk and the Minister of Justice at Durban Airport on 2 January 1990 in order to discuss the matter of the CCB with him at his request. As he puts it in his autobiography, I informed him, among others things, that I had "received disconcerting information about a secret defence front organisation, the so-called Civil Co-operation Bureau (CCB) ... that the CCB, which had been created in the mid-1980s within the framework of the SA Defence Force's underground structures ... [and that the CCB's Region 6 – M.M.] had apparently used totally unacceptable methods and strategies against the ANC and other revolutionary organisations".[35]

I assured the President that I would immediately take steps to investigate the CCB's activities, and that I would, if necessary, disband the organisation. In January 1990 I ordered an internal investigation into allegations regarding the CCB's Region 6 that had recently come to my attention.[36]

I addressed an enquiry to the Defence Force, and it was explained to me that this region was activated in 1988-1989 because the CCB would in some cases be able to act more efficiently if Region 6 were permitted to function inside South Africa on the same basis as in other regions. I was given the example of a hypothetical case where a terrorist cell is discovered and observed in a neighbouring state; if its members crossed the border into South Africa, the members of the cell have to be handed to the SA Police for follow-up and action, even though the Police have no intimate knowledge of the cell or its background. Consequently the CCB itself activated Region 6 without knowledge of and in contravention of the proper approval procedures.

The activation of Region 6 produced good results at times. An example of successful domestic action against a terrorist cell from outside the country was the case of Ms Jenny Schneider and eleven members of the Area Political Military Council (APMC) who were uncovered by the CCB in a neighbouring country and handed to Region 6 members. They followed the cell to Cape Town, trapped it there and had the members arrested.[37]

Pres. De Klerk appointed Mr Justice L.T.C. Harms as chairman of a one-man commission in January 1990 in order to, according to him, "investigate the involvement of members of the Security Forces in violence which could no longer be adequately handled by means of normal legal processes".[38] One important alleged victim of the CCB who was referred to during the Harms investigation was Anton Lubowski. He was SWAPO's Secretary General and was murdered on 12 September 1989 – presumably by an assassin. Of course there was much speculation about who was responsible for the murder and what the motive may have been, and many allegations were made.

Mainly as a result of adverse publicity, rumours, the negative image of and perceptions regarding alleged CCB operations, the presence of certain undesirable elements within the CCB, and a reduction of the revolutionary threat outside South Africa, I gave the Defence Force instructions in February to suspend the activities of the CCB with immediate effect. The organisation had to disband by 30 July 1990. These instructions were carried out.[39]

I was chastised by Mr Justice Harms even after I had tried to correct this matter in public by quoting facts. This was in the wake of a snap debate in the House of Assembly on 26 February 1990 when I revealed the true facts concerning Anton Lubowski. Mr Justice Harms alleged that I had compromised the Defence Force's channels of intelligence in this case.[40]

One needs to keep in mind that the Government, with F.W. de Klerk as its new leader, was experiencing a great deal of pressure during House of Assembly debates at the time. During the no-confidence debate the right-wing opposition parties, in particular, were very critical of the new President's actions of 2 February 1990.

At that stage there was no agreement or commitment between the Government and the ANC Alliance regarding negotiations that could lead to peace between the two groups. The Groote Schuur Minute between the Government and the ANC was only signed in May 1990, and prior to this, the ANC was therefore under no obligation to renounce violence.

At the same time the ANC was executing Operation Vula in order to supply the so-called "People's Army" in South Africa with weapons and ammunition; it was therefore creating a greater capacity for violence. The Defence Force was deliberately being blackguarded by means of propaganda and accusations, which included those of assassination. In the circumstances I therefore felt that I had to act quickly to counter the assault.[41]

The allegations concerning the Lubowski murder formed part of a pattern of derogation aimed at the Defence Force and more specifically at the Military Intelligence Division, and to a lesser degree at me. I knew that Military Intelligence did not have the capacity to carry out such an operation, and there was absolutely no authorisation for such an action. Taking all this into account, I decided, after careful consideration, to reveal certain facts even though I would compromise a certain channel of intelligence by doing so.

Although Mr Justice Harms was correct in his judgement, I acted with other practical considerations in mind which influenced me; I had to take into account the broader political picture and the current internal situation.

It is not always pleasant to have to make decisions, and one may not like the consequences of those decisions, but one has to act in accordance with the requirements and the facts of the situation.

Because the CCB's actions were shrouded in secrecy, many dark deeds were and still are ascribed to it. One can hardly expect the uninitiated to be able to distinguish between fact and fiction in such circumstances, particularly since some cases were exaggerated by certain journalists.

Most of the amnesty applications handed in to the TRC by the Defence Force's CCB members from ten regions came from Region 6. These applications were based on the applicants' conviction that they had committed unlawful acts. There were five or six such cases, and in every case the TRC granted amnesty.

The contents of the confessions contained in the amnesty applications by most of the applicants from Region 6 reveal a sense of reckless indiscipline, fuelled by amateurish flights of fancy. Five or six of these members had acted on their own, without the proper competency and background knowledge regarding the nature of the struggle. This entire region acted on its own initiative and without the required authority, recruited members and apparently, on its own initiative, acted unlawfully inside the country. This region caused the CCB and the Defence Force a great deal of embarrassment and irreparably harmed its image. Its actions left an indelible disgrace.[42]

When the CCB case became public, I issued a press statement on 19 February 1990 to the effect that I had never approved of or recommended unlawful actions such as murder.[43] No request was ever addressed to me personally in my capacity as Minister, or in my presence to the Defence Force, for authorisation to kill anybody. If such acts were perpetrated, they were the unauthorised personal responsibility of the individual concerned.[44]

As a member of the State Security Council and the Cabinet, I can confirm with conviction that killing people, either by murder or assassination, was never Government policy. I knew my Cabinet colleagues very well, and I can speak for them and give the assurance that none of them would ever approve of such a despicable deed as cold-blooded murder.

Many accusations regarding the existence of so-called hit teams and hit lists were directed at me and the Defence Force during the revolutionary war. It is claimed that the hit lists contained the names of "victims" who were to become the targets of assassins in some sort of priority because of their political activities. It is claimed that the Defence Force and I drew up these lists and appointed the murderers.

In my period of service as Chief of the Defence Force, and later as Minister of Defence, senior Defence Force officers and I repeatedly gave the public the assurance that we did not regard the Defence Force or its personnel to be above the laws and regulations of the country. Anybody who was unwilling to accept this would personally have to bear the consequences.[45]

As former Chief of the Defence Force and former Minister of Defence, I testified as follows before the TRC: "Where members of the SA Defence Force (SADF) acted unlawfully during the period of the conflict I wish to offer my unqualified apologies. The background against which such acts were committed must, however, not be forgotten. The sound judgement of members of the SA Defence Force sometimes suffered in the heat of battle, owing to the abhorrence generated by the deeds of terrorism committed by the liberation movements. If, however, moral blame is to be attached to the lawful actions of the SA Defence Force, such blame must be levelled at the former governments and not at individual members of the Defence Force. I make the statement with the full realisation that I was part of those governments."[46]

In *The last trek - a new beginning* Pres. De Klerk says that the Harms Commission submitted its report to him on 13 November 1990. "Mr. Justice Harms sharply criticised the CCB. According to him this organisation claimed for itself the right to try, sentence and punish people without those people knowing the accusations made against them or having the opportunity to defend themselves. There was evidence linking the CCB to bomb attacks and attempted murder."[47] It was also said that the judge could find no evidence that the CCB was in fact responsible for the death of activists, but its behaviour prior to and during the Commission's enquiry raised the suspicion that it was involved in more violence than had been brought to light by the evidence. According to Harms, his problem was that the CCB had destroyed or removed its files, despite my instruction that the Commission be provided with the required documents.

In its report the Harms Commission also stated: "It is a normal phenomenon that a defence force should create a covert organisation for employment ... a covert organisation with an offensive capability or goals requires a strong control structure. Power should not be concentrated, and the greater the secrecy, the greater the danger of irregularities. There should also be proper measures in place to exert control over a covert organisation's money and documentation."[48]

After thorough discussion, and taking account of the lessons learned from the CCB events, the Government approved certain guidelines regarding covert organisations on 27 June 1990. This meant that the Government was convinced of the necessity for covert operations, and gave the Chief of the Defence Force the authority to continue with covert special operations, as in the past. In summary the guidelines were as follows: "... that the Government in principle accepts the execution of covert special operations; that these operations shall be applied only when the normal line-function operations of departments prove inadequate, or their supplementation is considered desirable; ... that only departments with the capacity in regard to personnel, funds, structures and expertise may operate covert special operations – that is the security departments and the Department of Foreign Affairs. Other departments need to obtain explicit authorisation by means of a Cabinet decision. No indemnity against criminal prosecution may be offered to anyone. The minimum number of persons should be informed with regard to special operations and covert programmes. The 'need to know' principle should therefore be applied."[49]

When one looks at the deeds perpetrated by persons in Region 6, and the evidence that came to the fore during their amnesty applications, it was clearly an error of judgement that the approval in principle of the structures of Region 6 was granted at the same time as the approval of the CCB. From the amnesty applications and the subsequent hearings it was quite clear that no Region 6 operations were submitted to the Chief of the Defence Force for approval, and that they were executed without authorisation. It is therefore not accurate to regard these actions as approved Defence Force actions. One also needs to take into account that the CCB's staff plan determined, in writing, that "in no uncertain terms ... CCB (Civil Co-operation Bureau) members must obey all the laws of the land".[50]

Mr Justice Harms could find no convincing evidence that the CCB was responsible for Lubowski's death, but he did find that Lubowski had received money from the Defence Force. However, he stated that the premise that the CCB would not have been involved in his murder because Lubowski had received money from the Defence Force's Military Intelligence Division (MID) is incorrect. The CCB may not have been aware of his involvement in MID, and it may have wanted to get rid of him as a political figure.

In 1997 the TRC requested me to submit to it all evidence regarding the Lubowksi assassination, and this was subsequently done by the Defence Force's legal representative (Adv. Piet de Jager SC). Despite certain media assertions during the sitting that Lubowski was not an agent, the TRC makes no comment on this evidence in its final report, nor on the facts presented to it. The evidence and facts presented to the TRC *in camera* have never been released so that the public can judge. It is astonishing that the TRC has not made this public, despite all the Defence Force's efforts to set this matter right.

No matter created as much painful embarrassment for myself and the Defence Force as the actions ascribed to the CCB.

By once again presenting certain background facts, I have tried to put into perspective certain allegations, and to explain why the SA Defence Force had to endure all those painful allegations in silence. Due to circumstances the allegations could not be contested in public at the time.

In spite of the unauthorised actions of some members, the CCB did, in general, do good work. Funds were annually budgeted for the organisation according to a prescribed procedure, and transactions were subject to an audit.[51]

As far as the other leg of Special Forces, namely the Reconnaissance Commandos, is concerned, I have described some of their outstanding achievements in the struggle in chapter 16. These actions were usually executed in life-threatening circumstances. (Paul Els's book *We fear Naught but God,* deals in a perceptive manner with the Reconnaissance Commandos and their activities during operations.)

As the Reconnaissance Commandos always executed such tasks efficiently, the present Government has very wisely decided to retain the Special Forces in the new SANDF.[52]

Chapter 20

THE ANC: ORIGIN, DEVELOPMENT AND STRATEGY

In this chapter, the primary focus is on the African National Congress (ANC). The ANC developed from a liberation movement to a terrorist organisation, and eventually to a political party. The organisation led the physical assault on South Africa, and for a large part of its existence it was therefore engaged in conflict with the Defence Force. Apart from the Government, the ANC Alliance was the most important participant in the negotiation process of the early 1990s. Although the physical struggle was abating at the time, the organisation did not cease its assault on the Defence Force.

BACKGROUND AND STRATEGY OF THE ANC

From the 1960s onwards, the internal actions of the Defence Force were very closely linked to the strategies and actions of the ANC, as described in Chapters 2, 4 and 9. This interaction originated in the country's constitution, which gave the Defence Force - as instrument of the State - the mission to defend the country's citizens against internal unrest and external threats. Similarly, the defense of the country was directed by the Defence Act. Among other things this Act (approved by Parliament, as was all other legislation) determined that the State may employ the South African Defence Force to defend the country; to prevent and suppress terrorism; to combat internal unrest; to protect life, health and property; to maintain essential services and to execute policing tasks (as prescribed).[1]

The ANC was established in Bloemfontein in 1912 as the South African Native National Congress, under the chairmanship of the Rev. J.L. Dube, and was only renamed the African National Congress in 1925. Initially the organisation had peaceful aims, with the extension of political rights and an improvement in the economic and social circumstances of black people as its main goals.[2]

The ANC's reaction to and actions with regard to government policy were reflected in various ways at various times. Initially the ANC had liberal aspirations, but it gradually became more militant. At first it tried to use passive resistance, and then it became a multiracial popular front, but was eventually overtaken by impatient black nationalism, and moved underground.[3]

During its conference in Bloemfontein in 1949, the ANC tried to join all black people into one mass movement and at the same time it made a concerted effort to involve all coloureds and Indians as well. This resulted in the Congress Alliance on which the Freedom Charter was based, and which included whites.

This congress also adopted the well-known ANC symbol of the African salute, with the right arm raised, the closed fist and raised thumb, with the slogan "Amandla ngawethu" (Ours is the power) and the refrain "Mayibuye Africa" (Africa, return). The fist represents the African continent; the thumb represents the horn of Ethiopia and the elbow the South African coastline. "Nkosi Sikelel' iAfrika", which has existed since 1925, was officially accepted as the ANC's anthem.

In 1952 the ANC used the Defiance Campaign to protest against Government policies by means of large-scale violation of laws that were regarded as oppressive. This phase was ended when the Government adopted the Criminal Procedure Amendment Act, which imposed heavy fines on those breaking the laws of the land or opposing them through protest or other actions. The Public Safety Act gave the Government the required powers to impose a state of emergency on a certain area or the entire country.[4]

As early as 1952 Mr Nelson Mandela had discussed the matter of violence as a means of achieving political ends with Walter Sisulu, but as a result of political pressure this debate became more urgent in the early 1960s.

Younger and, in many cases, less disciplined black leaders demanded greater militancy, broke away from the ANC and created a new organisation, the Pan African Congress (PAC), under Robert Sobukwe in 1959. They also organised a military wing, Poqo, which was later renamed APLA (Azanian People's Liberation Army). In their actions aimed at curbing terrorism, the SA Defence Force later had to deal with this organisation.[5]

The years 1960-1963 were decisive for the future of South Africa. The year 1960 saw the high tide of black nationalism in Africa, as 17 countries became politically independent. This was also the period when the British Prime Minister, Harold Macmillan, made his "Winds of change" speech in Parliament in Cape Town, and referred to the political forces that were taking hold in Africa. In this period, too, the ANC and PAC were declared banned organisations. South Africa became a Republic on 31 May 1961. Because of resistance to its domestic policies, it withdrew from the British Commonwealth.[6]

The Defence Force would increasingly become involved in the country's security from 1960 onwards. A march to the police station at Sharpeville in protest against the pass laws, created the impression amongst the police officers who were surrounded by the black crowd, that their lives were in danger. They fired on the crowd without any order to do so, and left 69 people dead and 180 wounded. This tragedy resulted in large-scale black unrest countrywide. The Government declared a state of emergency in most parts of the country on 30 March 1960, and the Defence Force was on standby between 30 March and 2 April 1960.[7]

Chief Albert Luthuli, who was president of the ANC at the time and was awarded the Nobel Peace Prize in 1961, was opposed to violence on moral grounds. He was convinced that a policy of non-violence should never be changed by circumstances, in contrast to Nelson Mandela, later our President, who believed that the tactic of non-violence should be changed if it did not serve its purpose. Eventually, at a meeting of the ANC's National Executive Committee (NEC) in Durban in 1961, Luthuli did agree that military action was inevitable. He, and the other members of the NEC, were convinced that the underground military movement needed to become a separate and independent organisation, linked to the ANC and subject to its total control, yet autonomous, i.e. two separate forces carrying out the struggle. The ANC therefore employed the logical incompatibility of preaching non-violence in public and employing violence underground in order to mislead the international community and to ensure their support.[8]

The Joint Executive Committee, which included the Indian Congress, Coloured People's Congress, South African Congress of Trade Unions and Congress of Democrats, furthermore decided at this Durban meeting to give Nelson Mandela instructions to create a new military organisation, nominally separate from the ANC, namely Umkhonto we Sizwe (MK – Spear of the Nation). A week later, on 16 December 1961, Hero's Day, a traditional day of ANC gatherings, MK announced its existence with organised sabotage attacks on symbolic targets by exploding bombs at electricity power stations and government buildings in Johannesburg, Port Elizabeth and Durban. The so-called high command consisting of Nelson Mandela, assisted by Walter Sisulu and Joe Slovo, took the lead in these attacks. A formal link between the ANC and MK was created in October 1962 when the NEC very clearly referred to MK as "the military wing of our struggle".[9]

In preparation for the military struggle to come, Mandela studied, among other things, South African military history and the vulnerability of the country's industries. He also slipped undetected out of the country and visited African countries who had been successful in their struggle against former colonial powers. In Algeria he was told that the Algerians realised that the French could not be defeated in a military struggle, but that "guerrilla victory was not designed to win a military victory so much as to unleash political and economic forces that would bring down the enemy". On returning to South Africa, Mandela was arrested on his way to Johannesburg and sentenced to five years' forced labour on 7 November 1962.[10]

The Organisation of African Unity (OAU) was established in May 1963, and this organisation would play a key role in the resistance offered to South Africa by African states.

The Police raided the Liliesleaf Farm at Rivonia on 11 July 1963 and confiscated hundreds of documents, among others the operational plans for Operation Mayibuye, a war of terrorism in South Africa. The introductory sentence to this plan states: "It can now truly be said that very little, if any scope exists for the smashing of white supremacy other than by means of mass revolutionary action, the main content of which is armed resistance leading to victory by military means."[11]

Four of the militant ANC members arrested at Rivonia were members of the Communist Party. In the wake of these arrests, many Alliance members fled abroad with ANC leaders such as Oliver Tambo and Govan Mbeki. There they applied their efforts to isolating South Africa on all fronts, namely politically, economically and militarily, and in the fields of the church and sport, and in so doing make the country more vulnerable. The eventual goal was to institute sanctions and embargoes against South Africa. Taking everything into account, there were eight "commandments" that were to be pursued with all possible means, namely intensifying the revolutionary climate; isolating South Africa; destroying South Africa's economy; undermining and eventually destroying the will and ability of the Government and people to resist the revolutionary on-slaught; activating and mobilising the population to offer resistance to the current dispensation; intensifying terrorist attacks and neutralising South Africa's Security Forces, particularly by sowing suspicion. In addition a wedge had to be driven between the Government and the Security Forces (SFs), and lastly the political dispensation had to be destroyed.[12]

The London section of the ANC used various organisations abroad to apply great pressure on the Defence Force. Seminars were arranged on an ongoing basis, for example one in Brussels in 1975, where South Africa's military situation was discussed. This seminar was actually planned by the so-called World Peace Council, a communist front organisation, which on this occasion included the ANC and SWAPO. During this seminar West Germany was also attacked for building a uranium enrichment plant and nuclear reactor in South Africa which would enhance the country's nuclear capability.[13]

The Soweto school uprising, which involved 15 000 schoolchildren, broke out in 1976. The alleged reason given for the uprising is that Afrikaans was to be introduced as a medium of instruction for some of the pupils' school subjects.[14] The uprising increased the violence throughout the country, which became more and more intense. In reaction the Government decided that the Defence Force needed to support the Police in preventing and containing internal rioting, and to ensure that the situation did not escalate. Should the situation deteriorate into organised firefights, the primary responsibility would be transferred to the Defence Force. Should it become necessary for the Defence Force to intervene, the situation had to be stabilised as quickly as possible through effective action to allow the SA Police to resume responsibility again.

In order to help maintain essential services in unrest-ravaged townships, the Army carried out escort tasks; provided medical help; carried out explosives clearance duties; and provided certain protection services at schools. However, the Defence Force had to use minimum force at all times.[15] Proactive and, where necessary, containment actions were planned and managed by instituting countrywide operations and intelligence centres. Where required, the Air Force, Navy and Medical Service were represented.[16]

The Air Force contributed through the rapid tactical and strategic deployment of ground forces, reconnaissance flights and casualty evacuation.

The Navy was given instructions to protect harbours and property against insurgency attacks, and the marines, in particular, were involved. In the Western Cape Navy fire engines were deployed to fight fires set by rioters.

The role played by the Medical Service in controlling unrest was mainly in the form of providing medical services to all Security Forces and to the local population as required, and aiding local authorities to maintain essential health services. This Service was deployed to evaluate crowd behaviour during the unrest and to give military commanders advice on how unruly crowds could be controlled in such circumstances. Specialist research was done in this regard.[17]

TERRORISTS OR FREEDOM FIGHTERS?

According to Nicholas N. Kittrie of the American University in Washington, a liberation movement which does not use internationally accepted methods to achieve legitimate political ends, is guilty of terrorism and therefore of a crime.[18] Because MK members did not adhere to the internationally accepted requirements or protocols that were in place up to 1977, in other words carrying weapons openly and wearing a uniform that was recognisable from a distance, they had to be regarded as terrorists rather than guerrilla fighters.[19]

Benjamin Netanyahu defines the concept of "terrorism" as follows: "It chooses innocent victims precisely because they are innocent. What distinguishes terrorism is the wilful, calculated choice of innocents as targets ... Terrorism is the deliberate and the systematic murder, maiming and menacing of the innocent to inspire fear for political ends."[20]

In this work the difference between terrorists and guerrillas is defined as follows: "Terrorists habitually describe themselves as guerrillas. Guerrillas are not terrorists. They are irregular soldiers who wage war on regular military forces – not on civilians. Actually, guerrillas are the very opposite of terrorists. While they put themselves against far superior combatants, terrorists choose to attack weak and defenceless civilians – old men, women, children – anyone, in fact, except soldiers if they can avoid it. Civilians then are the key to the terrorists' strategy. They kill civilians and more often than not they hide behind them, hoping that the prospect of more innocent deaths will help them escape retribution."[21]

Douglas Pike writes about terrorism as follows: "Even in warfare certain acts are illegal and may properly be named terror. This latter point rests in the belief that in all things there are limits, and a limit in warfare is reached at the systematic use of death, pain, fear and anxiety amongst the population (either civilian or military) for the deliberate purpose of coercing, manipulating, intimidating, punishing or simply frightening into helpless submission. Certain acts, even in war, are beyond the pale and can only be labelled as terror."[22]

Mahmood Mamdani wrote in 2004: "Despite important differences, genocide and terrorism share one important feature: both target civilian populations."[23]

There is no doubt that actions described by these definitions of terrorism made up an inseparable part of the so-called South African liberation movements. The main targets were those parts of the black population which would not co-operate – many of them chiefs with an influence that the ANC wished to neutralise in order to gain power. Secondly, a much more intense form of terrorism was used against the whole population of a town or area that was found not displaying the required enthusiasm for the revolutionary cause.[24]

The creation of the United Democratic Front (UDF) and the Mass Democratic Movement (MDM) in the 1980s brought about a change in activities. The UDF and MDM were loose assemblies of organisations intended to give direction to the protest actions (before the UDF was effectively banned). These umbrella organisations created an alliance of legal internal allies, who were to play a key role in the ANC campaign.[25]

The internal terrorist struggle spread abroad, where the terrorists hid. The Alliance terrorism groups who operated inside South Africa followed the international custom of terrorist organisations. Following a terrorism attack in South Africa, they returned to the country they had come from and hid amongst the civil population, where women and children were present. This meant that follow-up cross-border actions by the Defence Force usually caused civilian casualties. The terrorist organisation's propaganda media then immediately exploited these civilian casualties as calculated Defence Force attacks on the civilian population.[26]

A former Chief of the Defence Force, Gen. Constand Viljoen, pointed out on numerous occasions that the SFs would never have been able to fight if 85% of the population were sympathetic to the revolutionary forces and terrorists. Military initiatives alone were no defence against such an assault, but had to be supported by simultaneous economic and political actions.[27]

THE UNBANNING OF THE ANC

On 2 February 1990 Pres. F.W. de Klerk announced the release of Nelson Mandela from prison and the lifting of the ban on the ANC, SACP, PAC and a number of other organisations. The previous year had already seen preparations being made for the release of Mandela when the last prisoners who were sentenced during the Rivonia Trial of 1964 where released.[28]

Nelson Mandela was elected ANC President to replace Oliver Tambo in 1990. This occurred during the first ANC national convention to be held inside the country in 30 years. He had some success with his argument that negotiations were simply another level of the struggle, and that if they hesitated to grab the opportunity even for a moment, they would be playing into the enemy's hands.[29]

At that stage the ANC was caught off guard by the releases and the lifting of the ban on the organisation, because this signalled that the Government had, for no apparent reason, unilaterally ended the revolutionary war. In the violent struggle that had been waged up to that time, the ANC/SACP Alliance had, in their opinion, not been so successful as to warrant this drastic change of policy by the Government. According to De Klerk, Mandela thought it was clear to him that a military victory by the Alliance was "a vague and even impossible dream".[30] However, an inherent characteristic of any revolutionary organisation is that it must be able to handle unexpected events successfully in order to survive.

The 1980s and early 1990s made great demands on the Defence Force with regard to its adaptation to and strategic planning for the rapidly changing circumstances. At that stage the Nkomati Accord, which envisaged the ending of all forms of aggression between the two neighbouring countries, had been concluded with Mozambique. This meant that the Mozambican border, across which numerous acts of terrorism had been conducted against South Africa in the past, would be closed to terrorists. Furthermore South-West Africa was to become independent as Namibia on 21 March 1990, which signalled the end of the war against Cuba in Angola; as a condition of this event was that Cuba had to withdraw from Angola. Even the fight against SWAPO was something of the past.

One also needs to take into account international events of the time. The fall of the Berlin Wall in November 1989 symbolised the crumbling of the Soviet Bloc, and would eventually result in a worldwide loss of confidence in the communist ideology. The SA Communist Party was an exception to the rule, in that it still tried to cling to this outdated ideology. The crumbling of Soviet power meant that it was no longer capable of supporting revolutionary forces and using proxy forces such as the Cubans to promote their ideal of world domination. This would also have a major impact on the ANC Alliance.

The fall of the Berlin Wall certainly marked a watershed in world affairs. In hindsight it also drastically changed one's view of political and military conditions prevalent before that event. The colossus that had posed a threat to world peace through its imperialist goals suddenly collapsed like a house of cards. This also created the impression that all fears of Soviet power were simply an illusion, developed deliberately for selfish political ends.

I am often asked why the negotiation process had not started a number of years earlier. In my opinion this was not possible because the three main parties with the greatest influence on the negotiation process still followed their own agendas. The Soviet Union was still bent on taking control of South Africa's mineral bounty and the Cape sea route. The ANC Alliance was still bent on taking over South Africa with might and main, even if it meant that the country first had to be made ungovernable.[31] With Soviet and communist proxy military forces still present in Southern Africa, it was too much to ask of the South African government of the time, and too risky to consider negotiations with the ANC Alliance.[32] However, when the Soviet Union and international communism collapsed, F.W. de Klerk and the South African government could take the risk of reaching out to the ANC to start negotiations.

Despite the spectacular failure of communism in the USSR, the ANC/SACP Alliance still clung to the ideology. Even in his first speech following his release on 11 February 1990, Mandela did not, as expected, sever the ANC's ties with international communism, but expressed solidarity with the South African Communist Party and singled out its Secretary General, Joe Slovo, for special praise.[33]

As a result of their extended programme of struggle against the South African Government, the ANC/SACP Alliance continuously tried to refine and improve its techniques. When the Alliance realised, at a stage, that it was not making enough progress with the revolutionary struggle, it went to the notorious Gen. Vo Nguyen Giap of Vietcong fame for advice on how to ensure a better performance for the Alliance. By coincidence the strategy devised at that time was called "The Green Book". Was it a mere quirk of history that the approved national strategy of the P.W. Botha Government, which was contained in an official state document classified as "Top Secret" and known only to the Government inner circles and directors-general, was also called "The Green Book"? After all, moles such as Dieter Gerhardt were discovered in the South African civil service at the time.[34]

ANC STRATEGY AFTER UNBANNING

During the negotiation process which commenced at this time, the Alliance had one important characteristic it had learned by experience in its extended struggle against the South African Government: the importance of having a well-formulated and workable plan or strategy, and to follow this at all times. The Freedom Charter of 1955, for example, was of cardinal importance in achieving its ideals and goals. The Charter was even incorporated in the ANC's constitution of 1958 whereby its importance was emphasised. Strategically and philosophically the Alliance was therefore well equipped for negotiations. It was very aware of what its negotiation goals had to be, and what it had to work, fight and strive for jointly when the opportunity arose. Yet, depending on the circumstances, the Alliance did not hesitate to make adjustments to its structures, planning and actions.

One can distinguish three broad phases in the Alliance's strategy after the ban had been lifted: the one following Mandela's release in February 1990 up to the moment when it decided to engage in serious negotiations; the negotiations themselves; and the period following the negotiations, which includes the April 1994 general elections, the assumption of power in May 1994, and subsequent events.

Mandela's release did not end violence in the country. For example, 124 lives were lost due to violence in Natal in 1989, and this rose to 1888 lives in 1990. The Alliance relentlessly continued their verbal attacks on the SFs, and alleged that the SFs were involved in perpetrating violence. These allegations were used as convenient reasons to suspend the negotiations and to try to gain the moral supremacy – the so-called moral high ground – once negotiations were resumed again. The first example of this was the incident in the township of Sebokeng, which resulted in the Alliance suspending the bilateral talks that were to have taken place on 11 April 1990. The Defence Force was not involved in this incident – only the Police and demonstrators were.[35]

The first negotiations between the Government and the Alliance on 2-4 May 1990 took place at Groote Schuur, and the decisions made there were known as the Groote Schuur Minute. The essence of the Minute is summarised in its first and last paragraphs:

"The Government and the ANC have agreed jointly to commit themselves to ending the present climate of violence and intimidation, no matter by which side, and to stability and a peaceful negotiation process.

"Effective communication channels shall be created between the Government and the ANC in order to effectively curb violence and intimidation, no matter by which side." (This was the Alliance's clearest commitment to peace at that stage.)[36]

In judging the Alliance's activities, one must always keep in mind that its knowledge of propaganda, negotiation techniques and even revolutionary warfare was obtained mainly from the USSR and other communist countries. It is therefore understandable that the Alliance, its thinking, value systems and actions were strongly based on examples that had been presented and recommended to them in those countries. As a result, the point of departure of the Communist Bloc countries, namely "the end justifies the means", was often applied.

Despite the contents of the Groote Schuur Minute, the intense conflict in the country continued and constantly caused tension between the negotiating parties. Sometimes the Alliance tried to dismiss the role played by its cadres and supporters, sometimes it defended the actions of these participants, and sometimes it denied that it had any control over them. However, allegations were invariably made that the SFs instigated violence, were involved in it, or did not try to prevent it.[37]

Notwithstanding the agreement contained in the Groote Schuur Minute, Alliance radicals also clandestinely continued with what was called Operation Vula in an attempt to overthrow the Government. This rebellious wing of the Alliance was concerned that the Alliance was not making enough progress in the military sense, and launched this operation in the 1980s. Tim Jenkins, an ANC exile in London who faced a jail sentence in South Africa, in one of a series of six articles in *Mayibuye*, the ANC monthly, wrote that there was a good deal of soul-searching within the ANC in the 1980s: "... while there had been some spectacular attacks against the apartheid regime, the underground struggle had not really taken off." He writes that at that stage the cadres had been trained in hit-and-run operations, but that there were no real Alliance leaders in the country who could claim to be the leading force of the struggle. The foot soldiers were sent into South Africa, but the generals stayed at bases in foreign countries. As the number of incidents increased, so did the casualty count. Only after the Kabwe Conference of 1985 was there any drastic change in tactics.[38]

It was then realised that "armed propaganda" could not change the struggle into a "people's war". During the 1980s the Alliance remained relatively isolated from the increased mass protest. Its weakness was that it remained an "army in exile", with lengthy lines of communication, rather than a force which was completely integrated with the community. It was extremely difficult to establish communication with cadres in South Africa from abroad. Later the development of computers made it possible to establish contact far more efficiently and safely.

It was at the Kabwe Conference of 1985 that the ANC officially made the shocking decision that the distinction between "hard" and "soft" targets should disappear. In other words, the assault against civilians was approved. In 1981 the Alliance's choice of targets was 81% hard and 12% soft targets; in 1986 this had changed to 10,3% hard and 80,7% soft targets.[39] The Kabwe decision mitigated against the ANC's signed international undertaking to adhere to Protocol 1 of 1977 of the Geneva Convention of 1949; this undertaking bound the ANC to act only against the SFs or hard targets. Section 1.52(1) and 57 of the undertaking has special significance. In its final report the TRC tried to justify the ANC's attacks on soft targets, and claims that such attacks did not violate this Protocol.

With the Kabwe policy decision the ANC breached the trust between itself and the international community, and consequently it is difficult not to regard it as a terrorist organisation.[40]

The purpose of Operation Vula was to secretly develop structures inside South Africa for the Alliance and to establish a number of arms and ammunition caches for the envisaged "People's Army", which was supposed to support the "People's Revolt" against the government of the day at the initiative of the Alliance. To this purpose leading Alliance members such as the father of the idea, Mac Maharaj, as well as Siphiwe

Nyanda and Ronnie Kasrils, were smuggled into the country on various occasions to prepare for the revolution by organising an underground network. Despite the Nkomati Accord, Mozambique was the main supply route for this operation.[41]

As a result of the exposure of Operation Vula by the SFs, the negotiation parties were compelled to sign the Pretoria Minute on 8 August 1990, in which the Alliance unilaterally undertook to end the armed struggle against apartheid. Despite Mandela's statement that Vula was inactive, a year later he praised in public the members who had been involved in it because they had continued their activities and had escaped arrest. In this speech he also boasted about the operation's successes, including smuggling in weapons, ammunition and personnel. Fortunately the Police exposed these activities in time, and caught Maharaj and eight conspirators.[42]

The Alliance therefore agreed to something that it had always claimed to be impossible, namely abandoning the armed struggle. Mr Mandela announced that the Alliance had suspended the armed struggle that was launched 30 years before. However, the Alliance placed full-page advertisements in the press to sketch this ceasefire as a compromise and not a surrender. Naturally the suspension of the armed struggle was a contentious issue within the Alliance. Even though Umkhonto we Sizwe was not active, the armed struggle had always had a special meaning for many members of the Alliance because it provided visible proof that they were actually fighting the enemy. However, Mandela claims that he had told his followers time and again that the Pretoria Minute meant a temporary suspension of the armed struggle, not that it was being terminated. It would seem that he regarded it simply as an interim measure.[43]

Despite the Pretoria Minute, underground military activities continued. For example, Chris Hani (the MK chief) said: "The ANC will get everything it wants, because the weapons are here." He boasted at Uitenhage: "If Umkhonto we Sizwe receives the instruction, it will go back to the bush, no matter what the ANC's National Executive Committee says. We received our mandate from the people, and not from the National Executive Committee."[44]

However, the violence continued, and this could easily have derailed the negotiation process. The Government therefore appointed a working group to attend to all the outstanding matters flowing from the Alliance's decision to suspend the armed struggle, and to report back. The working group reported back during a meeting between the Alliance and the Government at what was then called D.F. Malan Airport in Cape Town on 12 February 1991. The agreement reached between the two parties at this meeting was known as the D.F. Malan Accord. The Alliance agreed to an immediate end to attacks using weapons, firearms, explosives and petrol bombs. There had to be an end to smuggling in personnel, arms and explosives and an end to the creation of underground structures for military training in South Africa. There should be no more violence with mass action; no party may have a private army; and there should be control over the Alliance's cadres and secret arms caches already inside the country.

The Alliance however, quite shamelessly failed to keep their promises. Mandela in turn claimed that the Government was largely to blame for the violence. He stated his case to the ANC's NEC, and on the strength of this the NEC wrote the Government a letter threatening to withdraw from the constitutional negotiations if the Government did not meet seven demands by 9 May 1991. Among others, these seven demands were that the Minister of Defence (myself) and the Minister of Law and Order (Adriaan Vlok) should be dismissed, that counter-insurgency units should be disbanded and that an independent Commission of Enquiry should be appointed to investigate the SFs. However, the Government dismissed these demands.[45]

Certain "revelations" began to appear in the press in July 1991 that the Government had for some time secretly supported the Inkatha Freedom Party, and the press soon dubbed this "Inkathagate". The ANC Alliance then tried to gain as much political advantage from this as possible and repeated their demands of 9 May, including the demand that the Security Ministers should be dismissed.[46]

The Government had in fact been giving substantial support to Inkatha for several years: for example, 200 persons were trained by Defence Force instructors to protect VIPs, government buildings and structures in KwaZulu-Natal. I will expand on this in Chapter 22.

THE ALLIANCE MAKES DEMANDS AND PRES. DE KLERK REACTS

Pres. De Klerk decided to relieve Adriaan Vlok and myself of our duties in the portfolios of Law and Order and Defence, respectively, in July 1991. The responsibility for Defence was therefore taken from me after eleven years, and I was entrusted with the activities of the Department of Water Affairs and Forestry.

This change of portfolios created the impression amongst the SFs that it was done to accede to the ANC Alliance's demands, and that Pres. De Klerk showed a willingness to bend his knee to them. A degree of uncertainty was immediately noticeable amongst the SFs. It was the Alliance's goal to undermine the Government's power base during the negotiation process and to achieve a psychological advantage. This was achieved in many ways, some of them very subtle. A wedge was to be driven between the Government and its most important power base, namely the SFs, and in particular the Defence Force, by sowing suspicion about their actions amongst the general population. The perception was to be created that the Defence Force was acting according to its own agenda, which was in direct conflict with that of the Government. (These actions of the Alliance were executed to satisfy the ANC seventh and eight commandments, as mentioned above.)

The Alliance was extremely successful in reaching its goals, levelling constant allegations, accusations and criticism against the SFs and the two Security Ministers, because the Government was slowly accepting that the propaganda may possibly be true.[47] The breach of trust between the Government and the SFs became worse when, at the end of 1992, Pres. De Klerk erroneously dismissed 23 well-trained, loyal senior Defence Force officers who could be depended on through thick and thin.

Since the Pretoria Minute in August 1990, the dispute between the Government and the Alliance over the ending of the armed struggle by the Alliance lasted some 16 months, until the eve of CODESA 1 (the Convention for a Democratic South Africa), which signalled the start of serious peace negotiations between the various political parties. It commenced on 20 December 1991 in a climate of crisis, and ended in stalemate.[48]

CODESA 2 commenced on 15 May 1992. One of the five working groups created during CODESA 1 could not reach agreement, and the conference adjourned the next day without having achieved anything.[49]

It is therefore not surprising that the ANC Alliance announced a four-phased rolling mass action campaign early in June 1992, with the goal of overthrowing the South African Government and replacing it with an interim government.[50]

This programme commenced on 16 June (Soweto Day), lasted until September and involved various sit-ins, rallies, and occupations of government buildings, general strikes and protest marches.

Among other things this programme of resistance included a countrywide general strike on 3 and 4 August 1992. Mandela led a march of 60 000 Alliance supporters to the Union Buildings on 5 August, and 70 000 Alliance supporters marched on Bisho on 7 September. This ended tragically when 28 protesters were killed and 200 were wounded. However, the Alliance gained much publicity and experience by such actions, which would stand them in good stead during future actions. It created a strongman image for the Alliance, particularly amongst the poorly informed. Despite the fact that the Alliance did not succeed in achieving its goal of an interim government, it had demonstrated that it could rely on the political support of many, and that its actions could harm the country a great deal, particularly with regard to the economy.[51]

Bilateral negotiations were resumed on 26 September 1992 amidst the persisting unrest and riot situation, and resulted in the signing of a Minute of Understanding by De Klerk and Mandela, which provided a blueprint for future negotiations.[52]

Up to that stage it was quite clear that the ANC Alliance was in control of events and dictated the initiative, while the almost totally silent Government was being bested.

Not much needs to be said about the negotiation process. The outcome was a clear political triumph for the Alliance. Its strategy had worked. This strategy had basically involved the following: create an awareness of the principles that were non-negotiable; create a psychological climate and achieve a position to one's advantage and beneficial to one's cause; ensure positive publicity; study one's opponents and know them (they most probably made the usual profile studies of their negotiation opponents, while it is not known whether the negotiators on the Government side did the same); try to put pressure on the opponents and try to drive wedges in amongst them; make sure one has the abilities and skills for successful negotiations.

In contrast to P.W. Botha, who had once been Minister of Defence, F.W. de Klerk never showed any real interest in security matters, and had no exposure to the security culture and thinking. As a minister De Klerk was never involved in the formulation or application of security strategies, and he therefore felt himself to be on the periphery of the State Security Council. He himself said that he was identified as a "dove" ever since he became a member of the State Security Council in the early 1980s, and that he was somewhat marginalised. He was never fully involved in deliberations, and never had a clear insight into its activities.[53]

One needs to keep in mind that a member of the Defence Force, whether a national serviceman, a Citizen Force or Commando member, or a member of the Permanent Force, puts his life on the line when executing his duties, and therefore the results of political decisions have a far more direct effect on him. Due to circumstances F.W. de Klerk unfortunately missed an opportunity to be a part of military life, and to experience its culture, distinctive manner of thinking and doing.

He informs us in his autobiography that shortly after his election as President he began to dismantle the "structures of power that the so-called securocrats" had developed under P.W. Botha. "I was determined to normalise the role of the security forces." This statement implies that the Defence Force had had improper and abnormal powers. He adds that he wanted to put an end to the special decision-making process his predecessor had granted the Defence Force.[54]

However, De Klerk was later to admit: "The South African Defence Force represented the Government's eventual power base, and was the final guarantor of the constitutional process we had initiated. At that stage we did not have the assurance that the entire process could be finalised in a peaceful manner. Anything was still possible prior to the election of April 1994. The ANC could once again unleash mass action. Its radical faction could once again gain the upper hand and revive Operation Vula and the armed struggle; KwaZulu could try to secede. The right wing could rebel."[55]

It is accepted the world over that a defence force represents a country's final power base. During a crisis situation the defence force must act in accordance with the country's acknowledged constitution in order to avert a crisis and to restore law and order. It is difficult to reconcile F.W. de Klerk's later positive pronouncements on the Defence Force with the negative attitude towards and actions against the organisation and its command structure he displayed during his term of office as President and therefore Commander-in-Chief of the Defence Force.

The negotiation process and views expressed there did not escape the consequences of the fall of Soviet communism and the disappearance of that country's imperial goals. From 1990 onwards, events that occurred earlier were approached in an entirely different political climate and from a different point of view. Due to ideological and political ulterior motives, historical events were henceforth often distorted. These calculatedly distorted perceptions were meant to contribute towards establishing a particular frame of mind amongst those participating in the major events of the time – particularly at the military level. A feeling of frustration, hopelessness, despondency and guilt had to be created amongst them in order to rob them of their self-confidence and belief. Like the walls of Jericho, the walls of confidence and trust had to come tumbling down following a loud trumpet-call of accusations.

ALLIANCE ACTIONS WITH AN INFLUENCE ON THE SA DEFENCE FORCE

Since the ANC Alliance became a political party and came to govern the country, a specific modus operandi regarding their political actions pertaining to the Defence Force became evident.

It would seem that once the Alliance has formulated a view, it is very difficult or even impossible to change that perception, even if the original view is based on incorrect observations and facts. If the contrary is later proved with facts, the Alliance will persist with its original conviction; one sometimes gets the impression that it does not wish to be confused with facts. After all, Adv. Dumisa Ntsebeza, a former TRC commissioner, has declared: "... perceptions are more important than facts".[56]

For example, there is the perception that the Alliance had achieved military victories over the Defence Force during the revolutionary war. Certain ANC supporters with no knowledge of military events still seem to harbour the perception that the previous Government was compelled by force of arms to negotiate with the ANC on the future of South Africa. As against this, Joe Slovo, later an Alliance minister with direct ties to MK, declared in the October 1992 edition of the *African Communist* that the Government of the day was not defeated in the armed struggle. As late as 1997 Mandela declared in public that the Alliance had not won the military struggle: "... the military and paramilitary forces of apartheid remained undefeated when power passed to the ANC ..."[57]

In Chapter 18 I referred to the stubborn perceptions regarding the air crash in which Pres. Samora Machel of Mozambique had died.

Certain pronouncements and findings of the TRC with regard to the Defence Force confirm this inability to change perceptions or views on the grounds of new facts. This Commission's attention was drawn, in writing, to false allegations, accusations and pronouncements, yet despite this, the TRC has published these falsities. This means that a distorted version of actual facts has become public record, and will probably be accepted as the truth.

Public pronouncements of TRC members on untested allegations made before the Commission have also contributed to the creation of false perceptions. For example, the chairperson, Archbishop Desmond Tutu, has alleged that chemical and biological experts of the Defence Force sterilised black women without these women knowing about it.[58] Such a selective type of birth control is highly unlikely, and furthermore statistical evidence of a decline in the birth rate of this population group is totally lacking.

This is how perceptions, misrepresentations, disinformation, propaganda, etcetera are created, developed, pronounced, spread and believed. In turn the media feel compelled to publish these sensational revelations made by prominent people. This means that the rumours, inventions or perceptions reached an even greater number of members of the public, and one cannot blame them for believing it. In such cases the reputations of the previous Government and the Defence Force were seriously damaged in a quite deliberate manner.

Once a perception or misrepresentation has been fixed in the mind of a person or a community, the trend is unconsciously to take note only of additional information that reinforces the already established impression. Should information not match an existing impression, it is usually easier to discard it. The facts concerning a case make little impression on an existing misperception.

There has been a concerted effort to cast the Defence Force and the so-called "apartheid regime" in a bad light. With regard to the Defence Force, these efforts have concentrated on aspects such as "political murders" that have allegedly taken place with the approval of "the highest authority", or allegations of "third force" activities allegedly committed by the Government or the Defence Force, and which they still shroud in secrecy. Eventually these allegations have resulted in members of the Defence Force being compelled to present evidence under oath before the TRC, the country's High Courts and certain amnesty committees.

Certain buzzwords were also created with the exclusive goal of helping to develop and establish negative feelings towards the Defence Force; words such as "total onslaught", used entirely out of context, and "securocrats", to indicate a bunch of power-hungry militarists.

THE ALLIANCE'S STRATEGY

At that time the Alliance broadcast the idea that the Defence Force, with the approval of the Government, had acted unlawfully, and had continued in this manner after February 1990. Prior to and during the negotiations objections were raised by the highest levels of the Alliance to certain crimes the Defence Force had supposedly committed and was still committing without them being investigated or solved. Most of these allegations were totally unfounded or were based on rumours.

Where facts and evidence did prove allegations to be correct, the Defence Force acted immediately and instituted legal action against the perpetrators. In the cases where these allegations were false, providing accurate facts relating to the allegations brought about no change in the ANC Alliance's perceptions – the misconceptions continued.

The perception the Alliance had of the Defence Force, and of course of other Government departments, with regard to so-called atrocities was shocking, to say the least. This perception came as a particular shock to those who had not been involved in the struggle and did not have the facts to counter the allegations. One must also take into account that the acts perpetrated by both sides should be judged in context of the extent of the violence. Necklacings and murder occurred daily everywhere in South Africa two decades ago. If one takes into account the circumstances prevalent at the time, one could perhaps even produce mitigating factors for the atrocities committed by the Alliance. The alleged unlawful acts of the Defence Force took place, for the most part, in the heat of battle against a terrorist organisation. This was in contrast with the actions of the terrorist organisation, which quite calculatedly ignored rules and protocols; an enemy which, with only a few exceptions, attacked and tried to destroy only soft targets.[59] The alleged misdeeds of the SFs are now being judged, some 20 years later, in an atmosphere of calm, with virtually no danger of terrorism, and in a society which does not live in mortal fear. It is therefore more difficult and sometimes impossible to justify those acts as they took place in very different times and in non-comparable circumstances.[60]

The political winner, namely the party with the political power, usually has the privilege of defining the term "legitimate". Pronouncements on the concepts of "just" and "justice" then bear the meanings assigned to them by a particular political force within a particular society. The TRC's investigations, findings and pronouncements are typical examples of how this privilege may be applied in practice. George Orwell said: "He who controls history, controls the future. Who controls the present, controls history."

Probably in anticipation of a victory in the general election of April 1994, the Alliance considered certain steps for implementing its strategy. Most important was that its members' and supporters' most basic needs had to be satisfied. Experience and sympathy with the masses brought the Alliance to the realisation that quite apart from the implementation of its Africanisation policy, its members and supporters urgently needed roofs over their heads, jobs, running water, electricity, education and training, as well as social services such as medical care.

A second step, which could be executed with far less trouble and financial expense, was to ensure that voices should be raised against the SFs, and that steps should be taken against them for their alleged unlawful activities.

The ANC Alliance would have calculated that it would be able to obtain enough examples of unauthorised acts to satisfy its goal of negative publicity. This publicity had to create a negative psychological impact. The successful creation of such a state of mind would lead to a feeling of uncertainty amongst former Defence Force members and supporters of the former regime. This would leave these target groups vulnerable, would undermine their honour and pride, and would cause them to hang their heads in shame at so-called malpractices of the past.[61]

By this time, of course, the ANC Alliance had had enough practice to become quite proficient at creating defeatism, sowing suspicion and undermining the morale of the population.[62]

In order to undermine the former Government, its departments, agencies and all those who had any part in the former dispensation, a process of public legal actions was launched against them. At the same time this was meant to rob the political opposition parties and their supporters of any political initiative and place them on the defensive. The KwaMakutha trial and the TRC hearings resulted from this process.

The TRC was a commission appointed by the then Government of National Unity (GNU) to unravel events that had taken place during the conflict, to make and publish findings on them and, at its discretion, to make recommendations for any further steps. The members of the TRC were mainly ANC/SACP members and their sympathisers. Despite the fact that the National Party was a member of the GNU, and F.W. de Klerk was an executive vice-president of the country, no supporter of the National Party was appointed to the TRC.

In a certain context the Alliance's publicity campaign was extremely successful. Although the judgement in the KwaMakutha trial did not meet with expectations, it did create uncertainty concerning the former Government and Defence Force actions. For almost a year during 1996 the public was treated by the media to unproven allegations of atrocities that the Defence Force had supposedly perpetrated with the full knowledge of the Government of the day.

The unprecedented publicity generated by the TRC's investigations, and its emphasis on SF actions, played havoc with the confidence, self-respect and trust of South Africans who had served in the former Government and the SFs. The TRC deviated from globally accepted legal procedures during the proceedings, particularly in regard to the presentation of evidence. When allegations were made against individuals, the person incriminated (or his or her legal representative) did not always receive prior warning as is usual practice. As a result those involved, or their legal representatives, were not always present when allegations were levelled against them during a TRC hearing. There was no cross-examination in such cases, and in most cases evidence was accepted as the truth and recorded as such. Similarly the TRC often did not question the admissibility of evidence, or measure it against acknowledged standards, but simply accepted it, despite a declaration by the Secretary of the Amnesty Committee as follows: "[C]ross-examination is one of the rules of natural justice. It is a fundamental right. It is one of the basic methods by which the truth can be established."[63]

On the other hand, Adv. Denzil Potgieter, a TRC Commissioner, said the following during a television interview on 14 April 2002: "… the TRC began about six years ago … there was no legal process in the true sense of the word".[64] One can therefore question which of these gentlemen's position is the correct one. One can almost state that the TRC process reminds one of an inquiry by a contemporary Inquisition.

The sword of publicity resulting from the activities of the TRC by and large cut to one side only, namely that of the former Government, the SFs and their supporters. Surely this unbalanced publicity must have exceeded even the Alliance's wildest expectations. The unproven allegations used in the publicity campaign aimed at Wouter Basson (partly as a result of TRC proceedings) serves as another good example of such an assault.

There is a clear rising line in calculated opinion forming which began from the moment the ban on the ANC/SACP was lifted in 1990 and lasted throughout the negotiation and pre-election periods. This well-thought-out ANC/SACP strategy was even continued for some time after the 1994 elections.

The tragedy of the events in the period from 1990 to the turn of the century is that the SA Defence Force, once the ideal image of South Africa's efficient and successful military machine, was unfairly damaged by the creation of figments of the imagination.

The blame for this must firstly be placed at the door of the previous

Government, which the Defence Force primarily had to serve. An example is the poor knowledge of the SA Defence Force illustrated by F.W. de Klerk in *The last trek – a new beginning* (1998), and his apparent mistrust of it. There were also malicious people who publicly proclaimed half-truths without having any real factual knowledge – the proverbial little foxes in the vineyard. An example of this was the regular special TRC report on television during the TRC hearings. I personally objected to this propaganda programme to the Chairman of the TRC, without any avail.

Secondly, the ANC/SACP Alliance and its agencies also contributed in that its well-planned propaganda campaign was largely responsible for creating false impressions of the Defence Force, which have lasted to this day. During the negotiations and the subsequent processes, the Government of the day, and particularly the Defence Force, accepted that both parties would act in good faith. Both the participating parties would have to give up something to ensure a peaceful transition to full democracy, but this was predicated on mutual trust. Not only were the principles that they agreed to of importance, but there also had to be a mutual assurance that all promises would be kept. In other words, there could be no hidden agenda. This would not only determine the success of the negotiations, but also ensure the success of future efforts to foster mutual acceptance, understanding and reaching out to one another.

However, the principle of good faith was certainly not clear from the ANC Alliance's subsequent actions. Operation Vula and the TRC hearings are two cases in point. The TRC was intended as a Government instrument to promote unity, mutual respect and understanding by means of the fairness of its inquiry into and judgement of past events. Instead the Commission became an instrument of revenge, without any good faith whatsoever.

The fact remains, however, that during the most critical period in the existence of South Africa, the Defence Force managed to create for all parties a climate which promoted political negotiations.[65] Yet, in exchange for its peaceful surrender of military power and its support in installing the newly elected Government in terms of the Constitution, the Defence Force was rewarded with denigration and persecution!

If one were to view the course of the political and revolutionary events in Southern Africa in the years 1960 to 1990 quite objectively, one is again impressed by the enormous support given to the ANC Alliance and SWAPO by the USSR, East Germany and Cuba in the form of training, arms and armaments supplies, propaganda and finances. These two organisations would not have been able to exist without this generous support. Furthermore it is internationally and politically accepted that countries have no friends, only interests. Against this background one may well ask whether the ANC Alliance and SWAPO had realised that once the struggle had ended, they would have been required to support the promotion of Soviet Imperialism. Fortunately these forces were stopped – thanks to the Defence Force – or no democratic processes would have been possible in South Africa. The ANC Alliance and SWAPO can be grateful that they are now under no obligation to repay their debt to the Soviet Union.

In conclusion it cannot, however, be denied that the ANC Alliance did manage, through the revolutionary war and with deft footwork, to engender an humiliating feeling of guilt amongst the "political losers". If nothing is done to address this feeling of guilt and subservience, it may last for generations to come. My effort at combating this feeling of guilt and to promote the very important spirit of reconciliation, has been to record the truth as experienced by myself and the Defence Force of the time. At the same time I wish to leave the past where it should be and to embrace and participate in the future, with its extraordinary challenges, which is rushing towards us like an express train.

If one does not take note of the ANC Alliance's tactic of creating a debilitating sense of guilt amongst its target group, it may in future be dismissed as a mere flight of fancy. This is why I have used three flagrant examples to illustrate how the Alliance acted against the Defence Force. These are discussed in later chapters. These actions were very successful, and helped to undermine the existence of most of the ANC Alliance's political opponents.

I hope that my contribution, by means of this book, will prove the truth of the ANC's well-known motto, namely:

> The word will never get lost,
> The truth will conquer the lie.

Chapter 21

RETIREMENT FROM POLITICS

APPOINTMENT TO WATER AFFAIRS AND FORESTRY

I already mentioned in Chapter 20 that I was moved from the Department of Defence to the portfolio of Water Affairs and Forestry on 11 July 1991. As I had initially entered politics with some reluctance, as indicated in Chapter 15, and had agreed to it only under certain circumstances, this new twist gave me food for thought. When I initially accepted my appointment as Minister of Defence, my goal was to help with our country's national defence, and at the same time to ensure a continued connection with the Defence Force for myself. This unexpected move, as described in Chapter 20, severed this connection. So what next?

In my opinion it is the prerogative of a country's Head of State to decide how he wishes to govern the country, and with whom. As part of Pres. De Klerk's team I therefore did not protest against his decisions regarding the changes to his team. Seen against the background that he had never been involved in national security and Defence Force activities, and therefore had no experience in this field, I decided to accept the new appointment, for the time being at least.[1] It would afford me some opportunities in the future to ensure that the new Cabinet would not nullify former Cabinet decisions concerning important facets of security without thorough input from me. At a later stage, I was glad that I had taken this task on myself.

One of the high-risk Cabinet decisions that had been made earlier involved approved cut-backs in the financial requirements of the Defence Force and Armscor, as well as Cabinet approval for sensitive projects and actions, for example Defence Force training for some 200 members of Inkatha. Without such approval this could have been regarded as a high-handed Defence Force action.

In the next 18 months a number of proposals were put to the Cabinet which would have nullified previous Cabinet decisions made during my period of responsibility for the Defence Force. For example, a Cabinet decision was proposed which would impact on new approved Headquarters for the Air Force, and the purchase of new training aircraft. Fortunately my presence and knowledge of the events leading up to the approval of these matters helped to prevent a backwards step with regard to national security.

When Pres. De Klerk announced my transfer from Defence to Water Affairs and Forestry, the media asked to me to comment. I could not reveal my actual inner feelings to them, because I regretted that after 41 years of close involvement with the Defence Force, my path would now diverge from it. The main reason for the transfer was that even at that stage (i.e. 1990 and 1991) I was one of the few members of the Cabinet who was prepared to publicly criticise the Alliance's demands, pronouncements and actions. This was before the Government and the Alliance settled their dispute over the continuation of the armed struggle and the Alliance set in motion its four-phased rolling mass action protest. The Alliance's Operation Vula was in full swing at the time, and the ANC was trying to create the perception that the Defence Force had its own agenda in direct conflict with that of the Government.

My media comments were therefore limited to the facts, and I merely said: "The cause is always bigger than the man. I served the Defence Force and Armscor to the best of my ability for many years. The Defence Force's military successes in Angola paved the way for the present political processes. Armscor's achievements in the 1980s ensured South Africa's political independence. I gave these two organisations my all in the interests of the security of all our people. I have now been called to serve South Africa in another field. I will do this with the same dedication. I defeated the Reds: now I'm joining the Greens."

Having been relieved of all Defence Force duties for some 18 months,

I was in Pretoria on Thursday 17 December 1992, occupied with my tasks as Minister of Water Affairs and Forestry, when I was urgently requested to see Pres. De Klerk in Cape Town on Friday, 18 December 1992.

THE CASE OF 23 DEFENCE FORCE OFFICERS

This incident is also known as the Steyn Enquiry, or "Night of the generals".

In F.W. de Klerk's office I was handed a document of about four or five pages to study. According to him the contents of the document served as basic information for a media statement he intended to release the next day. I read it very briefly, and noticed it concerned the dismissal of certain Defence Force officers. However, it also dealt with a matter of which I had no knowledge, and I asked him to sketch the background to this matter for me. He said that he intended to get rid of these 23 officers because they had apparently been involved in an inadmissible right-wing intrigue aimed against the State.

He explained that he had on an earlier occasion appointed Gen. Pierre Steyn of the Defence Force to conduct a special investigation into certain irregularities which had apparently occurred within the Military Intelligence Division (MID). Apparently Steyn had briefly and verbally reported to him that there were signs of third force activities, or otherwise that there had been an unofficial rebirth of the Civil Co-operation Bureau. Furthermore he alleged that the Defence Force was involved in intimidation and the instigation of violence. Steyn advised Pres. De Klerk to act as soon as possible at all levels, and handed him a list of names of Defence Force members who should be confronted, together with recommendations on steps to be taken against them. Furthermore he recommended that certain matters be referred to the South African Police, the Attorneys General, the Auditor General and the Goldstone Commission.[2]

Apparently the President had accepted most of Steyn's recommendations.

My next question was why I had to come and see him with regard to the matter, and what purpose this would serve. He answered: "These activities commenced and took place when you were still Minister of

Defence." I answered: "If they did happen, it would definitely not have been during my term of office as Minister of Defence, because I had my finger on the pulse of the Defence Force. I knew what was happening in the Defence Force." I again gave my opinion by saying that he was making a mistake in his assessment of these officers. I even went so far as to say that some of the persons included in the list displayed greater integrity than I could lay claim to for myself.

I then asked him whether he wanted any further reaction from me, and his advice was that I could resign as Minister immediately, could resign after he made his media statement over the weekend, or could try to weather the storm. My reaction to this was: "I know most of these 23 officers very well. I know they are honourable, and I certainly harbour no suspicions in regard to them. I know they would never conduct any improper activities, and certainly none aimed at the State."

I also made it clear that I was definitely planning to retire from politics, but that I would decide for myself when this would occur. I made it quite clear that I did not wish to be associated with his actions in any way. I would nevertheless telephone him after the media release and convey my views on the matter to him. I realised, however, that had I retired from politics in July 1991, when I was transferred from Defence to Water Affairs and Forestry, I would no doubt have been publicly branded alongside these 23 officers.

After I had taken note of his media statement and had watched the various media presentations, I contacted Pres. De Klerk telephonically on the afternoon of 20 December 1992. I informed him that I stood by my opinion that he had committed an error of judgement. The publicity surrounding the matter did not influence my opinion.

The President referred Steyn's recommendations and certain aspects of his investigation to the South African Police, the Attorney General, the Auditor General and the Goldstone Commission.[3]

The South African Police, the Attorneys General of the Transvaal and Witwatersrand, and members of National Intelligence (NI) began their investigation into the Steyn allegations in co-operation with Gen. Steyn early in January 1993. Apart from the allegations themselves, and in spite of Steyn's participation in the investigation, they could at that stage find no factual evidence that would stand up in a court of law to confirm the allegations. Because of this lack of evidence, none of the possible suspects could even be approached to testify in this regard. According to the MID and NI one suspect (a certain Terblanche) was quite willing to talk about the matter and had already taken a polygraph test which provided negative results.[4]

Adv. B.J. Bredenkamp, Deputy Attorney General of the Transvaal, was appointed to the investigating team in a full-time capacity. In his opinion there was no possibility of prosecution unless new information regarding the allegations was found.

The departmental investigating team came to the conclusion that there was no evidence; the allegations sounded like loose talk that could have originated around a coffee table or after a drink in a bar, to which certain people had attached too much weight.

The representatives of NI, Dr Kobus Scholtz and Mr Mervyn Markram, could not present any further information when requested to do so by the investigating team.

The task that I had taken upon myself regarding national security – as mentioned earlier in my discussion of my transfer from the Ministry of Defence – was largely completed by the end of 1992. As I was not involved or included in any of the negotiations between the Government of the day and the ANC Alliance, I went to see Pres. De Klerk in January 1993 and informed him that I intended to retire from politics at the end of February 1993. Of course I had no idea of the horrible, demeaning and emotional events that awaited me.

All in all one has to accept that the dismissal of the 23 officers was based merely on perceptions, allegations and accusations. According to the Attorney General of the Witwatersrand, the allegations had no basis. A year later, on 14 April 1994, during a television debate in the run-up to the 1994 election, Mr Mandela requested F.W. de Klerk to make available the evidence that had resulted in the dismissal of the 23 Defence Force officers. He could not do so. The fact is that on a later occasion and on legal advice F.W. de Klerk apologised to some of the officers in writing. The State was also compelled to offer certain officers financial compensation for this presidential *faux pas*.[5]

Chapter 22

OPERATION MARION AND THE KWAMAKUTHA COURT CASE

When it assumed power in 1994, the ANC Government took certain steps aimed at former members of the Defence Force. The aim, as part of its divide and rule strategy, seemed to be to embarrass participants in the previous political dispensation by accusing them of complicity in alleged atrocities that members of the Defence Force were supposed to have perpetrated on instructions of the previous Government.

The three most blatant examples of such public embarrassment, which contributed to the disintegration of support for the Defence Force (and the former Government), involved two sensational trials and the public pronouncements and reports of the Truth and Reconciliation Commission (TRC).

The two trials were the trial of the KwaMakutha murders, in which certain members of the Defence Force's top echelons and I were accused of murder and tried in KwaZulu-Natal, and the trial of Dr Wouter Basson on charges relating to chemical and biological warfare. The trial of and accusations against Dr Basson raised questions about the authorisation given to obtain South African expertise to counter weapons of mass destruction. Questions were also raised about the way in which he did this.

THE KWAMAKUTHA TRIAL: OPERATION MARION

The mid-1980s were characterised by violence, unrest and terror, and KwaZulu was the focal point. The Government instructed the Defence Force to accept certain protection tasks that the Police could not properly handle, as additional tasks. This is normal in most developed countries.

At the time there was serious concern, particularly amongst leaders of the Inkatha movement, about an increasing number of assassinations of their members. It was a matter of urgency to devise a plan to improve the security situation, and Operation Marion was the result of this plan. The purpose of the operation was to provide trained personnel who would protect government property. These personnel were also to be trained to ensure the safety of Mr Mangosuthu Buthelezi, the Chief Minister of KwaZulu, and other important persons – mostly members of Inkatha.

The Government therefore decided that the Defence Force should provide basic military training for 200 Inkatha-aligned Zulus so that they would be able to operate as security personnel.

As early as 1985 Mr Buthelezi was a very important leader in South Africa and abroad. Both the USA and Britain classified and treated the ANC/SACP Alliance of the time as a terrorist organisation. On the one hand Buthelezi was a political rival of the ANC, but on the other he was a leading critic of apartheid and the policies of the Government of the day.[1] From a security point of view it was clear that he was in great danger of losing his life in an assassination attempt or in some other violent way. It was ANC policy that the structures of the KwaZulu Government and those of the Inkatha movement should be destroyed. If this could be achieved, the ANC/SACP allies could let loose their insurgents on the rest of South Africa. The small number of KwaZulu policemen was no match for these attempts by the enemy.[2]

The South African Government regarded it as its duty to protect the citizens of this area, and their leaders in particular. An extraordinary meeting of the State Security Council (SSC) was therefore arranged for 20 December 1985 in Cape Town, and urgent protection for Chief Minister Buthelezi was placed on the agenda. At that meeting it was decided that I, as Minister of Defence, assisted by Chris Heunis, the Minister of

Constitutional Development and Planning, and Louis le Grange, the Minister of Law and Order, had to assist Mr Buthelezi so that a security force could be established in KwaZulu. This was of particular importance in light of the deteriorating security situation on the border with Mozambique. Despite the Nkomati Accord, larger numbers of ANC terrorists were entering KwaZulu illegally from Mozambique.[3]

In accordance with the SSC's recommendations, the Government gave instructions that the three of us were to meet Chief Minister Buthelezi in Cape Town on 9 January 1986. The Chief Minister's view of the threat that he, the traditional leaders and the Inkatha movement faced, accorded with information supplied to me by the Defence Force. He also requested the formation of a paramilitary force to manage the situation, and requested that he should be given the authority to issue firearms licences.[4]

After having heard the Chief Minister, the three of us requested expert advice on implementing the SSC's recommendation. The joint implementation proposals drawn up by the three of us were presented to the SSC on 3 February 1986, and were accepted by this body. The proposals were approved at the next Cabinet meeting.[5]

In brief the proposals involved the following: A Security Management System similar to the National Security Management System (NSMS) had to be created for KwaZulu. This would primarily be the responsibility of the Department of Constitutional Development and Planning. Furthermore the SA Police Force would be responsible for training 500 additional members of the KwaZulu Police Force, while the Defence Force would be responsible for training a paramilitary force after a detailed assessment of needs and goals had been drawn up in consultation with Mr Buthelezi. Lastly Mr Buthelezi's request that this support should be implemented covertly was to be respected. The project, to be co-ordinated by Min. Heunis, was accordingly classified "Top Secret".[6]

The implementation of the protection was an urgent matter, and for this reason Gen. Tienie Groenewald, of the staff of the Chief of Staff Intelligence of the Defence Force, discussed the matter with the Chief Minister on 12 February 1986. During this visit another assessment of needs and requirements was made on instruction of the SSC. Gen. Groenewald provided me with this information on 17 February 1986.[7]

Consequent to these events, I constituted a Defence Force Committee under the chairmanship of Gen. Kat Liebenberg to finalise the details of implementing the aims of the execution of the Defence Force's task in accordance with the Cabinet decision and the Chief Minister's needs. I verbally presented the subsequent Liebenberg Report to Min. Heunis. I also informed him that senior staff officers had cleared the concept of a paramilitary force with Mr Buthelezi, and that it was exactly the same concept that the Defence Force had applied in South-West Africa/Namibia when it was given a similar instruction, namely to protect Ovambo chiefs against SWAPO terrorism attacks.[8]

As Minister of Defence I gave formal permission for the provision of basic military training to 206 security and protection personnel on 8 April 1986, and the operation was given the code name Marion. One needs to bear in mind that at this stage Inkatha was a cultural organisation with underlying political objectives. Its name changed to the Inkatha Freedom Party (IFP) only a few years later, in 1990.

I met the Chief Minister in Durban on 17 April 1986. He said that he was satisfied with the Defence Force's arrangements, and expressed his sincere thanks towards the South African Government.[9]

I then verbally informed the State President, Mr P.W. Botha, and Min. Heunis that all aspects with regard to the formation of a paramilitary capability had been cleared with the Chief Minister, and I also conveyed his thanks to the Government.

The training of the protection personnel took place in a continuous period from April to October 1986. Because the Defence Force had training facilities suitable for this purpose in the Caprivi, the personnel training took place there. The remoteness of the area made it possible to conduct the task covertly, as was required by the Government.

According to evidence given at a later stage by the main State witness, Defence Force officer Capt. J.P. Opperman, the Zulus undergoing the training did not know where the training was being conducted. They were flown from Natal to the Caprivi by aeroplane, and some of them believed themselves to be in Israel. They were also under the impression that they were being trained for employment by the KwaZulu Police Force. After completion of the training the group was flown directly from the Caprivi to Ulundi in Northern Natal, where it was to remain temporarily until it received further instructions.

At that stage Opperman was a Defence Force liaison officer in Natal, appointed to handle Operation Marion, and Sgt André Cloete was his assistant. Following their appointment, the two of them travelled all over Natal in an unmarked vehicle for two or three weeks on reconnaissance. Apparently they also carried out liaison visits to Col Jacobus Victor, the Defence Force intelligence officer in Natal, and to Maj. Louis Botha of the SA Police. Within their own departments the latter two officers were responsible for gathering, evaluating, co-ordinating and disseminating intelligence. They operated from Durban and were responsible for the whole of Natal.

Opperman claimed that on completion of the reconnaissance he drove to Pretoria to see Col John More of the Military Intelligence Division (MID). He wanted to prepare the way for planning and executing military operations in Natal, because he was convinced that in view of the successes of ANC assaults on Inkatha such operations were essential.

He claimed that More listened attentively to his presentation, left his office for a few hours, and assured Opperman on his return that permission had been granted for planning such operations. However, Opperman had to make quite sure that the operations would have a positive impact on Inkatha, and would prove to be an asset to the South African Government. Subsequently Opperman met, amongst others, Messrs M.Z. Khumalo and Daluxolo Luthuli (both members of the Inkatha movement) and told them that permission for military operations had been granted.

Opperman also claimed that he had identified four possible targets, and that a target dossier had been opened for each of them. With the help of Col Victor, it was then ascertained that none of the chosen persons was a Defence Force informant or had had contact with the Defence Force. Following a thorough evaluation of the target dossiers by Opperman, Cloete and Luthuli, it was decided that Victor Ntuli, a United Democratic Front (UDF) activist, was to be the first target.

There was another visit to Col More in Pretoria, who was allegedly informed of the reasons why Victor Ntuli was chosen as the first target. He gave his approval for the operation and said the planning had to go ahead. Arms and ammunition for the operation were to be obtained from the Ferntree Defence Force Base in Natal. Opperman also purchased ten flashlights for the operation.

Opperman and Cloete travelled directly from Pretoria to Ferntree and collected the arms and ammunition. They then travelled to Ulundi and arranged to meet ten of the Zulus who had received military training in a dry riverbed. AK-47s were issued, and flashlights were attached to the rifles with insulation tape. Each person fired a few shots, and practised the actions that would be required for such an operation.

The ten Zulus earmarked for the operation were instructed to meet Opperman and Cloete near the Louis Botha Airport in Durban at 02:00 the next morning, where a ten-seater vehicle and a driver would be waiting.

After the practice, Opperman and Cloete left for the Natal Command Army Base in Durban, apparently to inform Col Victor of the intended operation, and to request him to meet them at the old Durban Prison about an hour after the conclusion of the operation. He would then take into safe custody all the weapons used in the operation. Maj. Louis Botha of the SA Police was apparently also visited, as he had to ensure that no Police officers would be present in the area during the operation. If the persons executing the operation were to leave empty cartridge cases or anything else at the scene of the attack, the Major was to arrange that these were quietly removed.

Everything went according to plan. Opperman, Cloete and the ten Zulus in the microbus met at the pre-arranged place, and the AK-47s were issued. In order to obstruct any later identification, advertising boards were attached to the microbus, and the number plates were replaced with a false set. The team then moved to the target area in Kwa-Makutha to execute the operation, while Opperman and Cloete waited for them at a pre-arranged place. The team returned about half an hour later. The operation had apparently been executed successfully. The weapons were returned, the advertisements were removed from the vehicle, and the original number plates were restored. Opperman and Cloete accompanied the team beyond Umhlanga, from where it returned to Ulundi on its own. Opperman and Cloete then disposed of the advertising material and false number plates.

Opperman claims that he then met Col Victor at the old Durban Prison and returned the weapons to him. Victor promised to keep them at Natal Command, where they would be collected to be melted down at Iscor in Pretoria.

According to Opperman, More received a report that the operation had been a success. opperman was informed that a certain Cmdt Van der Merwe would collect the weapons in Natal, and this indeed happened. Opperman and Cloete collected the weapons at the Command while Van der Merwe waited for them outside the Command's premises. Opperman and Cloete then travelled north to Ulundi by car, while Van der Merwe followed in his vehicle. The weapons were transferred to Van der Merwe's car on the outskirts of Ulundi, and he travelled to Pretoria on his own.

In the days thereafter, dramatic reports of the attack of 21 January 1987 on a house in the KwaMakutha township appeared in the media. According to these reports, a group of persons armed with AK-47s launched a bloody attack on the house and gruesomely murdered 13 persons and wounded at least 4 others.

After Mr Nelson Mandela's release and the lifting of the bans on organisations such as the ANC, the SACP and the PAC, a negotiation process followed which ended in the countrywide elections of 1994. The ANC Alliance won the elections, and a Government of National Unity (GNU) was formed.

One of the first things the new central government undertook in KwaZulu-Natal was to instruct the SA Police Service's so-called Investigation Task Unit (ITU) to investigate alleged unlawful actions by the State in Natal, and particularly the KwaMakutha massacre. The Minister of Safety and Security also appointed an independent civilian board in September 1994 to help with the investigation into alleged State-aided violence. One of the reasons for creating this civilian board, known as the Investigation Task Board, was that the authorities feared that certain senior members of the Security Forces, who were suspects in the case, would be able to misuse their ties with the Security Forces in order to manipulate or influence matters in their favour. The Investigation Task Board consisted mainly of members or strong supporters of the ANC/SACP Alliance. The convenor of the Investigation Task Board was a legal expert, Mr Howard Varney. The Investigation Task Unit and Investigation Task Board worked very closely together in the Natal investigation.[10]

The *Financial Mail* had the following to say about the Investigation Task Unit: "The ITU has been given carte blanche to seek revenge against former political adversaries from Varney's days as United Democratic Front Leader in the Eastern Cape ... The ITU is a Trojan horse for the ANC."[11]

Unfortunately for the ANC, serious differences of opinion were soon evident amongst the crew of their Trojan horse. At the time media speculation was rife about tension in the office of the Attorney General (AG) in KwaZulu-Natal. As befits a good jurist, the AG, Mr Tim McNally, apparently wanted to act only against those who, according to the available evidence, were directly involved in the massacre. This would clearly make it much more possible to obtain a verdict of guilty. On the other hand a very junior official seconded to the Investigation Task Unit apparently took the rigid view that the highest possible authority of the time should also be included. This would mean that members of the SSC and Chief Minister Buthelezi would also have to be charged. Rumours were rife at the time that the official concerned, Adv. Karl König, went directly to his political master, Dullah Omar, the Minister of Justice, without the knowledge of the AG, in order to air his views as to who was responsible for the KwaMakutha murders.[12]

Because Operation Marion had been approved by the Cabinet of the time, König probably thought that if members of the SSC could be found guilty, it would implicate the entire Cabinet, and that this would cause such a political embarrassment that they would find it hard to recover from it.

König probably had insight into documents that had a very high security classification. Those documents were probably from the SSC and the SA Defence Force and the State Archives, which would have carried the usual restricted security classification. It is very possible that an uninformed person may have interpreted the military terminology in the documents incorrectly and could have deduced that the documents showed malicious intent. When the High Court studied the documents pertaining to Operation Marion during the trial, it could find no instructions for or description of unlawful actions. The court found: "It must be obvious that at the time they were written and received, the documents were not subjected to the minute and critical analysis either by the authors or signatories or by the receivers that has befallen them before this court." Furthermore: "Nowhere in the documents will one find any express mention of KwaMakutha, murder, unlawful killing, hit squads or indeed any consent or authorisation to commit any unlawful acts or any killings whatsoever."[13]

Even before the commencement of the trial, there was media speculation on the differences between the AG and his subordinate. Apparently these differences had serious repercussions within the ANC. According to the *Financial Mail* of 10 November 1995 McNally was summoned to appear before a Parliamentary committee, and *Die Burger* of 12 November 1996 asked questions about ulterior political motives.

In the same article, headed "Suspicion of selective prosecution" the *Financial Mail* commented on the matter as follows: "McNally's decision to charge Malan and his co-accused came after he had been sharply criticised by ANC leaders ... for 'protecting' Inkatha Freedom Party leaders and the security officers from prosecution and then interrogated by the parliamentary committee on Justice for his 'political bias'."

The accused in the trial themselves began to suspect that all was not well in the AG's office. In fact, during the trial Varney's body language clearly expressed his disgruntlement to all those present.[14]

In the meantime Opperman had confessed to the Investigation Task Unit that he and certain other persons had been involved in the KwaMakutha massacre. He averred that he and Cloete, who had assisted him, did execute the repulsive murders, but that it was done on command of the highest authority in the Defence Force. According to him, the directive also had the political approval of the Government of the day.

The Investigation Task Unit offered not to prosecute them for this offence on condition that they should act as State witnesses and give evidence against those about to be charged. Opperman, Cloete and one of the Zulus who had been trained in the Caprivi, A.B. Khumalo, accepted the offer.

The Investigation Task Unit offered to accommodate Opperman (the principal State witness) and later Cloete (the second main State witness) in the State's witness protection scheme. In addition Opperman was promised that if he testified satisfactorily during the trial, he and his family would be permanently resettled in a foreign country of his choice, under an assumed name if he wished, with State aid, including financial support. Opperman indicated that he and his family would prefer to be resettled in Denmark.

The bomb burst on 5 June 1995. Without any warning, the first senior Defence Force officer, Col John More, was arrested at night at his home in Pretoria in a degrading and shocking manner.

Subsequently certain former and serving senior Defence Force officers were invited to tea at Defence Headquarters in Pretoria by Gen. Georg Meiring, the Chief of the Defence Force at the time, on the afternoon of Friday 27 October 1995. He informed us that the State intended arresting and trying us for our share in Operation Marion. It was upsetting news for all of us.

My first thoughts were about the effect that this news could have on the families of those involved, including my own; they would surely experience it as a great dishonour. Those directly involved in the incidents would find it easier personally to fight such a set-back with the facts, but it would be very difficult for the families who did not really know what was going on to be confronted on the matter by strangers. Children can also be very cruel towards one another, and the children of all those involved would suffer. All we could do at that stage was to hope and pray that everything would turn out all right.[15]

Furthermore all those present were informed that the Government planned to keep secret the proposed arrests until after they had actually occurred. We stared at each other in confused silence. We all realised that this was part of a large-scale political plot. It would hardly be possible to hide proposed arrests such as these. I also believed, and said so to the others, that the ANC would deliberately leak this sensational news to the media just prior to the countrywide municipal elections, and that the media would make it public with great fanfare within two days, that is not later than Sunday 29 October 1995. This prediction proved to be quite correct: the Sunday newspapers carried the story under banner headlines.[16]

The municipal elections in KwaZulu-Natal had been postponed until the first half of 1996. It was very clear that the news of the proposed arrests would place the ANC in a favourable light. This advantage would be particularly evident in the ANC's contest with Inkatha in KwaZulu-Natal. Of course the ANC would be able to get a good deal of political mileage from the revelations; its timing was perfect. Col More had been arrested as early as June, but now – four months later and only a few days before the important elections – the rabbit of mass arrests was pulled from the hat. Even the media were critical because the arrests had not been made five or six days or even a week later.

As one could expect, the news received huge publicity in the days following 29 October. Of course there was speculation that it was simply an election ploy by the ANC to make sure that incorrect perceptions about the Defence Force and the previous Government would be strengthened among the public at a time that would be very inconvenient for the previous Government.

Pres. Mandela personally had a difficult time answering to these accusations. He had clearly not been informed that his Minister of Justice had for some months been contemplating a trial of persons who could possibly be accused. With the elections just around the corner, and possibly as a result of pressure from the ranks of the ANC, the Minister or his Department decided to act. Pres. Mandela could only say that an unfortunate set of circumstances had caused the news of the arrests and the elections to follow one another so soon.[17]

The curiosity of the foreign media had also been piqued. Their representatives in South Africa, known as the Foreign Media Association, extended an invitation to me, as one of the accused, to have breakfast with them on 28 November 1995, and I accepted. I was able to use the occasion to state my case, to inform them fully about the much-discussed atrocities and to answer their questions. The event proceeded in good spirit, and at least offered me the opportunity to make my voice heard in the international arena. Five manned television cameras and about a hundred members of the international media were present. The only discordant note was a very hostile Allister Sparks, at the time a member of the SABC Board, who had provided some of the gathered reporters with barbed questions in order to corner and flay me. Furthermore an Australian reporter tried to get at me with personal remarks. Fortunately it was not difficult to cope with them. Question time lasted some two hours, and I felt satisfied with the way the session had gone. Despite many rumours, bits of gossip and perceptions prevalent at the time, I had the feeling that I had satisfied the foreign media. I was able to clear up many things that were unclear or uncertain, and place the entire matter in its proper perspective. When question time was over, I was thanked, and many of the journalists then personally wished me well with the trial. It was remarkable that not one of the foreign television stations who had recorded the event consequently broadcast a negative view of the proceedings, or indeed of the trial that followed.[18]

At the time there were widespread rumours – some of them reported in the newspapers – that certain political and other leaders wanted to petition the authorities to grant me and my co-accused amnesty, or had indeed done so. The *Financial Mail* even involved former Pres. F.W. de Klerk in this regard.[19]

I then decided to pay Pres. Mandela a personal visit on the matter of such an appeal for amnesty, because I was convinced that every one of the accused in the military had a clean conscience. This visit took the form of a dinner on 28 November 1995. I made a very simple request: that those responsible for these acts of terrorism had to be prosecuted and punished. The accused Defence Force officers and I were innocent and required no amnesty. He listened attentively and granted my request, and consequently the law took its course.[20]

F.W. de Klerk, who was at that stage a deputy president in the GNU, also became embroiled in the KwaMakutha matter, in that he called several meetings with the Ministers who had been members of the SSC in the former Government; some of these Ministers were also Cabinet members in the new GNU. The meetings were mostly to ascertain their views on the manner in which the ANC/SACP Government would possibly handle the TRC and amnesty question in the time to come.

During the first meeting called by Deputy President De Klerk in 1995, Adriaan Vlok, the former Minister of Law and Order, and I got the impression that our former colleagues who were present could perhaps conclude that the two of us may possibly be guilty of murder as a result of the instructions that had been given by us. I tried to make it clear that we were as innocent of murder as the other former colleagues who were present. After all, Project Marion was a joint decision of the SSC and the Cabinet.

Adriaan Vlok and I also wanted to know whether the present and former ministers at the meeting would accept responsibility for any previous actions by their departments, and whether the State would accept the legal costs for any future trials and appearances before the TRC.

The two of us stated very clearly to those present that if at any future date any differences of opinion were to appear amongst former members of the Cabinet and SSC, and the then heads of the two Security Departments, we would stand by our former Heads of Department. I also emphasised that the former Heads of Department should be present at any future meetings of this nature.

The meeting discussed all these matters, but made no definite decisions. It was, however, decided that the former Heads of the Security Departments could attend the next meeting. F.W. de Klerk acted as chairman at all times, and indicated that he was inclined to agree that the Ministers and former Ministers should consider accepting responsibility for the actions of their Departments.

A subsequent, similar meeting was then held, and some of our former Heads of Department, mainly those of the Security Departments, attended. On this occasion it was decided that F.W. de Klerk needed to see Deputy President Mbeki on the issue of the TRC and other matters, including the question of amnesty.

It was then provisionally decided that another meeting should be held round about November 1995; the exact date was to be determined later. As a result of the KwaMakutha arrests that had been made in the meantime, the meeting was postponed a number of times, and eventually apparently cancelled. In any case, neither I nor the former Heads of Department for which I was responsible, were invited to attend any further meetings.

Adriaan Vlok and I still stood by our former departments, and during the TRC hearings we publicly testified that we accepted the moral responsibility for their actions. This is how it should be.[21]

The Operation Marion trial, also known as the KwaMakutha or Malan trial, began in the Durban Magistrate's Court on 1 December 1995. The title of the formal charge sheet read, "The State versus Peter Msane and 19 others". The charges were entered and heard, and then referred to the Natal Division of the Supreme Court and postponed to 4 March 1996. I was released, along with the others, but had to pay bail of R10 000, hand in my passport and report to my nearest police station every week.

When the accused and a small group of Defence Force supporters tried to leave the Durban Magistrate's Court to return to Pretoria, a large press contingent and a mass of dancing and shouting people awaited us at the building's front door. Our appearance was greeted with screaming and yelling from the crowd. Many people in the mass pulled an index finger across their throat to indicate that we should die. It was clear that we had been found guilty by the crowd even before the trial had begun.[22]

Some of the journalists asked me to make some sort of statement or comment. In order to be heard above the noise of the crowd, I bellowed – with a voice well trained on the parade ground: "Those who are guilty of this heinous deed must be punished. What happened here today could become a grave crisis for South Africa's new-found democracy ... I am a democrat ... I am a Christian ... and I am proud of it."[23]

Fortunately the security personnel quickly took us to our waiting transport, because what I felt at that stage could have induced me to say a great many other things as well. I felt like rebelling against these demeaning circumstances and to tell the world that the accusations and imputations were false. At the same time I also felt helpless.

One's nerves are rubbed raw in such circumstances. Phrases such as: "... committed on the orders of the highest authority, and with political approval ..." were freely used. Sometimes it is very difficult to keep your composure and not to protest your innocence out loud. I have always been prepared to accept the consequences if I had done something wrong, but absolutely not if I was not guilty of anything.

In the meantime the municipal elections which had not taken place in KwaZulu-Natal in November, together with the rest of the country, had been postponed to June 1996. The start of the trial would therefore coincide with the pre-election period. As is the case in most criminal trials, the state witnesses present their evidence first, and this would provide the ANC with juicy, untested propaganda material to use during the elections. One must keep in mind that the two main opponents in the municipal elections were the IFP and the ANC. M.Z. Khumalo, a prominent IFP member, and six Zulus trained in the Caprivi (all of them Inkatha supporters), would be in the dock.

The countrywide municipal elections were held on two different dates: just after the arrests, and then again at the start of the KwaMakutha

The Defence Force accused. Front row, from left to right: Cmdt Jan van der Merwe, Brig. Cornelius van Niekerk, Col Jacobus Victor and Capt. Dan Griesel. Back row, from left to right: Adm. Andries Putter, Gen. Tienie Groenewald, Cmdt Jakes Jacobs, Gen. Kat Liebenberg, Gen. Magnus Malan, Col John More, Gen Neels van Tonder, Gen. Jannie Geldenhuys.

trial, which suited the ruling ANC perfectly from a political propaganda point of view.

The trial started in Durban on 4 March 1996 before Mr Justice Jan Hugo, assisted by two assessors, namely retired magistrate T.N. Kruger and Attorney H.Q. Msimang.

The 20 accused consisted of seven Zulus, one member of the SA Police, Brig. Botha, eleven senior Defence Force officers and I, as former Minister of Defence. There were five generals amongst the eleven senior Defence Force officers, of whom two were former Chiefs of the Defence Force, namely Gen. Jannie Geldenhuys and Gen. Kat Liebenberg. The others were Gen. Neels van Tonder, Gen. Tienie Groenewald, Adm. Andries Putter, Brig. Cornelius van Niekerk, Col John More and Col Jacobus Victor, Cmdt Jakes Jacobs and Cmdt Jan van der Merwe, and Capt. Dan Griesel.

Seven top defence teams represented the accused. Each team consisted of a seasoned senior counsel, assisted by a junior counsel and attorney. The legal teams were led by Adv. Sam Maritz (SC) of the Pretoria bar.

According to the original charge sheet, the 20 accused were charged with 13 counts of murder, four of attempted murder or alternatively conspiracy to commit murder, in terms of the Riotous Assemblies Act 7 of 1957.[24]

The first charge concerned an incident which took place in the Kwa-Makutha township south of Durban on 21 January 1987 in which 13 persons were murdered and 4 were wounded. The charge also stated that the alternative charge of conspiracy to commit murder was made to ensure that if the State could not prove the involvement of the accused in the KwaMakutha incident, it could aver that the actions of the accused in the period from 19 December 1985 to June 1989 formed a conspiracy to commit murder against members of the ANC/UDF and related organisations in general.

The trial lasted eight months. During the first part of the trial, the State called witnesses, who were then cross-examined. During this first part of the trial I got the impression that the State's evidence was very convincing, and at the same time damning to the accused. The evidence agreed to such an extent, and sounded so convincing, that I began to doubt whether the court would find us not guilty. If there had been no cross-examination, any outsider would surely have been convinced of the accused's guilt.

Most of the media were shocked by the evidence given by the State witnesses concerning the KwaMakutha massacre, and found it credible and acceptable (without any critical analysis), and reported it as such. The presence of a strong foreign media contingent at the trial meant that the State's evidence enjoyed strong coverage abroad as well.

The publicity helped to create the impression countrywide and even worldwide that all the accused, and myself as Minister at the time, surely must have had a hand in the massacre. The public must surely have thought: "But isn't the entire Cabinet accountable?"

On preparing Sgt Cloete for his testimony, the Investigation Task Unit had given him insight into the written testimony of Capt. Opperman, which is completely unacceptable in any court. Referring to the methods used by the Investigation Team, the judge said: "The uncritical use of modern technology is not always beneficial. It appears that the police had statements noted on laptop computers, when they interviewed Cloete, for example. Some paragraphs from these previous statements were simply 'cut and pasted' onto Cloete's statement. Most if not all examples quoted to us are fairly innocuous, but the danger of contamination – even if unintentional – remains present."[25]

The fact that the first six accused (the Caprivi trainees) were not identified by means of an identity parade also caused the court to doubt the identification process. The absence of such a basic identification process and the careless way in which the investigating officers handled this aspect upset the bench a great deal.

During the second phase of the trial the accused appeared one by one, presented their evidence, and were then cross-examined. However, at the commencement of this phase three of the accused Defence Force members, namely Groenewald, Van der Merwe and Griesel, were discharged by the court because there was insufficient evidence of their involvement.

From the evidence given by the main State witnesses, particularly under cross-examination, it was clear that there were inconsistencies in their versions of events. The testimony of the accused also differed substantially from that of the State witnesses.

THE SUPREME COURT'S MAIN FINDINGS

The following findings concentrate mainly on the most important State witnesses. These facts make it easier to understand why the Supreme Court was able to reach a unanimous verdict.

In its evaluation of the State witnesses, the Court pointed out that the State relied almost exclusively on the evidence of the three accomplices Opperman, Cloete and Khumalo. The credibility and reliability of these witnesses was therefore of the utmost importance. The Court further pointed out that the three were themselves liable to prosecution: "It is indeed possibly only because they agreed to be State witnesses that they themselves evaded prosecution."[26]

The court was very critical of the credibility of these witnesses: "All three the accomplices are such that we would have gravely doubted their veracity, even if they were not accomplices and not subject to the cautionary rule pertaining to such accomplices." According to the court, accomplices are usually self-confessed criminals who try to gain the greatest advantage from their revelations: "... in this case the manifest exemption from prosecution is and was present in the minds of all three of the accomplices."[27]

The court was of the opinion that Opperman, the main witness, was clearly tempted to tell the Police what, in his opinion, they wanted to hear. For example, there was evidence that Opperman told the Police that he would involve "very senior people".[28]

Initially, in his main evidence, Opperman accepted certain responsibilities for the actual execution of the operation. He testified that he had planned which type of weapon should be used, and how many. When he was cornered under cross-examination, he denied his own part in the planning of the weapons to be used, and ascribed this aspect, and the actual execution at the particular place, to Cloete. In this regard Cloete differed radically from him.[29]

Initially Opperman maintained that the operation was planned and executed perfectly, but on conclusion of the cross-examination he could no longer defend that view: "... Opperman's previous claims ... lay in tatters ... Some of his claims indeed had been shown to be false and others had been shown to be grossly inadequate or naive."[30]

"It is in our view clear that Opperman was lying when he said that the objective was to kill Victor Ntuli alone and indeed Mr McNally (the Attorney General of KwaZulu-Natal, prosecuting in this case) conceded this."[31]

During cross-examination Opperman made the sensational revelation that the operation in KwaMakutha was not a Defence Force operation, but "... an operation launched by Inkatha, with guidelines from our side". According to the judge, this statement was in stark contrast with the rest of Opperman's testimony, during which he testified about the approval and authorisation given: "It also raises the interesting possibility that the guidelines or advice might have been of his own making. If it is only advice or guidance that was being given, there seems to be no reason to involve his superiors."[32]

Opperman boasted in court that he was the commander of the KwaMakutha gang of murderers, to such a degree that in the judge's view Opperman displayed self-aggrandisement. It was found that Opperman was a liar who gave the court unreliable answers under oath.[33]

The court was also of the opinion that Opperman's chief co-witness, Sgt Cloete, was an unreliable witness. According to the court's judgement, McNally was also of this opinion.[34]

There were also significant differences between the versions that Opperman and Cloete gave of certain events.

The third State witness was the Zulu member of the KwaMakutha attack group, who tried to support Opperman and Cloete with his testimony regarding the events. The Court found: "Khumalo's support is in our view based upon a clear lie."[35]

The court made meaningful comments on certain matters pertaining to KwaMakutha. The first concerned the training of Zulus in Caprivi. According to the court, certain allegations were made that the training was illegal, but no evidence was presented that this was in fact so. Neither was there any evidence that the recruits' training was exclusively aimed at the unlawful killing of people, or that it differed from similar training undergone by ordinary soldiers. There was no indication that the training they received on returning from Caprivi was of an offensive nature, or that it was aimed at unlawful operations.[36]

The meaning of the word "offensive" elicited a good deal of discussion. It was clear from the beginning that the military world, and civil society as represented by the prosecuting authority, attached different meanings to this word. In this regard the court found: "The importance of this description can hardly be over-emphasised. It shows that in 1986 a senior member of the SADF could quite naturally ascribe to the word 'offensive' a meaning quite innocent and far removed from what the State alleges. When this document was written, and this also goes for most of the documents in this case, there was no reason to believe that a hostile reader would ever get access to them. The Security Forces must have believed that they and they alone would control these documents for the foreseeable future. There can therefore be no suggestion that they were written for the purpose of showing an innocent face to any future hostile readers."[37]

Moreover there was no doubt that at the time no Defence Force or State instruction had been given for the KwaMakutha tragedy. "It would have become abundantly obvious by now that we have found no proof of any express authorisation of the KwaMakutha incident, nor, indeed, on the *viva voce* evidence have we found any indirect or tacit approval, authority or ratification of the raid."[38]

The court concluded that there was no doubt that on 21 January 1987, the KwaMakutha victims were shot dead at KwaMakutha by trainees recruited by Inkatha and trained in the Caprivi. There could also be no doubt that Opperman and Cloete, between them, had planned the operation and had trained and instructed the participating trainees to do what was done. Of equal significance was the fact that the group that had been trained in the Caprivi was, in the wake of the KwaMakutha incident, never again activated. Neither were they at any stage supplied with arms and ammunition by the Defence Force.[39]

It was also found that Opperman could never have been under the impression that he was carrying out instructions or that he was given the authority to act in the manner that he did. Opperman either acted on his own authority, or he had incorrectly interpreted his instructions in order to achieve his own goal. (As shown above, Opperman had earlier testified: "... KwaMakutha was not a Defence Force operation ..."[40]

The court also found that, apart from the group which had perpetrated the crime, the other accused were not involved in a conspiracy and had not colluded to ensure that the crime was committed.

Mr Justice Hugo presented the judgment on behalf of the Court on 10 and 11 October 1996. He presented a detailed, clear and well-founded verdict of "not guilty".

There is no doubt that the outcome of the KwaMakutha trial was of the greatest importance to the ANC/SACP Alliance.[41] The strong reaction of ANC spokespersons following the judgment leads one to conclude that the ANC Alliance was convinced that a guilty verdict would be reached. This is why they questioned Attorney General McNally's initial decision to prosecute only certain persons, and pressured him into including the alleged planners.[42] It is possible that the lawyers, König and Varney, played a role in the decision to cast the net more widely. A verdict of guilty in the KwaMakutha case would have made it possible to forge a direct link between the previous Government, the Defence Force and political murders, which would have been seen as a bonus for the ANC/SACP Alliance's future plans. However, the court case itself enjoyed so much publicity that one can assume that trust in the previous government was seriously shaken.

I had a great deal of appreciation for Pres. Mandela's even-handed view on the matter. He said: "We were not in court and we did not have the benefit of hearing the evidence and cross-examination. The Judge had all those opportunities and I fully accept the decision." His office added: "Without confidence in the court this society will degenerate into private vengeance and extra-legal activities."[43]

However, the case was not laid to rest on conclusion of the trial. The convenor of the Investigation Task Board, Howard Varney, as well as other lawyers who supported the case against the "accessories", regarded the TRC as an opportunity to conduct a re-trial and as a platform to regain lost esteem. Varney therefore compiled a report of 160 pages in which he not only expressed his strong doubts about the correctness of the Supreme Court's acquittal, but also expressed criticism of KwaZulu-Natal's Attorney General.[44]

The TRC must have been sympathetic to his view, and agreed to a public hearing, which took place in the Durban City Hall in June 1997. According to the media, Archbishop Desmond Tutu, the TRC Chairperson, had on occasion said that if the court could not ascertain the truth, the TRC would.[45]

This hearing, under the chairmanship of TRC Commissioner, Dumisa Ntsebeza, lasted about 14 days, and reinforced misperceptions of the Defence Force. The original accused and some of the previous witnesses were not even asked to testify or be present at the TRC hearing, and virtually no cross-examination or questioning of the new witnesses was permitted.

The result of this hearing was a finding of "guilty" in the form of a very long list of accusations against the original accused, and against a new list of accused, including former Pres. P.W. Botha and former Chief Minister Mangosuthu Buthelezi.[46]

According to media reports the TRC had been pressurised to do something visible, hence the hearings.

However, I am convinced that the primary purpose of this "re-trial" was to reinforce the negative image of the accused amongst the public. The "re-trial" also created the impression that the TRC had at its disposal a great deal of time and money.

Not one of the parties involved in the original KwaMakutha trial objected to the court's findings. It seems that the TRC undertook the "retrial" at its own initiative, but it did raise questions about the TRC's position within the South African legal system. On whose authority was the TRC able to "re-open" cases that had already been finalised? And why did it summon witnesses to the hearings in such a selective manner? I was under the impression that if a party wanted to object to a Supreme Court verdict, an appeal to the Appeal Court was the way to do this. What had happened in this case?

If one takes into account the differences of opinion between the AG of KwaZulu-Natal and certain ANC Members of Parliament prior to the KwaMakutha Trial, it is not surprising that McNally resigned shortly after the court's judgement. The general impression was that his resignation was not voluntary.

One cannot help but wonder whether the events in the office of the KwaZulu-Natal Attorney General in the wake of the KwaMakutha trial had something to do with the over-hasty appeal following the trial of Wouter Basson. In the Basson case, as discussed in the next chapter, it would appear that the Attorney General concerned had seen neither the concise nor the complete findings of the court, and was not fully informed of the facts. Even the judge was amazed at the haste with which the notice of appeal was lodged, and asked: "… why so quick to lodge an appeal? First read the judgement."

Chapter 23

CHEMICAL AND BIOLOGICAL WARFARE: PROJECT COAST

All warfare is based on deception. A skilled general must be the master of the complementary art of simulation and dissimulation; while creating shapes to confuse and delude the enemy he conceals his true disposition and ultimate intent. His primary target is the mind of the opposing commander. An indispensable preliminary to battle is to attack the mind of the enemy.
– Sun Tzu, *The Art of War*, 500 B.C.

Few things in the post-modern era have captured the imagination of people so much, and have caused such waves of panic and fear to wash over continents, as the concepts of chemical and biological warfare. The Americans have recently launched a controversial war on Iraq, partly in fear of so-called weapons of mass destruction.

Few people in this country, and certainly even fewer in the rest of the world, know that in the late 1970s and early 1980s such weapons were used against South Africa's allies and also at a later stage against the Defence Force.[1] Fortunately the attempts were unsuccessful, due to climatological phenomena. (There is more information on this in the account of the Battle of the Lomba River in Chapter 16.)

During the revolutionary war in Angola in the 1980s, intelligence reports and electronic intercepts indicated at an early stage that the Cubans were stockpiling and moving chemical warfare stores. Medical reports gathered from our troops in the border area mentioned that strange symptoms had been observed amongst UNITA troops. These reports engendered suspicions that chemical weapons had been used, because many of the symptoms could not be explained in purely medical terms. It was very difficult to determine the precise nature of these weapons. Because of the vast distances, the affected persons only reached their home bases a week or so after the fighting had occurred. By that time various stages of paralysis and infection of the respiratory tracts had occurred.

The Defence Force was entirely ignorant as far as chemical weapons were concerned, because at that stage it had never even thought about deploying such weapons. The only available information was found in textbooks, and these were not very instructive. On the other hand the Cubans and the Soviet Union were well versed in the use of chemical weapons – the latter had used chemical weapons in Afghanistan, and had freely experimented with them. They therefore had the capability of supporting the MPLA and FAPLA forces with such weapons.

Project Coast, the Defence Force's chemical and biological weapons research project, was therefore launched in 1981 under these circumstances. I gave my written permission, because at that stage South Africa had very little expertise, and no chemical and biological capability, and it could not rely on the support of any other power should such a threat develop. In view of the extensive United Nations embargo, this was quite understandable. However, at no stage did I authorise the offensive application of the chemical and biological capabilities that were to be developed by Project Coast.[2]

Brig. Dr Wouter Basson, the project officer for Coast, therefore had official approval to develop a Defence Force capability to defend South Africa and all its people against a possible chemical and/or biological attack. I attested to this under oath before the TRC on 7 May 1997, and handed in a copy of my letter of authorisation.[3]

Basson was a brilliant, capable and dedicated member of the Defence Force. He was a medical man with exceptionally good academic and practical qualifications. I knew him as a reliable man of great integrity. Over a long time he had been subjected to labelling by the media, and had to endure drawn-out trials.

Right from the planning stage, Project Coast was aimed at developing a defensive capability in the field of chemical and biological warfare. South Africa has never supported the axiom that everything is fair in war. Although it was not the aim of the project to develop an offensive capability in this field, it was necessary to try to gain some knowledge of the application of chemical agents. This was difficult in the case of a defence force with no culture of chemical warfare and which possessed no methods of detection nor any decontaminants. Among other things Project Coast had to help determine the offensive capabilities of such weapons, and in so doing gain knowledge about ways in which we could defend ourselves against them. After I had given my evidence before the TRC, *Die Burger* correctly reported that there was nothing sinister about the chemical project.

Should an area be contaminated with poisonous gas, the relevant knowledge is needed to be able to determine the type of poison and to decontaminate the area, or one's forces moving through the area could be destroyed, thus losing the battle. No commander would want to become involved in such a scenario without the required knowledge.

At that time the enemy regarded Angola as the ideal terrain for experiments with chemical warfare. This theatre of war was remote and isolated, and the access routes could be controlled. They could deploy their chemical agents, wait for the results and then sterilise the area with napalm and incendiary bombs.

There is no such thing as the most effective chemical weapon; the value of each lies in the perceptions you wish to create in the mind of your enemy by employing the weapon. As in any game of chess, you make a move and then wait for your opponent to react. For example, you could fire coloured smoke containing no deadly agents whatsoever, but if the enemy is unsophisticated or inadequately trained, he will immediately turn and run. By employing such psychological methods, you could achieve your objectives at minimal cost and without killing anybody.

If your opponent is somewhat more sophisticated and has been trained in chemical warfare, he will immediately order his troops to don their cumbersome protective gear, which limits their mobility and effectiveness.

It is therefore quite clear that for each scenario in which the use of chemical weapons is being considered, one must very clearly determine what you wish to achieve, in other words which weapon best suits the particular circumstance. No commander wishes to kill 20 000 or more of the enemy in a single action, because it would create enormous logistical problems for himself. For example, how would one dispose of all the corpses littering the battlefield?

The latest research on chemical warfare is therefore not so much aimed at killing people, but rather at affecting their ability to fight.[4]

One can divide chemical weapons into two main categories, namely those that are lethal, and those that affect your capabilities and render you unable to fight properly. (Various tear gas agents are used to achieve the latter goal.)

As regards the lethal weapons, some are more poisonous than others, but applying them may be problematic due to factors such as climate. In the late 1970s the USA and the Soviet Union realised that in light of a more sensitive social conscience, the large-scale loss of life that would result from the application of lethal chemical weapons would no longer be acceptable. Since then they have occupied themselves with developing non-lethal chemical weapons that would rather affect the brain functions of the target groups in order to render them incapable of efficient functioning (incapacitating agents). The goal is to ensure that the enemy is not even aware that chemical weapons have been used – the more subtle the effect, the better. It is amazing that the Geneva Convention has not yet defined the use of these weapons.

Incapacitating agents affect people by robbing them of their will to live, because they can no longer see, hear or control their emotions. They cannot remove this stimulant themselves, and therefore remain trapped by its effect until they receive help.

The so-called psychotropic agents render people incapable of properly interpreting information gathered by their senses, particularly their ears, eyes and skin, or of rationally reacting to such information. They may become completely apathetic, or overreact, to the degree that they may begin arguing with their comrades about petty things, which may even result in their shooting these comrades.

Sometimes chemical agents are also used in tear gas. These agents cause irritation and also affect people's capabilities. Their sight is affected most, and they experience trouble breathing, so they try to escape the effect by running away. These agents are suitable for riot control, and the dispersal of crowds. At the time, tear gas was the only capability the Defence Force had.

In the early 1980s the Security Forces used only the outdated tear gas method, but it was very inefficient. Crowds normally taunted the Security Forces and pelted them with stones and other objects. When tear gas was used in reaction, the crowd was irritated for only a brief period, and then returned to take part in the rioting with greater vigour – angrier than before! The fact is that tear gas did not affect the cohesion of the crowd.

Eventually such riotous crowds were so well organised that a barrel of water was placed on each street corner of the block where the riot was taking place, so that the tear gas could be washed off to neutralise its effect.

The effective counter-measures used by the ANC Alliance against the old tear gas method gave them greater prestige and promoted their strongman image, to the detriment of the Security Forces and the State. This situation could not be allowed to continue, because in this sort of revolutionary struggle the population's loss of trust is fatal. It was necessary to do something drastic, because it was quite clear that the Security Forces were coming second; the Alliance followers were exploiting such situations in a quiet, calculated manner. I therefore requested the Project Coast project officer to develop a more efficient type of tear gas.

After thorough research and even testing of the effects on members of the Security Forces, a new type of tear gas was developed. Apart from a burning sensation, the smoke caused visual nausea and a slight headache. This undermined the will to do what you had planned, because you felt too ill to continue. It caused the crowd to fall apart, and undermined its cohesion. It also functioned best in the presence of sweat or other moisture. The barrels of water quietly disappeared, and the crowds no longer moved from one place to another, growing all the time. The chain was broken and the core destroyed, because this core soon felt that it "had had enough". Enthusiasm for rioting evaporated, and everybody soon went home.

It was also found that incapacitating agents could be used as chemical weapons against equipment. Experiments on this aspect were mainly conducted in the USA, with the aim of using such weapons to destroy the enemy's means of communication and structures such as bridges, stainless steel structures, the tar on runways and certain weaponry. Half a litre of mustard gas applied to certain strategic points on an aircraft's wing causes the wing to rust and fall off within minutes. Some of these agents can be used to incapacitate the enemy's military capability without killing or wounding a single person.

A major misconception amongst the general public is that chemical warfare is aimed at killing thousands of people on the battlefield. However, the actual purpose is to ensure parity on the battlefield, or to obtain the advantage. The following serves as an example: We are the commanders of two opposing forces. We are of equal strength, which leaves neither with the possibility of freedom of movement. You wish to gain an advantage over me, and use a non-lethal blue gas, which smells of almonds and causes slight nausea amongst the troops. What do I do? I have to accept that it is a deadly gas, and that a third of my troops will die within minutes, or otherwise be incapable of action. How do I react? I immediately order my troops to protect themselves against the threat. This means that they must don their protective gear, and put on their masks and gloves.

This almost immediately robs my troops of proper sight and hearing, and tires them very quickly. Under the African sun it also means that heat exhaustion will render them even less capable of action within half an hour. If you attack now, you will have at least a 60% advantage over me. In turn I could try to trump you by firing some other gas of a different colour and odour. This will compel you to take counter-measures (donning suits, masks and gloves), which would cancel out your previous advantage over me. In a conventional situation, where both forces have been trained for this type of warfare and both have protective gear, the level of training is crucial. Such chemical weapons can be deployed strategically and tactically to try to gain the upper hand on the battlefield.[5]

Should a country find itself pitted against an enemy with superior expertise and a greater chemical and biological capability, it could suffer very grave consequences, especially in a situation where capabilities may differ significantly. An example of such a significant difference is where one side has gunpowder, and the expertise to use it, while the other side has to make do with bows and arrows.

It is extremely difficult to act efficiently while wearing these suits, which provide protection against chemical weapons. (Photo: *Salut*, Nov. 1997.)

The difference between chemical and biological weapons is that the latter are transmitted by people, animals and the atmosphere. Biological weapons are living weapons that can replicate themselves and can spread without any human assistance. A chemical weapon cannot replicate and spread on its own; it needs people, air, wind, water, etcetera for this to happen.

The earliest biological weapons were diseases well known to humans, such as smallpox, plague, anthrax and animal diseases.

In Africa, where proper hygiene is often lacking, it is difficult to determine whether illnesses are caused by natural phenomena or by biological weapons. Incorrect food preparation and handling, for example, can cause many diseases. It is also difficult to control biological weapons in Africa because of the continuous and widespread movements of groups and individuals.

In the early stages of Project Coast it was found that biological weapons are not suited to deployment in the Southern African conflict situation. The possibility of using various types of biological weapons, including bacteria, viruses and parasites, was investigated in order to gain the knowledge required, should such weapons be used against us. For example, it was found that few viruses are suited to biological warfare, and that bacteria such as cholera are very vulnerable, because they can be neutralised by adding a minimal amount of chlorine to the water.

In 1994, when it became clear that the ANC Alliance would be taking over from the previous Government, F.W. de Klerk requested that Pres. Nelson Mandela be informed of Project Coast. This request was acceded to, because the previous Government had no wish to hide anything concerning the project. Subsequently all Project Coast's research activities and results, progress and recommendations were loaded onto computer disks and handed to the ANC Government so that it could decide what to do with this information on chemical and biological warfare.[6]

I was later informed that the Defence Force members responsible for Project Coast had fully informed Pres. Mandela on the nature, goals and extent of the project, and that he had approved its continuation.

During the Basson trial evidence was given that a foreign delegation reported to Pres. Mandela, in the presence of personnel from National

Intelligence, on South Africa's progress in the fields of chemical and biological warfare. The delegation apparently claimed that South Africa had advanced even further than the United States in this regard, and that they could not say with certainty whether South Africa was further advanced than the Soviet Union. It appears that it was at their insistence that the President offered to reinstate Dr Wouter Basson in a position in the Public Service, thereby breaking Public Service regulations.[7]

The success of Project Coast and the scientific advances made have to be accredited to the leadership, initiative and enterprise of Wouter Basson. He provided exceptional service.

The TRC investigated Project Coast in July 1998, but failed miserably to analyse the project properly and to gain an accurate understanding of it. The Commission attempted to investigate a technical project, but did so with little technical support and with very few experts and specialists present. It was impossible to place the activities of Project Coast in any proper perspective, because only about 2 or 3% of its activities were touched on, and the remaining 97 or 98% remained unexplored. It seems as if a sense of the dramatic dominated the TRC's pronouncements. The TRC became hopelessly entangled in consideration of only a few concepts – perhaps because these concepts did not suit its predetermined aims.

Wouter Basson, the project officer for Project Coast, said a number of things about the TRC at a news conference in Pretoria on conclusion of his High Court trial. Apparently the TRC had offered him a new identity and another job abroad if he "laid his cards on the table and well and truly sank all the generals and the Minister". He would not even have to testify, "but sit behind a curtain and tell them what questions to ask". This is truly a very strange procedure and approach for an open-minded commission appointed to promote truth and reconciliation.[8]

It is sad that Dr Basson had to handle his trial in the High Court for almost 2½ years all alone, with very little moral support from the previous government. Eventually Mr Justice Hartzenberg found him not guilty on 46 counts of murder, attempted murder, fraud, drug trafficking and obstruction of justice.

In brief the State's case against Wouter Basson can be divided into three subsections, namely:

Violent crimes. This encompassed the greatest part of the State's charges, and included charges of murder and attempted murder against Basson. The most notable aspect during this part of the trial was the flagrant contradictions by various State witnesses concerning the same incident. Taken as a whole, it gave the State's evidence a disquieting lack of reliability. For example, for every State witness who testified to Basson's conduct or to his presence during certain occurrences or incidents, there were two or three State witnesses who testified, under oath, to something completely different. These testimonies usually contradicted the evidence of the main State witness, consequently rendering the testimony of the main State witness useless.

Commercial crimes. The State alleged that Basson concluded a number of fictitious transactions and that he possibly misused the funds earmarked for these, or may have used the funds to his own advantage. During the trial it became quite clear, however, that the facilities or items that these funds were destined for, were found in possession of the Defence Force, although the sensitivity of the transactions made it difficult to determine in detail the exact manner in which the funds were spent. The High Court could find no case of corruption or self-enrichment.

Drug-related crimes. The manufacture of certain ingredients of certain drugs was an official project that I had approved. As mentioned earlier, this project provided the material required for the development of a new and efficient type of tear gas used by the Security Forces in riot situations. The new tear gas disrupted the cohesion of riotous crowds and broke the chain of violence, calmed emotions and eliminated violence. This new method of crowd control was very successful, and it contributed towards minimalising the loss of life amongst South Africans during riots. However, the State claimed that Basson had manufactured drugs under the guise of chemical and biological warfare, and had then sold these to obtain funds to finance the further waging of war, or for self-enrichment. The court found Basson not guilty on these charges.

The TRC hearings, the court's findings and reporting in the media inflamed emotions with regard to this case. I find it regrettable and in fact totally unforgivable that people in high places were not able to display greater judgement and self-control in their pronouncements on this matter. For example, the former Minister of Justice, Penuell Maduna, had the following to say a few days after the conclusion of the trial: "Judge Hartzenberg is a good judge, I respect him, however I disagree with his findings in this court case." In a later interview the Minister admitted that at that stage he had not seen the judge's complete findings or even an abridged version thereof.

The privatisation of the facilities that the State had acquired and erected for Project Coast received a good deal of publicity during the trial. However, the previous government first launched a thorough investigation involving various Government Departments before making an official decision in this regard. This investigation recommended the privatisation, and certain guidelines according to which it had to occur. The recommendation was then ratified by the Auditor General, and at least three Heads of Government Departments and their respective Cabinet Ministers.

For many years the Wouter Basson saga continued. After having had to testify before the TRC, after a High Court trial and after the Appeal Court dismissed the State's appeal, the case was eventually even referred to the Constitutional Court. Each time the State refused to accept the findings of that particular court. Each time the higher court needed to grapple anew with the facts of the case. And each time the taxpayer had to foot the bill.

Apparently the State was brimming with confidence before the commencement of the trial in the High Court, and foresaw Basson's conviction. The finding, it would appear, did not meet the State's seemingly subjective expectations. The State then immediately appealed against these findings, seemingly (as I mentioned earlier) without first properly analysing the written judgement and findings. This creates the impression that the State was intent on playing the man (i.e. the judge who had delivered the judgement) instead of the ball.

The Appeal Court delivered a unanimous finding against the State. Once again the State was not satisfied with the judgement and findings, and referred the case to the Constitutional Court on appeal. After the Basson case had been submitted to the Constitutional Court two years previously, the National Prosecution Authority decided in October 2005 not to prosecute any further. This was because in South Africa it was not legally admissible to prosecute a person for a second time on the same criminal charges that had already been heard and rejected by a high court, in this case the Pretoria High Court.[9]

On the periphery of the decisions of the various courts concerning Wouter Basson, there is still the questionable success achieved by the TRC during its hearings.

Chapter 24

THE SA DEFENCE FORCE AND THE TRUTH AND RECONCILIATION COMMISSION

BACKGROUND

The Truth and Reconciliation Commission (TRC) excelled in creating and broadcasting perceptions of and allegations about the Defence Force by making comments and pronouncements while their investigations were still in progress. It is incomprehensible that the chairperson, deputy chairperson and commissioners of such an important government commission could make such pronouncements at so many public events even before the investigations had been completed and the TRC had reported to the Government. Surely this equates with a judicial inquiry where a presiding judge of the High Court or Supreme Court of Appeals makes public comments and pronouncements even before all the evidence has been heard and the court's investigation has been completed. One of the reasons for such inexplicable behaviour may be that the TRC wanted to help the ANC Alliance to promote its strategy of creating divisions amongst certain sections of the population by creating perceptions. These actions by the TRC covered many fields and caused a great deal of division, alienation and strife, even in church circles.[1]

Furthermore the TRC published incorrect reports and findings concerning the Defence Force, and disseminated these internationally, even though these errors were brought to the Commission's attention in writing and well in time.²

I will now expand on some of the matters I have touched on.

Otway Hayes once said:
Let not winning be your aim.
It is important how you play the game.

If the TRC had kept in mind Otway Hayes' truth during its investigations and as it formulated its reports, it would not have been necessary for me to react to the TRC's reports so critically. From the way in which the TRC acted, and from the contents of its reports on the Defence Force, it would appear that the TRC followed the opposite approach. It looks as if the goal of the investigation was to win, instead of conducting the investigation honestly and formulating its reports in a manner that speaks of integrity.³

I do not intend to denigrate the TRC's status or dignity, or to belittle the important task the TRC had to carry out. Most of my comments were submitted to the TRC in writing before and after the release of its first report in 1998, but the TRC did not take them to heart. The TRC did not even reply to our correspondence. Some additional comments could not be made before, because the TRC's final or second report (Vol. 6) appeared only in March 2003.

The President promulgated the Promotion of National Unity and Reconciliation Act (Act 34 of 1995) on 26 July 1995. Among other things it provided for "... an enquiry into and the gathering of as complete as possible a picture of the nature, causes and extent of gross violations of human rights perpetrated within or outside the Republic as a result of the conflicts of the past in the period from 1 March 1960 to the cut-off date envisaged in the Constitution".

In order to ensure quick and efficient liaison between the TRC and the SA National Defence Force (SANDF), Gen. Georg Meiring, at that time the Chief of the National Defence Force, created a nodal point, which was a contact point or office which could be contacted easily in order to obtain any information or communications from the organisation. Among other things it was intended to help the TRC to liaise with all the SANDF's elements or structures. Initially it provided the TRC with a facility for gaining access to the personnel and documents of both the SA Defence Force (SADF, that is the Defence Force prior to 1994) and the SANDF (the Defence Force after 1994).

THE SA DEFENCE FORCE'S FIRST WRITTEN SUBMISSION TO THE TRC, OCTOBER 1996

The first report of 80 pages submitted to the TRC by the SANDF's Nodal Point in October 1996 elicited sharply negative comments from some TRC commissioners. This showed quite clearly that the commissioners had little knowledge of or expertise regarding military organisations, procedures and customs. It also became clear that whereas the former Defence Force had been politically neutral, that is to say loyal to the Constitution and the Government of the day rather than to a political party,[4] the TRC, which was charged with investigating the Defence Force's past, was highly politicised. Not only were the political affiliations of the vast majority of the TRC members well known, but they displayed a hostile attitude towards the Defence Force at all times.[5] Among other things, this hostility was reflected in the politically coloured remarks of its vice chairman, Dr Alex Boraine, and the manner in which the TRC handled and disregarded later submissions and suggestions by the Defence Force.

Dr Boraine's negative comments were reported in the media. Among other things he referred to the Defence Force as "South Africa's apartheid military machine", and "... that defence force that – thank God – no longer exists".[6]

With reference to the Defence Force's submission he claimed that "... the submission flies in the face of facts", and "... it was breathtakingly one-sided and audacious in its failure to acknowledge culpability".[7] This comment was made even before the TRC could establish the "facts" or could determine "culpability".

The Star reported on 22 October 1996 on the following comments made by Dr Boraine with regard to the Defence Force's submission: "I find it almost unbelievable that in 80 pages there is no acknowledgement or acceptance of responsibility for a single death during the apartheid era." According to the *Mail & Guardian* of 25 October 1996 Mr Ronnie Kasrils, Deputy Minister of Defence, was "angry and extremely disappointed to say the least, at the insensitivity of the presentation". One can only assume that this reaction was because the facts presented by the Defence Force did not correspond with the perceptions that the ANC Alliance and the TRC had already formed.

Members of the former Defence Force were extremely dissatisfied with the TRC's handling of matters, and the uncalled-for negative criticism aimed at them. Some of them approached the former Chiefs of the Defence Force and insisted that the matter should urgently be discussed.[8]

During a meeting of members of the former Defence Force held on 20 February 1997, it was insisted that a contact bureau be created to protect the interests of former SADF members, in the same way that the SANDF's Nodal Point was handling interaction with the TRC. The purpose of the Contact Bureau would be to handle communication and liaison with former SADF members and the SANDF's Nodal Point, the TRC and other Government bodies, for example the Justice Ministry, the Public Protector and non-governmental organisations in South Africa and abroad. It did indeed greatly facilitate liaison and co-operation with these bodies, and provided, in writing, all the information that the TRC requested or which it generated at its own initiative.

Initially the Contact Bureau consisted of the former Chiefs of the Defence Force, Gen. Viljoen, Gen. Geldenhuys and Gen. Liebenberg, and the Sergeant Major of the Defence Force, WO1 Jan Holliday. They were assisted by Gen. Raymond Holzhausen and a deputy, Gen. Dirk Marais, as convenors. Initially I was not involved in the Contact Bureau, so that I could act in my personal capacity and independently in my dealings with the TRC.[9]

FIRST EVIDENCE BEFORE THE TRC ON BEHALF OF THE SA DEFENCE FORCE, 7 MAY 1997

Following discussions with the former Chiefs of the Defence Force, I offered to give voluntary evidence to the TRC in the interests of the Defence Force. The approach was that we would give evidence in order

I take the oath during the TRC sitting of 7 May 1997, in the presence of Gen. Viljoen.

of rank, from the top down, in contrast to the SA Police, where evidence was apparently given from the bottom to the top. Following an interview in the presence of my lawyer, Mr Ernst Penzhorn, my request for voluntary evidence was granted personally by the chairperson of the TRC, Archbishop Desmond Tutu.

My first appearance occurred on 7 May 1997, and lasted some four hours. I was placed under oath, and the session was concluded with a lengthy question-and-answer session. During this session I testified, among other things, about a so-called Third Force, the project involving chemical and biological weapons, the Civil Co-operation Bureau (CCB) and cross-border operations. I answered all the questions put to me there and then, and also offered to reply in writing to any further questions concerning the SA Defence Force that the TRC cared to put to me. I did not receive any further questions or requests from the TRC, apart from a subpoena to appear before the TRC again on 4 and 5 December 1997. During this hearing I answered all the questions put to me, as I had done at the first hearing, and offered to respond to any future questions or clear up any uncertainties. I never heard anything from the TRC thereafter, and read only their negative and incorrect comments in their reports. One thing is certain: the Commission had no reason whatsoever to complain of a lack of co-operation from the Defence Force, or any lack of willingness to assist them at all levels. The Defence Force and I were always willing or ready to fully inform them.

My voluntary presentation before the TRC on 7 May 1997 ensured that any Defence Force members who appeared subsequently would not be unprepared. Furthermore the content of my testimony was meant to ensure that members of the Defence Force would gain a clear understanding of the motives for Defence Force actions. Members were also better equipped to understand their own actions within this framework. They could then use this knowledge in motivations for amnesty, or for when they themselves were required to testify. I am convinced that my appearance made it easier for Defence Force members to decide for themselves whether they wished to appear before the TRC or not.[10]

I tried, in this way, to set an example to those who had served under me, and also to those who followed me. I did it because I still considered those serving in the Defence Force to be honourable men and women and respected them as such, and also because I was determined to always stand by them.[11]

In my submission I clearly stated, among other things, that with regard to any foreign operations, the TRC had no authority to grant amnesty for prosecution in the countries concerned.[12]

There was no reason why I should apply for amnesty, and I conveyed this view to the TRC. However, I also indicated that if I had unwittingly violated any human rights, I was more than willing to offer a sincere public apology. I believe that our country's welfare and future depends a great deal on reconciliation between the various citizens of South Africa. I emphasised this conviction during my appearance before the TRC.[13]

I did not expect the TRC to agree with everything that the Defence Force had done. I only requested the TRC to accept the bona fides of Defence Force members, in the same way that I and my fellow citizens had to be prepared to accept the bona fides of Umkhonto we Sizwe (MK) in regard to their endeavour to achieve their ideal, difficult as this may be and despite what I may think of their methods.[14]

In view of this, I said that both the Defence Force and the ANC Alliance had succeeded in their endeavours: the ANC had achieved its initial political goals, and the Defence Force had ensured that a climate conducive to negotiations aimed at achieving a true democracy was maintained.[15]

SYMPOSIUM OF THE SA DEFENCE FORCE, 30 AUGUST 1997

In the wake of my submission, a symposium was organised for members of the former Defence Force on 30 August 1997, at which various experts as well as former Chiefs of the Defence Force, including myself, were afforded an opportunity to speak.

During the symposium each of the former Chiefs declared that they were willing to accept full moral responsibility for all actions by former subordinates in the execution of their duties that occurred during the terms of office of those respective Chiefs. Only actions undertaken out of self-interest or self-enrichment were excluded. During my opportunity to speak, I recounted my submission to the TRC on 7 May 1997 in regard to the Defence Force. In it I had also declared: "... I take moral responsibility for the actions of members of the Army and South African Defence Force, during the respective periods when I was involved, and for the execution of tasks of the South African Defence Force to uphold the then constitution and to preserve the sovereignty of the Republic of South Africa."[16]

Those present, who represented the old Defence Force, unanimously accepted the following motion: "The symposium expresses its unequivocal support for the process of reconciliation now taking place in South

Africa and which must continue to take place. As in the past, we – as former SA Defence Force members – shall continue to lend our full cooperation to the creation of a peaceful State for all its inhabitants. However, the Symposium would like to express its concern and dismay over the unfair and apparent one-sided process adopted by the TRC."

SECOND WRITTEN SUBMISSION TO THE TRC BY THE SA DEFENCE FORCE, 1997

The other former Chiefs of the Defence Force and I were still prepared to co-operate with the TRC as it pursued its mission. After hearing from the TRC which additional information concerning the Defence Force they wished to receive, a second supplementary report of 272 pages was submitted.

Although the report was based on facts, Dr Boraine and senior members of the TRC were apparently disappointed because it was not what they wanted to hear. Their subsequent remarks revealed the TRC's political leanings, which corresponded with well-known ANC sentiments. This was a further revelation of the TRC's animosity towards the Defence Force.

It was therefore fortunate that I had warned those present at the symposium not to appear before the TRC without good legal representation, particularly because evidence given before the TRC could easily leak and could therefore be exploited elsewhere, to their detriment.[17]

It also became clear that the methodology used by the TRC in its investigation was that a hypothesis consisting of a patchwork of mottos, slogans, clichés and propaganda themes of the struggle was created and that information was then selected to prove the truth of this hypothesis. The 200 page "charge sheet" of the ANC's National Executive Committee of August 1996, *Statement to the Truth and Reconciliation Commission*, probably played an extremely important role in determining the TRC's questionable working method. It is significant that this comprehensive ANC declaration, with its many false accusations and allegations against the SA Defence Force, corresponds largely with the requests for information put to the Defence Force by the TRC. One cannot exclude the possibility that this declaration served as the guideline for the TRC in formulating its accusations against the Defence Force – which could for the most part not be proven! Perhaps this sort of document was also the reason why the TRC could generally achieve very little reconciliation.

SECOND TESTIMONY BEFORE THE TRC ON BEHALF OF THE DEFENCE FORCE, 7-10 OCTOBER 1997

The TRC informed the Defence Force Contact Bureau on 3 September 1997 that the date for the second testimony by the Defence Force was to be 8 October 1997 (i.e. after my own appearance before the Commission), to coincide with a number of hearings in the period 7 to 10 October 1997. This date was preceded by repeated written and verbal TRC notices that the focus of the questioning during the hearings would be on determining the motives and perspectives for the actions of the various forces, specifically the SA Police, the Defence Force, Umkhonto we Sizwe (MK) and APLA. Dr Boraine and other members of the TRC confirmed this proposed procedure to Gen. Geldenhuys' legal representatives, late on the afternoon of 7 October. They were informed that there would only be an hour for the presentation or verbal introduction to the submission of the Defence Force's supplementary documents.

The verbal introduction to the Defence Force's submission, presented by Gen. Viljoen, was constantly interrupted by Dr Boraine with admonishments to finish within the hour. Clearly he and other commissioners, for example Dumisa Ntsebeza, were not interested in the contents of the Defence Force's submission. Ntsebeza quite openly and shamelessly dozed off.

Then, during the continuation of the presentation of evidence by the Defence Force and the SA Police, the attention focused almost exclusively on individual responsibility. For example, Gen. Geldenhuys was cross-examined in a most irritating and, in fact, incriminating manner for almost one and a half hours on his actions when he was Chief of the Defence Force and after he became aware of Defence Force involvement in the murder of the Ribeiro couple of Mamelodi. No questions were put to Gen. Geldenhuys or Gen. Joubert of the SA Police to determine motives and perspectives as originally requested by the TRC. The TRC emotionally and sensationally concentrated only on individual responsibility, clearly in an attempt to find a basis for negative publicity regarding the Security Forces.

In contrast, the focus of the questioning of MK and APLA did indeed fall on motives and perspectives regarding their actions. On 10 October, when MK appeared before the TRC, any member of the MK delegation who wished to reply to a TRC question was permitted to do so. Self-incriminating replies regarding the Church Street bomb and the Magoo's Bar bomb by Mr Mac Maharaj, the leader of the delegation, were not, as was the case with Gen. Geldenhuys, followed up with a thorough cross-examination.

There was no attempt whatsoever to gain information about violent actions by members of the liberation movements between 1 September 1984 and 31 August 1990.

In this regard I would like to refer to the TRC's finding in Vol. 6, Section 3, Chapter 2, paragraph 52: "The stated objective of MK was never to engage in operations that deliberately targeted civilians ..." I furthermore refer to the evidence presented by Mr Aboobaker Ismail on 4 May 1998 regarding the Church Street bomb: "... whilst Umkhonto we Sizwe (MK) had the means to attack civilians, it would have been very easy to come to various houses and shoot people. Umkhonto never did that sort of thing." As mentioned elsewhere, statistics in this regard tell a very different story. The very opposite is true as far as MK's actions against black officials were concerned, and as the Commission quite rightly finds in the next paragraph: "Despite their noble intentions, the majority of casualties of MK operations were civilians." The finding in paragraph 52 shows that most of these "civilians" were black: "Attacks on collaborators form a significant proportion of MK armed actions." Blacks in uniform, black members of local, regional and national government authorities and black civilians with views differing from those of the ANC were wrongfully labelled "collaborators" and were murdered.

In practice the struggle operations were mostly black on black. A small minority element consisting of the ANC/PAC/SACP leadership forced the black mass into submissive obedience with the help of militant terrorists and the Self Defence Units (SDUs) and spurred them on to act against the State.

Missing and dead people cannot vote. Why would the TRC, as the instrument of the ANC government, concern itself with matters that could result in negative publicity for the Alliance and the revolutionary approach prevalent at the time? It was more convenient to try the former "enemies" of the time and to exploit the publicity this created to the advantage of the "cause".

It would appear that the TRC's approach was to forget about those who had been killed and wronged by MK, APLA and their cohorts, or to ignore them. Instead, the TRC concentrated on the once peaceful black masses that were forced, through intimidation, to abandon the democratic process and a peaceful political evolution. These were the ones who had to make a political about-turn in order to support the ANC's quick option of a violent revolution. After all, the vast majority of the people who died as a result of the Alliance's actions were opponents of the option of violence, or were law-abiding black citizens who put their life on the line for the maintenance of law and order.

As regards attacks on so-called "collaborators with apartheid political structures", the TRC found: "MK applicants tended to describe such attacks as 'intimidation' rather than attempted assassinations."[18]

The submissions by the MK and APLA took the view that everything they did as terrorist organisations was justified. They placed extraordinary emphasis on the fact that apartheid was condemned as a crime against humanity by the international community, i.e. the General Assembly of the United Nations, and that these organisations' brutal and barbaric actions were therefore justifiable and excusable. MK's emotional answers and accounts, in particular, even if it related to irrelevant matters, were listened to with attention and patience. This contrasted sharply with the treatment of Gen. Viljoen, despite the fact that his submission contained extremely important information on motives and perspectives, as was the case, too, with the first Defence Force submission in October 1996.

FURTHER ACTIONS

As the Defence Force's second written submission (1997) of 272 pages had no real influence on the TRC's one-sided approach, the Contact Bureau submitted a complaint titled "Complaints in respect of the TRC's handling of the former SADF and its members" to the Public Protector, dated 29 January 1998. At the same time an assessment of the TRC, titled "Assessment of the probable results of activities of the TRC as perceived by former Chiefs of the SADF in respect of the SADF", dated 6 February 1998, was handed to the TRC Chairperson. Apart from substantiated criticism of the TRC's treatment of the SADF, it also contained constructive suggestions that would help the TRC to promote real reconciliation and national unity. As confirmed in the above-mentioned document, we were still prepared to co-operate with the TRC.

As a further reaction to the criticism, and in order to satisfy the extensive need for information, the Contact Bureau made another written submission (the third report). It was titled *Supplementary submission by former Chiefs of the SADF: Factors determining the volume and quality of information supplied to the TRC by them and the number of applications for amnesty by members who served in the SADF* (hereafter referred to as the Supplementary Submission).

In this Supplementary Submission, dated 14 May 1998, all the information which the TRC could possibly still wish for (in the opinion of the Contact Bureau), was included. Concerning the TRC commissioners' scepticism about the few applications for amnesty, the report expressed understanding for their limited knowledge and experience of the military world, and we said: "To us it is normal that the history of a well-organised and disciplined military force should not be scattered with long lists of serious offences."

As we had done so many times in the past, we once again emphasised that the ultimate responsibility for the effective management of the Defence Force during our periods of office rested with us as commanders of the Defence Force.

We also, once again, confirmed that positive results can be ascribed to our leadership – directly or indirectly. We thus also, of course, accepted responsibility for negative results, direct or indirect.

It is a common phenomenon that, in the wake of the conclusion of peace, former defence forces are targeted to be discredited and even persecuted by the new rulers. It is sometimes claimed: "The generals carried the responsibility; they must now take the punch!" We agree.[19] It is quite normal that the responsibility for military actions is borne by those who order them. Our willingness to do so rested on our faith in the discipline and competence of our trained Defence Force members.

SUPPORTING HUMAN RIGHTS

The former Chiefs of the Defence Force are convinced that the Defence Force would not easily and deliberately have violated human rights. Our conviction rests on various characteristics unique to the Defence Force.

Firstly: The vast majority of the Defence Force consisted of national servicemen and voluntary part-time Citizen Force and Commando members who served for brief periods. They were drawn from all spheres of civil society, and had various political views. It would therefore have been impossible for large-scale transgressions of the law and human rights abuses to have occurred without them becoming known.

Secondly: As early as 1960/61 the Defence Force made a thorough study of terrorism and revolutionary war, and even then realised the importance of sound relations with the population – and made this its policy.[20] There was no room for gross violations of human rights in such a policy. (This is in stark contrast to our enemy of the time. They stamped their authority on the population only through human rights violations. Most of the applications for amnesty should therefore have come from that side.)

Thirdly: It was our policy to plan all operations in such a way as to cause the least possible harm to civilians. In contrast to our opponents, we respected the population. We did not cause 194 local authorities to stop functioning; we did not destroy or damage 7187 houses of black citizens of South Africa; we did not destroy or damage 1770 schools, and 1265 shops owned mainly by blacks; nor did we destroy or damage 12 188 private vehicles owned by blacks, or the delivery vehicles driven by them; nor 10 318 buses transporting black people. We did not kill 399 blacks by necklacing, or 372 by setting fire to them or their houses. We did not force blacks who bought groceries at white shops to drink paraffin or to eat the soap they had bought.[21]

Fourthly: The training of our Defence Force of the time was so thorough that high standards of discipline and action were to be expected. Transgressors were charged in accordance with the Military Disciplinary Code, and were tried and punished. If Defence Force operations resulted in death or injury, these incidents were investigated by the SA Police. The SA Police opened case files and handed them to the Attorney General, who decided on prosecution at his or her discretion.

CULTIVATING THE PROPER ATTITUDE TOWARDS THE POPULATION

Numerous examples of the actions continuously undertaken to cultivate the proper attitude towards the population amongst soldiers of the Defence Force can be quoted. Only a few cases are mentioned here.

Four appendices were attached to the Supplementary Submission of 14 May 1998 referred to above, among them two letters by the Chief of the SA Defence Force (CSADF) to "fellow soldiers", which were submitted to the TRC.

One letter, written by Gen. Geldenhuys as Chief of the Defence Force, reads as follows:

Dear Fellow Soldier

Your presence in the unrest areas in these times is vital for our country and all its peoples. You must do your share to return our country to normal. This we do, amongst others, by protecting the vast majority of people from a small element of murderers, arsonists and those seeking violence. So that those who want to go to school can go; those who want to go to work can go; and those who want to travel on busses can travel. Be firm and decisive but courteous and just. Carry out your superiors' orders and respect people and property. Stay calm. Set the example. It is not easy, but I know you can – I trust you.

[Signed]
Jan Geldenhuys
Chief SADF

The other letter is dated 6 September 1990. I quote only a part: "Violence is now being used not to achieve political objectives against the State; it is being used rather to settle underlying differences. Law and good order is essential for stability and for the future of our country and all its people. Be firm and friendly; decisive, but still impartial; and above all, be fair. Show respect to all people and their property!"

Other attachments to the Supplementary Submission were two copies of signed and dated (7 January 1986 and 7 January 1992) declarations by two ordinary soldiers that they were properly informed of the critical role played by the local population in a revolutionary war, and that they realise that the revolutionaries are in practice intent on creating frustration amongst the Security Forces in order to provoke retaliation and abuse. These letters were but two examples of many to show the manner in which important official Defence Force policies were executed, from the Chief of the Defence Force down to every member of the Defence Force. The declarations (only two examples from among thousands) contain the following undertaking: "During my operational service I undertake at all costs to refrain from misconduct against the local population, and strictly to apply the recipe of maximum force against the enemy and maximum friendship towards the local population ..."

The circumstances as explained above were included in the abovementioned Supplementary Submission to the TRC in order to explain the small number of amnesty applications. Furthermore it was clearly stated that members could not apply for amnesty in relation to actions that were executed correctly or in good faith, on instructions or in accordance with policy or doctrine. The high expectations the TRC had with regard to amnesty applications by members of the Defence Force were clearly because the TRC regarded the Defence Force as transgressors in the conflict, and wanted to prove this, probably in order to cast a more friendly light on the atrocities and abuse perpetrated by the Defence Force's enemies of the time.

THE TRC AND INFORMATION ABOUT THE ANC

Amongst the correspondence handed over by the Contact Bureau to the TRC there was a letter written about investigations into human rights abuses in ANC camps abroad. The reply to this letter was one of the very few, and perhaps the only, that the Contact Bureau received from the TRC concerning its correspondence. On 15 July 1998 Archbishop Desmond Tutu responded as follows: "Let me make it quite clear that the TRC has not sought to ignore or cover up any violations that happened in ANC camps." Also: "The TRC has said that we have considerable material relating to the violations that took place in those camps." Furthermore: "It is a great deal more than we have been able to get from other less cooperative bodies and I hope that you will, like a reasonable person, concede that where there is 'pressure for time', we have enough evidence oral and written to make findings about violations in ANC camps and you will desist from suggesting that no hearings have been held." (He is referring to evidence about alleged abuses in ANC camps and possible applications for amnesty in this regard.) However, it remains inexplicable why they did not make public the information on these camps in the same way that allegations against the SA Defence Force were made public.

The TRC's report shows that it did take note of "significant information from the ANC through its submissions, its own commission report and certain internal files" regarding "ANC violations against its members outside South Africa". Only 21 members of the ANC's Security Department (NAT) and camp commanders applied for amnesty. Nine of them later withdrew their applications. The remaining 12 applications concerned 19 offences against suspected infiltrators in ANC/MK ranks and against persons who wished to withdraw from MK ranks.[22]

Clearly these make up the sum total of the "considerable material relating to the violations in these camps" referred to by Archbishop Tutu in the above-mentioned letter.

DEFECTS IN THE TRC HEARINGS CONCERNING PERSONS INVOLVED IN ANC ATROCITIES

Judging by the names of almost 900 persons in the list handed to the TRC by the ANC and included in the final TRC report as "Appendix 2; List of ANC members who died in exile", they were all blacks. There was no trial of those who were responsible for thousands of blacks in South Africa being robbed of their future right to vote because they were murdered on the instigation of the ANC/MK, or whose lives were ruined by gross human rights violations.[23]

There were no in-depth investigations into the 898 ANC members who did not return alive from abroad. The TRC's excuse of "pressure for time" is difficult to understand if one takes into consideration that when the KwaZulu-Natal High Court concluded the KwaMakutha trial, the TRC did have enough time and investigation capacity to complete a "Case Study" of Operation Marion, and to ensure a retrial of the KwaMakutha case.

It is also strange that the problem of "pressure for time" only stopped the TRC from investigating alleged abuses by the ANC/SACP/MK/PAC/APLA factions. But there was never any "pressure for time" syndrome when unproven Defence Force "atrocities" were concerned.

Chapter 25

PUBLIC REPORTS OF THE TRC CONCERNING THE SA DEFENCE FORCE

To be conscious that you are ignorant is a great step towards knowledge
– Benjamin Disraeli

In this chapter the TRC's treatment of the Defence Force is briefly discussed. The TRC's prejudice and unfair procedures are clearly illustrated in its two reports, namely the first dated October 1998 and the final report of March 2003. Some of the factual errors that were made, notwithstanding the correct information that the Defence Force submitted at the TRC's request, will also be pointed out.

THE TRC'S FIRST PUBLIC REPORT, OCTOBER 1998

In an effort to promote reconciliation and national unity, the Contact Bureau and the Nodal Point undertook various initiatives to bring the TRC to other insights regarding the Defence Force, yet the first TRC Report that was released proves that the opposite happened.

The first public TRC Report contains inaccuracies and misperceptions about and unfounded accusations aimed at the Defence Force and some of its members. Furthermore, some members were linked to certain actions without having received prior notification, as required by the TRC Act. Other members were informed in time, but the TRC ignored their rebuttals.

Inaccuracies and contraventions of the legal principles in the TRC's report were brought to the Contact Bureau's attention by a number of former members of the SA Defence Force and some legal representatives. These inputs provide an insight into the way the TRC treated the Defence Force and its members. Together with other inputs of the Contact Bureau they were subsequently included in a document titled *The Contact Bureau's analysis of the TRC report*, dated 19 April 1999. This document was signed by all the members of the Contact Bureau panel, namely myself, Gen. Viljoen, Gen. Geldenhuys, Gen. Meiring, Gen. Marais (Secretary) and Warrant Officers Holliday and Röhrbeck, and forwarded to the TRC.

This concise signed document of the panel consisted of 60 pages and was delivered to the TRC in April 1999 (attached as Appendix A). The TRC ignored it, as it did with most inputs. To date no mention of it has been made at all, not even by means of the normal acknowledgement of receipt. Later, when we enquired about when a reply could be expected, and whether this was likely before the publication of the TRC's final report, we were informed that the TRC was no longer functioning, and that the commissioners were not available. No comments regarding our attempts to correct errors in the first TRC Report were therefore forthcoming. The final TRC Report that appeared in March 2003 makes no mention of our representations and objections.

In order to give the reader an opportunity to form an opinion of our objections to the TRC's first report (October 1998), some examples of the accusations are quoted verbatim from this first public report, together with our related comments as contained in the document produced by the Contact Bureau in April.

For the sake of authenticity this part of the *The Contact Bureau's analysis of the TRC report* is reproduced at the end of this book as Appendix A.

From Appendix A it should be clear that the TRC has made public a report riddled with errors, misperceptions, accusations and allegations against the Defence Force and it does not appear as if the TRC is planning to consider any corrections.[1]

THE TRC ACT OF 1995

This Act was promulgated "to promote National Unity and Reconciliation", and as mentioned before, it provides for a Truth and Reconciliation Commission. The Act clearly spells out the aim of the Commission.

As indicated in the title, reconciliation and the promotion of national unity lay at the heart of the legislation. These were noble goals, and there is no reason to believe that this was not the real goal of the legislators.

To determine the truth about a specific historical event, the historical context in which the event took place must be taken into consideration. To do this it is essential to understand the perceptions and motives of those involved at the time. To really determine the truth – one of the aims of the TRC – integrity, impartiality, equity and objectivity are non-negotiable requirements.

We have seen what happened to the truth where the Defence Force was concerned. We have seen that equity, impartiality and objectivity fell by the wayside. It now appears that the TRC also failed in regard to reconciliation. Along with other South Africans who still strive for reconciliation, I was shocked to see and hear Adv. Denzil Potgieter, a TRC commissioner, telling the presenter and the public on television that the TRC process had not brought about reconciliation.[2] The question is: What has the TRC brought about? Does this mean the TRC exercise was simply a massive, fruitless expense borne by the taxpayers? Perhaps the exercise merely furthered the ANC Alliance's expressed strategy to mortify the Defence Force and the previous Government for so-called Security Force atrocities in order to cause shock, disbelief and suspicion amongst their supporters?

Can the failure to achieve reconciliation be partly ascribed to the fact that the TRC did not always concern itself with the truth, or that it had its own agenda? The experience of the members of the Contact Bureau in their dealings with the TRC make it seem as if the TRC was subjective and ignorant of military matters,[3] and that it allowed itself to be led by its preconceived perceptions, unsubstantiated allegations and accusations. The selective quotations from Gen. Geldenhuys' book also make one wonder about the degree to which they selectively used facts (see Appendix A).

THE TRC'S SECOND AND FINAL PUBLIC REPORT, MARCH 2003

The Defence Force had expectations that the TRC would correct errors in its first report in Volume 6 of the second or final report, which dealt with the activities of the Amnesty Committee. Despite the fact that inaccuracies were brought to the TRC's attention in writing, and were accompanied by supporting documents, these hopes were dashed.

Volume 6, the last part of the final TRC Report, also contains indications of partiality and manipulation of facts, and I wish to refer briefly to these.

A particular feature is the loose manner in which the TRC refers to the SA Police, the SA Defence Force and the Security Forces by using an umbrella term, Security Forces. Incidents involving SA Police activities are often described, but in the findings on these incidents the activities are ascribed to the Security Forces, which includes the Defence Force. This increases and reinforces the effect of negative perceptions of the SA Defence Force.

COMMENT ON AMNESTY APPLICATIONS BY THE SA DEFENCE FORCE

Volume 6 of the Final Report mentions that "… despite the fact that the South African Defence Force (SADF) was responsible for numerous violations, especially outside of South Africa, very few SA Defence Force members and operatives applied for amnesty".[4]

This remark by the TRC about the small number of amnesty applications is placed on record even after the Contact Bureau had handed to the TRC its written submission of 14 May 1998, titled *Supplementary submission by former Chiefs of the SADF: Factors determining the volume and quality of information supplied to the TRC by them and the number of applications for amnesty by members who served in the SADF*. This once again shows how little attention was paid to information supplied by the former Defence Force in the final TRC Report.

The TRC was repeatedly and fully informed of the reasons why few amnesty applications were submitted. Only the most important ones are mentioned below:

Firstly: The Commission had no jurisdiction to grant indemnity for alleged human rights abuses committed during operations abroad.

Secondly: The Defence Force was mainly responsible for operations abroad, while the SA Police was charged with maintaining law and order internally.

Thirdly: Defence Force members were aware that correctly carrying out one's legitimate duties was not a violation of human rights, and that the former Chiefs accepted responsibility for these actions. Only actions executed out of self-interest or for self-enrichment were not covered by this principle.

Fourthly: The TRC's effectiveness was inhibited by the perceptions it created as a result of its one-sided and hostile treatment of the Defence Force. Most members of the Defence Force were very reluctant to co-operate with the TRC.

Fifthly: The Defence Force followed a very progressive training policy. In the course of their careers commanders were regularly re-trained in order to adapt to changing tasks and strategies. This ensured a high standard of command, and resulted in high standards and good discipline throughout the Defence Force.

The small number of applications submitted involved a handful of irregularities that did occur and for which the Defence Force expresses its regret.

The TRC would have created a far greater impression of objectivity had the reasons for the small number of amnesty applications been mentioned in its report. These reasons had in fact repeatedly been made known to the TRC in numerous documents.

Despite all the Defence Force's efforts, the Commission writes: "The dearth of applications reflects the general reluctance of SA Defence Force members to participate in the amnesty process." [5]

The Commission's concern that so few Defence Force members (only 10,6% of all applications) requested amnesty for internal actions, must be ascribed to an absence of military background and insight amongst the ranks of the TRC – and in particular its limited knowledge of "motives and perspectives" which the Defence Force clearly set out in its submission to the TRC, but which the TRC chose to ignore or dismissed with negative comments.[6]

This proves that the Commission did not read the Defence Force's submissions, because the Defence Force did not create violence; the Defence Force tried to prevent it. The Commission acknowledges that "... the limited evidence makes it difficult for the Commission to make specific findings, especially on the role of the military".[7] However, this did not prevent the Commission from making unfounded accusations and implicating the Defence Force in such cases under the collective term of "Security Forces".

If this was the result of ignorance, the members of the Defence Force would have had sympathy for such misperceptions. However, they are quite aware of the efforts that were made to co-operate with the TRC, and of all the information that was provided both voluntarily and at the request of the TRC. One must therefore suspect a degree of deliberate malice.

Despite a complete exposition in our submissions of the development and course of the conflict and the counter-strategies developed as a result thereof, the TRC interprets the Defence Force's involvement in the National Security Management system as a gross violation of human rights.[8]

In fact, it is clear from the approach in the report that in the eyes of the TRC the former Defence Force achieved nothing positive.

There is widespread suspicion amongst the ranks of the Defence Force that the TRC was really trying to gather evidence to be used in the prosecution of senior leaders.

FUTURE RECONCILIATION

The ANC's short-term and long-term strategy may result in a continuation of the political advantage it gained from the TRC process. It is therefore no surprise to me that the TRC's Committee on Restitution and Rehabilitation recommended in the final report that a "Secretariat" be established in the Office of the President to create "... a Presidential Award for innovative and inclusive projects aimed at keeping the memory of the past alive in schools, research centres and institutions of higher learning". A "past" aimed at reconciliation or division? Will it be based on the hearsay information and speculation the TRC has produced?

The Commission further recommends that the curriculum of the South African Human Rights Commission Education Centre should include projects that will encourage children "to keep the past alive".[9]

The question is: How will the execution of these recommendations contribute to building, as required by the Constitution, a "historic bridge between the past and a deeply divided community characterised by dissention, conflict, extreme suffering and injustice"? If the recommended projects are to be based on the truth, the question would be: Who caused the suffering during the struggle? Who tried to combat it? Who made possible the peaceful transition to a full democracy?

A THIRD FORCE?

One aspect to which the Committee devoted ten pages, is the so-called "third force".[10] In this case the TRC's methodology, which it followed in other cases as well, was first to formulate a hypothesis, and then to collect information to prove its correctness.

In the case of the "third force" the correctness of the hypothesis could not be proven with facts. The hypothesis probably originated in a State Security Council discussion in November 1985 at which consideration was given to the creation of a statutory third force, like the one created in Germany in the 1970s, in other words a statutory force which would be charged with responsibilities relating to international borders. Mr Adriaan Vlok, who was Chairperson of a committee appointed by the State Security Council, recommended that such a third force should not be established in South Africa, but rather that the capacity of the SA Police should be expanded to keep pace with the unrest situation, which was indeed done.[11]

The increase in violence after 1990 gave rise to rumours that such a third force had indeed been created. "As attacks continued, allegations were made that a 'hidden hand', or 'third force', was involved in orchestrating and fomenting violence – to derail the negotiation process and/or to undermine the ANC's efforts to consolidate its political presence."[12]

Although the "Security Forces" were once again blamed for this, the

Commission declared: "Unlike the police, the military made no disclosures to the Commission about its role in violations ..."[13] In the next paragraph the Commission admits: "Such denials and the limited evidence available make it difficult for the Commission to make specific findings, especially on the role of the military."

Operation Marion, which resulted in the KwaMakutha trial (discussed in more detail in Chapter 22) is also mentioned in this context. However, the SADF's involvement, as approved by the State Security Council, was limited to the training of 200 members of Inkatha to protect VIPs. The TRC, however, classifies this approved support for Inkatha as a so-called third force activity.

The Defence Force stands by the facts as mentioned in the Contact Bureau's second submission to the TRC on 8 October 1997.[14] This clearly shows that there was an over-eagerness amongst certain bodies, such as National Intelligence, to link the SA Defence Force to Third Force activities. Investigations launched by F.W. de Klerk in reaction to these allegations could find no confirmation of them. Despite the fact that the Steyn enquiry into the allegations was never completed and did not make any final findings, Dr Boraine probably leaked a non-official and incomplete interim version of provisional suspicions to the press. The dismissal of 23 senior SADF members ordered by De Klerk in consequence of the Steyn investigation was based on unsupported allegations, as indicated above.

Despite these and more complete information being provided in submissions to the TRC, and despite Archbishop Tutu's claim that the Commission experienced "pressure for time", the TRC did find enough time to waste its energy as far as the Defence Force was concerned. For example, with reference to the Harms Commission, the TRC alleged – without any proof – that "... security force personnel were instructed by their seniors to lie ...". The TRC tried to gain advantage from a generalised and unsupported statements in this way.[15]

The TRC does show a limited degree of understanding for the motives and perceptions of unnamed elements in its admission: "The need to defend frequently and rapidly against attacks metamorphosed into offensive action."[16]

The ten pages concerning the third force are riddled with vague statements, as shown in the following phrases: "less clear", "to some degree", "generally thin", "not established", "unable to establish", "it is probable", "The Commission believes" etcetera.

In general the value of the TRC's investigations, and therefore also it findings, are reflected in the following admission – an affirmation of its admission in the final report, namely that "... whilst it has made adverse findings on the basis of the evidence it received, it remains a commission of enquiry and, as such, is not bound by the same rules of evidence as a court of law".[17]

I do not wish to comment on the validity of this statement, apart from saying that it was not applied consistently. The "rules of a court of law" were indeed sometimes applied when members of the Defence Force were treated like accused, and when it could be to their detriment. On the other hand, evidence was often heard without any or with only limited cross-examination – in other words, whatever the witnesses said would be included in the report as the truth.[18]

DECLARATION OF ACCEPTANCE OF RESPONSIBILITY

As indicated many times in this book, the former Chiefs of the Defence Force reaffirmed to the TRC their conviction that the Defence Force was extremely successful in the role it played in facilitating constitutional transformation. We also reaffirmed that we accepted responsibility for those who served under us and acted in the execution of their duties at our command or with our direct or indirect written or oral instructions within the military chain of command.[19]

On the other hand one also needs to look at the ANC's "Declaration of Responsibility". This involved the following: "In line with the ANC's position that its leadership accepted full political and moral responsibility for the actions of its members, large numbers of the National Executive Committee (NEC) members and those involved in ANC hierarchies submitted collective amnesty applications to the Commission." These amnesty applications, which contained no specific misdeeds or gross violations of human rights, were initially granted and subsequently set aside. This implies an involvement by those concerned in unspecified violations of human rights.[20]

Nowhere in the TRC report is the authenticity of the ANC's declaration doubted. By its silence the Commission confirms that no cases of ANC offences that resulted in disciplinary action being taken against the perpetrators were brought to its attention.[21] In the same paragraph the ANC's submission in this regard is quoted: "Maintaining discipline in guerrilla and conventional armed forces is also fundamentally different. In the case of a guerrilla force, discipline flows from a thorough understanding of the political objectives of the armed struggle, not from the threats of court martials or punishment." My experience makes it clear to me that this ANC view means that ANC leaders condoned undisciplined actions and also tried to be granted amnesty for these actions in an illegitimate manner.

As an experienced soldier I find it impossible to believe the ANC's suggestion that in the absence of any legal processes, and with only a political goal, its forces would not act in an undisciplined manner. Such an approach means that there was probably no distinction between disciplined and undisciplined actions.

However, according to *Beeld* of 30 October 1998, the TRC also found that: "A lack of control over such elements ... resulted in many misdeeds against people by means of kangaroo courts, necklacings and other cruelties."[22]

THE DIFFERENCE BETWEEN A GUERRILLA AND A TERRORIST

What is also striking in the final TRC report is that the ANC's reference to Umkhonto we Sizwe (MK) as a guerrilla force is never questioned.[23] As early as my submission to the TRC of 7 May 1997 I clearly stated an internationally accepted distinction between terrorists and guerrilla forces. For example, one of the great differences is that terrorists do not wear uniforms or display identifying markings, while guerrillas openly and without any fear wear uniforms and openly display identifying markings in order to make identification possible (see the discussion in Chapter 20). Nowhere in the TRC report is any definition given to distinguish between these two types of armed resistance movements.

IN SUMMARY

Only time will tell to what degree the TRC succeeded in bringing about reconciliation in South Africa. The admission by one of the commissioners referred to earlier is, however, a cause for concern. Did the Commission fail in its most important instruction?

A second important instruction was that the Commission should try to establish the truth. It was therefore assumed that the Commission would rely on facts, and that obvious errors and contradictions would prevent it from arriving at the truth. Concerning the Defence Force, only a small number of the errors in the official TRC report are pointed out in Appendix A. These inaccuracies and errors form the basis of false accusations and allegations made against the Defence Force by the TRC. Such clear errors and contradictions cause one to wonder about the rest: Which parts of the report are credible and reliable, and which ones are not?

At this stage, with the Government not yet having given any indication of its intentions with regard to amnesty or legal action against members of the Defence Force, it is unwise to react to further allegations and accusations by the TRC concerning the Defence Force. However, I am of the opinion that the few cases I have indicated should suffice to shed light on the actual situation and to highlight the TRC's false, biased and unsupported accusations and portrayals.

In my opinion every person in possession of the real facts concerning the Defence Force's actions can only shake his or her head in disbelief when considering how any reliable commission appointed by the Government could present a report and distribute it internationally without making absolutely sure that it does not contain any questionable facts, particularly since the Commission's attention was specifically drawn to the questionable nature of certain of those "facts".

In view of the TRC's actions and handling of the incidents discussed, I cannot but conclude that the TRC looked at the SA Defence Force as if the Defence Force was a part of this country's Government of the day. The TRC was constantly looking for Defence Force actions that would justify criminal prosecution, in order to further neutralise the previous regime and denigrate its achievements. Even the publicity that unsuccessful prosecutions enjoyed in the media, as was the case with the Kwa-Makutha and Wouter Basson trials, contributed towards ensuring that the ANC's support base did not become alienated from it. However, the support base of the previous government and the Defence Force became demoralised as a result of these trials, the contents of the charge sheets and the evidence of state witnesses, and did become alienated. Even the verdicts of not guilty did not nullify the negative effects of bad publicity over a long period of time. The negative impressions caused by the unsuccessful prosecutions had a negligible effect for the present Government and cannot even remotely compare with the propaganda mileage achieved through reports during the course of the lengthy prosecutions, which gave a very negative impression of the previous government. The war may have ended, but the political struggle continues. *A luta continua!*

Chapter 26

CONCLUSION

The 42 years of my life that were inextricably entwined with the Defence Force constituted a long but very fruitful period. Mine was a career with many wonderful memories, crammed with a great many challenges. It unfolded in many interesting places, and exposed me to a variety of situations and informative experiences. There were numerous challenges, and I crossed paths with many people from all walks of life, from heads of state to the ordinary man in the street.

In South Africa I served in Pretoria, Cape Town, Robben Island and Saldanha for periods longer than two years. My later appointments as Chief of the Army, Chief of the Defence Force and eventually Minister of Defence meant that I had to travel a great deal in order to execute my responsibilities concerning the country's internal security, and in connection with its role in Southern Africa. Some of my duties were carried out over shorter periods in many African countries as well as the Middle and Far East, South America, the USA and Western Europe.

As early as 1950, when I joined the Defence Force as a candidate officer (cadet), I was particularly impressed with the high quality of the military training. In those early years my fellow-students and I had excellent instructors under the leadership of Warrant Officer (later General) Frits Loots.

The high standard and quality of the military training was a pleasant surprise to me throughout my career. From the most elementary to the most advanced, the training was conveyed in a simple and practically orientated manner, and rehearsed and applied where possible. In the case of officers and non-commissioned officers retraining was periodically done to ensure that the leadership remained informed about the practical application of current knowledge, and at the same time stayed in touch with new developments. The Defence Force was intensively geared towards military training.

Combat-readiness also formed part of this training at all times. This training and preparation for combat meant that when actual fighting took place, our men were not caught unawares. They were ready from the start, and knew what to expect and how to act.

One of the most gratifying experiences during my career was probably when the Government handed the Defence Force a written planning instruction. The tasks that flowed from it, and the planning and execution thereof, formed part of a set of ordered state goals and capabilities. It took a great deal of time and energy to implement this part of the national strategy and to align the Defence Force with it so that this organisation could carry out its responsibilities efficiently. The Defence Force's top management realised that a decentralised management style needed to be introduced. Delegations had to be spelled out clearly, and the organisational culture had to be adapted throughout. The Defence Force's top management accomplished this task with efficiency and enthusiasm.

This was one of the reasons why the entire Defence Force was reorganised. At the same time the improvement of the organisational frame of mind and the normalisation of human relations received attention. The latter two actions made good progress, together with the streamlining of the Defence Force's management ability. The proper frame of mind and the maintenance of sound human relations are of cardinal importance for any defence force, particularly during a revolutionary assault.

On completion of the reorganisation of the Defence Force, the State approved the National Security Management System and its subdivisions, and administered its implementation. Persons from various government departments, parastatals and the private sector, from various backgrounds and cultures, were part of the system. Accordingly it took some time to develop an efficient working method and sense of common purpose. However, as soon as the system began functioning efficiently, it provided the State with an excellent internal co-ordinating capability, at the same time developing an indispensable management capability. This co-ordinating capability was instituted across the length and breath of the country, a management capability that was essential for any country, whether at war or not, to assess and co-ordinate stumbling blocks or prevailing conditions, or the internal challenges concerning sensitive matters that affect the population, such as poverty, housing, unemployment, health services, etcetera. This provided the State with the ability to have and keep its finger on the pulse of the nation. For me, who was well versed in this system and constantly co-operated with it, the termination of the system was a great disappointment.

The success achieved by the Defence Force in these three fields, namely reorganisation, frame of mind and human relations, together with the quality of the trained manpower, resulted in great things. Add to this the production of sophisticated weaponry of great quality delivered by Armscor, and the reasons for the operational successes achieved by the Defence Force become quite clear. These military successes contributed to driving the Soviet Union and the Cubans from Southern Africa. The SA Defence Force won the physical encounter, which gave the various internal political leaders the opportunity to negotiate South Africa's future in peace and safety.

To my mind the battle at the Lomba River at the end of 1987 was the culmination of all military successes of the past 30 years. Soviet commanders were in control of the enemy forces, including Cuban and Angolan (FNLA) troops, and Soviet tactics as applied to conventional warfare were used in Africa probably for the first time. During this battle the combined communist military force was five to six times larger than our own combined forces. The enemy forces were equipped with far more sophisticated weaponry than we had, yet we hammered them. This marked the start of peace for Namibia, and also required the withdrawal of foreign forces from Southern Africa.

Few countries in the world will be able to equal our military successes. We were largely involved in a revolutionary war that switched over to conventional actions every now and then. The outstanding achievement was that we never suffered a defeat during this lengthy physical struggle. It is a remarkable achievement for any country to be successful against a superior force for such a long period, without suffering any military defeat.

Initially few South Africans realised the significance for the West of the fall of the Berlin Wall in 1989, and the role it was destined to play in South African politics. The symbolic destruction of international communism, and the end of the Cold War between the East and the West, occurred without the majority of South Africans realising that the SA Defence Force had made a significant contribution to this historic transition to a new political dispensation.

The rousing of suspicion that has subsequently been directed at the Defence Force does not take into account the dramatic changes on the national and international political stages. Against the background of my involvement in the Defence Force and its people over many years, and the extensive knowledge I acquired, I also felt a need to put the SADF's case to the TRC. As part of my testimony I said the following:

> Those who served in the South African Defence Force (SADF) were honourable and decent men and women. I respect them and shall stand by them. I do not expect you to necessarily agree with all that was done by the SADF. Neither do I expect the family and the friends of people who died in the SADF operations to forget. My appeal to you and to them is only to accept the bona fides of the members of the SADF involved.

I am grateful that I was afforded the opportunity and privilege to have been able to serve my country and its people during such a watershed period.

ENDNOTES

CHAPTER 2
MY MILITARY CAREER BEGINS IN EARNEST (1953-1965)
1. *Review of Defence and Armaments Production 1960-1970*, Apr. 1971, p. 25-26.

CHAPTER 3
APPOINTMENT TO COMMAND (1966-1972)
1. *Quotations from Chairman Mao Zedong*, 1976.
2. *Hansard*, 15 Sept. 1987, col. 5909, 5911.
3. *Ibid.*, col. 5908-5910.
4. *White Paper on Defence and Armaments Production, 1973*, p.10.

CHAPTER 4
DEPUTY CHIEF OF THE SA ARMY
1. *Hansard*, 24 Sept. 1981, col. 4674, *Hansard*; 16 Feb. 1981, col. 1465.
2. *White Paper on Defence and Arms Production, 1984*, p. 1-3.
3. Greig, Ian. 1977. *The Communist challenge to Africa: An analysis of contemporary Soviet, Chinese & Cuban policies*, p. 55-56.
4. *White Paper on Defence, 1977*, p. 7; Barnard, S.L. 1991. 'n Historiese oorsig van die gewapende konflik aan die noordgrens van Suidwes-Afrika/Namibië, *Acta Academica*, 23(1), Mrt. p. 113.
5. De Villiers, Dirk and Johanna. 1984. *PW*, p. 234.
6. Olivier, C.G. 1977. *Suid-Afrika se buitelandse beleid*, p. 77.

ENDNOTES

7. De Villiers and De Villiers, 1984, p. 232.
8. Van der Waals, W.S. 1990. *Portugal's war in Angola*, p. 244.
9. See for example Chabal *et al.*, 2002. *A history of postcolonial Lusophone Africa*, p. 14-15.
10. Van der Waals, 1990, p. 247.
11. De Villiers and De Villiers, 1984, p. 320.
12. *Hansard*, 24 Sept. 1981, col. 4494; *Hansard*, 16 Feb. 1981, col. 1463-1465.
13. *Hansard*, 24 Sept. 1981, col. 4495.
14. Walker, Sir Walter. 1978. *The bear at the back door*, p. 9.
15. Greig, 1977, p. 162-164.
16. De Villiers and De Villiers, 1984, p. 279; Greig, 1977, p. 246-248.
17. Greig, 1977, p. 248-249.
18. *White Paper on Defence and Armaments Supply, 1986*; Van Zyl, Frans. 1997. Groot lieg: waarheid of leuen? *Insig*, Des., p 16-18; Greig, 1977, p. 86.
19. ANC. 1981. *In Combat, Jan. 1980-Aug. 1981*. Sept.
20. Greig, 1977, p. 152-153.
21. *Hansard*, 24 Sept. 1981, col. 4684.

CHAPTER 5
THE NATIONAL SERVICE SYSTEM

1. Chief of the SA Defence Force. 1985. *Report of the Ministerial Committee of Enquiry with regard to the future planning of the SA Defence Force and related Military Aspects*. HSAW/503/1/B. Top Secret. 29 Nov., p. 10-1-10-23.
2. *Review of Defence and Armaments Production, 1960-1970*, 1971, p. 14-16.
3. *White Paper on Defence and Armaments Production, 1973*, p.10; 1975, p. 12; 1979, p. 4-8.
4. *White Paper on Defence and Armaments Supply, 1982*, p. 19.
5. *Ibid.*, p. 18-19.
6. *Review of Defence, 1960-1970*, 1970, par. 71-73; *White Paper on Defence and Arms Production, 1984*, p. 11-13.
7. *White Paper on Defence and Armaments Supply, 1982*, p. 17.

CHAPTER 6
DIVERSE CHALLENGES FOR THE CHIEF OF THE SA ARMY

1. *White Paper on Defence and Armaments Production, 1975*, p. 8-9.
2. *White Paper on the Planning Process in the South Africa Defence Force, 1989*, p. 8.

CHAPTER 7
AN INCREASE OF TERRORISM ACROSS THE BORDER OF SOUTH-WEST AFRICA
1. Spies, F.J. du T. 1989. *Operasie Savannah:Angola 1975-1976*, p. 33, 34.
2. In this regard see Fourie, Brand, 1992, *Buitelandse Woelinge om SA, 1939-1985*, p. 193 and De Villiers and De Villiers, 1984. *PW*, p. 265.
3. Spies (1989) mentions pronouncements by Adm. Rosa Coutinho and the Cuban deserter Gen. Rafael del Rino Diaz that there were Cubans in Angola even before the Alvor agreement of 15 January 1975 (Venter, Al J. (ed.) 1989, p. 122-123). He furthermore refers to pronouncements by former CIA member, John Stockwell, and the articles by Robert Moss, former editor of *The Economist*, that confirm that Cubans were present in Angola months before 5 November 1975 (Spies, p. 52).
4. Barnard, S.L. 1991. 'n Historiese oorsig van die gewapende konflik aan die noordgrens van Suidwes-Afrika/Namibië. *Acta Academica*, 23(1), Mrt. 109. Also see Spies, 1989, pp. xiv and 52.
5. *White Paper on Defence, 1977*, p. 6.
6. *Ibid.*
7. Malan, M.A. de M. 1987. Council of South Africa, Cape Sun, Cape Town. 11 Nov.
8. *White Paper on Defence and Armaments Production, 1973*. p. 2; *Hansard*, 24 Sept. 1981, col. 4684.

CHAPTER 8
OPERATION SAVANNAH
1. Barnard, S.L. 1991. 'n Historiese oorsig van die gewapende konflik aan die noordgrens van Suidwes-Afrika/Namibië. *Acta Academica*, 23(1), Mrt. p. 113.
2. See, for example, Du Preez, S.J. 1989. *Avontuur in Angola*, p. 118-119 and Spies, F.J. du Toit, 1989. *Operasie Savannah:Angola 1975-1976*, p. 138.
3. *Hansard*, 17 Apr. 1976.
4. Spies, 1989: p. 171.
5. *Ibid.*, p. 293.

CHAPTER 9
BASIC REQUIREMENTS FOR A SUCCESSFUL DEFENCE FORCE
1. *White Paper on Defence, 1977*, p.4-7.
2. *White Paper on Defence and Armaments Production 1960-1970*, Apr. 1971, p. 4-5.

3. *Ibid.*, p. 11-14.
4. *Ibid.*, par. 10, 11.
5. *White Paper on Defence and Armaments Supply, 1986*, p. 4-7.
6. *White Paper on Defence and Armaments Supply*, 1979, p. 25-26.
7. *White Paper on Defence and Armaments Supply, 1986*, p. 33-38; Malan, M.A. de M. 1987. Speech delivered on the 75th anniversary of the SA Defence Force, Potchefstroom, 1 Jul.
8. *White Paper on the Organisation of the SADF and Armscor of SA Limited, 1984*, p. 30-32.
9. Cabinet of the Republic of South Africa. 1980. *Die RSA se Belange en die RSA Regering se Doel, Doelstellings en Beleid vir Ordelike Regering asook Riglyne vir die uiteindelike Staatkundige Bestel van Suider-Afrika.* Minutes of a Cabinet Meeting held on 4 March 1980 in Cape Town. Secret (the so-called *Green Book*); *White Paper on Defence, 1977*, p. 7-11; *Hansard*, 24 Sept. 1981, col. 4683-4684.
10. Republic of South Africa. 1992. *Official Yearbook 1991-1992*, p. 39.
11. *Green Book*, 1980. p. 3-1; *White Paper on Defence, 1977*, p. 8.
12. *Green Book*, 1980. p. 3-1, 3-2; National Defence Force Nodal Point. 1997. *Defence Force involvement in the internal security situation in the Republic of South Africa from 1976 to 1994*. Confidential submission to the Truth and Reconciliation Commission.
13. National Defence Force Nodal Point. 1997. *Additional submission to the TRC*, p. 1-10-1-14.
14. *White Paper on Defence and Armaments Production, 1973*, p. 2-3.
15. Malan, M.A. de M. 1997. Voluntary evidence before the TRC, 7 May, p. 2-3.
16. *White Paper on Defence and Armaments Supply, 1986*, p. 13-14.

CHAPTER 10
MANAGEMENT AND COMPOSITION OF THE SA DEFENCE FORCE

1. *Hansard*, 15 Sept. 1987, col. 6016-6024; Malan, M.A. de M. 1985. The relationship between the Defence Force and the State. Speech to the Joint Staff Course (JSC) on the occasion of handing over certificates, Defence College, Pretoria, 29 Nov.; Malan M.A. de M., 1990. The relationship between the SA Defence Force and the State. Lecture delivered at the JSC, Defence College, Pretoria, 27 Aug.; Malan, M.A. de M. 1997. Voluntary evidence before the TRC, 7 May, p. 11.
2. Malan, 1997. p. 15; *Hansard*, 16 Feb. 1981, col. 1462; *Hansard*, 14 May 1986, col. 5502-5504; *Hansard*, 24 Sept. 1981, col. 4682-4683; *Briefing Regarding the Or-*

ganisation and Functions of the SA Defence Force and Armscor of South Africa Limited, 1990, p. 25.
3. The authority for this action first came from the *White Paper on Defence* (1977) and at a later stage from the *Green Book* (1980), according to which the national goal of South Africa was "to improve the living standards of all peoples and population groups in the RSA". Also see *Hansard*, 24 Sept. 1981, col. 4668-4669; Malan, M.A. de M. 1987. Speech delivered during the Sports Prestige Dinner of the University of Stellenbosch, 16 Oct.; *White Paper on the Planning Process of the SA Defence Force, 1989*, p. 8; Malan, 1997, p. 15.
4. *The Friend*, 29 Jul. 1976; *Pretoria News*, 30 Jul. 1976; *Die Transvaler*, 13 Aug. 1976; *The Cape Times*, 24 Oct. 1977; *Briefing Regarding the Organisation and Functions of the SA Defence Force and Armscor of South Africa Limited, 1990*, p. 11.
5. *Hansard*, 26 Feb. 1990, col. 1628.
6. *White Paper on Guidance Regarding the Organisation and Functions of the SA Defence Force and Armscor of South Africa Limited, 1984, 1986, 1990*.
7. *White Paper on the Organisation and Functions of the SA Defence Force and Armscor, 1984*, p. 41.
8. *Ibid.*, p. 44.
9. *Ibid.*, p. 47.
10. *Hansard*, 24 Sept. 1981, col. 4674-4678.
11. *White Paper on Defence, 1977*, p. 4-11.
12. *White Paper on Defence and Armaments Production, 1973*, p. 5, par. 8.
13. *White Paper on Defence, 1977*, p. 8-9; *Green Book*, 1980, p. 3-3.
14. *Hansard*, 24 Sept. 1981, col. 4682-4684.
15. *Hansard*, 24 Sept. 1981, col. 4684; *Rapport*, 10 Mei 1996.
16. *White Paper on Defence, 1977*, p. 10.
17. *Green Book*, 1980, p. 3-9-2; *Hansard*, 28 May 1985, col. 6380-6381.
18. *Hansard*, 20 Feb. 1989, col. 1068-1069; *Hansard*, 20 Apr. 1989, col. 5908.
19. Minutes of a Meeting of the State Security Council, 21 Oct. 1985.
20. *White Paper on Defence, 1975*, p. 6; *White Paper on Defence, 1977*, p. 31.
21. *White Paper on Defence, 1960-1970, 1973, 1975, 1977, 1986*.
22. *Hansard*, 24 Sept. 1981, col. 4684.
23. *Die Transvaler*, 13 Aug. 1976.
24. *Die Transvaler*, 13 Aug. 1976; *Pretoria News*, 13 Jun. 1979.
25. *Cape Times*, 24 Oct. 1977.
26. *Cape Times*, 24 Jan. 1978.

27. *White Paper on Defence, 1984*, p. 16.
28. *White Paper on Defence, 1977*, p. 33; *White Paper on Defence, 1982*, p. 19.
29. African National Congress. 1996. Submission to the Truth and Reconciliation Commission, 19 Aug., p. 4.7.3.1-4.9.1.

CHAPTER 11
OPERATIONAL AND RELATED MATTERS
1. *Sunday Times*, 13 Mar. 1977; Malan, M.A. de M. 1980. Die totale aanslag teen die RSA. C.R. Swart Lecture, Bloemfontein, 19 Sept.
2. Prinsloo, Daan. 1997. *Stem uit die Wildernis*, p.132-133; National Defence Force Nodal Point. 1997. *Defence Force Involvement in the Internal Security Situation in the RSA: A Confidential submission to the Truth and Reconciliation Commission, Part 4, Annexure B (The Total Onslaught)*, p. 2-7.
3. Roherty, James Michael. 1991. *State Security in South Africa. Civil-military relations under PW Botha*, p. 41-43; *White Paper on Defence and Arms Production, 1975*, p.3; *White Paper on Defence, 1977*, p. 3-5; *Hansard*, 20 Feb. 1981, col. 1975-1976; Hough, M. 1981. *Nasionale Veiligheid en Strategie met spesifieke verwysing na die RSA*, Aug., p.1-21.
4. *Defence Force Involvement in the Internal Security Situation in the RSA, Part 4, Annexure B (The National Management System)*, 1997, p. 10-11; Stadler, H.D. 1997. *The Other Side of the Story*, p. 148-153.
5. Stiff, P. 2001. *Warfare by other means*, p. 275.
6. De Klerk, F.W. 1998. *Die laaste trek - 'n nuwe begin*, p. 132.
7. *Ibid.*, p.137.
8. Translated as: "These were the first volleys in which financial, military, technological and diplomatic methods will be used in the Bush Administration's 'unconventional war' against international terrorism."
9. Steenkamp, Willem. 1990. *Borderstrike!*, p. 6; Barnard, S.L. 1991. *'n Historiese oorsig van die gewapende konflik aan die noordgrens van SWA/Namibië, 1966-1989*, p. 117.
10. Barnard, p. 118.
11. *White Paper on Defence and Arms Production, 1986*, p. 14.
12. *Militaria*, 19 Feb. 1989, p. 8, 9, 11.
13. Geldenhuys, Jannie. 1995. *A general's story from an era of war and peace*, p. 73.
14. *Ibid.*, p. 73-74.
15. *Citizen*, 9 Nov. 1998.

16. Steenkamp, 1990, p. 77.
17. Heitman, Helmoed-Römer. 1985. *Die Suid-Afrikaanse krygsmag*, p. 144.
18. Geldenhuys, 1995, p. 95.
19. De Villiers, Dirk and Johanna. 1984. *PW*, p. 325-326.
20. Van Bergen, C.J. 1981. *Die vyf Wesmagstate en die SWA-skikkingsonderhandelings (1978-1979)*, p. 102-106.

CHAPTER 12
THE NATIONAL SECURITY MANAGEMENT SYSTEM
1. Stadler, H.D. 1997. *The other side of the story*, p. 148-153.
2. *Hansard*, 15 Sept. 1987, col. 5912.
3. Murphy, G.H.P. 1987. *Geskiedenis van die Witwatersrandse Gesamentlike Bestuursentrum (WITGBS), 1984-1986*.
4. *Hansard*, 15 Sept. 1987, col. 5912; Berger, P.L., Godsell, Bobby (eds.). 1988. *A future South Africa: Visions, strategies and realities*, p. 36-37.
5. De Klerk, F.W. 1998. *Die laaste trek - 'n nuwe begin*, p. 133, 135.

CHAPTER 13
NUCLEAR AND RELATED TECHNOLOGICAL DEVELOPMENT
1. Stumpf, Waldo. 1996. South Africa's nuclear weapons programme: From deterrence to dismantlement. *Arms control today*, Dec. 1995/Jan. 1996, p. 3-4.
2. Van der Westhuizen, L.J., Le Roux, J.H. 1997. *The leading edge*. Unpublished manuscript in possession of the Institute for Contemporary History, University of the Free State, p. 172.
3. Van der Westhuizen and Le Roux, p. 172-173.
4. Steyn, Hannes, Van der Walt, Richard, Van Loggerenberg, Jan. 2003. *Armament and disarmament: South Africa's nuclear weapons experience*, p. 14-15.
5. Stumpf, 1996, p. 5.
6. Steyn, Van der Walt and Van Loggerenberg, 2003, p. 12-13.
7. Van der Westhuizen and Le Roux, 1997, p. 173; Steyn, Van der Walt and Van Loggerenberg, 2003, p. 40-42.
8. Van der Westhuizen and Le Roux, 1997, p. 174; Stumpf, 1996, p. 4.
9. Fourie, 1992, p. 417-424; Van der Westhuizen and Le Roux, 1997, p. 174; Stumpf, 1996, p. 4.
10. Fourie, Brand. 1992. *Buitelandse woelinge om Suid-Afrika, 1939-1985*, p. 362; Stumpf, 1996, p. 4.

11. Steyn, Van der Walt and Van Loggerenberg, 2003, p. 65.
12. Steyn, Van der Walt and Van Loggerenberg, 2003, p. 92-93.
13. Fourie, 1992, p. 418.
14. Steyn, Van der Walt and Van Loggerenberg, 2003, p. 43; Van der Westhuizen and Le Roux, 1997, p. 174.
15. Stumpf, 1996, p. 5; Steyn, Van der Walt and Van Loggerenberg, 2003, p. 87-88; Van der Westhuizen and Le Roux, 1997, p. 175.
16. Van der Westhuizen and Le Roux, 1997, p. 174, 177; Stumpf, 1996, p. 5.
17. Van der Westhuizen and Le Roux, 1997, p. 179.
18. Atomic Energy Corporation (AEC). *Official Yearbook 1983*, p. 714.
19. Van der Westhuizen and Le Roux, 1997, p. 177; Stumpf, 1996, p. 6.
20. Steyn, Van der Walt and Van Loggerenberg, 2003, p. 88.
21. Stumpf, 1996, p. 6.
22. Steyn, Van der Walt and Van Loggerenberg, 2003, p. 65.
23. *Ibid.*, p. 98-99.
24. *Hansard*, 24 Mar. 1993.
25. Steyn, Van der Walt and Van Loggerenberg, 2003, p. 76.
26. *Ibid.*, p. 75-82.
27. *Ibid.*, p. 69-70.

CHAPTER 14
ARMSCOR, THE OTHER MEMBER OF THE DEFENCE FAMILY

1. *White Paper on the organisation and functions of the SA Defence Force and the Armaments Corporation of SA Limited, 1984*, p. 57-63; *White Paper on the organisation and functions of the SA Defence Force and the Armaments Corporation of SA Limited, 1990*, p. 64-70.
2. *White Paper on Defence and Arms Supplies, 1979*, p. 26-27; Steyn, Hannes, Van der Walt, Richard, Van Loggerenberg, Jan. 2003. *Armament and disarmament: South Africa's nuclear weapons experience*, p. 50.
3. Malan, M.A. de M. 1987. Speech delivered on the occasion of the celebration of the 75th year of the South African Defence Force, Potchefstroom, 1 Jul.
4. *Hansard*, 17 May 1988, col. 10010-10011; *White Paper on Defence and Arms Supplies, 1979*, p. 23-24.
5. Steyn, Van der Walt and Van Loggerenberg, 2003, p. 51.
6. *Ibid.*, p. 46, 49.
7. *Ibid.*, p. 49.

8. *Ibid.*, p. 50-60.
9. *White Paper on Defence and Arms Supplies, 1986,* p. 33-38.
10. See Steyn, Van der Walt and Van Loggerenberg, 2003. *Armament and disarmament: South Africa's nuclear weapons experience,* p. 54-55 for a list of locally manufactured arms, ammunition and equipment.
11. Malan, M.A. de M. 1990. Lecture delivered at the Institute for Strategic Studies, University of Pretoria, 16 Oct.

CHAPTER 15
ADAPTING TO MY NEW POSITION AS MINISTER OF DEFENCE
1. *Financial Mail,* 5 Sept. 1980, Malan into the fire.
2. *Rapport,* 25 Jan. 1981.
3. *Hansard,* 29 May 1985, col. 6440-6441.
4. Prinsloo, Daan. 1997. *Stem uit die Wildernis,* p. 149.
5. *Hansard,* 24 Sept. 1981, col. 4672.
6. *White Paper on Defence and Arms Supplies,* 1982, p. 17-20.

CHAPTER 16
THE GREATEST SOUTH AFRICAN DEFENCE FORCE VICTORY IN BATTLE
1. *Hansard,* 29 May 1985, col. 6432.
2. Bridgland, Fred. 1990. *The war for Africa,* p. 18-19; Hamann, Hilton. 2002. Ek skaam my nie, *Insig,* Aug. 2002, p. 52-53.
3. Hamann, Hilton. 2001. *Days of the Generals,* p. 85.
4. Bridgland, 1990, p. 18-19; Hamann, 2001, p. 85-86.
5. Bridgland, 1990, p. 23.
6. Geldenhuys, Jannie. 1993. *Dié wat wen,* p. 167.
7. *Ibid.,* p. 168.
8. Bridgland, 1990, p. 1; Hamann, 2002, p. 52-53.
9. Geldenhuys, 1993, p. 172-174. Bridgland, 1990, p. 369.
10. Bridgland, 1990, p. 62.
11. *Ibid.,* p. 62-63.
12. *Ibid.,* p. 262.
13. Hamann, 2001, p. 89.
14. Bridgland, 1990, p. 162.
15. Bridgland, 1990, p. 260; Hamann, 2001, p. 89.

16. Geldenhuys, 1993, p. 170.
17. *Ibid.*, p. 170.
18. Bridgland, 1990, p. 180.
19. *Ibid.*, p. 67.
20. *Ibid.*, p. 180; Geldenhuys, 1993, p.173.
21. Geldenhuys, 1993, p. 174.
22. *Hansard*, 17 May 1988, col. 10012-10014; *Hansard*, 7 Feb. 1989, col. 184; Barnard, S.L., 1991, 'n Historiese oorsig van die gewapende konflik aan die noordgrens van Suidwes-Afrika/Namibië 1966-1989, *Acta Academica* 23(1), p. 123.
23. Hamann, 2002, p. 52-53.
24. Hamann, 2001, p. 97.
25. Renwick, Sir Robin, *Unconventional diplomacy in Southern Africa*, quoted in *Beeld*, 15 Aug. 2002.
26. Bridgland, 1990, p. 267; Hamann, 2001, p. 96.

CHAPTER 17
DESPERATE ATTEMPTS TO TRUMP THE SA DEFENCE FORCE
1. Bridgland, Fred. 1990. *The War for Africa*, p. 342; Geldenhuys, Jannie. 1993. *Dié wat wen*, p. 190-191.
2. Hamann, Hilton. 2001. *Days of the Generals*, p. 99.
3. Geldenhuys, 1993, p. 190; Hamann, 2001, p. 99.
4. Bridgland, 1990, p. 343.
5. *Ibid.*, p. 343-344.
6. Geldenhuys, 1993, p. 195; Hamann, 2001, p. 99.
7. Geldenhuys, 1993, p. 196-198; Bridgland, 1990, p. 358.
8. Geldenhuys, 1993, p. 199.
9. Hamann, Hilton. 2002. Ek skaam my nie. *Insig*, Aug., p. 52-53.
10. *Ibid.*, p. 52.
11. Bridgland, 1990, p. 374-375.
12. Geldenhuys, 1993, p. 210.
13. *Ibid.*, p. 213-214; *Beeld*, 25 Nov. 2005.
14. Stiff, Peter. 1991. *Nine Days of War*, Preface.
15. *Hansard*, 21 Apr. 1989, col. 6132-6143; Barnard, S.L. 1991. 'n Historiese oorsig van die gewapende konflik aan die noordgrens van Suidwes-Afrika/Namibië, 1966-1989, *Acta Academica*, 23(1), p. 124.
16. *TRC report*, par. 128-131, chapter 2, vol. 2.

17. *TRC report*, par. 127-128, chapter 2, vol. 2.
18. *Hansard*, 7 Feb. 1989, col. 188.
19. *Hansard*, 20 Apr. 1989, col. 5906-5909; *Hansard*, 21 Apr. 1989, col. 6138-6139; Steenkamp, Willem. 1990. *South Africa's Border War*, p. 184.
20. Geldenhuys, 1993, p. 220.
21. *Hansard*, 18 May 1988, col. 10103-10105; *Hansard*, 3 May 1989, col. 7475.
22. *Hansard*, 11 Feb. 1986, col. 5, 7-8.
23. *Hansard*, 18 May 1988, col. 10092-10093.

CHAPTER 18
TWO CONTROVERSIAL MATTERS: DIETER GERHARDT AND THE DEATH OF PRESIDENT SAMORA MACHEL

1. *Ha'aretz Magazine*, 7 Apr. 2000, p. 6-9, 13.
2. *Ibid.*, p. 7.
3. *Ibid.*, p. 8.
4. *Ibid.*, p. 8.
5. *Ibid.*, p. 13.
6. Prinsloo, Daan. 1997. *Stem uit die Wildernis*, p. 135.
7. *Ha'aretz Magazine*, p. 13.
8. *Ibid.*, p. 13.
9. *Ibid.*, p. 8.
10. *Ibid.*, p. 9.
11. The death of Pres. Machel, *ANC News Briefing*, vol. 10(44), 2 Nov. 1986, p. 14-15; The death of Pres. Machel, *ANC News Briefing*, vol. 10(46), 16 Nov. 1986, p. 14.
12. Hamann, Hilton. 2001. *Days of the Generals*, p. 116-118.
13. *Hansard*, 4 Feb. 1986, col. 168-170.
14. Margo, Cecil. 1998 (1999), *Final Postponements: Reminiscences of a Crowded Life*, p. 216.
15. *Ibid.*, p. 217-218.
16. Margo, 1998, p. 223-225; Hamann, 2001, p. 119-121.
17. Margo, 1998, p. 225; Hamann, 2001, p. 122.
18. Margo, 1998, p. 228; Hamann, 2001, p. 121-122.
19. Margo, 1998, p. 229; Mackenzie-Hoy, Terry. 2003. Samora Machel: Did we do it? *Engineering News*, 24-30 Jan. 2003, p. 63; 31 Jan.-6 Feb. 2003, p. 53; 7-13 Feb. 2003, p. 82.
20. Hamann, 2001, p. 116-117.

21. *Die Burger*, 24 Oct. 1996, Editorial; *Hansard*, 15 Sept. 1987, col. 5943-5946.

CHAPTER 19
THE EMINENT PERSON'S GROUP AND THE CIVIL CO-OPERATION BUREAU
1. Prinsloo, Daan. 1997. *Stem uit die Wildernis*, p. 113, 310.
2. *Ibid.*, p. 311.
3. Prinsloo, 1997, p. 314; Botha, R.F. 1997. Main points of Statement: TRC Hearing of State Security Council, 14 Oct., p. 3.
4. *White Paper on Defence and Arms Procurement, 1986*, p. 13-16.
5. State Security Council. 1986. Minutes of the State Security Council Meeting, 12 Dec., p. 8. Top Secret.
6. *Hansard*, 18 May 1988, col. 10092.
7. State Security Council. 1985. Minutes of the State Security Council Meeting, 20 Dec., p. 8. Top Secret.
8. Geldenhuys, Jannie. 1993. *Dié wat wen*, p. 149.
9. Schedule 1 to Cabinet Resolution of 11 Jun. 1986, dated 15 Aug. 1986, p. 5.
10. *Hansard*, 4 Feb. 1986, col. 160-162; 11 Feb. 1986, col. 4-6.
11. State Security Council. 1986. Minutes Regarding Target Briefing, 18 Mar. Top Secret; Schedule 2 (dated 10 Apr. 1986) to Minutes 5/86 of State Security Council Meeting, 14 Apr. 1986, Item 7, Top Secret.
12. Cabinet Resolutions of 11 Jun. 1986 via HSAW/Cape/UG/309/1, 15 Jul. 1986, p. 5.
13. Botha, 1997, p. 12; Roherty, James Michael. 1991. *State Security in South Africa. Civil-military relations under PW Botha*, p. 130.
14. *Hansard*, 18 May 1988, col. 10092.
15. De Klerk, F.W. 1998. *The last trek - a new beginning*, p. 138-139.
16. *Hansard*, 26 Feb. 1990, col. 1629.
17. *Ibid.*, col. 1627.
18. National Defence Force Nodal Point. 1997. *Additional submission with regard to the former SADF*, p. 2-9-2-12.
19. *Hansard*, 26 Feb. 1990, col. 1629-1630; *Sechaba*, Aug. 1985; Malan, M.A. de M. 1997. Voluntary evidence before the TRC, 7 May, p. 49.
20. Ministerial press release, 7 Mar. 1991; Malan, 1997, p. 56; Harms, the Hon. Mr Justice L.T.C. 1990. *Commission of inquiry into certain alleged murders*, p. 39-43.
21. Ministerial press release, 7 Mar. 1991; Malan, 1997, p. 56; Harms, 1990, p. 63.
22. Contact Bureau of the former SADF. 1998. *Sworn statements by former chiefs of the*

SADF before the TRC, Jun., p. 1-17, par. 53; Sechaba, Nov. 1985, p. 25-26; P.W. Botha in an interview with *Washington Times*, 1986; *Sechaba*, Aug. 1985.
23. Malan, 1997, p. 30.
24. *Ibid.*, p. 31.
25. *Hansard*, 18 May 1988, col. 10091-10093.
26. Malan, 1997, p. 31.
27. *Ibid.*, p. 32.
28. *Hansard*, 29 May 1985, col. 6511; 4 Feb. 1986, col. 161; Malan, 1997, p. 40, 41.
29. *Sechaba*, Aug. 1985.
30. Malan, 1997, p. 35; *Sechaba*, Aug. 1985.
31. Cited by Agence France Presse, 13 Apr. 1986; Malan, 1997, p. 38.
32. Malan, 1997, p. 35-36; *The daily news*, 16 Sept. 1986, p. 6; *Sunday Times of London*, 14 Sept. 1986.
33. *Sechaba*, Nov. 1985, p. 25-26; *Sechaba*, Dec. 1986, p. 15-16.
34. *Hansard*, 18 Mar. 1986, col. 2160; BSB kry nie sluipmoordopdragte, *Die Burger*, 8 Mei 1997; *Rapport*, 11 Mei 1997.
35. De Klerk, 1998, p. 211; Hamann, Hilton. 2001. *Days of the Generals*, p. 142.
36. Hamann, 2001, p. 148.
37. *Africa Confidential*, vol. 29, no. 16.
38. De Klerk, 1998, p. 211.
39. *Hansard*, 6 Feb. 1991, col. 256-260.
40. *Hansard*, 26 Feb. 1990, col. 1627/1628; Harms, 1990, p. 163-178.
41. *Hansard*, 18 Mar. 1986, col. 2161.
42. *Hansard*, 6 Feb. 1991, col. 260.
43. *Die Burger*, 8 Mei 1997, p. 3.
44. *Hansard*, 26 Feb. 1990, col. 1627.
45. *Hansard*, 26 Feb. 1990, col. 1627; *Die Burger*, 8 Mei 1997: SAW nie verhewe bo gereg nie.
46. *Ibid.*, p. 9; *Pretoria News*, 8 May 1997; *Beeld*, Redaksioneel, 9 Mei 1997.
47. De Klerk, 1998, p. 220.
48. Harms, 1990, p. 198.
49. Minutes of Cabinet Meeting no. 10/90, 11 June 1990, Attachment A to KKVS 11/90. Top Secret.
50. Harms, 1990, p. 63.
51. *Hansard*, 26 Feb. 1990, col. 1627/1628; *Hansard*, 6 Feb. 1991, col. 259; Hamann, 2001, p. 142.

ENDNOTES

52. *Salut*, Apr. 1995, Special Forces: "They are here to stay", p. 17-20.

CHAPTER 20
THE ANC: ORIGIN, DEVELOPMENT AND STRATEGY
1. *Official Yearbook of the Republic of South Africa 1984*, p. 313; *Hansard*, 24 Sept. 1981, col. 4682- 4684.
2. Benson, Mary. 1994. *Nelson Mandela. The man and the movement*, p. 13; *Suid-Afrikaanse Biografiese Woordeboek*, Volume II, p. 248.
3. *Official Yearbook of South Africa 1991-1992*, p. 45.
4. Stadler, H.D. 1997. *The other side of the story: A true perspective*, p. 21; Muller, C.F.J. 1975. *Vyfhonderd jaar Suid-Afrikaanse geskiedenis*, p. 443.
5. Stadler, 1997, p. 22-24; *Amptelike Jaarboek van Suid-Afrika 1991-1992*, p. 45-46.
6. Kotze, D.J. 1975. Kommunisme in Suid-Afrika, verlede, hede en toekoms. Paper delivered at the Autumn School, University of Stellenbosch, 1-4 April 1975, p. 39; Campbell, Keith, 1986. *ANC - A Soviet Task Force?* p. 7-9.
7. Defence Force Nodal Point. 1997. *Defence Force involvement in the internal security situation in the Republic of South Africa from 1976 to 1994, Annexure A*, p. 3-4; Mandela, Nelson. 1995. *Long Walk to Freedom*, p. 281.
8. Mandela, 1994, p. 322-324.
9. *Ibid.*, p.323; Benson, 1994, p. 89.
10. Mandela, 1994, p. 347-365; p. 372-373.
11. Greig, Ian. 1977. *The Communist challenge to Africa*, p. 205-206.
12. Greig, 1977, p. 206; Kotze, 1975, p. 13; *White Paper on Defence and Armaments Production, 1973*, p. 4-5 and 1986, p. 12-14.
13. Greig, 1977, p. 242.
14. Suzman, Helen. 1993. *In no uncertain terms*, p. 176.
15. Mandela,1994, p. 575; *White Paper on Defence and Armaments Provision, 1986*, p. 16.
16. Cabinet of the RSA, 1980. *Green Book*, p. 3.9.2.
17. *White Paper on Defence and Armaments Provision, 1986*, p. 17.
18. Quoted by Venter, Albert. 2002. Is die een se terroris die ander se vryheidsvegter?
19. *Rapport*, 11 Mei 1997, ANC het self terro-opsie gekies; Greig, 1977, p. 183.
20. Netanyahu, Benjamin (ed.). 1986. *Terrorism: How the West can win*.
21. The character, extent and nature of the revolutionary assault on South Africa is outlined in *Hansard*, 17 May 1988, col. 10020-10022 and 18 May 1988, col. 10090-10097; Malan, M.A. de M. 1997. Voluntary evidence before the TRC, 7 May, p. 27.

22. Pike, Douglas. *The Viet Cong strategy of terror*. Quoted in Greig, 1977, p. 184.
23. Mamdani, Mahmood. 2004. *Good Muslim, bad Muslim*, p. 11.
24. Greig, 1977, p. 184.
25. Stadler, 1997, p. 46-55.
26. *Hansard*, 18 May 1988, col. 10092.
27. Benson, 1994, p. 176.
28. *Hansard*, 6 Feb. 1990, col. 148; De Klerk, F.W. 1998. *The last trek - a new beginning*, p. 180.
29. Benson, 1994, p. 232.
30. De Klerk, 1998, p. 191.
31. ANC. 1987. Towards a people's war and insurrection, *Sechaba*, Apr., p. 2-6.
32. *Hansard*, 15 Sept. 1987, col. 5914.
33. De Klerk, 1998, p. 187; Scholtz, Leopold. 1997. Die oorlog was nie tevergeefs nie, *Insig*, Sept., p. 24.
34. Stiff, Peter. 1999. *The silent war*, p. 314.
35. De Klerk, 1998, p. 216-217.
36. *Ibid.*, p. 199; *Official Yearbook of South Africa 1991-1992*, p. 47.
37. Stadler, 1997, p. 42-44; De Klerk, 1998, p. 216.
38. Jenkins, Tim. 1995. Talking to Vula: The story of the secret underground communication network of Operation Vula, *Mayibuye*, May 1995-Oct 1995; Waldmeir, Patti. 1997. *Anatomy of a miracle*, p. 162.
39. Stadler, 1997, p. 67; *Rapport*, 11 May 1997; Mamdani, 2004: 11.
40. *Sechaba*, Aug. 1985; Malan, 1997, p. 34; *Defence Force involvement in the internal security in South Africa from 1976 to 1994*, 1997, Part 2: The violent component of the revolution; Stadler, 1997, p. 66-67.
41. Waldmeir, 1997, p. 162; Stadler, 1997, p. 42-48, 90-97; De Klerk, 1998, p. 218-219.
42. De Klerk, 1998, p. 218-219; Mandela, 1994, p. 702; *Official Yearbook 1991-1992*, p. 47.
43. Waldmeir, 1997, p. 165; Mandela, 1994, p. 702.
44. De Klerk, 1998, p. 233.
45. *Ibid.*, 1998, p. 222-233.
46. *Ibid.*, 1998, p. 225.
47. *White Paper on Defence and Armaments Provision, 1986*, p. 14; Ministerial news release, 5 Sept. and 4 Oct. 1990. See also letter from Col Jan Breytenbach with regard to these allegations, *Citizen*, 9 Nov. 1998.
48. Waldmeir, 1997, p. 192; De Klerk, 1998, p. 236.

49. Mandela, 1994, p. 594; De Klerk, 1998, p. 255.
50. Mandela, 1994, p.724; *Official Yearbook 1991-1992*, p. 48.
51. Waldmeir, 1997, p. 207; Stadler, 1997, p. 98-101; De Klerk, 1998, p. 257-261.
52. Mandela, 1994, p. 726.
53. De Klerk, 1998, p. 135.
54. *Ibid.*, p. 170-171.
55. *Ibid.*, p. 283.
56. *Cape Times*, 24 Mar. 2004.
57. *Hansard*, 6 Feb. 1990, col. 152; Owen, Ken. 1997. So what did they do in the war, daddy? *Leadership* 16, p. 52; De Klerk, 1998 p. 274; Johnson, R.W. 1997. South Africa's new problems. *Wall Street Journal*, 19 Sept.
58. *Beeld*, 15 Jun. 1998; *Beeld*, 10 Aug. 1996; *Rapport*, 9 Aug. 1998.
59. *Pretoria News*, 8 May 1997.
60. *Hansard*, 6 Feb. 1990, col. 150; Stadler, 1997, p. 66-67, 175, 197.
61. Scholtz, 1997.
62. *Hansard*, 24 Sept. 1981, col. 4672-4673.
63. *Beeld*, 21 Okt. 1989.
64. kykNet-broadcast, 14 Apr. 2002, 20:00.
65. Malan, 1997, p. 3.

CHAPTER 21
RETIREMENT FROM POLITICS
1. De Klerk, F.W. 1998. *The last trek - a new beginning*, p. 135.
2. Steyn-verslag, *Beeld*, 11 Apr. 1997.
3. *Beeld*, 20 Jan. 1997; *Sunday Times*, 19 Jan. 1997.
4. SAP Report, 15 Apr. 1993, p. 18-20; Dokumente wys daar was geen getuienis, *Rapport*, 19 Jan. 1997.
5. *Rapport*, 6 Jun. 1999; *Beeld*, 2 Jun. 1999.

CHAPTER 22
OPERATION MARION AND THE KWAMAKUTHA COURT CASE
1. Court Record, p. 3481.
2. *Ibid.*, p. 3482.
3. Minutes of SSC meeting, 20 Dec. 1985, Top Secret.
4. Minutes of meeting of Chief Minister Mangosutho Buthelezi, Min. Chris Heunis, Min. Louis le Grange and Min. Magnus Malan, 9 Jan. 1986.

5. Minutes 1/86 of SSC Meeting, 3 Feb. 1986. Top Secret.
6. Minutes 1/86, Appendix A.
7. MID Report ST/UG/311/7/17, 14 Feb. 1986.
8. Report of the Chief of the Army, HLeër/503/2/1, Mar. 1986.
9. MID Report ST/310/4/ Marion, 16 Apr. 1986. Top Secret.
10. Varney, Howard (convenor: ITB). 1997. *The role of the former state in political violence. Operation Marion: A case study*, Mar.
11. *Financial Mail*, 10 Nov. 1995, "Suspicion of selective prosecution", p. 22, 25.
12. Varney, 1997, p. 10 footnote 27; p. 11 par. 5.
13. Court Record, p. 4487.
14. *Sunday Times*, 30 Mar. 1997.
15. *Rapport*, 10 Mrt. 1996; *Die Burger*, 14 Okt. 1996. Magnus oor sy nagmerrie; Malan sê krag van Bo het hom deur saak gedra.
16. *Rapport*, 29 Okt. 1995; *The Sunday Times*, 29 Okt. 1995.
17. *Beeld*, 2 Nov. 1995.
18. Hamann, Hilton. 2001. *Days of the Generals*, p. 216-217.
19. *Financial Mail*, 10 Nov. 1995.
20. Hamann, 2001, p. 216-217.
21. *Beeld*, 8 May 1997.
22. SA Institute of Race Relations. 1996. Malan: A disgraceful episode. *Fast Facts*, Nov., p. 6.
23. *International Herald Tribune*, 3 Nov. 1995. SA Charges Ex-Defence Chief, p. 7.
24. Court Record, p. 4382.
25. *Ibid.*, p. 4385.
26. *Ibid.*, p. 4383-4384.
27. *Ibid.*, p. 4385.
28. *Ibid.*, p. 4386.
29. *Ibid.*, p. 4404.
30. *Ibid.*, p. 4404.
31. *Ibid.*, p. 4407.
32. *Ibid.*, p. 4408.
33. *Ibid.*, p. 4419.
34. *Ibid.*, p. 4419, 4435.
35. *Ibid.*, p. 4461.
36. *Ibid.*, p. 4457-4458; p. 4462; p. 4484.
37. *Ibid.*, p. 4472-4479; p. 4517-4521.

38. *Ibid.*, p. 4486.
39. *Ibid.*, p. 4447.
40. *Ibid.*, p. 4408.
41. *Saturday Star*, 12 Oct. 1996. Outrage and dismay over Malan finding; *Die Burger*, 11 Okt. 1996. ANC ontplof oor Malan-uitspraak; *Die Burger*, 14 Okt. 1996, p. 10; *The Times*, 12 Oct. 1996, p. 19.
42. *Pretoria News*, 14 Oct. 1996, Editorial.
43. *Citizen*, 12 Oct. 1996; *Pretoria News*, 12 Oct. 1996; SA Institute of Race Relations, 1996, p. 6.
44. Varney, 1997, p. 10-12, footnote 27-28.
45. SA Institute of Race Relations, 1996, p. 6; *Citizen*, 12 Oct. 1996; *Pretoria News*, 14 Oct 1996.
46. Anon. 1997? Findings i.r.o. the involvement of members of the SADF, SAP and members of Inkatha in Operation Marion, p. 17-26. Unpublished document in possession of the author, presumably submitted to the TRC.

CHAPTER 23
CHEMICAL AND BIOLOGICAL WARFARE: PROJECT COAST
1. *Beeld*, 12 Feb. 1997.
2. Report by the Project Officer, HSF/Top Secret/302/6/C123, 16 Mar. 1990; *Hansard* 14 May 1986 col. 5506.
3. Malan, M.A. de M. Voluntary evidence before the TRC, 7 May 1997, p. 57-59.
4. *Die Burger*, 8 Mei 1997. Chemiese projek was nie sinister, p. 13.
5. Armscor. 1998. *Salvo* 1, p. 21-22.
6. Hamann, Hilton. 2001. *Days of the Generals*, p. 170.
7. *Beeld*, 16 Jun. 1998.
8. *Rapport*, 23 Okt. 2005.
9. *Ibid.*

CHAPTER 24
THE SA DEFENCE FORCE AND THE TRUTH RECONCILIATION COMMISSION
1. *Beeld*, 15 Jun. 1998.
2. *Pretoria News*, 30 Apr. 1999; *Beeld*, 1 Mei 1999, WVK lees nie alles.
3. *Citizen*, 28 Jul. 1999.
4. *Hansard*, 14 May 1986, col. 5503.

5. *Rapport*, 2 Aug. 1998. FW lewer skerp kritiek op WVK-proses.
6. Quoted in: SANDF National Defence Force Nodal Point, 1997. *Additional submission with regards to the former SADF*, p. 9 and Contact Bureau of the former SADF, 1998. *Complaints in respect of the TRC's handling of the former SADF and its members*. Unpublished documents submitted to the TRC, 29 Jan.
7. *Die Burger*, 26 Okt. 1996; SAPA report, Boraine angry at SADF submission, 21 Oct., which reads: "TRC deputy-chairman Dr Alex Boraine has slammed the bland and 'soulless' submissions made by former SADF members in Cape Town yesterday.

    'My overall impression is that the submission is breathtaking in its one-sidedness', Boraine said.

    'I find it almost unbelievable that in 80 pages there is no acknowledgement or acceptance of responsibility for a single death during the apartheid era.'"

    Die Burger of 22 Okt. 1996 reported as follows (see translation below): "Die WVK het gister die voorlegging van die voormalige Weermag verwerp omdat dit te feitlik was en te min 'siel' bevat het.

    'Die voorlegging was asembenewend eensydig en byna vermetel daarin dat geen aanspreeklikheid hoegenaamd vir enige gebeure aanvaar word nie. Die Weermag tree as die ridder op die wit perd na vore,' het dr. Alex Boraine gesê.

    Volgens dr. Boraine skrei die voorlegging teen die feite soos die WVK dit aangehoor het van verskeie getuienis oor verskeie maande."

    ["Yesterday the TRC rejected the submission of the former Defence Force it was too factual and had too little 'soul'.

    'The submission was breathtaking in its one-sidedness and is almost audacious in that there is no acknowledgement whatsoever of responsibility for any events. The Defence Force is portrayed as the knight on the white horse, Dr Alex Boraine said.

    According to Dr Boraine the submission flies in the face of facts as heard by the TRC over many months from various witnesses." - my translation]
8. *Beeld*, 17 Mrt. 1997. WVK kies kant, sê Jannie Geldenhuys.
9. Contact Bureau of the former SADF. 1999. The Contact Bureau's analysis of the TRC report, 19 Apr., p. 6.
10. *Pretoria News*, 8 May 1997.
11. Malan, M.A. de M. 1997. Voluntary evidence before the TRC, 7 May, p. 2.
12. Malan, 1997, p. 59-60; *Pretoria News*, 8 May 1997.
13. Malan, 1997, p. 8, p. 60; *Beeld*, 9 Mei 1997. Editorial.
14. Malan, 1997, p. 2-3.

15. *Ibid.*, p. 3; *Rapport*, 10 Mrt. 1996.
16. Malan, 1997, p. 9.
17. *Rapport*, 26 Jul. 1998.
18. TRC report, Vol. 6, Section 3, Chapter 2, par. 62.
19. *The Contact Bureau's analysis of the TRC Report*, 19 Apr. 1999, p. 1-3.
20. *Hansard*, 14 May 1986, col. 6522.
21. Extracts from sworn evidence by former Chiefs of the SADF before the TRC. 1998, p. 1-17, par. 53; *Sechaba*, Nov. 1985, p. 25-26; *Sechaba*, Aug. 1985; *Rapport*, 11 Mei 1997.
22. TRC report, Vol. 6, Section 3, Chapter 2, par. 79.
23. *Rapport*, 30 Mei 1998. WVK bekyk nie ANC-moord op 'verraaier'.

CHAPTER 25
PUBLIC REPORTS OF THE TRC CONCERNING THE SA DEFENCE FORCE

1. *Rapport*, 2 Mei 1999. Generaals se verslag wys WVK se foute.
2. kykNet, 14 Apr. 2002, 20:00.
3. *Beeld*, 24 Apr. 1997.
4. *TRC Report*, Vol. 6, Section 3, Chapter 1, par. 4.
5. *Ibid.*, Vol. 6, Section 3, Chapter 1, par. 6.
6. *Ibid.*, Vol. 6, Section 3, Chapter 1, par. 9.
7. *Ibid.*, Vol. 6, Section 4, Appendix, par. 8.
8. *Ibid.*, Vol. 6, Section 3, Chapter 1, par. 5.
9. *Ibid.*, Vol. 6, Section 5, Chapter 7, par. 12.
10. *Ibid.*, Vol. 6, Section 4, Appendix.
11. Malan, M.A. de M. 1997. Voluntary evidence before the TRC, 7 May, p. 50-56; *Die Burger*, 8 Mei 1997; *Beeld*, 9 Mei 1997, Editorial.
12. *Ibid.*, Vol. 6, Section 4, Appendix, par. 3.
13. *Ibid.*, Vol. 6, Section 4, Appendix, par. 7.
14. National Defence Force Nodal Point. 1997. *Defence Force involvement in the internal security situation in the RSA*, p. 6-3-6-18.
15. *TRC report*, Vol. 6, Section 4, Appendix, par. 33.
16. *Ibid.*, Vol. 6, Section 4, Appendix, par. 35.
17. *Ibid.*, Vol. 6, Section 5, Chapter 2, par. 3.
18. *Rapport*, 5 Mei 1996, p. 2.
19. *Rapport*, 10 Mrt. 1996.

20. *TRC report*, Vol. 6, Section 3, Chapter 2, par. 29.
21. *Ibid.*, Vol. 6, Section 3, Chapter 2, par. 85.
22. *Beeld*, 30 Okt. 1998.
23. *Ibid.*, Vol. 6, Section 3, Chapter 2.

APPENDIX A

EXTRACTS FROM *THE CONTACT BUREAU'S ANALYSIS OF THE TRC REPORT,* 19 APRIL 1999.

The Contact Bureau of the SA Defence Force analysed those sections of the TRC Report that were published in October 1998 in which reference was made to the SADF. Comments were incorporated in a document entitled "The Contact Bureau's analysis of the TRC Report". This analysis, dated 19 April 1999, was forwarded to the TRC for their information and reaction.

A number of representative instances are quoted below in order to give an indication of the various incidents, analyses and comments presented to the TRC.

All page numbers refer to the text that follows and all references to the TRC Report are to the first part that was published in October 1998.

1 Quotation from p. 16, par. 72-103:

The TRC's interpretation of the post-1979 military strategy in Angola

The TRC's interpretation of the post-1979 SA Defence Force strategy is as follows:

"The Angolan War was an ongoing, thirteen-year-long occupation, enabling the SA Defence Force to achieve one of its aims namely, the de facto secession of the South from the central government control. This is certainly the view of the former Army and SA Defence Force chief, General Geldenhuys. Writing in his autobiography (*A General's Story,* Chapter 7) he states:

> A few specific cross-border operations made headlines ... Each in turn had a positive influence on the course of the war ... in the end ... it was the overall effect of the almost unseen ... day-to-day general operations that brought us success" (*TRC Report,* Vol. 2, Chapter 2, par. 58).

General Geldenhuys' attention was drawn to this paragraph.

The quote comes from his book, *A General's Story,* Chapter 7. His comments are summarised in the following paragraphs.

This part of the TRC Report is false, deceptive and factually incorrect both in respect of the generalities as well as the specifics.

The view expressed by the TRC in the main body of the paragraph was never the view of the general (Geldenhuys) – not then and not now. And, most importantly, the view as presented to the public by quoting from the book does not, and can not, substantiate the TRC's view. The view and the quotation are chapters and poles apart. They erroneously relate to different **time-periods and places.**

The passage from Chapter 7 of the book, especially in the composite form into which it is juggled in the Report, **reflects on an earlier period!** And the last sentence of the quote does not refer to the operations north-of-the-border, Angola. **It refers to south-of-the-border, Namibia.**

To demonstrate this wilful misinformation, and for ease of reference, the original relevant text from the book, as well as paragraph 58 of the TRC's report (including the composed quote from the book) are given.

Note: The words printed in bold in the left-hand column (see p. 440) are those parts selected and joined together by the TRC. The remainder of the text was left unquoted.

APPENDIX A

The general's book, original text	The TRC Report, text and quote
1. The post-1979 period Quote from Chapter 12 *The cross-border operations up to 1985*, were necessary and well executed. I still believe though, that the accumulated effects of relentless *day to day operations south of the border was vital for our overall success.*	The post-1979 period No quote
2. The period mid-1977 to June 1980 Quote from Chapter 7 **A few specific cross-border operations made headlines.** Operation Reindeer on 4th May 1978 and Operation Sceptic, or Smokeshell on 10 June 1980. Both were particularly significant. **Each, in turn, had a positive influence on the course of the war**. In time other cross-border operations further strengthened our position. The cumulative result of all these operations was one of the most successful counter-insurgency campaigns since World War II. Before providing details of Operation Reindeer, I want to make it clear that **in the end** it was the general ground and air operations that earned us international acclaim. The large scale specific cross-border operations with aim of gaining a winning advantage were dramatic and spectacular. Some of these operations or part of them, were professional phases of war - the subject of books and videos. However, in my opinion **it was the overall effect of the almost unseen** but incessant **day-to-day general operations that brought us success.**	The post-1979 period Text and quote (Chapter 7) The Angolan war was an ongoing thirteen-year-long occupation, enabling the SADF to achieve one of its aims, namely, the de facto secession of the south from the central government control. This is the view of the former army and SADF chief, Gen. Geldenhuys. Writing his autobiography he states : (Quote) **A few specific cross-border operations made head lines** ... [sentence omitted] ... **each in turn, had a positive influence on the course of the war** ... [omission] ... **in the end** ... [omission] ... **it was the overall effect of the almost unseen** ... [omission] ... **day-to-day general operations that brought success** (Unquote)

As can clearly be seen the book very specifically did cover the post-1979 period, namely in Chapter 12, which begins as follows: "The cross-border operations up to 1985 were necessary and well executed. I still believe, though, that the accumulated effects of the **day to day operations south of the border** was vital for our overall success." (Ironically, this chapter is titled "*INFORMATION AND DISINFORMATION*: The massacred village.")

This fits like hand-in-glove with the time frame and subject matter which the TRC addresses. However, they do not quote from this chapter, instead they prefer to quote from chapter 7 fraudulently, implying that it deals with the post-1979 period, and more importantly, that it is all applicable to north-of-the-border, Angola.

This is absolutely unbelievable. Why did those responsible for writing the TRC's reports not quote from the relevant chapters? (It is so easy. The book was written in chronological order. Chapter 6, 7, 8, 9, and 10, all inclusive, deal mainly with the period up to June 1980, while chapters 11, 12, etc. deal with the period thereafter.)

There is only one logical answer to the question why the TRC quoted from the wrong chapter. The main view of the TRC as stated in its paragraph 58, Chapter 2, Vol. 2, is that an ongoing occupation enabled the Defence Force to achieve its aim of forcing a de facto secession of the south of Angola – for which the general claimed success in his book.

On the one hand the general's book is often internationally quoted as an authoritative source on the subject. Quoting from it would give the TRC's view credibility.

On the other hand, however, even a lay person would know that to successfully maintain a long occupation and force a secession would require massive continued force levels, executing extensive and high density, incessant operations over a long period, on a daily basis.

The TRC creates the false impression that this was indeed the case, firstly by **piling operations from the pre-1979 period onto those of the post-1979 period as if it all happened in the post-1979 period.**

Secondly, **the TRC jams day-to-day operations which took place in Namibia into the Angola scene as if it all happened there.**

The quote from the book under discussion relates specifically to the pre-1980 period. When it was the Defence Force's aim to keep acts of terror in Namibia at a manageable level until the political solution was found. That was certainly what was achieved and what he described as successful.

The 1979/1980 yearbook of the Institute for the Study of Conflict in London described South Africa's military action in SWA/Namibia as follows: "An outstanding example of a successfully counterinsurgency offensive taken at an early stage of the conflict."

This is very serious.

General Geldenhuys did not study this part of the TRC's report with a magnifying glass seeking for hidden microscopic bits of petty human error.

If the misrepresentations were merely the result of cut-and-paste fluffing by naïve innocent ignorants it might have been overlooked. But the TRC has already denied the accusation that researchers, compilers and their overseers were young and inexperienced university students. They were competent and well suited for the task.

If the consequences of the deliberate distortions were not so far-reaching and damaging that it cannot be overlooked.

While the **obvious** play with words, paragraphs and chapters results in such deliberate misrepresentation of **factualities**, one squirms to think how the **less obvious** play with logic results in false **argument**. In any event one cannot reach a truthful view if it is based on distorted fact.

If one writes that a statement is certainly the view of a person, quoting him to support that statement, then the quote must do that. If it does not, then something is seriously wrong, as in this case, especially since the TRC's reports are regarded nationally and internationally as extremely important documents.

It contains the TRC's views after close on three years of research, investigation, hearings and deliberations. The writers and overseers of this part did not have to write it in a hurry as it was not dependent upon last minute-hearings. They must surely held accountable.

The compilers would have known that at least Gen. Geldenhuys would pick up the trickery. Maybe they argued: So what? He is only one person but thousands of other readers are unlikely to know better.

Perhaps they were careless and insensitive to bungling even if it did affect the lives of other people. On the other hand, this type of arrogance is more often than not found in persons holding high positions of authority.

In trying to find an explanation for this deliberate distortion of the facts, it would almost seem as if a key figure had made up his mind how the truth in the reports should read and then ordered the researchers and writers to do it.

Perhaps another or complementary possible explanation may be found in the general's book.

2 Quotation from p. 20, par. 100-103

The reality of disinformation to be reckoned with in investigating the truth about the past.

(General Geldenhuys) writes many passages in his book (A General's Story) about how thick the air was with propaganda during the armed conflict, about the trickery with information, misinformation, disinformation etc., the propaganda about creating perceptions of who the good guys were and the bad ones. He included lists of factually false perceptions created in the process. He claims that South Africa and the SA Defence Force certainly lost the propaganda war around the armed conflict.

In Chapter 12, "Information and Disinformation: *The Massacred Village*, he quotes the architect and engineer of a sensational hoax to the effect that a Namibian village was "wiped out by the Boers". The man responsible for this was SWAPO's Secretary for Information, Andreas Shipanga. The latter tells in detail in his book, *In Search of Freedom*, how he managed to create this lie which caused a sensational commotion.

The General also states in his book, Chapter 20, "Revolutionary Politics: Perceptions and False Perceptions – 'The Pig in the middle'": "The problem is that propaganda is being used during times of conflict to create false perceptions for political gain. However, in the following phase of reconciliation, they are being kept alive and obstructing the peace process."

The TRC fell into a trap of trying anew to substantiate old false perceptions.

3   Quotation from p. 26, par. 126

Unspecified allegations of torture at Osiri

The TRC reports that "captured combatants were kept in makeshift detention centres, such as the camp at Osiri, 160 kilometres north of Windhoek, where they were interrogated and often tortured …" (TRC Report, Vol. 2, Chapter 2, par. 102). The report does not mention that the SA Defence Force was not the responsible authority at Osiri. It also fails to mention that there were two places called Osiri. The other Osiri was at Oshakati where the Defence Force Sector 10 Headquarters was situated. It was also a place of detention, initially constructed in a temporary fashion but later replaced with a permanent building. The detainees in this Osiri were frequently visited by a representative of the International Red Cross, who did not find reason to complain. The allegation of gross violation of human rights by the Defence Force in Osiri is therefore not substantiated and rejected.

4   Quotation from p. 26-28, par. 127-131

Substantiation of TRC findings based on lies

The following is a paraphrase of paragraphs 127-131.

The TRC relies on the amnesty application by a SA Defence Force conscript, Mr. Kevin Hall, to report certain **atrocities** by himself and some other troops in **May/June 1975** (TRC Report, Vol. 2, Chapter 2, par. 105-107). He was allegedly ordered to **carry out a contact**. This allegation as well as the **execution of the contact** as described by himself, is a false concoction. Research was done to determine Mr Hall's credibility. The results are as follows:

According to his personal file:
- Did his basic training at Walvis Bay, 7 January to 14 March 1975.
- Served at Equestrian Centre, Potchefstroom, 17 March 1975 to 6 January 1976.
- Joined Potgietersrust Commando in April 1976 where he attended a number of camps, this includes:
- Five one month camps at the Northern Transvaal border.
- One three month camp at Sector 20 (Kavango), i.e. NE area of SWA/N during period 19 August 1982 to 7 November 1982.

His service record reveals the following;
- He had long stints of light duty/hospitalisation. Started during basic training and continued as he served in the Potgietersrust Commando.
- His training results were poor. Failed in most tests and courses.

He has a questionable disciplinary record. Twice convicted, once for absence without leave, and once for failing to obey a lawful command.

Rifleman Hall never served on the SWA border in 1975. A border service record completed by Hall himself also made no mention of such a stint of border duty. Furthermore, the unit to which Hall belonged until his departure to the Equestrian Centre at Potchefstroom, was scheduled to deploy in the SWA border area for the first time during August 1975, at least two months later than his alleged experience.

No incident, described by Hall, occurred anywhere in the border area during 1975.

Research was done to establish whether the incident perhaps occurred in Kavango during Hall's border duty from August to November 1982, the only time that Hall served on the SWA border as a member of 1 RNT (First Northern Transvaal Regiment). It was found that:
a. Mapungeerela base never existed ...
b. The nature and pattern of incidents which took place in Kavango over this period did not even remotely coincide with the incident described by Hall. Colonel G.C. van Rooyen who served at Rundu at the time, stated that a contact of that magnitude would have established an all time record for Sector 20 and would have been known and reported in the media.

APPENDIX A

c. The action alleged to have taken place by the Security Forces is in total contrast with all practices and drills practiced by them at the time, e.g.
   i. The "dead combatants" would have been identified and follow-up operations, involving helicopter gun ships would have been launched as a matter of great urgency.
   ii. Captured insurgents, particularly the wounded, were the most valuable sources of information. The killing of wounded as described by Hall would have resulted in severe disciplinary steps against him and his superiors.
   iii. Hall's patrol would have been replenished and most likely relieved after such a contact. The incident would most certainly have been exploited to the full for propaganda purposes.
   iv. Captured insurgents were never kept in holes in the ground, but were always evacuated to the Sector Headquarters for secondary phase questioning by intelligence specialists as a matter of urgency.
   v. Hall was clearly unsuitable to serve in a position of authority. It is inconceivable that he would or could unilaterally take such action.

Deductions:

a. It can be proved that the incident reported by Rifleman Hall never took place. This information is readily accessible and available.
b. If one mistake of this nature could be made by the TRC, the credibility of other reported occurrences, based on untested hearsay evidence, which appear frequently in the report, must be questioned.

5 Quotation from p. 31, par. 143

Commandant Salmon Pienaar incorrectly implicated

The TRC Report stated that Commandant Salmon Pienaar (SA Defence Force) was "amongst those who decided on and tasked the ten members of the SA Railway Police (SARP) task force to obtain a railway vehicle and conduct the first Trojan Horse operation." The Commission subsequently finds that Pienaar as one of the "thirteen senior and junior members of the SA Police, SA Defence Force, SA Railway Police, [who] in conjunction with the relevant structures of the Joint Management Centre planned and executed an action in Athlone which resulted in several gross violations of human rights" (TRC Report, Vol. 3, Chapter 5, par. 173).

The facts of the situation are:

a. As SA Army representative on the Joint Operation Centre, he could not have been involved in authorising a SA Railway Police operation.
b. He was, surprisingly, subpoenaed to appear in the Cape Supreme Court on a charge of murder where no evidence was brought against him, and where he was found not guilty.
c. At a TRC hearing he again explained his position with respect to the incident. His legal advisor at the hearing, Advocate Piet de Jager, requested the TRC to refrain from implicating him in this case.
d. The TRC, however, persisted in implicating him as a perpetrator in its report.

6 Quotation from p. 32-33, par. 149, 152 and 153:

Other improper accusations

SA Defence Force blamed for SA Police actions in Queenstown. In the TRC's reporting on the killing of people in Queenstown in November 1985, it is to be noted that throughout the text, preceding the summary, allegations of massacres are levelled at the police. Yet in the summary and in the finding the SA Defence Force is blamed together with the SA Police for "criminal negligence for the lives of human beings, and is held accountable for the killing of an estimated number of eighty people during the five named massacres in 1985 (TRC Report, Vol. 3, Chapter 2, par. 197-202).

Par. 152
Untested evidence used to make findings. A certain Captain Nel is extensively quoted regarding TREWITS and target intelligence. No proof can, however, be found in the TRC Report that any of his statements were ever substantiated by any of the other persons mentioned. **It appears that his untested statements were found "more suitable" in their raw and untested form.** This attitude in the TRC allowed it to find the Minister of Defence and the Chiefs of the Defence Force, officers commanding Special Forces, etc. to be accountable for the extra-judicial killing of political opponents (TRC Report, Vol. 2, Chapter 3, par. 509).

Par. 153
Unreliable sources led to unsubstantiated allegations by the TRC. The TRC appears to have had to rely on any source, no matter how unreliable, as long as the source would serve the TRC's prejudged ideas, perceptions and and its obvious determination to attempt to completely ridicule the SA Defence Force. In this respect the following questions still need to be answered:
a. Who was the Military Intelligence member who was in Kosi Bay, who alleged that they all thought: "This is it, ...the kaffirs, this is the time to sort them out." (Paragraph 500, Chapter 7, Volume 2)? Who were the "we" he claimed to quote?
b. Who was the faceless Military Intelligence operative quoted regarding the train violence, taxi wars, Boipatong and the creation of anarchy? Why was his evidence accepted for inclusion in the first report without any substantiating evidence or cross-examination (TRC Report, Vol. 2, Chapter 7, par. 504)?
c. Why were the deductions/allegations as alleged to have been put by a former deputy chief of staff intelligence regarding the "increased tendency to tell the politicians what they wanted to hear", and a "culture of covering up illegal actions", which gave "'certain sectors" of the security forces "carte blanche to engage in operations that are clearly dubious" not substantiated by other evidence/witnesses? Our experience in general is that this perception which was found acceptable by the TRC for inclusion in their report was in contrast to the Defence Force's convictions (TRC Report, Vol. 2, Chapter 7, par. 528).

BIBLIOGRAPHY

A

African National Congress. *s.a. Die herkoms van die African National Congress.* Unpublished document in possession of author.

African National Congress. 1986. Death of Pres. Machel. *News Briefing*, 10(44), 2 Nov.

African National Congress. 1986. Death of Pres. Machel. *News Briefing*, 10(46), 16 Nov.

African National Congress. 1987. Towards a people's war and insurrection. *Sechaba*. Apr.

African National Congress. 1996. *Submission to the Truth and Reconciliation Commission.* 19 Aug.

Anonymous. 1990. Waardes van genl. Magnus Malan. *Modderfonteiner.* Nov.

Armscor. *SA Defence Industry Directory 2002-2003.* Pretoria: Armscor.

B

Barnard, S.L. 1991. 'n Historiese oorsig van die gewapende konflik aan die noordgrens van SWA/Namibië, 1966-1989. *Acta Academica*, 23(1): 102-127.

Benson, Mary. 1993. *Nelson Mandela: The man and the movement.* London: Penguin.

Berger, P.L.; Godsell, Bobby (eds.). 1988. *A future South Africa: visions, strategies and realities.* Cape Town: Human & Rousseau.

Birmingham, David. 1995. *The decolonization of Africa*. London: University College of London Press.
Botha, R.F. 1997. Main points of Statement: TRC Hearing of State Security Council, 14 Oct.
Breytenbach, Jan. 1986. *Forged in battle*. Cape Town: Saayman & Weber.
Breytenbach, Jan. 1990. *They live by the sword: 32 "Buffalo" Batallion - South Africa's foreign legion*. Alberton: Lemur.
Bridgland, Fred. 1990. *The war for Africa: Twelve months that transformed a continent*. Gibraltar: Ashanti Press.
Bruwer, J.P. van S. 1966. *South-West Africa: The disputed land*. Cape Town: Nasionale Boekhandel.

C

Cabinet of the Republic of South Africa. 1980. *Die RSA se belange en die RSA-regering se doel, doelstellings en beleid vir ordelike regering asook riglyne vir die uiteindelike staatkundige bestel van Suider-Afrika* (die *Groenboek*). Unpublished minutes of a Cabinet meeting held on 4 March. Secret.
Cabinet of the Republic of South Africa. 1986. Minutes of a Cabinet meeting held on 16 July 1986. Attached to Memo HSAW Kaap/UG/521/2/2/3.
Cabinet of the Republic of South Africa. 1986. Minutes of a Cabinet meeting held on 11 June 1986.
Cameron, Trewhella (hoofred.). 1987. *Nuwe Geskiedenis van Suid-Afrika*. Kaapstad: Human & Rousseau.
Campbell, Keith, 1986. ANC - *A Soviet Task Force?* Norfolk: Thetford Press.
Chabal, Patrick; Birmingham, David; Forrest, Joshua; Newitt, Maly; Seibert, Gerhard; Nadrade, Elisa Silva. 2002. *A history of postcolonial Lusophone Africa*. London: Hurst & Co.
Chief of the SA Defence Force. 1981. Briefing to the Cabinet of the RSA. Unpublished document. 4 Jun.
Cilliers, Jackie; Reichardt, Markus. 1995. *About Turn*. Pretoria: Institute for Defence Policy.
Coetzer, J.P.J. 2000. *Gister se dade, vandag se oordeel*. Pretoria: JP van der Walt.

Contact Bureau of the former SADF. 1998. Complaints in respect of the TRC's handling of the former SADF and its members. Unpublished documents submitted to the TRC. 29 Jan.

Contact Bureau of the former SADF. 1998. Assessment of the probable results of activities of the TRC as perceived by the former Chiefs of the SADF. Unpublished document submitted to the TRC. 6 Feb.

Contact Bureau of the former SADF. 1998. Supplementary submission by former Chiefs of the SADF: Factors determining the volume and quality of information supplied to the TRC by them and the number of applications for amnesty by members of the SADF. Unpublished document submitted to the TRC. 14 May.

Contact Bureau of the former SADF. 1998. Memorandum by former Chiefs of the SADF. Unpublished document submitted to the TRC. Jun.

Contact Bureau of the former SADF. 1998. Complaints i.r.o the TRC's handling of the former SADF and its members. Unpublished document submitted to the TRC. 25 Aug.

Contact Bureau of the former SADF. 1999. The Contact Bureau's analysis of the TRC Report. Unpublished document submitted to the TRC. 19 Apr.

Contact Bureau of the former SADF. 1999. Press release: Release of the Contact Bureau's analysis of the TRC Report. 29 Apr.

D

Departement van Verdediging. 1957. *Verdedigingswet no. 44 van 1957*. Cape Town: Parliament.

De Klerk, F.W. 1998. *Die laaste trek – 'n nuwe begin*. Kaapstad: Human & Rousseau.

De Kock, W.J.; Krüger, D.W. 1972. *Suid-Afrikaanse Biografiese Woordeboek*. Vol. II. Kaapstad: Tafelberg.

De Villiers, Dirk & Johanna. 1994. *PW*. Kaapstad: Tafelberg.

Du Preez, Sophia. 1989. *Avontuur in Angola: Die verhaal van Suid-Afrika se soldate in Angola 1975–1976*. Pretoria: J.L. van Schaik.

E

Els, Paul. *We Fear Naught but God: The story of the South African Special Forces.* Johannesburg: Covos Day.

F

Former Chiefs of the SADF. 1997. Second appearance before the TRC. 7-10 Oct.

Fourie, Brand. 1992. *Buitelandse Woelinge om SA 1939-1985.* Unpublished manuscript in posession of author.

Frankel, Philip H. 1984. *Pretoria's Praetorians: Civil-military relations in South Africa.* Cambridge: Cambridge University Press.

Fraser, genl. C.A. 1958. *Revolusionêre oorlogvoering: Grondbeginsels van opstandsbekamping* (revised edition of *Lesson learnt from past revolutionary wars*). Pretoria: SAW.

G

Geldenhuys, Jannie. 1993. *A General's story.* Pretoria: J.L. van Schaik.

Geldenhuys, Jannie. 1993. *Dié wat wen. 'n Generaal se storie uit 'n era van oorlog en vrede.* Pretoria: J.L. van Schaik.

Giniewski, Paul. 1966. *Die stryd om Suidwes-Afrika.* Kaapstad: Nasionale Boekhandel.

Greig, Ian. 1977. *The communist challenge to Africa: An analysis of contemporary Soviet, Chinese & Cuban policies.* Richmond: Foreign Affairs Publishing Co.

H

Hamann, Hilton. 2001. *Days of the Generals.* Cape Town: Zebra Press.

Hamann, Hilton. 2002. Ek skaam my nie. *Insig,* Aug.: 52-53.

Parliament of the RSA. *Hansard*:
  17 Apr. 1978 (The USA and Angola);
  24 Sept. 1981 (Government's security policy);
  24 Sept. 1981 (Onslaught against Southern Africa);
  28 and 29 May 1985 (Gathering of information; allegations about the

SADF's destabilising neighbouring states; so-called violation of Lusaka Accord; SADF caused a credibility crisis for SA);
2 Feb. 1986 (The "need to know" principle and Parliament);
4 Feb. 1986 (Government policy and co-operation with neighbouring states);
11 Feb.1986 (Right to know and cross-border operations);
14 May 1986 (Requirements set to the SADF and chemical needs);
14 Sept.1987 (SADF and internal actions);
15 Sept.1987 (Security needs to ensure national security);
15 Sept.1987 (Propaganda onslaught and Pres. Samora Machel's aeroplane accident);
17 May 1988 (Armscor and operations at the Lomba River near Cuito Cuanavale);
18 May 1988 (Terrorists and guerillas);
17 and 18 Sept. 1988 (Specific tasks and directives to the SADF; nature, extent and essence of revolutionary onslaught);
Feb. 1989 (South-Western Africa and Angola);
20 Feb. 1989 (Defence posture and finances);
3 May 1989 (Armaments trade);
20 and 21 Apr. 1989 (SWAPO's violation of the Genève Protocol and South Africa's investment in SWA/N);
26 Feb. 1990 (The CCB and the Lubowski case);
6 Feb. 1991 (CCB);
24 Mar. 1993 (Dismantling of nuclear capability).

Harms, the Honourable Justice L.T.C. 1990. *Commission of Inquiry into Certain Alleged Murders*. Pretoria: Staatsdrukker.

Heitman, Helmoed-Römer. 1985. *Die Suid-Afrikaanse krygsmag*. Johannesburg: Bison Books.

Heitman, Helmoed-Römer. 1990a. *South African armed forces*. Cape Town: Buffalo.

Heitman, Helmoed-Römer. 1990b. *War in Angola. The final South African Phase*. Gibraltar: Ashanti.

Heitman, H.-R; Dörning, W.A. 1988. The Joint Monitoring Commission. *Militaria*, 18(1).

Holtzhausen, Raymond. 2001. Utilization of Human Resources. *History Project: Former SADF 1960 to 1990*. Aug.

Hough, M. (ed.) 2004. *The external threat.* Instituut vir Strategiese Studies, Universiteit van Pretoria. Unpublished research report.
Hough, M. (red.). 1981. *Nasionale veiligheid en strategie met spesifieke verwysing na die RSA.* Instituut vir Strategiese Studies, Universiteit van Pretoria. Aug.
Howlett, Darryl; Simpson, John. 1993. Nuclearisation and denuclearisation in South Africa. *Survival,* 35(3): 154-173.

I
International Defence and Aid Fund. 1988. *Review of 1988: Repression and resistance in South Africa and Namibia.*

J
Jeffery, Anthea. 1999. *The truth about the Truth Commission.* Johannesburg: South African Institute of Race Relations.
Jenkins, Tim. 1995. Talking to Vula: The story of the secret underground communication network of Operation Vula. *Mayibuye,* May-Oct.
Johnson, Paul. 1994. *Modern times. A history of the world from the twenties to the year 2000.* Guernsey: Guernsey Press.
Johnson, R.W. 1997. South Africa's new problems. *Wall Street Journal,* 19 Sept. 1997.

K
Kittrie, Nicholas N. 1998. *The war against authority: From the crisis of legitimacy to a new social order.* Baltimore: Johns Hopkins.
Koster, J.D. 1986. *The influence of the South African Communist Party on the African National Congress.* RAU: Centre for the Investigation into Revolutionary Activities.
Kotze, D.A. 1975. Kommunisme in Suid-Afrika: Verlede, hede en toekoms. Herfsskool van die Universiteit van Stellenbosch, 1-4 Apr. 1975. Unpublished paper.

L

Liberman, Peter. 2001. The rise and fall of the South African bomb. *International Security*, 26(2): 45-86.

Lord, Dick. 2000. *Vlamgat*. Pretoria: Covos Day.

Lord, Dick. 2001. *Fire, Flood and Ice*. Pretoria: Covos Day.

M

Mackenzie-Hoy, Terry. 2003. Samora Machel: Did we do it? *Engineering News*, Jan./Feb. 2003.

Malan, M.A. de M. 1980. Die totale aanslag teen die RSA. C.R. Swart lecture no. 13, University of the Orange Free State, Bloemfontein, 19 Sept.

Malan, M.A. de M. 1987. Die uitdagings wat SA in die uitvoering van sy nasionale veiligheid in die gesig staar. Speech delivered to the Council of South Africa, Cape Sun, Cape Town, 11 Nov.

Malan, M.A. de M. 1990. 'n Veiligheidsvisie vir Suider-Afrika. Lecture delivered to the Instituut vir Strategiese Studies, University of Pretoria, 16 Okt.

Malan, M.A. de M. 1990. Speech delivered at the celebration of the 75th birthday of the South African Defence Force, Potchefstroom, 1 Jul.

Malan, M.A. de M. 1997. Voluntary evidence before the TRC, 7 May.

Malan, M.A. de M. 1997. Second session of voluntary evidence before the TRC, 4-5 Dec.

Mandela, Nelson. 1994. *Long Walk to Freedom*. Randburg: Macdonald Purnell.

Margo, Cecil. 1998. *Final postponements. Reminiscences of a crowded life*. Johannesburg: Jonathan Ball.

Mamdani, Mahmood. 2004. *Good Muslim, bad Muslim*. New York: Pantheon Books, Random House.

Maritz, Sam. 1997. Operation Marion: Submissions on behalf of Genls. Malan and Van Tonder to the TRC. Jul.

Ministerial press releases. 1990. Sebokeng incident; the CCB; report of the Harms Commission of Inquiry. 5 Sept., 4 Oct., 13 Nov.

Ministerial press release. 1991. The CCB. 7 Mar.

Ministeriële Komitee van Ondersoek. 1985. Verslag van die Ministeriële Komitee van Ondersoek in verband met die toekomsbeplanning van die SAW en verwante Krygkoraspekte. HSAW/503/1/B 29 Nov. (Uiters geheim.)

Muller C.F.J. (red.). 1975. *Vyfhonderd jaar Suid-Afrikaanse Geskiedenis.* Pretoria: Academica.

Murphy, G.H.P (Gen. Gerrit). 1987. *Geskiedenis van die Witwatersrandse Gesamentlike Bestuursentrum (WITGBS), 1984-1986.* Unpublished interdepartemental Defence Force Report. Sept.

N

Netanyahu, Benjamin (ed.). 1986. *Terrorism: How the west can win.* New York: Farrar, Straus & Giroux/London: Weidenfeld & Nicolson.

Nöthling, C.J. 1989. Kort kroniek van militêre operasies en optredes in SWA en Angola (1914-1988). *Militaria,* 19(2).

O

Olivier, G.C. 1977. *Suid-Afrika se buitelandse beleid.* Pretoria: Academica.

Osanka, Franklin Mark. 1962. *Modern guerrilla warfare: fighting communist guerrilla movements, 1941-1961.* New York: Free Press of Glencoe.

Owen, Ken. 1997. So what did they do in the war, daddy? *Leadership,* vol. 16.

P

Prinsloo, Daan. 1997. *Stem uit die Wildernis. 'n Biografie oor oud-pres. P.W. Botha.* Mosselbaai: Vaandel.

R

Renwick, Robin. 1997. *Unconventional diplomacy in Southern Africa.* Basingstoke: Macmillan.

Republiek van Suid-Afrika. 1984. *Suid-Afrika 1984: Amptelike jaarboek van die Republiek van Suid-Afrika.* Pretoria: Staatsdrukker.

Republiek van Suid-Afrika. 1992. *Suid-Afrika 1991-1992: Amptelike jaarboek van die Republiek van Suid-Afrika.* Pretoria: Staatsdrukker.
Roherty, James Michael. 1991. *State security in South Africa. Civil-military relations under PW Botha.* New York: White Plains.

S
SABC 2. *Forum.* Freek Robinson. 24 Jun. 1998.
SABC 1. TRC Special Report. 20 Apr. 1997.
Scholtz, Leopold. 1997. Die oorlog was nie vergeefs. *Insig,* Sept.
Schweizer, Peter. 2002. *Reagan's war: The epic story of his forty year struggle and his final triumph over communism.* New York: Doubleday.
South Africa. Defence Force. ±1985-1990. Monitoring of Radio Freedom and others. SADF: Unpublished internal reports.
South Africa. Department of Defence. 1971. *Review of Defence and Armaments Production period 1960-1970.* Pretoria: Government Printers.
South Africa. Department of Defence. 1973. *White Paper on Defence and Armament Production, 1973.* Cape Town: Parliament.
South Africa. Department of Defence. 1975. *White Paper on Defence and Armament Production, 1975.* Cape Town: Parliament.
South Africa. Department of Defence. 1977. *White Paper on Defence, 1977.* Cape Town: Parliament.
South Africa. Department of Defence. 1979. *White Paper on Defence and Armaments Supply, 1979.* Cape Town: Parliament.
South Africa. Department of Defence. 1982. *White Paper on Defence and Armaments Supply, 1982.* Cape Town: Parliament.
South Africa. Department of Defence. 1984. *White Paper on Defence and Armaments Supply, 1984.* Cape Town: Parliament.
South Africa. Department of Defence. 1984. *White Paper on the Organisation and Functions of the South African Defence Force and the Armaments Corporation of South Africa Limited, 1984.* Cape Town: Parliament.
South Africa. Department of Defence. 1986. *White Paper on Defence and Armaments Supply, 1986.* Cape Town: Parliament.
South Africa. Department of Defence. 1987. *Briefing on the Organisation*

and Functions of the South African Defence Force and the Armaments Corporation of South Africa Limited, 1987. Cape Town: Parliament.

South Africa. Department of Defence. 1989. *White Paper on the Planning Process of the South African Defence Force, 1989.* Cape Town: Parliament.

South Africa. Department of Defence. 1990. *Briefing on the Organisation and functions of the South African Defence Force and the Armaments Corporation of South Africa Limited, 1990.* Cape Town: Parliament.

South Africa. National Defence Force Nodal Point. 1996. Written submission in reference of the former SADF. Unpublished document submitted to the TRC. 8 Oct.

South Africa. National Defence Force Nodal Point. 1997. Answers to questions arising from the SADF submission of 8 Oct 1996. Unpublished document submitted to the TRC. 10 Jun.

South Africa. National Defence Force Nodal Point. 1997. Defence Force involvement in the internal security situation in the Republic of South Africa from 1976 to 1994. Confidential document submitted to the TRC. Aug.

South Africa. National Defence Force Nodal Point. 1997. Additional submission with regard to the former SADF. Unpublished document submitted to the TRC. Aug./Sept.

South Africa. National Defence Force Nodal Point. 1997. The Steyn Report. *Additional submission with regard to the former SADF.* Unpublished document submitted to the TRC. Aug./Sept., Chapter 6: 6-1-6-18.

South African Institute of Race Relations. 1996. Malan: A disgraceful episode. *Fast Facts.* Nov. Johannesburg: SAIRR.

Spies, F.J. du T. *Operasie Savannah: Angola. 1975-1976.* Pretoria: SAW (Direktoriaat Openbare Betrekkinge).

State Security Council (SSC). Minutes:
  SSC 3/79.
  SSC 6/79.
  SSC 14/79.
  SSC 12/83, Appendix B, ref. SSC/22/3/2/1.
  SSC 17/85.
  SSC 21, Oct. 1985.

SSC 20, Dec. 1985.
SSC 1/86.
SSC 5/86.
SSC 14/86.
SSC 20/86.
Stadler, H.D. 1997. *The other side of the story: A true perspective*. Pretoria: Sigma Press.
Steenkamp, Willem. 1990. *Suid-Afrika se grensoorloog 1966-1989*. Rivonia: Ashanti.
Steenkamp, Willem. 1983. *Borderstrike! South Africa into Angola*. Durban: Butterworth.
Steyn, Hannes; Van der Walt, Richardt; Van Loggerenberg, Jan. 2003. *Armament and disarmament: South Africa's nuclear weapons experience*. Pretoria: Network Publishers.
Stiff, Peter. 1989. *Nine days of war*. Alberton: Galago/Lemur.
Stiff, Peter. 2001. *Warfare by other means: South Africa in the 1980s and 1990s*. Alberton: Galago.
Stiff, Peter. 1999. *The silent war: South African recce operations 1969-1994*. Alberton: Galago.
Strachan, Alexander. 2002. Smokeshell, Askari, Savannah ... *Insig*, Aug.
Stumpf, Waldo. 1995. South Africa's nuclear weapons program. From deterrence to dismantlement. *Arms control today*, 25(10), Dec.-Jan. 1995/96.
Sun Tzu. 1963, 1971. *The art of war*. Griffith, Samuel B. (transl.). London: Oxford University Press.
Supreme Court of the Republic of South Africa (Durban and Coast Local Division). 1996. *Supreme Court records and judgement: Operation Marion*, vol. 57 and 58. Durban. October.
Sutherland, Frank. 1992. How the splitting of Armscor came about. *Krygcom*. March.
Suzman, Helen. 1993. *In no uncertain terms*. Johannesburg: Jonathan Ball.

T

Truth and Reconciliation Commission of South Africa. 1998. *Truth and Reconciliation Commission of South Africa Report*. Vol. 1-5. Cape Town: Juta.

Truth and Reconciliation Commission of South Africa. 2002. *Truth and Reconciliation Commission of South Africa Report.* Vol. 7. Cape Town: Juta.
Truth and Reconciliation Commission of South Africa. 2003. *Truth and Reconciliation Commission of South Africa Report.* Vol. 6. Cape Town: Juta.
Truth and Reconciliation Commission of South Africa. 1997. TRC findings in respect of the involvement of members of the SADF, the SAP and members of Inkatha in Operation Marion. TRC hearing in Durban. Jul.

V

Van Bergen, C.J. 1981. *Die vyf Wesmagstate en die SWA-skikkingsonderhandelings (1978-1979).* Unpublished M.A. thesis, University of Pretoria.
Van der Waals, W.S. 1990. *Portugal's war in Angola.* Rivonia: Ashanti.
Van der Westhuizen L.J.; Le Roux, J.H. 1997. *The leading edge.* Unpublished manuscript compiled for Armscor. In posession of the Institute for Contemporary History, University of the Free State, Bloemfontein.
Van Wyk, At. 1982. *Honoris Crux. Ons dapperes.* Kaapstad: Saayman & Weber.
Van Wyk, At. 1985. *Honoris Crux. Ons dapperes II.* Kaapstad: Saayman & Weber.
Van Zyl, Frans. 1977. Groot lieg; waarheid of leuen? *Insig,* Des.
Varney, Howard (convenor). 1997. The role of the former state in political violence. Operation Marion: a case study. Unpublished paper submitted to the TRC.
Venter, Al. J. (ed.). 1989. *Challenge: Southern Africa within the African revolutionary context: An overview.* Gibraltar: Ashanti.
Venter, Albert. 1997. Is die een se terroris die ander se vryheidsvegter? *Rapport,* 11 Mei.
Venter, A.J. 1988. Teorieë oor revolusie. Unpublished lecture to the SA Defence College. Jun.
Viljoen, G. van N. 1981. *Ideaal en werklikheid.* Kaapstad: Tafelberg.
Von Clausewitz, Carl. 1968. *On war.* Edited and with an introduction by Anatol Rapoport. Harmondsworth: Penguin.

W

Waldmeir, Patti. 1998. *Anatomy of a miracle: The end of apartheid and the birth of the new South Africa.* Harmondsworth: Penguin.

Walker, Walter. 1978. *The bear at the back door.* Sandton: Valiant.

Z

Zedong, Mao. 1976. *Quotations from Chairman Mao Tse-Tung.* Peking: Foreign Language Press.

NEWSPAPERS

Beeld: 29 Jul. 1976, 5 Feb. 1977, 11 Okt. 1982, 31 Okt. 1986, 23 Mrt. 1987, 31 Okt. 1988, 10 Mrt. 1989, 6 Sept. 1990, 15 Nov. 1991, 19 Nov. 1991, 4 Sept. 1992, 2 Nov. 1995, 6 Nov. 1995, 20 Jan. 1997, 5 Sept. 1998, 15 Jun. 1998, 30 Okt. 1998, 25 Jul. 1999, 25 Sept. 2001.

Burger, Die: 20 Feb. 1979, 17 Feb. 1981, 1 Mei 1984, 17 Mei 1988, 8 Feb. 1989, 20 Feb. 1990, 2 Jul. 1990, 27 Apr. 1991, 8 Mei 1997, 24 Des. 2001.

Business Day: 19 May 1989, 24/25 Mar. 1993.

Cape Times: 24 Oct. 1977, 24 Jan. 1978, 20 May 1983, 24 Mar. 2004.

Cape Argus: 24 Jan. 1978, 12 Mar. 1986, 3 Jun. 1987, 11 Nov. 1987, 27 Feb. 1990.

Citizen: 9 May 1979, 20 Feb. 1988, 26 Feb. 1990, 31 Jul. 1991, 4 Feb. 1993, 24/25 Mar. 1993, 22 May 1999.

Christian Science Monitor: 9 Jan. 1981.

Daily News: 16 Sept. 1986.

Financial Mail: 10 Nov. 1995, 28 Apr. 1989.

Financial Times (Weekend): 12/13 Oct. 1996.

Friend, The: 28 Jul. 1976.

Hoofstad: 19 Aug. 1977.

Mail and Guardian: 30 Oct. 1998.

New York Times: 7 Sept. 1981.

Pretoria News: 17 Oct. 1978, 13 Jun. 1979, 21 Apr. 1989, 5 Oct. 1990, 10 Oct. 1990.

Oosterlig: 29 1979, 15 Mrt. 1983.
Rapport: 24 Apr. 1988, 6 Nov. 1988, 15 Okt. 1989, 7 Feb. 1993, 29 Okt. 1995, 25 Nov. 1995, 22 Sept. 1996, 8 Des. 1996, 15 Des. 1996,19 Jan. 1997, 27 Apr. 1997, 11 Mei 1997, 26 Jul. 1998, 9 Aug. 1998, 11 Okt. 1998, 23 Okt. 2005.
The Star: 25 Jul. 1984, 12 Feb. 1986, 19 May 1989, 3 Dec. 1989, 18 Aug. 1994.
St. Petersburg Times: 14 Sept. 2001.
Suidwester, Die: 6 Apr. 1977.
Sunday Times: 13 Mar. 1977, Apr. 1977, 26 Aug. 1990, 19 Jan. 1997.
The Times of London: 12 Oct. 1996.
Transvaler, Die: 13 Aug. 1976, 23 Jan. 1978.
Vaderland, Die: 11 Okt. 1985.

JOURNALS

Africa Confidential, Volume 29, No. 16.
African National Congress. 1981. *In Combat, January 1980-August 1981*. Sept.
African National Congress. 1985. *Sechaba*. Aug.
African National Congress. 1990. *Sechaba*. Feb.
Armscor. 1981. *Salvo*, vol. 2. Pretoria: Corporate Communication, Armscor.
Armscor. 1989. *Salvo*, vol. 2. Pretoria: Corporate Communication, Armscor.
Armscor. 1998. *Salvo*, vol. 1. Pretoria: Corporate Communication, Armscor.
South Africa. National Defence Force. 1995. *Salut. Official monthly periodical of the SANDF.* Apr. Pretoria: SANDF.
South Africa. National Defence Force. 1997. *Salut. Official monthly periodical of the SANDF.* Nov. Pretoria: SANDF.
South African Defence Force. 1979. *Militaria.* Official professional journal of the SADF. Directorate Public Relations, 9(2).
South African Defence Force. 1976. *Paratus.* Aug.
South African Defence Force. 1993. *Paratus.* Mar.

INDEX

m = map
p = photograph

1 Military Area, 112-113, 118, 120, 128, 131, 135
101 Battalion, 268, 276
101 Task Force, 120-121, 133, 135
2 Battalion Group, 50
2 SA Infantry Battalion, 113
21 Battalion, 176
301 Air Component, 121
32 Battalion, 267-268, 275
61st Mechanised Battalion Group, 267, 275

Accra, 66
Ackerman, Ronnie, 28
Adis Abeba, 67, 131
Advena, 217
Afghanistan, 157, 263, 329, 392
Africa
    anti-communist countries, 249
    colonisation, 65
    communist countries, 113, 130
    decolonisation, 39, 65-66, 68, 74, 77, 108, 147, 341
    historical developments, 65
    independence from colonial powers, 66
    nationalism, 66
Africa Institute, Moscow, 68
Afrikaans Christian Women's Association (Afrikaanse Christelike Vrouevereniging or ACVV), 62
Afrikaner Broederbond, 25-26
Afro-Asian Bloc, 74
Ahtisaari, Martti, 295 (p)
aircraft, 190
    Antonov 22, 263
    Bosbok, 283
    Buccaneer, 192, 195, 217
    C-130 Hercules transport aircraft, 123, 124
    C-47 Dakota, 123, 313
    Canberra, 195
    Cheetah, 154 (p), 237, 238
    F28 Fokker, 248
    flossie, 123

INDEX

Hercules C-130, 50, 124, 192, 251
Ilyushin 76, 263
Impala, 274, 290
Mercurius, 123
MiG, 278, 279, 285, 292
   MiG-21, 262, 271, 283
   MiG-23, 238, 262-263, 271-272, 283, 289
Mirage, 166 (p), 192, 217, 238
   F1, 283
   F1AZ, 270
   F1CZ, 271
Seeker, 237, 238 (p)
Sukhoi Su-22, 285
Tupolev Tu-134A, 314, 315
Alexandra, 206-210
Algeria, 52, 74, 341
Aliwal North, 205
Allied Forces, 186
   North Africa, 24
Alvor Agreement, 109
Ambriz, 124, 126
Ambrizete, 135
Amin, Idi, 131
ammunition, 138, 232-237
ANC/ANC Alliance, 9, 12, 38, 67-68, 77, 79, 89, 98, 195, 206, 240, 319, 323-324, 327, 331, 338-363, 365, 370, 375-380, 382-384, 388, 390, 395, 398, 409-410, 412, 419, 429, 481
   "People's Army", 350
   "People's Revolt", 350
   Area Political Military Council (APMC), 332
   armed struggle, 82, 328, 347, 355-357, 363, 365, 410, 429
   ending of, 349, 351-353
   attitude towards violence, 341
   banned organisation, 340
   Bloemfontein Conference (1949), 339
   camps, 80, 190, 322, 324-325, 330, 342, 418
   civilian targets, 169, 328, 330-331, 350, 412-413
   communist ideology, 347
   Congress Alliance, 339
   constitutional negotiations, 200, 210, 327, 333, 338, 345, 347-349, 352-354, 368, 426
   Defiance Campaign, 339
   espionage, 324
   forays from Mozambique, 312
   government, 356-357, 375, 378, 398
      attitude towards SADF, 356-358
   Green Book strategy, 347
   history, 338-342
   human rights violations, 418-419
   Kabwe Conference, 326, 328, 330, 350
   leadership, 323, 340, 342, 428
   lifting of ban, 321, 345-348, 375
   mass action, 345, 352, 354-355, 365
   National Executive Committee (NEC), 340-341, 351-352, 410
   Operation Vula, 333
   propaganda campaign, 333, 349-350
   sabotage, 341
   strategy, 339, 348-352, 354, 360, 363, 358-363, 369-370, 422, 425
   suspicion-mongering against SADF, 365, 403, 406

(ANC/ANC Alliance *cont.*)
  symbols, 339
  terrorism campaign, 156, 172, 322, 324, 329-330, 333, 338, 345, 359, 371, 373
  training in the USSR, 79-80, 349
  TRC submissions, 410, 418, 428-429
  Umkhonto we Sizwe. *See* separate entry
Anderson, Billy, 28
Anglo-Boer War, 22, 25, 30, 58
Angola, 52, 131-132, 134, 152, 168, 297
  airfields and airports, 114, 126, 134, 274, 278, 279, 289
  anti-communist parties, 76, 116-117
  armed conflict, 76, 112, 200, 261-305, 391
  civil war, 75, 109-110, 114-116, 130-131
  communist forces in Angola, 113, 116, 118, 137, 138
  Cuban military involvement. *See* Cuba: military involvement in Angola
  deployment of chemical weapons, 269, 270, 275, 391, 393
  harbours, 114, 121, 135, 263
  independence, 109, 111, 122, 124, 128
  Joint Monitoring Commission (JMC), 256, 257
  liberation movements, 74-76
  mineral riches, 110
  MPLA government, 121, 131-132
  operational area, 179, 182, 191, 253
  peace talks, 256, 292, 293-295
    Cairo, 293
    Geneva, 294
  political parties and movements, 109, 111, 137
  Portuguese colonial era, 74-77, 110, 113- 114
    termination, 113
  refugees, 134, 136
  SA aid, 105
  SA military involvement, 40, 108-111, 115, 117-118, 121-122, 124, 131, 165, 242, 252, 256, 261-305, 365
  terrorist training camps, 80
  trilateral agreement, New York, 294
  USA involvement, 130
  USSR military involvement. *See* Soviet Union (USSR): military involvement in Angola
  withdrawal of SA troops, 130-133, 137-140, 189, 194, 256, 291, 294, 297, 303
Angolan forces
  16th Brigade, 266, 268
  21st Brigade, 266-269, 275
  25th Brigade, 266
  47th Brigade, 266-268, 275-276, 281
  59th Brigade, 266-268, 275-276
  strength, 266
apartheid, 39, 66, 67, 82, 158, 171, 188, 307, 320, 321, 349, 351, 357, 358, 370, 405, 406, 413
APLA (Azanian People's Liberation Army), 340, 411-413, 419
  terrorism campaign, 413
armaments, 114, 133, 138-140, 151, 237, 240, 267, 434
  captured, 121, 195-196, 253- 255, 266, 281, 283, 292

INDEX

arms embargo, 80, 149, 197, 225-229, 231, 240
   circumvention, 227-229, 234-235, 243
   positive and negative implications, 226
Armscor (Armaments Corporation of South Africa), 9, 11-13, 64, 133, 144, 147, 154, 179-180, 217, 221-222, 225, 227-237, 240-245, 253, 267, 271, 308-310, 365, 434
   armaments production, 226, 228, 231-232, 235-236, 237-242, 253
   arms exports, 241, 243
   arms procurement, 225, 233, 241
   cutback of funding, 154, 240-242, 365
   missile systems development, 219-222
   subsidiaries, 147, 217, 227, 228, 241
      Denel, 147, 241
      Sonchem, 99, 233
Army Foundation, 89
Army Headquarters, Pretoria, 36, 50, 60, 62, 64, 82-83, 92, 95, 112-113, 120, 172
artillery, 124-125, 231, 235, 243, 262-263, 267, 276, 281, 283, 290
   anti-aircraft guns, 33, 59, 190-191, 254 (p), 273
      12.7 mm, 194
      14.5 mm, 194
   cannons, 232-236. *See also* separate entry
   "space gun", 233
Atlantic Ocean, 79
Atomic Energy Board (AEB), 213, 217
Atomic Energy Corporation (AEC), 197, 217-218
avionics systems, 240

Barber, Simon, 299
Basson, Wouter, 361, 369, 390, 392, 399, 431
   trials, 392, 398-402
Battles
   El Alamein, 58, 284
   Elandslaagte, 58
   Gibeon, 58
   Lomba River, 160, 275, 284-286, 288-289, 292, 303, 391, 434
Beacon 5½, 113
Bekker, Adm. Burt, 169
Benguela railway line, 114, 121, 127-128
Berlin Air Lift, 134
Berlin Wall, 11, 217, 240, 346, 435
Berlin West Africa Conference (1885), 65
Bié (formerly Silva Porto), 121-122, 127-130, 136
Biermann, Adm. H.H. (Hugo), 94, 142-144, 306
   Chief of the SADF, 90, 94, 112-113, 130, 140
Biermann, Rear-Adm. S.C., 306
Bin Laden, Osama, 189, 329
biological weapons, 10, 43, 148, 270, 357, 369, 391-392, 396, 398-399
   diseases, 398
Bisho incident, 354
Black, Brig. Wally, 113
Boipatong, 468
bombs
   air-burst, 125
   mortar bombs, 36
Boraine, Alex, 405, 410-411, 427
Borcherds, Chaplain Vic, 57
border protection, 96-98, 301

485

(border protection *cont.*)
    electrified fence, 97, 98, 313
    sisal fence, 96-97, 313
border war, 71, 194, 256, 303
Borman, Col Frank, 314
Botha, Louis (Prime Minister of South Africa), 228
Botha, Maj. Louis (SAP), 373-374, 383
Botha, P.W., 162, 188, 191, 203, 275
    Minister of Defence, 73, 90-91, 107, 115, 128, 130, 132, 140, 146, 162, 171, 203, 245-246, 302, 355
    Prime Minister, 170, 174, 198-199, 216, 310
    State President, 72, 150, 205, 207, 210, 294, 304, 323, 347, 355, 372, 389
Botha, R.F. (Pik), 275
    Ambassador to the USA and UN, 130-131
    Minister of Foreign Affairs, 198-200, 293 (p), 294, 295 (p)
Botswana, 67, 90, 96, 152, 320
boycotts. *See* sanctions
Bradley, Gen. Omar, 292
Brazzaville Protocol
    Joint Military Monitoring Commission, 298
Bredenkamp, B.J., 368
Breytenbach, Col. Jan, 194
Brezhnev, Leonid, 67, 222, 309
Britain, 67, 77, 145-146, 198, 248, 310, 370
British Commonwealth, 145, 340
    Conference, 320
British Communist Party, 80
Brussels, 233
Bull, G.V., 63, 233

Bureau for State Security, 114
Burger, Alwyn, 24
Burger, Brig. Jannie, 40, 147
Burger, Steve, 209
Bush, George W., 189, 329
Buthelezi, Mangosuthu, 370-372, 376, 389

Cabinda, 110
Caetano, Marcello, 76
Cahama, 253, 287, 289
Calai, 136
Calueque, 111-113, 131, 289-292
Canada, 198
cannons, 234
    140 mm, 124-125, 140, 231
    20 mm anti-aircraft, 254 (p), 273
    23 mm anti-aircraft, 273
    9,2 inch, 34
    G2, 290
    G3, 234
    G4, 235
    G5 155 mm, 234, 236 (p), 237, 276, 277, 278 (p), 279, 290
    G6 155 mm, 165, 236-237, 277-278
    M2 155 mm Long Tom, 233
Cape sea route, 78-79, 347
Cape Town, 31, 34, 39-40, 58
Caprivi, 104, 107, 112, 138, 168, 195, 372, 377, 382, 385, 387-388
Caprivian African National Union (CANU), 74
car bombs, 329
Cariango, 129
Carpio, Victorio, 73
Carter, Jimmy, 309

Cassinga (Moscow), 191-193, 287
Castle, Cape Town, 39-40, 58, 64
Castro, Fidel, 110, 263, 285-288, 293-294
casualties
  Angolan forces, 195, 256, 275,
    281-283, 291
  Cuba, 257, 263-264
  MPLA, 275
  SA Police, 295
  SADF, 133, 140, 183, 193, 195, 255, 283,
    292, 326
  SWA Police, 298
  SWAPO (PLAN), 194, 253, 295, 298
Cela, 127, 136
Central African Federation, 77
Chand, Gen. Prem, 298
chaplain services, 135, 177, 179, 259
  church and prayer parades, 93, 178 (p)
Cheetah. *See* aircraft: Cheetah
chemical and biological warfare, 391-399
chemical warfare, 262
chemical weapons, 10, 43, 148, 269-270,
  275, 357, 369, 392, 395, 391-399
  deployment against UNITA, 269-270
  incapacitating agents, 394-395
  mustard gas, 396
  protective gear, 396, 397 (p)
  tear gas, 394-395, 400
Chetequera, 192, 194
China, 72, 74, 77
CIA (Central Intelligence Agency), 114,
  130, 310, 329, 481
Circle Complex. *See* Advena
Citizen Force. *See* SA Defence Force
  (SADF): Citizen Force (CF)
civil aviation, 313, 315

Civil Co-operation Bureau (CCB),
  327-337, 366, 408
  D-40, 328
  Project Barnacle, 328
  Region 6, 331-332, 334, 336
  structure, 328
  task, 328
Clark amendment, 130, 197
Clark, Dick, 130
Cloete, Sgt André, 373-375, 377, 384-388
Cockroft, Gen. Cockie, 169
CODESA (Convention for a Democratic
  South Africa), 200, 353
Coetzee, Brig. Jerry, 198
Coetzer, J.P.J., 211
Cold War, 66, 79, 222, 240, 435
Coloured People's Congress, 341
Coloured Representative Council, 175
Command and Staff Course, 39, 46
Commands
  Natal, 90, 374, 375
  South-West Africa, 51, 54, 108, 227
  Western Province, 39, 58, 83
communism, 187, 286
  communist countries, 72, 81, 110, 157
  communist forces in Angola, 110,
    138-139, 197, 240, 285, 434
  communist imperialism, 72, 157, 190,
    222
  communist parties, 68, 71, 79-80
  communist revolutions in Africa, 74,
    258
  communist spies, 307, 311
  front organisations, 342
  imperialism, 66
  influence in Africa, 67, 79, 110, 113,

(communism *cont.*)
 116, 248
 international, 81, 138, 286, 347
  collapse, 11, 217, 240, 293, 346-347,
   356, 435
 methods, 76, 77
 threat to South Africa, 145, 190
Communist Bloc countries
 support for revolutionary
  organisations, 79
Congress of Democrats, 341
Congress of South African Trade Unions
 (COSATU), 341
conventional warfare, 39, 43, 52, 84, 86,
 95, 98, 125, 138, 159-160, 165, 186,
 202, 240, 252, 270, 396, 434
 in Angola, 276, 284
conventional weapons, 190, 270
Council for Scientific and Industrial
 Research (CSIR), 305
Coutinho, Adm. António Rosa, 110
Coventry Four, 228
Crafford, Gen. Buks, 37
Craven, Col Danie, 24, 26-28
cross-border operations, 105, 110, 132,
 156, 158, 173-174, 189, 194, 253, 255,
 287, 303, 320, 323, 325-327, 345, 408,
 459-461
 approval procedure, 172-174, 324
Crous, Brig. Theo, 49
Cuanza River, 121, 128-129
Cuanza Sul, 127
Cuba, 74, 110, 263-264, 286, 289, 293,
 296-297
 Cuban soldiers, 263-264, 281
 deployment of chemical weapons in

  Angola, 270, 391-392
 military involvement in Africa, 263, 363
 military involvement in Angola, 13,
  110, 113-114, 121, 131-132,
  138-139, 145, 188, 191, 200, 231-232,
  240, 252, 256-258, 270, 281-282,
  286-287, 261-292, 293, 302, 346
 Order of Maximo Gomes, 263
 support to SWAPO, 137
 withdrawal from Angola, 198, 284,
  293-294, 346, 434
Cuito, 274, 288-289
Cuito Cuanavale, 160, 263, 265 (m), 266,
 271-273, 277-279, 284
Cuito River, 266, 268, 272-274, 279,
 281-283
Cunene River, 289
Cunzumbia River, 268, 282
Cupido, Cmdt. John, 61
Cuvelai, 256, 287

D.F. Malan Accord, 352
Dar es Salaam, 71-72, 80-81
Davis, Capt. Sam, 126
De Aar, 57, 227, 259
De Alva, Salvador Martinez, 73
De Cuéllar, Javier Pérez, 295 (p), 299
De Hoop Nature Reserve, 221
De Klerk, F.W., 154-155, 188, 200,
 210-211, 218-219, 275, 311, 326,
 331-332, 346-347, 353-356, 360,
 364-368, 380-381, 398, 427
 2 February 1990 speech, 154, 345
 dismissal of Defence Force officers,
  353

The last trek - a new beginning, 188, 335, 362
De Villiers, Dirk and Johanna, 72
De Vos, Brig. Piet, 38
De Wet, Gen. Christiaan, 228
De Wet, Jannie, 132, 140
deception in warfare, 278, 289-290, 300-301, 303
Defence Act, 151, 338
Defence College, 157, 208
Defence Force. *See* SA Defence Force (SADF)
Defence Force Act, 71
Defence Force Headquarters, Pretoria, 40, 83, 88, 112-113, 130, 164, 169, 172, 378
Delta Force, 329
Department of Defence, 12, 26, 36, 146, 163, 240, 364
Dos Santos, José Eduardo, 76, 267
Du Plessis, Barend, 209, 275
Du Preez, Frik, 87
Dube, J.L., 339
Durban, 78, 169
Dutch East Indies Empire, 65
Dutton, Gen. Jack, 15, 143
Duvenage, Floors, 28

Earp, Gen. Dennis, 318
East Germany
  military involvement in Africa, 363
  military involvement in Angola, 252, 261, 263, 271, 284
Eastern Bloc countries, 110, 349
  military involvement in Angola, 110, 145

Ebo, 127
Edwards, Adm. R.A. (Ronnie), 33-34, 169, 201
Egypt, 74
Eisenhower, Gen. Dwight D., 186
Elandsfontein, 36
Els, Ernie, 87
Emerson, Ralph Waldo, 184
Eminent Persons' Group, 320-327
equitation, 57
Erasmus, S Maj. WO1, 56
espionage, 68, 197, 305-306, 308-310
Ethiopia, 67, 72, 263
Etosha, 70
Europe, 65, 186
  colonial empires, 65-66
Eveleigh, sir Edward Walter, 314

FAPLA (Forças Armadas Populares de Libertação de Angola), 114, 116, 121, 125, 138, 195, 253, 256-257, 262-264, 267, 270, 275, 281-286, 292, 392
  clashes with SA forces, 253
  offensive against UNITA, 261
FBI (Federal Bureau of Investigation), 310
Ferreira, Gen. Deon, 281
First National Development Corporation (FNDC), 103 (p)
FNLA (Frente Nacional de Libertação de Angola), 76, 109-110, 114, 117, 121-122, 124-126, 138, 302, 434
  armaments needs, 115
  attack on Luanda, 124-126
  SA military assistance, 190
  USA support, 130

Ford, Gerald, 131
Foreign Media Association, 379
Fort Leavenworth, 42
Fourie, Brand
  Secretary of Foreign Affairs, 130-131, 198, 200, 230
France, 19-20, 65, 72, 198, 230
  provision of nuclear fuel, 215
Fraser, Gen. Pop, 46, 48
  Chief of the SA Army, 46
Freedom Charter, 339, 348
Frelimo (Frente de Libertação de Moçambique), 77
Frontline States, 78, 327

Gabon, 113
Gaborone, 322, 325
Gaddafi, Muammar, 329
Geldenhuys, Gen. Jannie, 266, 293, 383 (p), 406, 411-412, 421-422, 459, 462-463
  A general's story from an era of war and peace, 193, 283, 286
  Chief of the SADF, 258, 262, 266, 290, 411, 416, 459
Geldenhuys, Jacques, 315
Geneva Convention, 350, 394
Geneva Protocol, 53, 294, 297-298
  violation by Angola and Cuba, 299
Genscher, Hans-Dietrich, 198
Gerhardt, Alfred, 306
Gerhardt, Cdre Dieter, 197, 305, 306-311, 307 (p), 348
  Naval career, 310
  training in espionage, 308

German South-West Africa, 68. *See* South-West Africa, South-West Africa/Namibia *and* Namibia
Goldstone Commission, 366-367
Gomes, Gen. Francisco da Costa, 76, 109
Goosen, Retief, 87
Gorbachov, Mikhael, 262
Government of National Unity (GNU), 360, 375, 380
Gravett, Col George, 85
Great Britain, 65, 72
Green, Cdre, 142-143
Grenada, 263
grensoorlog, 252
Griesel, Capt. Dan, 383 (p), 385
Grobbelaar, Gen. P.H. (Chief of the SADF), 46
Groenewald, Gen. Tienie, 371, 383 (p), 385
Groote Schuur Minute, 333, 349
Grootfontein, 73, 120, 122, 128, 270, 273
guerrilla fighters, 188, 252, 344
guerrilla warfare, 341, 344, 429

Hague, The, 51
Hall, Kevin, 464-466
Hani, Chris, 331, 351
Harare, 322, 325-326
Harms Commission, 332, 335, 427
Harms, L.T.C., 332-333, 335-336
Hartzenberg, Willie, 399, 401
Havana, 110, 286
Heitman, Helmoed-Römer, 194
helicopters, 45, 123, 134, 136, 193, 262-263, 283, 285

Alouette, 285, 296
attack helicopters, 190, 274
  MI-8 Hind, 285
  MI-17 Hind, 285
  MI-24 Hind, 279, 285
  Rooivalk, 242
Hendrickx, B., 270
Herero tribe, 49
Heunis, Chris, 370-372
Heys, Douglas, 221
Hiemstra, Gen. R.C. (Chief of the SADF), 46
Hoare, "Mad Mike", 248-251
Holliday, S Maj WO1 Jan, 406, 421
Holtzhausen, Gen. Raymond, 15, 55, 94, 406
House of Assembly, 132, 248, 330, 332. *See also* Parliament
Huambo (formerly Nova Lisboa), 121, 127
Hugo, Jan, 383, 388
human rights violations, 184, 415, 418-419, 424-425, 428, 464, 466-467

Indian Congress, 341
Indian Ocean, 79, 152, 216, 248
Indonesia, 65
Inkatha Freedom Party (IFP), 352, 365, 370-373, 377-378, 382, 386, 388, 427
Institute for Military History, Moscow, 68
Institute for Social Sciences, Moscow, 68
internal unrest, 38-40, 74, 81, 206, 321-323, 326, 328-339, 343, 349, 354, 370, 426
International Atomic Energy Agency (IAEA), 215-216

International Court of Justice, 73
International Red Cross, 464
Iran, 157
Iraq, 157, 233, 391
Irish Republican Army (IRA), 329
Iscor, 375
Ismail, Aboobaker, 412
Israel, 230, 233
Italy, 20-21, 65
Ivory Coast, 113

Jacobs, Brig. Piet, 39-40
Jacobs, Cmdt Jakes, 383 (p)
Jamba, 257, 262, 264-266, 268, 285, 289
James, Justice, 251
Jansen, E.G., 37
Jansen, Mabel, 37-38
Jenkins, Tim, 349
Johannesburg City Council, 209
Johnson, Adm. Flam, 169
Johr, Ruth, 308, 310-311
Joint Management Centres (JMCs), 203-211, 326
  Alexandra, 206-210
  Eastern Cape, 205-26
Joubert, Gen., 411

Kaokoland, 112, 287, 298
Kapuuo, Clemens, 189
Karibib, 50
Kasrils, Ronnie, 351, 406
Katima Mulilo, 195
Kaunda, Kenneth, 131
Kavango, 103-104, 112, 465

Kennedy, John F., 44 (p), 45
Kenya, 52, 113, 248, 313, 318
KGB (Russian Secret Police), 311, 329
Khorab, 69
Khumalo, A.B., 377
Khumalo, M.Z., 373, 382, 385, 387
Kimberley, 26-27, 30, 100
Kirsten, Peter, 87
Kissinger, Henry, 132
Kittrie, Nicholas N., 343
Koeberg nuclear power station, 215-216
Komatipoort, 314
König, Karl, 376, 388
Kotze, Cmdt S.W.J., 132
Kriegler, Johann, 32
Kruger, T.N., 383
Kunene River, 107, 111, 132
KwaMakutha, 374-375, 377, 384
KwaMakutha trial, 10, 164, 247, 360, 369-370, 376, 381, 383, 390, 375-390, 419, 427, 431
   findings, 385-389
   Investigation Task Board, 375, 389

Lancaster House Summit, London, 78
Le Grange, Louis, 207, 313, 371
League of Nations, 69, 72
Lenz, 176
Lesotho, 152
liberation movements, 49, 68, 71, 73-74, 76, 78-81, 109, 118, 335, 343-344, 412
   in South Africa, 338
Liberia, 72
Liebenberg, Gen. Kat, 383 (p), 406
   Chief of the SADF, 157, 258, 372
   Liebenberg Report, 372
Light Horse Regiment, 58
Liliesleaf, 341
Limpopo River, 90
Lobito, 122, 135, 263
Loggin, Janet, 306
Lomba River, 262, 267-268, 275, 277-278, 282
Loots, Gen. Frits, 432
Loubser, Kobus, 230
Louw, Gen. Willem
   Chief of the SA Army, 63
Luanda, 110, 114, 120, 125-126, 261-263, 269
Luau (formerly Teixeira de Sousa), 128
Lubango (formerly Sá da Bandeira), 121, 289
Lubowski, Anton, 332-333, 336-337
   murder, 164
Lucusse, 265
Luena (formerly Luso), 128, 263
Lusaka, 49, 80, 322, 325-326
Lusaka Accord, 256
Luthuli, Albert, 340
Luthuli, Daluxolo, 373

MacArthur, Gen. Douglas, 186
Machel, Graça, 318
Machel, Samora, 77, 314
   aircraft crash, 10, 311-319, 357
   Board of Enquiry, 314-315, 318-319
      findings, 315-319
      Mozambican reaction, 316-317

Russian Board of Enquiry, 316, 318
SAAF involvement, 315-318
SADF involvement, 311, 317, 319
Soviet reaction, 316-317
US Federal Board of Aviation
Administration, 316
Macmillan, Harold, 67, 340
Maduna, Penuell, 401
Maharaj, Mac, 350-351, 412
Malan, Adolf Gysbert (Sailor Malan), 45
Malan, D.F., 30
Malan, Jacques, 19, 45
Malan, Magnus André de Mérindol
aide-de-camp for Governor-General (1958), 37-38
ancestry, 19-20
assistant military secretary, Defence Headquarters (1964), 46
Chief of the SA Army (1973-1976), 57, 91-107, 118, 121-122, 126, 140, 174, 308, 432
Chief of the SADF (1976-1980), 88, 140, 143-144, 164, 168, 170, 173-174, 176, 177, 185, 191, 194, 198, 200, 202, 204, 309, 334, 432
childhood, 19-25
Command and Staff Course, Pretoria (1960), 39
Command and Staff Course, USA (1962), 42
commencement of military career (1950), 32
Deputy Chief of the SA Army (1972-1973), 63
experience with negotiations, 198-201

first military experience, 26, 28-30
high school training, 24
intelligence officer, Army Headquarters (1957), 36
KwaMakutha trial, 378-390
marriage (1962), 41
Minister of Defence (1980-1991), 174, 176, 200, 204, 225, 245, 246 (p), 247-248, 252, 258, 293 (p), 295 (p), 334, 352-353, 364, 367, 370, 372, 383-384, 432
Minister of Water Affairs and Forestry (1991-1993), 353, 364-366
name, 19-21
Officer Commanding, infantry company, SA Army Gymnasium (1956), 36
Officer Commanding, Military Academy, Saldanha (1968-1972), 54-58
Officer Commanding, South-West Africa Command (1966-1968), 46, 48-54
Officer Commanding, Western Province Command (1972), 58, 61
parents, 19-22, 26, 28, 31, 143
participation in sports, 27, 31, 34
retirement from politics (1993), 364-368
SA Marine Corps (1952-1955), 32
second in command, Military Academy, Saldanha (1958), 38
South African Mariners Corps, 33-35
training instructor, SA Military College (1963), 46
TRC testimony, 336, 392, 406-410, 407

(Malan, M.A. de M. *cont.*)
   (p), 429
   university studies (1949-1952), 31-32
Malanje, 128
Mamdani, Mahmood, 344
Mamelodi, 411
Mancham, James, 248
Mandela, Winnie, 330
Mandela, Nelson, 318, 321, 330, 339-341,
   345-347, 351-352, 354, 357, 368, 375,
   379, 380, 389, 398
   ANC president, 345
   release, 345, 348
Maputo, 314-318, 322
Marais, "Cmdt" Piet, 227-228 (p), 240
Marais, Gen. Dirk, 406, 421
Marais, Org, 31
Margo, Cecil, 314, 319
Maritz, Sam, 383
Markram, Mervyn, 368
Márques, Gabriel García, 110
Marxism, 12, 66-68, 72, 76-79, 116, 157,
   249, 296
Mass Democratic Movement (MDM), 345
Matsapa, Swaziland, 248, 316-318
Mavinga, 262, 264, 265- 268, 287, 289
Mbeki, Govan, 342
Mbeki, Thabo, 381
Mbuzini, 314, 317
McHenry, Don, 199
McNally, Tim, 376- 377, 386-388, 390
Meiring, Gen. Georg, 404, 421
   Chief of the SADF, 378
Menongue (formerly Serpa Pinto), 263,
   271, 278-279
mercenaries, 248-250

Mexico, 73
Meyer, Hennie, 195
MI5 and MI6 (British Secret Service), 310,
   329
Military Academy, Saldanha, 32, 38, 54-58,
   64, 131, 202-203
military appreciations, 41, 94, 145,
   147-148
mines, 329
   anti-personnel, 81
   land mines, 74, 96, 194, 329
   limpet mines, 329
Minister of Defence, 54, 87, 90, 113, 123,
   163, 170, 172-173, 246, 328, 468
missile delivery systems, 220, 222
missiles, 35, 221, 273
   ground-to-air, 271, 274, 298
      Cactus, 289
      SAM-6, 271-272, 290
      SAM-7, 81
      SAM-8, 271
      SAM-9, 271
      SAM-13, 271
      RSA-3 (p), 220
      shoulder-fired, 271
      Stinger, 273, 278
Mogadishu, 80
Monument Koppie, 40
Moodie, Gen. Dunbar, 33
More, Col John, 373, 375, 378, 383 (p)
Moscow, 286, 311
Mount Etjo Agreement, 296
Mozambique, 52, 67, 72, 74-75, 77, 96, 152,
   157, 190, 200, 284, 311-315, 318, 357
   harbouring of terrorists, 80-81, 311,
   346, 351, 371

independence, 77
liberation movements, 312
MPLA (Movimento Popular de Libertação de Angola), 76, 109-110, 113-114, 137-138, 195, 252-253, 257, 261-262, 283-284, 293, 302
   collaboration with SWAPO, 137, 257
   offensive against UNITA, 267
   propaganda campaign, 284
Msane, Peter, 381
Msimang, H.Q., 383
Mugabe, Robert, 78, 323
Muller, Hilgard (Minister of Foreign Affairs), 130
Mussende, 128-129
Muzorewa, Abel, 78
Myburgh, Tertius, 208

Nairobi, 318
Namacurra, 237, 239 (p)
Namib Desert, 56
Namibe (formerly Moçâmedes), 114, 121, 135, 287
Namibia, 72, 78, 191, 295-296, 299, 346, 462- 463. *See* South-West Africa/Namibia
National Intelligence Service (NI), 249-251, 367-368, 399, 427
national key points. *See* South Africa: national key points
National Management System (NMS), 187, 203
National Party, 31, 203, 245, 247, 360
National Prosperity Management System (NPMS), 187, 203
national security. *See* South Africa: national security
National Security Management System (NSM), 187, 202-212, 326, 371, 425, 433
national service system (NSS), 64, 83-89, 151
   boycotts, 81
   civil conscientious objectors' committee, 89
   exemption board, 85, 86
   national servicemen (NSM), 12, 59-62, 83-86, 88-89, 93, 95, 100-101, 103-105, 123, 140, 148, 157, 194-195, 231, 260, 301, 355, 415
   hitchhiking, 61-62, 83, 87
      Call and Ride Scheme, 87
      Ride Safely Scheme, 87
navy vessels
   corvettes, 229-230
   submarines
      Agosta, 229
"need to know" principle, 14, 300, 304-305, 308, 323, 336
Nehru, Jawaharlal, 69
Netanyahu, Benjamin, 344
Neto, Agostinho, 76
New York, 304
New York Accord, 297
Ngubane, Tim, 331
Ngunza (formerly Novo Redondo), 122
Nicaragua, 263
Nicholson, Fred, 22
Nigeria, 321
Night of the generals, 365-368
Nixon, Richard, 130

Nkomati Accord, 200, 312-313, 346, 351, 371
Nkomo, Joshua, 78
Nkrumah, Kwame, 66
Non-Aligned States, 261-262
North Atlantic Treaty Organisation (NATO), 79, 309, 311
Northern Rhodesia (Zambia), 77
Ntsebeza, Dumisa, 356, 389, 411
Ntuli, Victor, 373, 386
nuclear capability of South Africa, 213-219, 222-224
   dismantling of nuclear weapons, 217-219
   nuclear delivery systems, 219
   nuclear energy, 213-215
   nuclear tests, 216-217, 305
   uranium enrichment, 197, 213, 216-217, 342
Nuclear Non-Proliferation Treaty (NPT), 215- 219, 222
nuclear weapons, 43, 148, 159, 197, 213-214, 216-219, 222-223, 270
   international control, 215, 218
   threat to South Africa, 223
Nujoma, Sam, 49-50, 71-72, 296-298
Nyanda, Siphiwe, 351
Nyassaland (Malawi), 77

Obasanjo, Olusegun, 321
Oberholzer, Obie (Oom Obie), 209
Okavango River, 103, 136
Olifant. *See* tanks: Olifant
Omar, Dullah, 376
Ondangwa, 253, 289-290
Ongiva (formerly Pereira de Eça), 136, 253
Operation Marion, 365, 369-376, 378, 380, 419, 427
Operation Mayibuye, 342
Operation Vula, 333, 349-351, 355, 362, 365
operational area, 99, 101, 153, 322. *See also* South-West Africa/Namibia: operational area
   visitors, 253, 275
operations of the SADF
   Askari, 252, 255
   Carnation, 252-253
   Daisy, 252
   Hooper, 261, 264, 268
   logistics, 118, 134
   Meebos, 252
   Modular, 261, 264, 268 (m), 277, 279
   Packer, 261, 264, 268
   Phoenix, 252, 255
   Protea, 175, 252-253, 255-256
   reasons for success, 258-260
   Reindeer, 191, 194, 460
   Rekstok, 194-195
   Safraan, 194-195
   Savannah, 40, 117-140, 144, 189-190, 194, 231
      attack on Luanda, 124-126
      combat groups, 126-130
         Alpha, 121, 127
         Bravo, 121, 127
         Foxbat, 121, 127
         Orange, 121, 128-129
         X-ray, 121, 128
      consequences, 137-140

logistics, 118, 120, 122-123, 133
   SA Army involvement, 124
   SA Navy involvement, 134-135
   SAAF involvement, 133-134, 136
   SAMS involvement, 135-137
   Task Force Zulu, 118, 121-122, 126-129, 134-135
   use of artillery, 124-126
   withdrawal of SA troops, 128, 130-133, 140
Sceptic (Smokeshell), 194-195, 460
Super, 252
Opperman, Capt. J.P., 372-375, 377-378, 384-388
Organisation of African Unity (OAU), 67, 78, 116-117, 122, 131-132, 249, 341
   establishment (1963), 67
   summit, 78, 128, 131, 137
Organisation of Independent African States (African Union), 67
Oshakati, 140, 289
Oshikango, 73
Ovambo People's Organisation (OPO), 71
Ovamboland, 71, 73, 75, 103-104, 111-112, 132, 255, 287, 289, 292, 297-298, 372
   assasination of leaders, 189
Ovambos, 71, 73, 77, 111-112
Overberg Missile Test Site, 221 (p)
Ovimbundu, 257
Owen, David, 198
Oyster Rocks, 56

Pama, Cor, 20
Pan Africanist Congress (PAC), 9, 82, 340
   banned organisation, 340
   camps in neighbouring countries, 80
   human rights violations, 419
   lifting of ban, 321, 345, 375
   terrorism campaign, 322, 324, 412
Pandit, Vijayalakshmi, 69
paratrooper attacks, 191-192
Paris Peace Conference, 69
Parliament, 9, 31, 39, 87, 115, 123, 154, 157, 163, 176, 179, 247, 253, 300, 304, 323, 338, 340, 390
Patrice Lumumba University, Moscow, 68
Patriotic Front, 78
Patta, Deborah, 319
Pelindaba, 197
Penzhorn, Ernst, 407
Permanent Force (SF). See SA Defence Force (SADF): Permanent Force (PF)
Persian Gulf, 67
Philippines, 73
Physical Training Brigade, 24-30, 42, 60-61, 99-100, 175
Pickard, Jan, 61
Pienaar, Cmdt Salmon, 466-467
Pietermaritzburg, 248
Pike, Douglas, 344
PLAN (People's Liberation Army of Namibia), 71, 74-75, 138, 194-195, 252-253, 256, 294, 296
   arms caches, 195
   camps in Angola, 194-195, 253, 287
      Chifufua, 195
   collaboration with MPLA, 256
   forays into SWA/Namibia, 255, 289-296
   losses, 194
Poland, 157

Pombuige River, 129
Ponte Salazar, 129
Poqo (later APLA), 340
Portugal, 109, 111-112
  colonies, 74-77. *See* Angola:
    Portuguese colonial era
  military forces in colonies, 75, 109
Potekhin, I.I., 68
Potgieter, Brig. J.D., 56, 131
Potgieter, Denzil, 361, 422
Pretoria, 21, 23-25
Pretoria Minute, 351, 353
Progressive Party, 187
Project Coast, 269, 392-393, 395, 398-399, 391-402, 408
Project Molteno. *See* SA Army: community projects
propaganda, 54, 66, 80, 81, 157
Putter, Adm. Andries, 383 (p)

Quibala, 127, 129

radar, 35, 240, 270-273, 283, 290, 316-317
Randall, Clarence, 45
Ratel. *See* vehicles: Ratel
Rautenbach, Piet, 231
Reagan, Ronald, 329
Reconnaissance Commandos (Recces).
  See SA Defence Force (SADF):
    Reconnaissance Commandos (Recces)
Red Eye. *See* rockets: Katyusha 122 mm MRL
Red Line, 70-71, 104, 108, 112
Renamo, 312

René, Albert, 248-249
Renwick, sir Robert, 285
revolutionary organisations, 53-54, 77, 82, 190, 205, 331, 345-346, 417
revolutionary warfare, 39, 41, 43, 46, 51-54, 58, 67, 79, 82, 84, 86, 93, 95, 98-100, 105, 146, 159-160, 169, 171, 173, 183, 186, 203, 205-206, 208, 210-211, 312, 327, 334, 342, 346, 349, 395, 415, 417
  creation of perceptions, 183-184
  propaganda, 183, 190
Rhodesia, 72, 77, 90. *See* Zimbabwe
Rhodesian Front Party, 78
Ribeiro incident, 411
Richard Bennet, 34
Ries, Alf, 208
Rive, Louis, 230
Rivonia Trial, 341, 342, 345
Robben Island, 33-34, 71
Roberto, Holden, 76-77, 124, 126
rockets, 35
  Bateleur rocket system, 232 (p)
  Katyusha 122 mm MRL, 81, 125, 139 (p), 195, 231-232, 253
  multiple rocket launchers (MRLs), 283, 290
  rocket systems, 231
  Valkiri 127 mm MRL, 232, 253, 276
Rodgers, Gen. Bob, 40, 132, 169
Röhrbeck, WO, 421
Rooikat. *See* vehicles: Rooikat
Roos, Brig. Ben de Wet, 124-126, 132, 135
Roosevelt, Theodore, 82
Roux, Mannetjies, 87
Royal Air Force (Britain), 45

Ruacana, 113, 115, 121, 132, 200
Ruacana-Calueque hydroelectric scheme, 105, 112-113, 115, 121
Rundu, 113, 120, 135-136, 465
Russia. *See* Soviet Union (USSR)

SA Air Force (SAAF), 12, 37, 50, 55, 83, 86, 113, 125, 133-134, 164, 166-167, 169, 217, 253, 262, 272, 274, 308, 313, 327
    1 Air Component, 133
    301 Air Component, 120, 133-134
    armaments procurement, 365
    armaments requirements, 242
    bases, 196
        Grootfontein, 270, 273
        Hoedspruit, 196, 313
        Ovamboland, 289
        Rundu, 271
        Waterkloof, 196-197, 251
    Chief of the SAAF, 40, 120, 166, 169, 173
    evacuation of casualties, 159, 183, 343
    in SWA/Namibia, 295
    involvement in Angola, 270-272, 274
    involvement in cross-border operations, 191, 193
    involvement in unrest areas, 343
    Mariepskop radar station, 313
    training, 271
SA Army, 12, 37, 42, 47, 55, 64, 82-83, 86, 92-98, 102, 107, 112-113, 118, 124, 140, 143, 164-165, 168-169, 232, 262, 308, 327, 467
    arms procurement, 92
    change of culture, 98
    Chief of the SA Army, 40, 47, 54, 60, 90, 91, 95, 165, 169, 173
    combat-readiness, 93, 95
    Command and Staff Course, 39, 46
    commands, 95
    community projects, 99-102
        Project Molteno, 100-101
    conventional force, 95
    counter-insurgency force, 95
    Headquarters. *See* Army Headquarters, Pretoria
    human relations, 98-100, 174
    in SWA/Namibia, 99, 102
    involvement in Angola, 274
    involvement in unrest areas, 343
    removal of discrimination, 99, 162
    Sappers, 124
    staff divisions, 164
    staff structure, 93-94
    volunteers, 176
    Women's College, 176
SA Cape Corps, 175-176
SA Defence Force (SADF), 9-10, 12, 15, 117, 136, 144, 147, 150, 161, 164, 169, 283, 304, 307, 323, 365, 376, 405, 409, 423, 427, 432, 435, 467
    actions against terrorism, 340, 343, 359
    adult education, 177
    amnesty applications, 423
    arms procurement, 92, 145-147
    attitude of ANC Government. *See* ANC/ANC Alliance: attitude towards SADF
    chaplain services, 177-179
    chemical and biological capability. *See* Project Coast

(SA Defence Force *cont.*)
  Chief of the SADF, 40, 46, 54, 84, 103, 112, 118, 121, 123, 143, 163-164, 173, 258, 309, 327, 336, 416-417, 468
  Citizen Force (CF), 12, 39-41, 58, 71, 84, 88-89, 95, 136, 148, 165-167, 176, 179, 182, 260, 294, 301, 355, 415
  civilian casualties, 322, 345, 415
  combat-readiness, 159, 433
  Commandos, 12, 39-41, 49, 58, 71, 84, 88-89, 148, 165-166, 176, 179, 227, 260, 301, 355, 415
  community projects, 88, 103 (p), 162, 181
  Complaints Office, 88
  Contact Bureau, 406, 411, 413-414, 417, 420-423, 427, 458
    submissions to TRC, 436-468
  counter-revolutionary strategies, 82, 188
  covert organisations, 335-336
  cross-border operations, 459
  culture change, 433
  defensive/offensive posture, 171, 387
  departmental strategy, 150-151
  Equestrian Centre, Potchefstroom, 57, 465
  Ferntree Base, 374
  function, 171
  General Staff Council, 46
  human relations, 105, 416-417, 433
  human rights, 415-416
  human rights violations, 424
    in Angola, 110, 112, 115-116, 138, 117-140, 145, 189-195, 252-258, 261-305, 434, 458-466. *See* Angola: SA military involvement
    in SWA/Namibia, 46, 48-51, 99, 101, 103, 106, 108, 120, 132, 140, 162, 172, 174, 177, 184, 189-195, 372, 464. *See* South-West Africa: SA military involvement
  instrument of the State, 157, 161, 338, 362
  liaising with opinion makers, 179-181
  manpower, 59-60, 83-84, 88, 96
  Military Intelligence Division (MID), 50, 114, 164, 196-197, 249-251, 309, 333, 336, 366, 368, 373, 468
  military requirements, 145, 149
    armaments, 92, 144-149, 151, 170, 227, 240-241, 308
    equipment, 14, 41, 60, 92, 145, 148-149, 152, 154, 226
    financial, 92, 145, 148-149, 151, 154, 170
    manpower, 92, 120, 145, 147-149, 151-152, 154, 170, 224
  military training, 32-33, 36, 49, 54, 59-60, 84, 95, 100-101, 107, 138, 162, 175-176, 370, 372, 415, 424, 432-433
  officer training, 32, 34, 39, 46, 55-56, 107, 162, 202-203, 424, 432
  organisation development, 93-94, 145, 169, 433
  organisational culture, 169-170
  organisational structure, 162-169
  perceptions, 332
  Permanent Force (PF), 12, 84, 88-89,

140, 167, 175, 179, 355
female members, 176
postal service, 182
power base of Government, 158, 204, 353, 355
Reconnaissance Commandos (Recces), 278-279, 327-328, 337
relations with civilians, 174-175
removal of discrimination, 107, 162, 175-177
Special Forces, 263, 271, 273, 278-279, 281, 327-328, 337, 468
sport, 87
staff structure, 93-94
success, 155, 152-160, 184, 190
support for UNITA, 257
supporting SAP, 322, 343
suspicion-mongering, 319, 333, 353, 357-358, 360-362, 367, 403, 410, 435
task, 74
TRC hearings, 421, 430. *See also* Truth and Reconciliation Commission (TRC): SADF
TRC submissions, 411, 413-414, 416, 421, 424, 430, 458
volunteers, 49, 54, 58, 85, 99-100, 107, 175, 176-177, 260, 415
withdrawal from Angola, 294
Women's Association, 259
Women's Organisation, 62
SA Indian Corps, 175, 176
SA Medical Service (SAMS), 12, 83, 86, 135-136, 164, 168-169, 327
Chief of the SAMS, 169
Citizen Force, 169

evacuation of casualties, 168 (p), 183
Field Ambulance units, 136
functions, 168
involvement in unrest areas, 343
military hospitals, 183
Surgeon General, 120
SA National Defence Force (SANDF), 10, 161, 171, 404-405
Nodal Point, 404-406, 420
SA Navy, 12, 55, 78, 83, 86, 120, 126-127, 134-135, 164, 166-167, 169, 306-308, 327
Chief of the SA Navy, 168-169, 309
Citizen Force, 168
harbour protection, 343
involvement in unrest areas, 343
Joint Maritime Operations Centre, Silvermine, 78
Navy Headquarters, 126, 170
SA Marine Corps, 32-34
vessels, 229, 237, 239
volunteers, 175
SA Police (SAP), 108, 165-167, 205-207, 295, 322, 328, 332, 343, 348, 366-367, 371, 373-374, 383, 411, 416, 423-424, 426-427, 467
and the TRC, 407, 411
SA Police Service (SAPS), 384
Investigation Task Unit (ITU), 375-377, 384
SA Press Union-SADF Liaison Committee, 302
SA Railway Police (SARP), 466-467
Salazar, António, 74, 76
Saldanha, 32, 38, 58, 202
Sanchez, Arnaldo Ochoa, 262, 285

sanctions
    economic, 172, 188, 320, 342
    weapons, 146, 222, 234. *See also* arms embargo
Sandton, 206, 208
SAS (British Special Forces), 329
SAS Drakensberg, 237
SAS Good Hope (p), 229
SAS President Kruger, 135
SAS President Steyn, 126, 127, 135
SAS Tafelberg, 135
satellites, 215, 219, 220
Saurimo (formerly Henrique de Carvalho), 128
Savimbi, Jonas Malheiro, 74, 76-77, 114, 128, 130-131, 253, 257, 266, 275, 285
Schaufele, William E., 110
Schneider, Jenny, 332
Schoeman, Hendrik, 24
Scholtz, Kobus, 368
Schultz, George, 295 (p)
Scorpions, 312
Scowcroft, Gen. Brent, 131
Sebokeng, 348
Secretary of Defence, 146-147
security, 36-37, 120, 135, 235, 300-301, 308-309, 325
Security Forces, 82, 88, 98, 151, 166, 183, 190, 208-209, 296, 321, 329, 332, 342-343, 345, 350-353, 355, 375, 387, 395, 417, 423, 425-426, 466, 468
    actions against terrorism, 330, 348-349
    armaments requirements, 242
    criticism of, 169
    in SWA/Namibia, 189
    provision of armaments, 227
    public relations, 183-184
    suspicion-mongering against, 342-353, 356, 359-361, 412, 422
    use of tear gas, 395, 400
    withdrawal from black townships, 321
security policy, 151
securocrats, 210, 355, 358
Seeker. *See* aircraft: Seeker
Serfontein, Sep, 94
Sese Seko, Mobuto, 76, 131
Seychelles, 248, 250
    failed coup d'etat, 248-252
Shaganovich, Gen. Constantin, 262-263
Sharpeville, 39, 340
Shipanga, Andreas, 463
Shirobokov, Gregori, 307, 310
Shiyagaya, Toivo, 189
Simon's Town, 34, 78, 126, 170, 310
Sisulu, Walter, 340-341
Slabbert, F. van Zyl, 187-188
Slovo, Joe, 341, 347, 357
Smith, Ben, 247
Smith, Ian, 77-78
Smuts, Gen. J.C., 25, 30, 69, 90
Sobukwe, Robert, 340
Somalia, 263
Sonchem, 99, 233
Sossusvlei, 56
South Africa
    airfields and airports, 27, 78-79, 152, 191
    armaments production, 146-147
        See also Armscor (Armaments Corporation of South Africa)
    border protection, 74

INDEX

buffer states, 67, 77, 81
constitutional negotiations, 12, 82, 146, 160, 171, 201, 210, 284, 327, 347-349, 351-358, 361-362, 368, 375, 409
Minute of Understanding, 354
counter-revolutionary strategies, 203
domestic policy, 39, 43, 68, 72, 117, 340
harbours, 33, 43, 78-79, 152
infrastructure, 152
national key points, 33, 36, 187
national security, 144-145, 151, 154, 161, 172, 203-206, 224, 245, 330, 364-365, 368
   policy, 150
   Soviet threat, 148, 157, 188, 190, 222, 347
   strategy, 154, 224, 355
   threat, 60, 147-148, 154, 156, 173, 188, 214, 226
national strategy, 150-151, 158, 170, 187, 224, 347, 433
neighbouring countries, 67, 81, 151, 158, 174, 188, 312, 327, 346
   harbouring of terrorists, 331
nuclear capability. *See* nuclear capability of South Africa
political reform, 210
railways, 79
revolutionary onslaught, 433-434
terrorism campaign, 169, 176, 321, 323-324, 326, 342, 346
South African Broadcasting Corporation (SABC), 57, 87, 206, 259, 379
South African Communist Party (SACP), 71, 79, 307, 323-324, 342, 346-347, 360-362, 370, 375, 380, 388, 412, 419
   lifting of ban, 345, 375
South African Military College, 32, 41, 46
South African Native National Congress (later ANC), 339
South African Women's Federation (SA Vrouefederasie or SAVF), 62
Southern Africa
   political situation, 64
Southern Cross Fund, 259
Southern Rhodesia (Zimbabwe), 77
South-West Africa, 19, 48. *See* South-West Africa/Namibia *and* Namibia
South-West Africa case, International Court of Justice, 51, 69, 72
South-West Africa/Namibia, 49, 70 (m), 73, 111, 118
   "Peace of Namibia", 252
   agricultural projects, 102-103
   airports and airfields, 49-50, 69, 192
   Angolan border, 54, 104, 111, 115, 120, 172, 182, 189, 195, 252, 288, 465
   border protection, 108, 110, 115-116, 120
   armed struggle, 73
   border war, 165, 188, 252
   ceasefire agreement, 297-298
   Citizen Force, 54, 71, 290
   Commandos, 54, 71
   counter-insurgency, 75, 105, 108
   cross-border operations, 191-193, 195, 460-461
   Cuban threat, 289
   elections, 198
   First National Development

503

(South-West Africa/Namibia *cont.*)
   Corporation (FNDC), 103
   harbours, 68-69
   human relations, 99, 102, 107
   independence, 346
   Joint Military Monitoring Commission, 298
   Mount Etjo Agreement, 296
   negotiations, 160, 199-200, 284, 289, 292, 294
   operational area, 57, 59, 99, 101, 104 (p), 105 (p), 106 (p), 104-107, 120-123, 134, 136, 162 (p), 168, 172, 175, 177-182, 191, 196, 200, 253, 259, 275
      postal service, 182
   operational plan, 49, 51, 54
   Police, 298
   refugees, 136
   revolutionary onslaught, 41, 48-51, 58, 71- 73, 77, 108
   SA administration, 49, 71-74
   SA aid, 105-106
   SA mandate, 67-69, 71-74, 109, 115
      security responsibility, 152
   SA military involvement, 49-51, 70, 108, 110, 112, 117, 140, 175, 179, 252, 255 (p), 298, 372, 464-466
   SA Police involvement, 49, 73, 108
   security threat, 48, 60, 71, 114
      Soviet threat, 190
   settlement plan, 190-191, 198, 257, 296
   SWAPO onslaught, 50, 71, 74, 110, 138, 157, 189, 194, 252, 255, 289-290
   Western Contact Group, 198-200

South-West African Territorial Force (SWATF), 255, 260, 267, 282-283, 286, 290-292, 295
South-West African Water and Electricity Corporation (SWAWEC), 112-113
Soviet Union (USSR), 12, 65-67, 72, 79, 195, 200, 255, 257, 262, 293, 305, 309, 311, 314-315, 318, 347
   arms provision
      to African countries, 147, 222
      to Angola, 81, 139-140, 190, 231, 253, 257, 263
      to MPLA, 135, 262-263, 302, 392
   chemical weapons, 269, 392, 394, 399
   destabilisation policy, 157, 190
   espionage, 197, 215, 307, 309-311
   expansionism, 78, 157, 363
   involvement in Africa, 67-68, 76, 78-80, 148, 171, 314
   loss of power, 11
   military involvement in Angola, 13, 110, 131-132, 137-139, 145, 188, 191, 223, 252, 257, 262, 264, 282, 284, 286, 292, 434
   presence in Indian Ocean, 249
   revolutionary warfare, 187
   Soviet Bloc, 66, 80
      collapse, 217, 222, 346
   Soviet Military Intelligence Division (GRU), 307
   support for revolutionary organisations, 67, 74, 79-80, 190, 193, 262
      ANC, 363
      MPLA, 110, 113-114
      SWAPO, 363

threat to South Africa, 214, 223, 347
withdrawal from Southern Africa, 217, 240, 284, 434
Soweto uprising, 342
Space Research Corporation (SRC), 233-235
Sparks, Allister, 379
Special Service Battalion (SSB), 100
Spies, F.J. du T., 14, 481
  Operasie Savannah: Angola 1975-1976, 14, 118, 127, 134
Spínola, António de, 109
  Portugal e o futuro (Portugal and the future), 76
St John, Canada, 234
Stalin Organ. *See* rockets: Katyusha 122 mm MRL
Stalin, Joseph, 66, 222
state of emergency, 39, 321, 323, 326, 339-340
State Security Council (SSC), 188, 202-206, 210-211, 252, 322-324, 334, 355, 370-371, 376, 380-381, 426-427
Steyn, Annette, 136
Steyn, Gen. Pierre, 367
  enquiry, 366, 367
    Night of the generals, 366, 427
Steyn, Hannes, Van der Walt, Richard, Van Loggerenberg, Jan
  Armament and disarmament, 214, 221
strategic minerals, 67, 78-79
Strijdom, J.G., 31
struggle, 11, 51, 78, 82, 154
Sun Tzu, 185, 391
Support Services Corps, 176
SWAPO (South-West African People's Organisation), 9, 48-50, 71-72, 74, 137-138, 191-192, 194-195, 256, 295, 297-298, 332, 342, 463
  camps
    in Angola, 115, 121, 137-138, 191, 195, 257, 287
    Cassinga, 191-193
    Vietnam, 192
    in neighbouring countries, 80
    in Zambia, 195
  clashes with SA Security Forces, 132, 190, 191, 194, 253, 296
  collaboration with MPLA, 114, 137, 253
  conventional assault, 256
    in Angola, 190, 256-257
  losses, 253, 255
  onslaught against SWA/Namibia, 194-195, 252, 287-289, 296, 346
  semi-conventional assault, 189-190, 195
  support from USSR, 363
  terrorism campaign, 74, 115-116, 157, 172, 189, 252, 372
  violation of Resolution 435, 294, 295-499
  withdrawal from border area, 294, 297
Swaziland, 96, 152, 248, 313, 316
Swemmer, Eben, 23
Syria, 263
Taiwan (Nationalist China), 72
Tambo, Oliver, 323, 342, 345
tanks, 190, 192, 253, 283, 285
  Olifant, 237
  T-34, 192, 196 (p), 262
  T-35, 255

T-54, 256
T-55, 262, 275
T-62, 281
Tanzania, 71, 74, 248
Techamutete, 192
Techipa, 289, 291-292
Tembisa, 208
terrorism, 79, 82, 95, 108, 147, 157, 187, 193, 324, 330-332, 335, 339, 342, 343-345, 359, 415, 429
   Al-Qaeda, 189, 329
   Church Street bomb, 412
   civilian targets, 326, 329, 344
   international, 189, 218
   Magoo's Bar bomb, 412
   terrorist organisations, 72, 75, 188, 326, 370
   camps in neighbouring countries, 322, 324
   terrorists, 252, 327
   training camps, 80
Thatcher, Margaret, 320, 329
third force, 358, 366, 408, 426-427
Thirion, Gen. Chris, 56
Thornberry, Cedric, 298
Toivo ja Toivo, Andimba (Herman), 71
total onslaught, 185-189, 358
   propaganda, 187
total strategy, 188-189
Toulon, 230
Treaty of Versailles, 69
Truman, Harry S., 186
Truth and Reconciliation Commission (TRC), 9-10, 13, 193, 311, 320, 356, 359-360, 362, 369, 381, 390, 403-431
   Act, 404

amnesty applications, 333-334, 358, 380, 408, 414, 417-418, 423-424, 429
Committee on Restitution and Rehabilitation, 425
credibility, 430, 461
distortions, 357
findings on violation of Resolution 435, 297, 299
KwaMakutha trial, 389-390, 427
Lubowski case, 336-337
members, 360
methods, 410, 421, 426, 430
Project Coast, 393, 399-402
publicity, 360-362
reconciliation task, 404, 411, 414, 420, 422, 426, 430
relation with ANC, 403, 410, 412, 417-419, 425, 431
reports, 350, 404, 412, 418, 420-421, 423-429, 458-459, 461-462, 464, 467-468
SADF, 357, 403-412, 413-418, 420-425, 430, 423-429, 435
submissions, 405, 410, 414, 416-417, 421-425, 427-428, 468, 458-468
suspicion-mongering against Security Forces, 360-362
task, 422
testimony of Magnus Malan. *See* Malan, Magnus André de Mérindol: TRC testimony
Umkhonto we Sizwe (MK), 409
Tumpo, 282
Tunney, John, 130

Tutu, Desmond, 206, 357, 389, 407, 418, 427

Uganda, 131
Ulundi, 372, 374, 375
Umkhonto we Sizwe (MK), 323, 329, 341, 344, 351, 357, 409, 411-413, 419, 429
  civilian targets, 412-413
  human rights violations, 418-419
  terrorism campaign, 413
Union Buildings march, 354
Union Defence Force, 24, 27, 31-32, 161
Union of Independent African States (African Union or AU), 66
UNITA (União Nacional para a Independéncia Total de Angola), 74, 76, 109, 114, 136, 253, 257, 269, 283, 302
  3rd Battalion, 268
  area of support, 109, 115, 121, 127-128, 261
  armaments needs, 115
  captured armaments, 196, 255, 281, 283, 285
  chemical weapons used against, 269-270, 392
  clashes with enemy forces, 257-258, 261-263, 265-267, 282, 284, 286
  collaboration with FNLA, 110
  collaboration with SA, 114, 117, 128, 279-282, 286
  conventional warfare, 128, 276
  guerrilla warfare, 128
  headquarters, 262
  military support from SA, 115, 122, 129, 132, 137-138, 190, 266, 281, 283
  USA support, 114, 130, 273
United Democratic Front (UDF), 161, 345, 373, 384
United Kingdom (UK), 314-315
United Nations (UN), 45, 67, 97, 226, 295, 298, 303
  arms embargo, 243. *See* arms embargo
  General Assembly, 72, 413
  resolutions, 243
    Resolution 2145, 72
    Resolution 435, 190, 198, 294, 296-298
    Resolution 558, 244
  Security Council, 190, 244, 299, 303-304
  Transitional Assistance Group (UNTAG), 298
United Nations Organisation (UNO), 67, 69, 72-74
  arms embargo, 226, 229
  Committee for South-West Africa, 73
  Council for South-West Africa/Namibia, 73
  General Assembly, 72
  resolutions, 230
    Resolution 418, 225
    Resolution 435, 200
  Security Council, 72-73, 226
United States of America (USA), 42-44, 46-47, 65-66, 72, 80, 94, 130-132, 186, 189, 197-201, 215-216, 218, 256, 273, 293-295, 309-311, 314, 329, 370, 391, 432
  chemical weapons, 394-395, 399
  espionage in SA, 195-198
  involvement in Africa, 110

(United States of America *cont.*)
   involvement in Angola, 116, 130, 302
   military attachés, 196-198
   military involvement in Vietnam, 75
   Operation Desert Storm, 233
   provision of nuclear fuel to SA, 215
   US Army Command and General Staff College, 42
   West Point, 45
   withdrawal of support from Angola, 132
University of Ghent, Belgium, 270
University of Pretoria, 32
University of South Africa (UNISA), 201
University of Stellenbosch, 31, 55
   Faculty of Military Science, 32, 38, 55
Uranium Enrichment Corporation, 217

Van der Merwe, Cmdt Jan, 375, 383 (p), 385
Van der Schyff, Jack, 28
Van Deventer, Gen. André, 15, 40, 120, 128, 143, 211
Van Heerden, Col J.S. (Koos), 121
Van Hoven, Piet, 315, 318
Van Niekerk, Brig. Cornelius, 383 (p)
Van Niekerk, Cmdt Gert, 113
Van Rooyen, Col G.C., 465
Van Tonder, Gen Neels, 383 (p)
Van Wyk, At
   Honoris Crux. Ons dapperes, 281
   Honoris Crux. Ons dapperes II, 281
Van Zyl, Gen. Koos, 93, 169
Vance, Cyrus, 198
Varney, Howard, 375-377, 388-389
Vastrap nuclear test site, 214-215, 309

vehicles, 144
   armoured troop carriers, 283
   armoured vehicles, 144, 190, 192
   BRDM-2 (p), 254
   Buffel, 292
   Casspirs, 283
   Kwêvoël, 283
   PT-76 amphibious vehicle, 262
   Ratel, 237, 283, 291 (p)
   Rinkhals, 283
   Rooikat, 237, 239 (p)
   troop carriers, 144
   Withings, 283
Verwoerd, H.F., 211
Victor, Col Jacobus, 373-374, 383 (p)
Vietnam, 80, 117, 186, 294
Viljoen, Cmdr Flip, 229 (p), 230
Viljoen, G. van N. (Gerrit), 24
Viljoen, Gen. Constand, 39, 130-132, 169, 406, 411, 413, 421
   Chief of the SA Army, 91, 193, 200
   Chief of the SADF, 252, 258, 262, 345
Vlok, Adriaan, 352-353, 380-381, 426
Vo Nguyen Giap, 347
Von Bismarck, Otto, 65
Von Clausewitz, Gen. Carl, 300
Voortrekkerhoogte, 24, 31-32, 142
Vorster, B.J. (John), 211
   Prime Minister, 74, 130-132, 172-173, 191, 214, 245
Walker, Gen. Sir Walter, 79
Walvis Bay, 50, 78, 112-113, 126, 135, 465
Warsaw Treaty countries, 309
Washington DC, 43-44, 198
Washington Post, 110
Watergate scandal, 130

INDEX

weapons
    AK-47, 81, 194, 374, 375
    ballistic systems, 235
    Degtyarev 12,7 mm heavy machine
      gun, 81
    glider bomb, 305
    mortars, 298
      120 mm, 290
      81 mm, 278
      82 mm, 194
    RPG-7, 194
    weapon systems, 146-149, 152, 232
weapons of mass destruction, 149, 159, 197, 369, 391
Webster murder, 164
Webster, Gen. Neil, 132, 169
Wessels, Kepler, 87
West Germany, 198, 342
West Indies, 234
West Rand Development Board, 209
Western Province Command, 58
Wilken, St. Elmo, 28
Wilkenson, Geoffrey, 315
Wilson, Harold, 80
Windhoek, 19, 48-51, 68, 464
Witvlei Committee, 216
Wolmarans, Chris, 36
Women's Agricultural Association (Vrouelandbouvereniging or VLV), 62
Women's Agricultural Union (Vrouelandbou-unie or VLU), 62
World Peace Council, Brussels, 342

World War I, 19, 51, 58, 68-69
World War II, 27, 45, 52, 56, 58-59, 65, 69, 71, 100, 125, 138, 140, 146-147, 159, 185-186, 202, 231, 284, 314
Wynberg, 207

Xangongo (formerly Roçadas), 253, 287, 289, 292

Yeltsin, Boris, 311
Youngsfield, 33, 59

Zaire, 76, 113-114, 116, 126, 128, 131, 302
Zambezi River, 152
Zambia, 50, 67, 104, 113-114, 116, 120, 128, 131, 195, 200, 284, 296, 302, 313-314, 320, 327
    SA aid, 105
    support for SWAPO, 137
Zanzibar, 81
Zedong, Mao, 51-53, 82
Zimbabwe, 52, 67, 96, 152, 157, 190, 284, 313, 320, 323
Zimbabwe African National Union (ZANU), 78
Zimbabwe African People's Union (ZAPU), 78
Zonderwater prison, 251

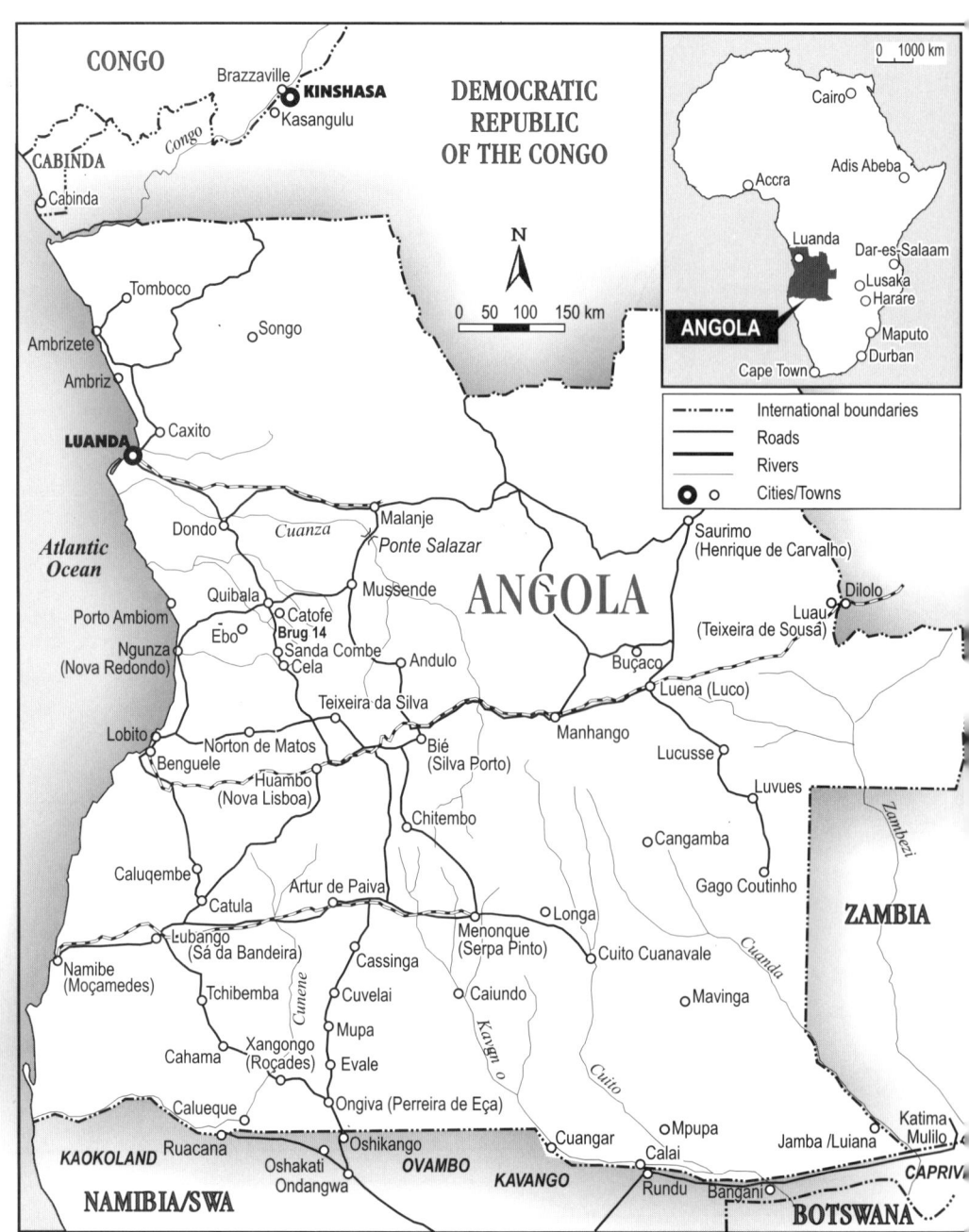